à Fantaisie " Les Grâcin
Isolde et Siegfried sont ici.
J'étais dans leur loge
hier soir au Rheingold. Je ne
veux pas critiquer, mais
vraiment la mise en scène
de ce chef d'oeuvre, et
les décors sont fort défec-
tueux, et mesquins!
Nous avons eu une tout
autre impression du
Rheingold, à Bayreuth.
Les oeuvres extraordinaires
ne s'accomodent guère au

The Letters of Franz Liszt
to Olga von Meyendorff
1871 – 1886
in the Mildred Bliss Collection
at Dumbarton Oaks

The Letters of Franz Liszt to Olga von Meyendorff
1871–1886

IN THE MILDRED BLISS COLLECTION
AT DUMBARTON OAKS

Translated by
WILLIAM R. TYLER

Introduction and Notes by
EDWARD N. WATERS

DUMBARTON OAKS
TRUSTEES FOR HARVARD UNIVERSITY
Washington · District of Columbia · 1979
Distributed by Harvard University Press
Cambridge, Mass. · London, England

Frontispiece: Liszt, candle in hand to light the dark entryway, welcomes Henry Wadsworth Longfellow and the American painter George Healy to his rooms in the Convent of Santa Francesca Romana overlooking the Forum in Rome, in 1874 (*see p. 151*). Longfellow was so entranced by this first impression of the composer-pianist that he persuaded Healy to record it on canvas. The portrait now hangs in Craigie House, the Longfellow home in Cambridge, Massachusetts.

LCC Card Number 77–082381 ISBN 0–88402–078–9

Printed in Vermont at The Stinehour Press, Lunenburg

CONTENTS

List of Illustrations ix

Foreword xi

Introduction xiii

LETTERS

1871 . . 3	1875 . . 179	1879 . . 332	1883 . . 441
1872 . . 34	1876 . . 224	1880 . . 365	1884 . . 456
1873 . . 75	1877 . . 262	1881 . . 393	1885 . . 475
1874 . . 115	1878 . . 306	1882 . . 415	1886 . . 491

Index 503

ILLUSTRATIONS

Endpapers

Original of letter of 27 August 1884, complete in four pages, set in sequence front to back of volume (*see p. 466*). His exaggerated longhand reflects Liszt's failing eyesight in his declining years.

Frontispiece

Liszt, candle in hand to light the dark entryway, welcomes Henry Wadsworth Longfellow and the American painter George Healy to his rooms in the Convent of Santa Francesca Romana overlooking the Forum in Rome, in 1874 (*see p. 151*). Longfellow was so entranced by this first impression of the composer-pianist that he persuaded Healy to record it on canvas. The portrait now hangs in Craigie House, the Longfellow home in Cambridge, Massachusetts (photo: courtesy of the National Park Service, Longfellow National Historic Site, Cambridge, Massachusetts).

Following p. 42

1. Olga von Meyendorff (1838–1926) (after a tinted photograph)
2. Concert in honor of Franz Josef, Emperor of Austria, in Budapest, 18 March 1872 (after oil painting by Schams and Lafitte)

Following p. 410

3. Liszt and his daughter (by Marie d'Agoult) Cosima, who, after her divorce from Hans von Bülow, married Richard Wagner (photo: Hanfstængl)
4. In 1881 Liszt visits his birthplace in Raiding, Hungary (after watercolor, Wagner Museum, Eisenach, E. Germany).

FOREWORD

IN his introduction to these letters, my colleague, Mr. Edward N. Waters, describes the fortuitous circumstances which combined to make possible this publication of an English translation from the original French. I first learned of their existence in October, 1970, when he informed me of the forthcoming visit to Washington of a lady who was a descendant of Liszt, and of her desire to come to Dumbarton Oaks and see them.

While it cannot be asserted that without Madame Ollivier de Prévaux' enthusiastic interest the letters would never have been published, it is certainly true that but for her they would not be appearing now. Thus, it is primarily to Madame de Prévaux that our thanks are due for this addition to the existing Liszt literature. As I listened to her in my office pleading for the publication of the letters which she and Mr. Waters had just been perusing, it occurred to me that this was a unique opportunity which should not be missed. The idea of collaboration—with direct access to the letters—between an internationally recognized authority on Franz Liszt and myself was irresistible. Mr. Waters, at the time Assistant Chief (and subsequently Chief) of the Music Division of the Library of Congress, and I were both already fully occupied, and it was nearly seven years before the results of our enterprise were ready for publication.

We wish to thank particularly Miss Marguerite Tise, who, from the beginning, has given unstintingly of her time and interest, and has made an outstanding contribution to this project. We wish also to thank Mrs. Irene Vaslef, Librarian of Dumbarton Oaks, and Miss Julia Warner, Associate Editor of Dumbarton Oaks, for their invaluable assistance, without which the task of research and editing could not have been completed within the time at our disposal. We also wish to thank Mrs. Ann Nuss who, while she was still at Dumbarton Oaks, collated the original letters and made enlarged copies of them for us to work from, thereby greatly facilitating our task.

Although it was at first intended to publish the letters in their original French as well as in translation, the cost of such a publication unfortunately proved to be prohibitive. However, the letters themselves are preserved in the Garden Library of Dumbarton Oaks, where copies of them or, when necessary, the originals may be consulted by qualified readers.

WILLIAM ROYALL TYLER
Director, Dumbarton Oaks
(1969–1977)

INTRODUCTION

THIS collection of letters became the property of Dumbarton Oaks on October 15, 1957. Shortly before that, the munificent collector Mrs. Robert Woods Bliss received them on approval from a New York dealer, and by telephone she invited me to inspect them. This I did, briefly and with alacrity, and when she asked if she should buy them I enthusiastically said *yes*! They fell into her possession, and now they are among the innumerable treasures at Dumbarton Oaks so generously donated to Harvard University by Mrs. Bliss and her husband.

In 1962–63 my wife and I were abroad for a year, researching Franz Liszt (1811–1886) and following his trail from city to city. It was a marvelous experience, and one of the great episodes was our visits with Baron Alexander von Meyendorff (1869–1964) living in London. He was the youngest and last surviving son of the Baroness, had enjoyed a distinguished political career, and was eager to know what had happened to the letters Liszt had written to his mother.[1] Forced to sell them in order to come to the financial aid of an ailing brother, he was unaware of their final depository. Ernest Newman tells us that they were put up for sale at Sotheby's in 1934;[2] so they had long since escaped the Baron's hands. The Baron greatly desired their publication, but he died in 1964 and his proffered editorial assistance vanished forever. He was a remarkable individual, and my wife correctly described him as a true noble-man.

1. See my short article, "Sur la piste de Liszt," in *Notes*, XXVII, No. 4 (Music Library Assoc., Ann Arbor, June 1971), 665–70.
2. *The Man Liszt* (London, 1934), 276 note.

On that same trip to Europe we met, in Paris, another unforgettable person of great intelligence and charm, Madame Blandine Ollivier de Prévaux, great-granddaughter of Liszt in the French line of descent. Speaking remarkable English, she chatted about many things. Naturally she was intensely curious about the Liszt-Meyendorff letters, but I could tell her little, having seen them only for a short time and *en masse*. I had had no opportunity to read any of them carefully.

In 1970 Mme de Prévaux paid her first visit to the United States and of course came to Washington. She, my wife, and I spent some memorable days together, and I arranged for her to see the treasured letters at Dumbarton Oaks. (They are all written in French.) A new Director, William Royall Tyler, was in charge, and our first contact was by telephone. He told me when to bring Mme de Prévaux to his office, and our first meeting created a lasting friendship. All of Mr. Tyler's early remarks to and continued conversation with the lady were in characteristically rapid and fluent French. She scanned the letters, waxed enthusiastic over them, and pleaded for publication in the original or in translation. Mr. Tyler acceded. As we left Dumbarton Oaks later, Mme de Prévaux said to me, and I quote the substance of her remark accurately: "Mr. Waters, never in my life, at home or abroad, have I ever heard anyone speak more perfect French. You must see that he translates those letters." The die was cast; this volume is the result.

It is difficult to explain why these letters have not been previously published, either in French or English. In his 1909 biography of Liszt,[3] Julius Kapp inserted a footnote (p. 500) referring to them: "A publication of these interesting letters is scarcely to be expected." Why such a presumption? The letters are warm and friendly, they deal with a variety of subjects, they imply a high degree of intimacy, but they contain nothing that would militate against their being published. Withholding them from the printer can only be interpreted as the determination of the recipient to allow no part of a valued friendship to be disclosed to the public. In 1909 the Baroness still had seventeen years to live, and such a decision killed the interest and hope that letter-editors normally evince.

But who was the Baroness Olga von Meyendorff and when did Liszt

3. *Franz Liszt* (Berlin-Leipzig, 1909).

first become acquainted with her? Writing to Agnes Street-Klindworth on September 19, 1863 (*Briefe* III, No. 98), Liszt said: "Among my few contacts whom I see less rarely than others I can mention . . . Baron Felix Meyendorff . . . (nephew of the [Russian] ambassador to Berlin and Vienna [who] came to Rome from Stuttgart as first secretary of the embassy). He has, I believe, all the qualities necessary for an excellent career. His wife (one of the daughters of Prince Gortschakoff of War-saw) joins to many other attractions a most original pianistic talent." By 1867 Meyendorff had been appointed ambassador to the court of Weimar, and Liszt saw the couple in Germany that year (August 28) when his *Elisabeth* was performed at the Wartburg. Transferred to Karlsruhe in 1870, Meyendorff seemed to be fulfilling the career Liszt had predicted, but he died suddenly, very early in 1871 (he was born in 1834), and his widow, with four sons, was left in a town that offered more novelty than comfort. She returned to Weimar where she had many friends and high social standing, and where Liszt was now return-ing every year to coach his group of "first-class pianists."

Surely Baroness Olga von Meyendorff (1838–1926) was a forceful, dominating, charming, and rather eccentric woman. Looking at her portrait in Robert Bory's *La Vie de Franz Liszt par l'image* (Geneva, 1936), 185, one sees the enchanting face of a person in whom intelligence and pulchritude are uniquely combined. She was destined to influence greatly the final sixteen years of the composer's life. He refers to her several times in writing to Princess Carolyne von Sayn-Wittgenstein (his second great romantic love) in Rome, generally in flattering terms. Once he ventured to be slightly critical and at the same time defensive. On May 7, 1871, he writes to his reclusive friend in the Italian capital that the Grand Duke has passed an hour with him, and he remarks that Carl Alexander wittily described Mme Meyendorff so: *Sie ist manch-mal nicht gerade liebenswürdig, doch immer sehr liebenswerth*, which might be roughly translated: "Sometimes she is not exactly amiable, but al-ways most deserving of affection."

Others, too, found her rather trying at times. Amy Fay (1844–1928), the American pupil of Liszt who supplied Liszt biographers with many of her master's personal characteristics, wrote home from Weimar on August 23, 1873, and referred to the Baroness as "Countess X":

"This haughty Countess, by the way, has always had a great fascination for me, because she looks like a woman who 'has a history.' I have often seen her at Liszt's matinées, and from what I hear of her, she is such a type of woman as I suppose only exists in Europe, and such as the heroines of foreign novels are modelled upon. She is a widow, and in appearance is about thirty-six or eight years old, of medium height, slight to thinness, but exceedingly graceful. She is always attired in black, and is utterly careless in dress, yet nothing can conceal her innate elegance of figure. Her face is pallid and her hair dark. She makes an impression of icy coldness and at the same time of tropical heat. The pride of Lucifer to the world in general—entire abandonment to the individual. I meet her often in the park, as she walks along trailing her 'sable garments like the night,' and surrounded by her four beautiful boys—as Count S. says, 'each handsomer than the other.' They have such romantic faces! Dark eyes and dark curling hair. The eldest is about fourteen and the youngest five.

The little one is too lovely, with his brown curls hanging on his shoulders! I never shall forget the supercilious manner in which the Countess took out her eye-glass and looked me over as I passed her one day in the park. Weimar being such a *kleines Nest* ['little nest'], as Liszt calls it, every stranger is immediately remarked. She waited till I got close up, then deliberately put up this glass and scrutinized me from head to foot, then let it fall with a half-disdainful, half-indifferent air, as if the scrutiny did not reward the trouble.—I was so amused. Her arrogance piques all Weimar, and they never cease talking about her. I can never help wishing to see her in a fashionable toilet. If she is so *distinguée* in a rather less than ordinary dress, what *would* she be in a Parisian costume? I mean as to grace, for she is not pretty.—But as a psychological study, she is more interesting, perhaps, as she is. She always seems to me to be gradually going to wreck—a burnt-out volcano, with her own ashes settling down upon her and covering her up. She is very highly educated, and is preparing her eldest son for the university herself. What a subject she would have been for a Balzac![4]"

4. *Music Study in Germany*, 14th ed. (Chicago, 1892), 259–60.

About a year earlier, on May 22, 1872, Cosima Wagner met the Baroness for the first time and found her most disagreeable. The occasion was the laying of the cornerstone of the Festspielhaus in Bayreuth. Liszt and the Wagners had been estranged for some time, although the Hungarian master had never ceased to acknowledge Wagner's supreme genius. Planned to coincide with Wagner's birthday (May 22), the cornerstone placement gave rise to a festive celebration, and Wagner wanted very much that Liszt be present. On May 18 Wagner wrote a most urgent and persuasive invitation to his father-in-law, and Liszt responded on May 20. The reconciliation was effected, but Liszt could not attend; his postscript added that, not wanting to entrust his letter of regret to the mail, he was sending it by a lady who, for several years, was familiar with his thoughts and feelings. The lady was the Baroness Olga.

In her recently published diary Cosima comments on the lady and the letter she brought with her.[5] Her entry for May 22 reads: "Before the concert a Frau von Meyendorff, just arrived from Weimar, had delivered Father's letter to R. The letter was lovely, but the woman, unfortunately, very unpleasant. She acts cold and repelling . . . I try to talk with Frau von Meyendorff—in French, thanks to her obstinacy." Cosima adds that her husband was highly provoked by the conversation and that it caused her considerable distress. Six months later, on November 21, she (Cosima) wrote that she had spent the evening with Marie M(oukhanoff-Kalergis) and *gar übles über Frau von Meyendorff gehört* ("heard much that was unfavorable about Frau von Meyendorff"). Gossip was as rife then as it is now! But as the years passed, Cosima and Olga became quite congenial and good friends.

These criticisms show the Baroness to be strongly independent, subservient to no one, fearlessly speaking her mind, and probably somewhat autocratic in demeanor. In these letters Liszt occasionally used expressions confirming this judgment.

La Mara (pseudonym of Marie Lipsius) wrote an interesting book entitled *Liszt und die Frauen*,[6] and the final chapter is devoted to the Baroness. Paying insufficient attention to Olga's personality, the author

5. C. Wagner, *Die Tagebücher, I, 1869–77* (Munich-Zurich, 1976).
6. *Liszt und die Frauen. Zweite neubearbeitete Auflage* (Leipzig, 1919).

truly states that the Baroness fortunately filled the gap in Liszt's life opened by Princess Carolyne's seclusion in Rome. By settling in Weimar Olga provided him with a center of hospitality and domesticity which his "bachelor" quarters there—the Hofgärtnerei—no longer offered and which he sorely needed. The Roman Princess, says La Mara, failed to realize what her self-imposed isolation would mean to the composer who, continuing his *vie trifurquée* (Weimar–Budapest–Rome), was dependent on a female anchor to keep him on course. For the most part the Baroness succeeded.

It is interesting to note that of the four women with whom Liszt maintained an extensive correspondence, it was the Baroness who received his last letter. His final missives were to: Princess Marie von Hohenlohe-Schillingsfürst (Carolyne's daughter), April 3, 1886; Carolyne, July 6, 1886; Agnes Street-Klindworth, July 7, 1886; the Baroness, July 17, 1886. The last-named meant a lot to him.

As Amy Fay wrote, Olga von Meyendorff was very highly educated. She was an omnivorous reader of both books and magazines; so was Liszt—and their conversations must have been extremely interesting. They were by no means of the same opinion, and discussions and arguments were surely frequent. They recommended books to each other and were continually sending separate periodical issues back and forth. His letters are full of personal observations, and he often commented with conviction on the views of authors with whom he might agree or disagree. It is easy to conclude from these letters that Liszt was the most intellectually curious and perhaps the most rational of all the great composers. He was, to be sure, an ardent and faithful Catholic, and while he could and would rejoice over clear defenses of the Church's position, he relished statements to the contrary—if only to try to refute them. In short, he was a thinking Christian, and he evidently found Olga to be a willing listener.

The intellectual and speculative content of the letters clearly reveals Liszt's widespread interests, his humility and humanity, his absorption in literary and philosophical movements. His references to and quotations from many authors attest the attention he paid to his reading. Mentally and spiritually he continued to develop, attaining a maturity beyond the reach of most. This could not have been easy, for he enjoyed, or suffered from, a masculine beauty and charm (not to mention his incredible talent) that irresistibly attracted the fair sex. He was human and succumbed to temptation, but not for long. He critically observed the whole world around him—literature, art, politics. He had firm views on what was happening. He was generously critical of less gifted musicians, and he played down his own gifts to an exemplary degree. Like all geniuses, he was unique, and his beneficent uniqueness extended far beyond the limits of the art he practiced.

From the strictly autobiographical point of view, perhaps, the most interesting letters are those of April 10 and 27, 1874. In these he informs the Baroness of his independence of Princess Carolyne, declaring that she had no influence over his decision to enter the minor ecclesiastical orders.

Most disappointing are his references to music. He refers frequently to composers and specific compositions. He suggests pieces that Olga should play (generally four hands or two pianos), he indicates his likes and dislikes, Wagner was his musical god and she apparently shared his enthusiasm. But there is little or nothing as far as aesthetic beliefs are concerned on how music should develop in the future. Wagner had achieved ALL; his works were sublime and divine.

Readers interested in Wagner will find numerous references to the *Patronatscheine* (patrons' vouchers) whereby the Bayreuth festivals were to be financed.[7] They were a clever and necessary device to raise money by forming an association of patrons who would each pledge 300 thalers. With the formation of Wagner Societies (*Wagner Vereine*) in various towns the scheme was changed. Several persons could combine their limited resources to purchase a single *Patronatschein*—and it is easy to see how lotteries would result. The whole effort was unsuccessful, and in 1882 Wagner himself announced the abolishment of the *Patronatverein*.

From a document typed by Baron Alexander von Meyendorff in February, 1933, when these letters must have slipped out of his hands, we learn that Carl Alexander, the Grand Duke of Saxe-Weimar, is often

---

7. Cf. E. Newman, *The Life of Richard Wagner*, IV, *1866–83* (New York, 1946), 306–9, 674, 690.

referred to as Sach(e)[8] and his wife, Sophie, as Mme S. In several letters Liszt confides to his correspondent dissatisfaction with his ducal patrons in no uncertain terms, and it may be assumed that she never betrayed his adverse criticisms.

There are numerous references to music festivals at which Liszt was invited to conduct or hear his music performed. Most of these have to do with events sponsored by the *Allgemeiner Deutscher Musikverein* (the General German Music Society) in which Liszt played a leading role from its very beginning (1859).

Liszt took great interest in the four Meyendorff children: Peter (Peterle), Michael (Mimi), Klemens (Clément), Alexander (Sachi). Clément, for thus Liszt always referred to him, was especially gifted as an artist, and there are many references to Clément-Rubens. His demise at the age of twenty-two was a grievous loss. It is easy to deduce that Michael, at the age of eighty, was the brother for whom Alexander parted with these letters to provide financial assistance. Liszt was fond of the boys and on several occasions sent his greetings to Olga's Quartet.

In the letters as a whole there are innumerable names of individuals—from the circles of royalty, nobility, and aristocracy. Liszt loved to drop names and vastly enjoyed the society in which fate had placed him. It was natural to express this pleasure to his intimate friend.

Summoned to Bayreuth at the time of Liszt's death, the Baroness arrived there the night of August 1–2, 1886. She was too late to see the master alive. At the funeral on August 3 she rode in a carriage that also conveyed Cosima, Daniela Thode (Cosima's daughter), and Princess Hatzfeld. Olga had certainly won a place of honor in the Wagnerian entourage.

In the aforementioned book by La Mara the author relates that the Baroness lived for almost thirty years in Weimar after Liszt's death, leaving the city at the outbreak of the First World War. She then settled in Rome without relinquishing her German dwelling, but in the Italian metropolis she seems to have lived in complete seclusion for, says

8. Liszt's spelling of proper names tended to be erratic. Throughout the letters, therefore, they are given, in his first use of them, as he spelled them, followed by the correct spelling set within brackets. Subsequently they are correctly spelled.

La Mara, in spite of manifold research, her later existence remained veiled.

The November, 1959, issue of *The Library of Congress Quarterly Journal of Current Acquisitions* (Washington, D.C.) contains a report on the notable additions to its Music Division during the preceding year. Pages twenty-eight to thirty describe a collection of Liszt autograph music manuscripts which were, at one time, in the possession of Baroness Olga von Meyendorff. There are twenty in all, and they date from 1865 to 1881. The Library of Congress acquired them from a gentleman in South America, but it is not known when or how they came into his possession. In any case, it is a rather strange coincidence that the two Meyendorff collections—one of music holographs, one of autograph letters—while in different institutions, are in the same city.

Olga von Meyendorff richly influenced Liszt's life. Whether he was writing music for her or letters to her, he was aware of his indebtedness. In signing these many letters he was always humbly affectionate, and he shared with her the great comforts of his religion. His laments, his complaints, his observations, his criticisms are here translated by Mr. Tyler and offered to all English readers.

Washington, D.C.   EDWARD N. WATERS
1977

Note: Annotation has necessarily been kept to a minimum.

The G and R numbers in the footnotes are references to Liszt's compositions derived from the two standard Liszt indices: *Grove*, v (London, 1954), by Humphrey Searle, and Peter Raabe's *Franz Liszt* (Tutzing, 1968).

Letters of Franz Liszt
to Olga von Meyendorff
1871 – 1886

1871

January 31, 71
Pest

Your words penetrate the depths of my soul—and awaken in it more than merely a memory. Will I be worthy of the sentiment, enigmatic but overflowing with conviction and loyalty, which you have vowed to me? I know not, and hardly dare think so. Since our last meeting in Rome my inner sorrows have deepened. To make others share them would weigh on me as a wrong, and for the years still allotted to me I feel capable only of a kind of passive perseverance in conformity with Christian precepts.

That which I still have to give is hardly worth the seeking; nevertheless I beg you to feel sure that no one honors more than I the lofty and sorrowful energies of your soul—and that I shall with predilection remain always,

Your wholly sincere servant,

F. Liszt

I'll be spending the winter here and shall probably come to Weimar in April if Their Highnesses[1] permit.

––––––––––

1. The Grand Duke Carl Alexander and the Grand Duchess Sophie.

3

February 7, 71
Pest

Yes, and with all my heart, "complete approval" of your W. project[2] unreservedly granted. Not knowing whether the major considerations which you must satisfy reconciled this project with your duties and convenience, I would not have risked raising the matter with you; but since you assure me that Weimar now suffices for you, and is even fairly well suited to the sum of the concerns and burdens of your existence, I wish to believe this and shall be very happy to come and seek you out there in the month of April (not August!).

Notwithstanding the residue of sadness markedly accumulated within me by twelve years of agitation, of fights, of passion in Weimar, I feel less ill at ease there than elsewhere, thanks to the long-standing kindness of Their Highnesses, whom I shall ever try to serve gratefully and faithfully. On one of her birthday anniversaries, I said to the Grand Duchess: "It is now some twenty years since I first ensconced myself here; deign to look on me as an old piece of furniture of the grand-ducal household; and may this piece of furniture be like mahogany, which improves with the passing years."

I shall beg my very gracious neighbor[3] of the Hofgärtnerei to plead the cause of W[eimar] with you. She is passionately devoted to you and will find the means of convincing you. So be it. When you have made your decision I hope you will notify your infirm and silent servant of it.

FL

Toward the end of next week, I shall pay a few days' visit to Mgr Archbishop Haynald, at Kalocsa.

Imre Széchenyi, whom I see a little more often here than in Rome, gave a musical evening on Sunday, when his musical compositions were greatly appreciated and applauded.

---

2. Presumably a reference to the Baroness von Meyendorff's settlement in Weimar, following the death of her husband two weeks earlier.
3. The Grand Duchess, on whose estate was Liszt's residence, the Hofgärtnerei.

March 7, 71
Pest

This week I had to take care of a little musical task, the instrumentation of a *Lied*, or rather Canticle, by Schubert: *Die Allmacht*,[4] and add to it a choir of male voices for a forthcoming concert of the *Société de Chant* of Buda. Now I have become terribly scrupulous and cautious in discharging my profession of musician. In order to go on writing I have to put everything else aside, and the setting down of my ideas, as such, takes an amount of time vastly disproportionate to their slight value. Moreover, there is then the matter of correcting copies and proof, the preliminary and dress rehearsals, correspondence with publishers, proofreaders, engravers, and a whole lot of endless worries imposed on me by the art and the craft of sound.

Forgive me for having delayed thanking you for your letter. Alas! I know only too well how little I am able to say what I would like, and how I would like to say it. I shall probably be kept here until after Easter. If possible I shall try to spend Holy Week in some nearby spot —and then I shall go to Vienna for a week or so.

Mme de Hell[dorf] had already told me that the aggressive insubordination of Father Hyacinthe had made a considerable impression on you. His eloquence and his successes have been stumbling blocks for him. The Catholic structure has no cement other than faith and absolute obedience. We no longer have enough of these left to us in Europe to be able to manage a schism. Consequently Father Hy[acinthe] will be reduced to that powerless isolation which is the most mortal sorrow of generous hearts. If you can part with his all too well-known last letter which I have not yet managed to obtain, you will be doing me a favor in sending it to me.

Let us speak of less important matters. Imre Széchenyi has composed a very pretty quartet—with a sparkling Moorish Serenade and Finale— for stringed instruments. We shall be hearing it tomorrow evening at his house in very charming company . . . who will probably yawn, at

---

4. G 376; R 652. Liszt's holograph is in the Library of Congress, Washington, D.C.

least *in petto*, during the audition of my *Orpheus*,[5] which is also to be performed, with harp, harmonium, violin, piano, etc., and I take the liberty of reminding you of its theme, heard in times gone by on the Corso:

From my heart and with conviction, your very respectful servant,

F. Liszt

<hr />

March 16, 71
Pest

Welcome to Weimar. In his recent letter to the Empress Augusta, Grillparzer endows our *Musensitz* [abode of the muses] with the glorious title of "Fatherland of all the cultivated minds of Germany," and Prince Pückler used to claim that all kinds of illustrations of this had of necessity and forever to meet there, both wholesale and retail. I hope you will find enough there which suits your mind and heart—and that you will include me with indulgence within this circle.

You ask who should be chosen as piano teacher for your children?[6] None other than my spirited and very worthy friend Gottschalg—un-

5. G 98; R 415, symphonic poem.
6. Peter von Meyendorff, called Peterle; Michael von Meyendorff, called Mimi; Klemens von Meyendorff, called Clément; Alexander von Meyendorff, called Sachi.

less Lassen should be willing and available. Do not let Gottschalg's not very aristocratic manners shock you, and overlook a certain prolixity on the subject of his friendship for me.

When I come to Weimar I shall beg you to have your pupils play the piano for me, and we shall settle everything for the best with my *legendarischen* Cantor,[7] now Hoforganist and Seminar Lehrer, with regard to the future course of their studies.

I have received from Rome Father Hyac[inthe]'s appeal to the bishops, which you read too much *ab irato* to form an accurate idea of it. It is a new version of the famous *Les Cinq Plaies de l'Eglise* by Rosmini, once a sensational opuscule in Rome to the point that the Cardinal's hat, already set aside for its author, fled in dismay. The basis of these ideas continues to ferment among foolhardy Catholics but I do not think that even an attempt at a schism will emerge from them.

In mid-April I shall go to Vienna, and shortly thereafter – – – it would be superfluous to say where.

Without enigma, your very devoted servant,

FL

———

March 27, 71
Pest

According to highly disagreeable reports, lodgings in Weimar are in short supply. I extend to you my sincere sympathy for the nuisance caused by your three changes of apartments, from the mezzanine to the floor between first and second, with the prospect of finally settling down on the first floor. There you will be tolerably housed. Heaven grant that I may help to make it restful and agreeable for you.

The picture you draw of your surroundings is most charming. All its elements blend in wonderful harmony with each other and we shall not be lacking in music with or without notes. What ideas for composition

7. Liszt often referred to Gottschalg as "my legendary cantor."

do you have for me? Write to me frankly about this. *Psalm 13*,[8] which you mentioned to me, should not be sung by a female voice; it calls for a virile register combined with the feminine sentiment of the anguish of things divine. I hear that Walther sang it admirably in Vienna this winter.

I hope that Mme de Moukhanoff will come to Weimar in June. She has a singularly true and subtle understanding of the soul. You will get along very well with each other.

I shall stay here until Easter—and shall write to the Grand Duke only after the jubilant ceremonies in Germany. Wagner is bringing out a *Kaiser Marsch* which he and I shall be playing four hands at the Tuileries[9] where you reside—in May.

umilissimo servo,

FL

My very affectionate homage to Mme de Helldorf.

———

Monday, April 1, 71

Pest

While I do not share your views with regard to an "official" announcement of my arrival at Weimar, I willingly heed your repeated admonitions and beg you to be so kind as to have the enclosed note delivered to His Excellency Count Beust.

It was my intention to arrive more or less unexpectedly, and I have never asked anyone to deliver a message at a high level on this subject. Were there to be any difficulty in locating the keys of the apartment which people have been so kind as to make available to me with the assurance that it would always remain at my disposal, I shall solve this

8. G 13; R 489.
9. The German equivalent: *Ziegelei.*

little difficulty by taking a room at the Erbprinz or at some other hotel.

Since I fear setting forth on Fridays, I'll leave Vienna only on Saturday (because of a little musical entertainment arranged for Thursday) and shall arrive in Weimar some time on Sunday.

Forgive me this enumeration of dates and pray believe me to be very wholly your obedient servant,

FL

Tomorrow morning I'll be in Vienna.

Please continue to send me *L'Univers* there – Schottenhof, c/o Hofrath v. Liszt.

I did not neglect to do what you asked of me for last Thursday.

————

Easter Sunday [April 9]
9 o'clock

This morning I took communion. On my return I opened your last letter and am replying effusively from my heart. What you ask of me was done long ago, simply, completely, and with no merit on my part, for I am as much a stranger to sentiments of rancor as of envy.

Besides, the way I understand forgiveness will not, I trust, displease you; a witty woman defined forgiveness as "a form of contempt": I am far from treating it thus, and feel that it must be free of all presumptuousness and arrogance, thus retaining only Christian humility and gentleness.

The love and obedient devotion you had for your husband[10] entitled him to my respectful—and sorrowful affection. It has never failed him; I have already sincerely prayed for him—and shall continue to do so in the future, united with you in heart.

The prayer of Pope Clement XI is very beautiful and embraces all the goals of Christian life, both active and passive. I recited it again

10. The Baron Felix von Meyendorff.

yesterday evening in its original version, which is far more concise and vigorous: *Credo, Domine, sed credam firmius. Spero, sed sperem securius. Amo, sed amem ardentius. Doleo, sed doleam vehementius*, etc. At Weimar I shall take the liberty of bringing you the German translation which is much preferable to the French, and there is also in the same volume a prayer which I often recite. It is by the abhorred St. Ignatius:

> "Soul of Jesus Christ sanctify me,
> Body of Jesus Christ save me,
> Blood of Jesus Christ exalt me," etc.

The copy of Pascal, which I thank you for remembering, has been mislaid somewhere, but we'll be able to share the pleasure of annotating another copy together at your Tuileries, where I also look forward to benefiting amply from your very obliging and much appreciated role of reader—beginning with Hübner's book.

Now, dear and awe-inspiring letter writer, don't scold me for writing to you so little and so seldom. You are familiar with my brachylogical [laconic] infirmity; I am the first to suffer from it, but am incapable of correcting it; so please be indulgent. Yesterday I sent a telegram to Beust for the birthday of the Grand Duchess, and I shall be writing next week to Monseigneur.[11] Please send me news of yesterday's festivities. I must stay here until the 20th–22nd of M[ay] because of a comedy to be given by amateurs, combined with a concert (for a children's charity); then I shall spend a week or so in Vienna (without any concert). Write to me c/o my cousin: Hofrath Ed. Liszt, Schottenhof.

The formulation of your musical plan for chapter III of the *Lamentations of Jeremiah* is astonishing. I'll be very careful not to duplicate Mme Viardot's irreverence, and would be much inclined to follow all your indications with regard to the allocation of the stanzas to the bass, the tenor, the baritone ("whose notes are most suitable for the passage which appeals to reason"), provided that I be given the time necessary to undertake a composition of this sort. I'll soon be turning to you for

11. The Grand Duke.

more extensive instructions on the same subject, and till then I implore you not to indulge in any more jeremiads.

Khristos Voskres [Christ is Risen]—without the yeast of old, but with the unleavened bread of sincerity and truth.

FL

———

April 24, 71
Vienna

Count Beust's telegram in reply to mine (for the anniversary of the G[rand] D[uchess]) pleased me greatly in giving me the assurance that my forthcoming stay at Weimar is not unwelcome to Their Highnesses. This morning I thanked the G[rand] D[uke] for this, while announcing my arrival in about ten days' time. Will you allow me to accept your very gracious offer to be of service with regard to the Hofgärtnerei, and will you be so kind as to settle matters pertaining to my lodging with Mme de Helldorf and Mme Merian? Last year they kindly undertook to take care of the necessary preliminaries so that the doors of my quarters should not be locked on my arrival—and Mme Merian knows the worthy creature named Pauline[12] who, with my valet, has been running my little household for years. The former one, Fortunato, went back to Rome in October but his successor, Miska,[13] my compatriot, will be more to the liking of Weimar. He has a pleasant manner and style without any false pretentions or ill humor. He will thus fit in harmonically[14] with Pauline who will, I hope, be happy to resume her former service in my household provided that Mme Merian is so kind as to tell her this.

Please excuse these almost too explicit details.

If I am able to leave Vienna Sunday next, I shall be in W[eimar] by

12. Pauline Apel, FL's housekeeper in Weimar, later caretaker of Liszt Museum there.
13. Miska Sipka.
14. Liszt writes *harmoniquement,* not *harmonieusement.*

Tuesday or Wednesday—for I am spending a half-day in Prague and in Leipzig.

To my very understanding one, greetings, respects, and homage.

FL

Until April 30 I shall be at my cousin's:
  Hofrath Ed. Liszt
  Schottenhof, Vienna.

[undated]

Let us first of all banish the "familiar demon" with his discordant comments and cart him off to burial on the "hearse" of a no less discordant phraseology, which must also be interred.

It goes without saying that you will fulfill all your duties. For this, calm is needed and you seem to be remarkably agitated. Will you talk reasonably with me? I am entirely at your command, whether in Eisenach where you have to stop off if you are taking Clément to Salzungen, or in Weimar. Only let me know the day and hour by telegram or letter and I will arrange matters according to your orders.

Besides, it seems to me that the doctor is exaggerating causes for concern and I do not usually place much faith in recommendations of climate, baths, travel, etc., which I have only too frequently found to be foolish. But I will avoid harping on so sensitive a point and I entrust myself completely to your own deliberations which will prompt you to take the best and wisest decisions. If I can be of the slightest help to you, call unreservedly on

your very humbly
devoted servant,

FL

Friday

I will answer at some other time a few minor points in your letter of yesterday.

Thursday morning, July 20
Weimar

I need not tell you that I haven't looked at a single syllable of the enclosed letter. I permitted myself only to change the envelope, for after having tried to correct the address on that of your correspondent, I found the result fuzzy and untidy, both of which I always dislike, whatever the circumstances or whatever form they take.

From Sunday evening until Tuesday I spent two peaceful days at Schwerstedt,[15] thanks to the fondness which your friend lavishes on me. Your Roman son, Clément, makes a very good impression and seems to be enjoying himself very much at Schwerstedt in spite of being deprived of strawberries, etc., in accordance with your orders. Mme de Hell[dorf] had already written to you before my arrival, and I was there when she mailed her letter.

Tausig has died in Leipzig. This is a great loss for me, both in terms of friendship and of art. He was an individual of great quality and skill. He had the ability to fill a most difficult position and would have carried it through to the end successfully. Men such as he are so rare that one does not know where to come across them.

I intended to go to Wilhelmsthal today; but Mme Moukhanoff, who was at Tausig's deathbed, is being so friendly and kind as to come here this morning and I will try to keep her here until Saturday. I'll probably accompany her as far as Eisenach and go from there to Wilhelmsthal.

L'Univers and the *Débats* reach me regularly. I read them with all the more interest in that I owe them to your generosity; also I like to hope that underlinings will not be wanting for too long.

You lost your last little bet, and will certainly lose all similar bets with

Your *umilissimo servo*,

FL

---

15. Estate of the Baron von Helldorf.

July 26, 71
Wilhelmsthal

On Sunday, the day after my arrival, Mlle de Watz[dorf] sent you news about Wilhelmsthal. Her pen will certainly have had more charm and liveliness than mine which is, alas, so gloomy! And yet it is not for lack of practice that I do not acquire more epistolary talent. For the last three days I have been doing nothing but laboriously penning words, which is harassing to me. Other than this I have only praise for everything here; my existence is most agreeable and peaceful, and Their Highnesses are most graciously affable to me.

I gratefully accept your "presumptions and rapacities" and shall come to thank you for them on Sunday at Weimar.

Princess Wittgenstein has sent me her latest book which she has paid me the honor of dedicating to me. It is a bulky tome (of about 700 pages) entitled *La Matière dans la dogmatique chrétienne*, published in Rome with the imprimatur of ecclesiastical censorship. The author writes to me: "it makes neither for easy reading nor for pleasant reading . . . but in one or two decades, it may be that this book will make its mark in the history of science."

I learn from the last issue of *L'Univers* that the "gentle and generous attempt by R. P. Ronald de Card" to lead Father Hyacinthe (to whom *L'Univers* always refers as M. Loyson) back to the fold has failed. He is leaving Rome and is going to Munich, the capital of the "neo-Protestantism which styles itself old-Catholicism."

With very sincere regards and humble devotion,

FL

———

Wednesday, August 13, 71

During the journey from Eisenach to Wilhelmsthal, I read some forty pages of the *Commentaire sur l'Evangile* by Gratry, which you had recommended to me. There are some beautiful and gentle things in it, nobly expressed. I found, scored with your fingernail: "gentleness is the fullness of strength"—a luminous aphorism, which should not be pressed too far in order not to spoil it. Prosaically speaking, true strength is accompanied by gentleness, just as true justice leans toward mercy. Truly great men are those who combine contrary qualities within themselves. You will find this thought vigorously expressed in Pascal: "I do not admire a man who has only great qualities if he does not at the same time have contrary qualities," etc. (I am not quoting the exact words, but the idea.) Indeed, we know by experience that gentleness without strength degenerates into weakness, justice without mercy into harshness and cruelty, and every gift, every quality, every virtue without charity becomes sterile!

Moreover, Father Gratry seems to me greatly to exaggerate the possibility of the immediate effect of Christianity on the peoples of Europe, and I do not really believe as he does that at the burning words of a "small number of men, the crowd, a heroic and simple mass, would follow the call as it did for the crusades." In my humble view the great results of our time are achieved principally through work and organization. This is slower and strewn with more difficulties than the enthusiastic approach which has unfortunately shown itself to be powerless in many circumstances, starting with the crusades themselves! In a recent letter to the Municipal Council of Lyon, M. Gambetta summarizes the present policy in a couple of words: *La nation toute entière instruite et armée*. The program is valid, but too restricted; let us add that the nation, educated and armed, must also be properly fed and housed, usefully occupied, and above all religiously minded. In the latter respect the clergy has an immense task before it.

Day before yesterday at dinner we were saying how empty Weimar is in summer. The Grand Duchess observed to me: "Mme de Meyendorff is there," on a half-questioning note. I replied, "Yes, Madame," in the most respectful and final manner. Later on, while we were alone together Countess Kalkreuth [Kalckreuth] reverted to the same theme, which I adorned, in measured terms, with a few embellishments concerning the apartment in the Tuileries, the project of acquiring the Zedlitz house, etc.

I spend the days in my room except for mealtimes (noon and 5 o'clock) when there are usually six or seven of us—Count Beust, Mme de Konneritz, Mme Kalckreuth, Mauderode, and Their Highnesses. In the evening we foregather at the Grand Duchess'. She has good news of the Grand Duke from Ostend. In the same issue of the *Revue des deux mondes* which contains the final part of Caro's *La Bohème*, an article by Laveleye on forms of government struck the Grand Duchess as most remarkable—which is high praise.

I want to believe in the "balm."

(unsigned)

September 6, 71
Eichstätt

From morning till night our time is taken up with those musical festivities in which, more than any others, I risk being given no respite. After the performances come public and private gatherings, speeches and resolutions, visits, meals, and entertainments. Besides, there really is something extraordinary at Eichstätt. In terms of church music it is the grain of mustard seed of the Gospel. Some thirty voices (just barely) of both sexes have recently performed in four days a program from which choral groups far larger and more famous than that of the *Dom Chor* of Eichstätt would shrink. We heard five masses by Palestrina, Witt, Ett, Greith, and some thirty church pieces, ancient and modern, psalms, motets, lamentations, litanies, etc. All this was sung with highly remarkable feeling and discipline under the baton of a most meritorious ecclesiastic, F. Witt, *Kapellmeister* of the Cathedral, President of the Cecilian Society (founded at Ratisbon in 1868, and differing greatly, much to its advantage from a musical point of view, from the Roman congregation of St. Cecilia), and a true and ardent confessor of church music, both by his written compositions and by his choral teaching.

This evening I arrive in Munich and leave again tomorrow, as soon as my passport has been visa'd at the Italian legation. Sunday I shall be back at Santa Francesca Romana, Campo Vaccino.

I was deeply touched by a pronoun[16] in your letter; it begins not with J—but with N; let us retain this pronoun, with a pure and lofty heart.

Since you order me to command, I beg you to moderate as much as possible your worries about Clément, so that you may discharge all your duties judiciously. Please let me know if the Salzungen cure, which was favored by fine weather, was a success. In October, I'll inform you of Bobrinski's arrangements with regard to Clément.

Louis Philippe's remark about M. Thiers rates a blue pencil mark, and no less Veuillot's comment: that after having always found a way to thrust himself into the King's place, even into the bed which His Majesty had reserved for himself while at the same time leaving the choice between the two beds up to M. Thiers, this devilish little man has again gone from bad to worse, and now wants to get into all the beds simultaneously, while insisting that everyone sleep standing up.[17]

I will miss the blue pencil marks in Rome, but perhaps you will nevertheless be sending me some now and then—and in November in Pest I'll dare once again to ask if I may share *L'Univers.*

Prostrate before you,

FL

The important document just now in the "Old Catholics" affair is the rescript of Cultural Minister Lutz to the Archbishop of Munich (see the *Allgemeine Zeitung* of Augsburg for August 30).

---

16. Liszt is referring to the initial letter *J* (for *Je*), instead of which Baroness von Meyendorff uses the letter *N* (for *Nous*).

17. A pun on a French expression for boring people to death: *C'est à dormir debout.*

Sunday morning, September 17, 71

Having left Munich on Thursday, September 7, at eleven in the evening, I arrived in Rome on Saturday the ninth at half-past five that evening, with no other stop than the three or four hours' wait at Padua and Bologna imposed by the railroad regulations.

Here at Santa Francesca I found my quarters again—and even my two cats—just as I had left them. The six or seven Olivetan Fathers who run the convent have not yet been expropriated. The Order is harmless and small; its principal convent was at Monte Oliveto in Tuscany; it also owns three or four houses in France, to whose growth a very congenial man who entered the Order rather late in life, but with sincere and active piety—the Marquis de Bainville—greatly contributed under the "corrupting" regime of Napoleon III. The founder of the Olivetans is St. Bernard Tolomei, born in Siena in 1272, died in 1348. He adopted the rule of St. Benedict, as the founders of the Cistercian and of the Camaldolese Orders, Robert, Abbot of Molesmes, and St. Romuald, had done two centuries earlier. Under Gregory XVI (who was a Camaldolese monk), there had been a question of merging the Olivetans with the Camaldolese who are far more numerous. Although both wear white habits and basically follow the same rule, they agreed only so far as to remain, if not divided, at least distinct from each other.

St. Frances of Rome, of a noble family, in founding the institution of the Colettines or Oblates in the fifteenth century, placed it under the direction of the Fathers of the Congregation of Monte Oliveto. If I am not mistaken, this institution had from its origin an aristocratic stamp which it has retained. The principal house of the Oblates is at Tor de' Specchi (at the foot of the Capitol), where these ladies long kept the body of St. Frances. It was translated in recent years to the church under the auspices of the Saint at the time of the erection there of the elaborate monument of the patroness, carved by the Cavaliere Meli, and paid for with the bequest for this purpose by an Oblate lady—Princess Pallavicini. The popular image, enclosed herewith, of St. Frances with her angel provided the theme of the monument. In the church to the right of the high altar there is also the tomb of Pope Gregory XI who, solicited by St. Catherine of Siena, brought the Holy See back from Avignon to Rome (January 7, 1377).

One of these days, I shall send you a fairly large photograph, taken at my expense, of the church of St. Frances. It was built on the site of the Temple of Venus and of Rome (the ruins of which are visible from one of the rooms of my apartment) between the Temple of Peace (or Basilica of Constantine?) and the Colosseum, twenty feet from the Arch of Titus and the Palatine hill—the Tuileries of the Caesars—over which the archaeological science of Senator Salvator Rosa now reigns supreme. Someone told me that he retains a feeling of profound gratitude toward the Emperor Napoleon, and that he had wept bitterly on learning of the disaster of Sedan.

I have as yet paid no calls. Unusually for me, I have caught an ailment which has forced me to spend a couple of days in bed for the first time in years. Let's say no more about it, for when I got up this morning I felt adequately recovered.

My very humble thanks for your two letters full of charm and sadness. I'll inquire at the Salviatis (at the end of the month) about the arrival of the Bobrinskis. Father Hyacinthe is not in Rome, and M. de Maguelonne is still awaiting his expulsion order. To give you an idea of the tone of the so-called clerical or popish press, I am sending you under separate cover yesterday's number of the *Correspondance de Rome*. Please keep me informed on the new and very important functions of M. de Loën as manager of the Nibelungen theatre at Bayreuth. Fifty thousand thalers would be one-sixth of the sum required. Is it true that the German Emperor[18] has given 15,000 thalers? . . . In what form? Have the names of the first subscribers already been published? When you see Loën, ask him for specific and printed information, if there is anything authentic on this subject.

Sunday, half-past five

Your telegram has just been handed to me, and I should almost scold you for it; but how can I? Please do me the favor never to worry about

18. Wilhelm I.

me at all. I intend to last and endure for some time yet on this earth; if I am wrong, no matter. I am quite ready to obey elsewhere the Father of Mercy, to whom I pray that he bless you and strengthen you in the holy peace of the "gentle and humble of heart."

FL

My greetings of lasting friendship to Lassen. Tell me how things stand with regard to his score for Hebbel's *Nibelungen*, and when it is to be performed in Vienna.

———

September 25, 71

Thank you for having anticipated my non-curious request by answering it before it reached you with the account of your walk with M. de Loën. The major recommendation I took the liberty of making to you of never worrying about me implied that of never paying attention to most of the things being said about my humble person.

Let us right away apply this recommendation to the confidences volunteered by L[oën] on my state of mind with regard to the performance of the *Nibelungen* in Bayreuth. I think I have already talked to you about this fairly explicitly, but since you do not seem to have understood me clearly, and since this goal interests you, I turn to it once again while asking you to forgive me for indulging in my turn in "*perissologies*" [pleonasms].

First of all, I am very glad that Loën has accepted the post of manager of the new model-theatre of Bayreuth. His capacity and experience, his vigilant zeal, effectively guarantee the sound conduct of the project and its ultimate success. Besides, since Weimar formerly had the honor of retaining Wagner's works in its repertory during the few years when other theatres with greater advantages did not pay much attention to them, it is more appropriate that the manager of Weimar, rather than any of his colleagues, should be the executive director of the great undertaking, full of difficulties and complexities, of the *Nibelungen*. Mme de Schleinitz and Tausig spoke to me at length about it at Weimar (last June). I did not conceal from them the fact that the funds—300,000 thalers—will prove inadequate for the task after a dozen or so dramatic performances; and that a more or less temporary theatre, newly erected on top of the old and renowned theatre of a small town, would generate great expenditures and many difficulties, still more greatly increased by the necessity of recruiting elsewhere the roughly two hundred members of the staff of singers, musicians for the orchestra, painters, decorators, machinists, etc., required for the production of ideal performances as intended by Wagner. Obviously if, for this task, he could have at his disposal and be satisfied with one of the large theatres of Germany currently active, disposing of proper material and artistic resources, to which one would need to add only extras, this would be at the same time more sound, more convenient, more economical, and . . . frankly speaking, more reasonable.

Nevertheless the project is grandiose, and the work of the *Nibelungen* more grandiose still. Nothing comparable has shone forth heretofore in the loftiest spheres of art. So let all efforts be bent toward the performance of such a masterpiece; nothing could be better and I associate myself with it very willingly, as I at once told Mme de Schleinitz and Tausig, by subscribing to three shares of three hundred thalers each—which, given the modesty of my income, is no easy matter for me—only requesting: 1) that one should be assured of the benevolent attitude of the King of Bavaria,[19] as supreme protector and promoter of the *Nibelungen*—failing which, in my opinion, one should abstain from proceeding further; 2) that some twenty people—Mmes de Schleinitz, Moukhanoff, Metternich, Meyendorff, at their head—should appear on the same subscription list as myself and should total roughly a tenth of the sum required by Wagner's program, for it would be unseemly for the champions of his genius to stimulate public sympathy (perhaps a little vague and hesitant?) to pay up before having themselves set a good example.

19. Ludwig II.

As a matter of fact, I have arranged with my friends Riedel and Gille that the *Allgemeiner Deutscher Musikverein*[20] would take at least one share (*Patronatschein*)[21] and, as an additional gesture, I have sent six thalers to the publisher Fritsch [Fritzsch] in Leipzig as a contribution to the Leipzig *Wagner Verein* of which he is the director.

This is exactly what I have said and done with regard to this matter. Now let everyone who will suspect me of malevolence toward the *Nibelungen* project: "Auf solche Einzelheiten kann ich nicht eingehen" [I cannot go into such details], the late Prince Metternich used to say, nor can I accept that my friends should call on me to justify myself, when their first duty should be not to accuse me wrongly.

———

Count Kalnocki [Kálnoky] told me yesterday that the Bobrinskis have just arrived. I'll tell you about this soon.

Saturday I saw again Duke Gaetani [Caetani] at Frascati, in good health, and still most intelligent and perspicacious. His daughter-in-law, Princess Teano, is about to have her second child. I am to have the honor of being the child's godfather—and shall return to Frascati on Friday, St. Michael's Day, the Duke's Saint's day.

My very sincere thanks for your kind "shipments" and supply of newspapers. Please stop sending me *L'Univers*, which I have now been reading as a subscriber since September 16; but if you would be so kind as to send me from time to time outstanding articles by Lemoinne and others in the *Journal des débats*, this will be pleasant and useful to me. Later on in Pest I will beg you to lend me Daniel Stern's[22] Dialogues (Diotima![23]) on Dante and Goethe,[24] so highly praised by the *Débats*,

20. From its beginning in 1859, Liszt played a leading role in this organization, the purpose of which was to foster and promote German music.

21. A method of raising money for Wagner's Bayreuth enterprise. A share was called a *Patronatschein*.

22. Pseudonym of the Countess Marie d'Agoult.

23. A priestess of Mantinea, to whom Plato, in *The Banquet*, attributes Socrates' theories on love and vanity. This literary fiction was popular with Goethe, Hölderlin, et al.

24. *Dante et Goethe: dialogues* (Paris, 1866).

and of which I read only half, some time ago, in the *Revue germanique*.[25]

In order to keep yourself informed on the trend among the *vieux catholiques*, I urge you to get the *Allgemeine Zeitung* of Augsburg, the official monitor of the new schismatic-orthodoxy, of the last week of this September. Father Hyacinthe, whom you now consider only a Mister, brings to it the aid of his "eloquent" personality, and your compatriots have sent delegates to Munich.

In the September 23 issue of the *Allg. Zeit.*, you will find the *Erwägungen eines Protestanten angesichts des Münchener Katholikencongresses* [Reflections of a Protestant concerning the Munich Congress of Catholics], signed J. F.-Jéna.

I remain, immutably and forever, your very humbly beholden servant,

FL

Thursday, October 5, 71

This time the fault is not mine. Registered letters are always subject to a slight delay in Rome. I answered yours the day after it arrived, and you will have received this last letter at the same time as the one from Bobrinski, whom I had also urged to place three seals on it for greater security. Thus the error arises from your calculation of time, preceded by a slip of geography. Bozen [Bolzano] is not on my way to Pest nor even Vienna (where I do not intend to go before Pest). If you look at the map you will see that I have to pass through Mestre, Unbresina, etc., without touching Verona or crossing the Brenner. . . .

Let us go back to the Bobrinskis. You can be sure of their friendliest sentiments, and I am convinced that they will very much welcome the opportunity of proving this to you. Unfortunately they are already very cramped in their Casa Margherita; the Countess complains of not being able to unpack a substantial portion of her belongings and the

25. It appeared in 1864 in the *Revue germanique et française*.

Count is concerned, from a humane point of view, at the too small living quarters of his servants. Furthermore, you know he is expecting his brother from Petersburg, whom he promised to put up, less than comfortably, in the room formerly occupied by their son.

If you have something to tell them which you would sooner not write down, please let me know, for I shall be seeing them fairly frequently until the end of this month. Thanks for the news of the *Nibelungen*, which I beg you to go on sending me now and then. I'll also be much obliged to you if you will keep me a little up to date on events at Court, which interest me, and on which my only correspondent in Weimar, Gottschalg, is not able to inform me accurately. Is the Grand Duchess at Heinrichau? Is the Grand Duke traveling? What is the date of Mlle de Watzdorf's wedding?

Speaking of marriage, people here are talking with some surprise about that of Count Larderelles (whom you saw in Rome as attaché at the French Embassy) to the daughter of Duke Salviati. It seems that Lard[erelles] had the ambition of marrying a Roman princess, and people say that he had already asked for the hand of the daughter of Prince Doria. On the other hand, it is rumored that Princess Sciarra's son has turned down a very brilliant Russian match.

Day before yesterday, at the Holy Father's[26] audience, I came across Baron Visconti in the guise of "the courtier of misfortune" (as he styles himself). *Roma capitale* has deprived him of everything save the honor of his imperishable glory. Milord Rosa, superintendent of monuments, director of excavations, Senator, etc., etc., is even in command at Ostia! A few right-thinking newspapers, such as the *Osservatore*, the *Voce della verità*, are publishing articles inspired by Visconti and Vespignani (they say) reminding Rosa of his lowly origins—which circumstances would seem conducive to excavating—of his former bread-winning job at the Borghese Gallery, where Visconti claims to have given him *la mancia*; and they bury him far deeper than any past, present, or future excavations with this triumphal quip: "M. Rosa has achieved far more through the sweat of his feet than through the sweat

26. Pius IX.

of his brow!" Forgive me for quoting this shockingly coarse item, which in no way detracts from the merit of my illustrious and peaceful neighbor in the palace of the Caesars.

The Holy Father is in wonderfully good health and in full strength of faith and authority. Notwithstanding the necessary tugging and hauling, some very well-informed acquaintances of mine forecast complete calm of the status quo in Rome during the winter. There was no more unrest on October 2, the anniversary of the plebiscite, than on September 20. *L'Italia fa da sè!* [Italy is making it on her own!]

All your letters have reached me. I hardly write or work. Send me neither *Débats* nor *Univers* any more: people lend me a lot of newspapers which I struggle to read. Veuillot replied in person to your criticisms of his article about the "hole" of the Mont Cenis. Frankly I don't much care for his first article and still less for the last one, in spite of my unwavering admiration for his intellectual dexterity. On the other hand, several shafts in his *La Gouaillerie en politique* (*L'Univers* for Sunday, October 1) seem to me well aimed.

Monday evening Princess Marie Hohenlohe arrived. She will be spending a few weeks with her mother—bedridden these last two weeks, but not dangerously sick—and has given me news of the performance of Hebbel's *Die Nibelungen* which she attended in Vienna. Lassen's music was a great success despite the very modest resources of the Burgtheatre orchestra.

Your very humble and silent servant,

FL

———

October 23, 71
Rome

For want of better, let me at least repeat to you once again at Bolzano my wishes, greetings, and thanks. Were they as efficacious as they are sincere you would certainly have nothing to complain about in this world—not even my sad self.

Something really pleasant happened to me yesterday. Bülow came to convey his wishes to me on my birthday. No man is as close to my heart as he. He is practically my son and has been, for some twenty years, the most spirited and intimate of my friends. The natural nobility of his character is such that heroism seems to be a familiar condition for him.

We had not seen or written to each other in two years. The painful circumstances of his separation from Cos[ima][27] have greatly impaired his health; but he is now recovering his full strength and intends to start on a round of performances next winter beginning with Vienna, Pest, Prague, Dresden, Berlin, Leipzig, and ending in London in May. In the fall he will be sailing to America.

Yesterday, Princess Wittgenstein and her daughter did me the honor of inviting themselves to dinner at Santa Francesca Romana. Teano, Count Kálnoky, Father Ferrari (now Archbishop of Lepanto), and Father Theiner were among our guests—and since Sgambati had taken the trouble to have a second piano brought to the house, we played *Mazeppa*[28] together. I then treated the audience to some movements from the *Carnevale di Milano*[29] (*Polonaise, Dormiveglia, Sospiri danzanti*) of Bülow, who also sat down at the piano thereby giving extreme pleasure to us all and to me in particular. Our little improvised concert ended with *Orpheus*,[30] with Bülow. This morning he is offering us a Beethoven session at the Sala Dantesca and leaves again tomorrow for Florence. Mme Laussot, who accompanied him here, asks to convey to you her respectful compliments.

To tell you all, let me add that I wrote again to Cosima at the end of last month. In her letter of yesterday she mentions M. de Loën, with whom she seems to be much pleased. Among other things she feels he

27. Cosima Wagner, wife of Richard Wagner, Liszt's second daughter. Her first husband was Hans von Bülow.

28. G 100; R 417, symphonic poem. G 640; R 362, for 2 pianos.

29. Opus 21.

30. G 638; R 360, for 2 pianos. *See also* note 5, letter of March 7.

has the advantage of not being unduly awed by the difficulties of the Bayreuth undertaking and of "seeing things through rose-colored glasses," an advantage I appreciate all the more in that I have it so little. I am usually given to seeing things neither in rose nor in black, but in gray—half in mourning: and even so I have to make a certain effort of will not to see things more somberly still.

I am staying here until November 9, and shall spend one day in Florence with Mme Laussot on my way to Pest.

May your new "Weimar chapter" be agreeable and beneficial to your soul, in accordance with the desire of

Your FL

Do not fret at the scarcity of my letters; this week I shall have to send off a dozen or so letters which take all my time.

November 2, 71
Rome

The hotel-keeper Badl at Gries seems to have been even more negligent than I. Following your indications, I wrote to you at that address on October 23 (I recall the date because of the evening before) but my letter probably did not reach you, as you accuse me of treating you too much as academies do their corresponding members, whose privilege consists in writing without receiving a reply.

Your day in Munich is full of interest. Far from ridiculing your curiosity, I permit myself to approve highly of it and thank you for sharing it with me. Your comment that you find Father Hya[cinthe]'s sincerity not quite "impartial and impersonal" is shrewd. These two qualities are too lackluster for him at this time; they would embarrass rather than help him. Moreover, you were entirely truthful in assuring him that I would never dream of calling him insane. Summary and violent judgments are repugnant to my nature, especially where persons are concerned to whom I am bound by sentiments of admiration and respect.

Do you recall the verse in the Gospel (Matthew, 5:22): "But I say unto you, that whosoever is angry with his brother shall be guilty at the judgment; He who shall call him *raca*, shall be condemned; and he who shall say to him, madman, deserves the gehenna of fire."[31] I try not to violate this precept and even tend to hold excessively mild opinions with regard to the conduct of others . . . being aware how much indulgence and compassion would be needed in order to absolve mine!

Notwithstanding your very witty criticism of Lenbach's portraits, I continue to believe that he would succeed wonderfully well in rendering the ideal essence of a certain face—the "mug" included. I shall perhaps have the pleasure of attending the materialization of this masterpiece next summer.

Day after tomorrow is St. Charles's day. Princess Hoh[enlohe] will be leaving for Vienna two days later, and as for me I expect to arrive in Pest on the sixteenth to seventeenth of the month. On the way I shall stop over for one day with Mme Laussot (whose compliments I conveyed to you in my Gries letter), and at Lamporecchio (near Pistoja) if Princess Rospigliosi will allow me to do so. Countess Bobrinska told me day before yesterday—at the dress rehearsal of the Brazilian opera *Il Guarany*[32] by the Brazilian maestro Gomes—that she had written to you recently. Her drawing room continues to be one of the most brilliant and sought after.

Be so generous as to forgive me my mournful "politeness," and my deplorable inadequacy in all matters.

Entirely yours,

FL

I'll be here until the tenth.

---

31. King James version: "But I say unto you, That whosoever is angry with his brother without a cause shall be in danger of the judgement: and whosoever shall say to his brother, Raca, shall be in danger of the council: but whosoever shall say, Thou fool, shall be in danger of hell fire."
32. First performed March 19, 1870, in Milan.

November 20, 71
Pest

Perfect and most amiable logic. Please go on writing to me at Pest. These last three days I have been occupying myself solely with unpacking and settling in. My quarters, Palatingasse 20, are most suitable and comfortable. Old friends of thirty years take the trouble to spare me all household drudgery. I am beset by enough other worries from outside. Enough of this; but send me from time to time the *Débats*—in which you will have noticed the incisive articles by Lemoinne on Favre, with the quotation: "I revealed my heart to the God of innocence . . . the wretched are his children. . . ." This article relieves you of the necessity of reading Favre's book—to which you may add Daniel Stern's volume on Dante and Goethe. Speaking of which, in Florence I again saw Hillebrand, who writes for the *Débats* under the name of Faxelles, and who asked me to convey his homage to you.

Last Monday I was at Lamporecchio, three hours from Florence, a princely residence enhanced by the infinitely witty and gracious Princess whom you know. She will spend the whole winter there.

There is no need for you to make an effort to feel carried away by *La Muette de Portici*[33] on the basis of Wagner's reminiscences. It merely acts for him as a nail on which to hang some bauble of his golden doctrine, which I follow with conviction and zeal—aside from some reservation of common sense.

Since you protest against "indulgence" and "politeness," I ask you bluntly to keep up your epistolary favors to your very insignificant and infirm servant.

FL

M. de Bièvre once said, I believe to Marie Antoinette, who had asked him to make up a pun about her green shoes, "*Madame, l'univers est à vos pieds.*" This had to do with a more or less imaginary universe. As far as that of Veuillot is concerned, I am so bold as to pray you,

33. Opera by Auber, first performed February 29, 1828, in Paris.

Madame, simply to have it mailed to the address mentioned below until January 1. Next year I shall claim the honor of laying l'univers at your feet.

———

December 1, 71

Pest

No, Madame, I was not appalled by the enormous package "decorated with your handwriting"; only I hoped to find in it still more of this same handwriting. Having said this much in praise of your "epistolary favors," I beg you to keep them up *mordicus* [with might and main], as well as your generosity as regards newspapers, which I accept with all the more gratitude in that you assure me that you derive pleasure therefrom. So send me after reading, and without any hurry, *L'Univers* (to which your pencil-strokes and notes add incomparable value) and continue sending the *Débats* in '72, since you intend renewing the subscription for yourself independently of me. As soon as I have read Wagner's and Laveleye's articles, I shall be honest and return them to you. For several days I was incapable of taking care of such matters. A specter[34] appeared here ready to commit a double murder—spare me the pain of a more detailed account. The specter vanished; my guardian angel protected me; and I am taking up again my usual way of life.—

Yesterday, I received a little gem of a letter from Mme Moukhanoff, who is staying at her daughter's at Ottensheim bei Linz, Ober Oesterreich. I shall perhaps be seeing her again in Vienna in a few weeks' time if, as I am told, my *Weihnachts Oratorium*[35] (the first part of *Christus*) is to be performed on December 31 at the *Musik Freunde* Society, with

34. The Countess Olga Janina, a gifted but uninhibited, very troublesome, and very amorous pupil of Liszt. She threatened to kill Liszt and then herself. The 6th edition of her book *Souvenirs d'une Cosaque*, written under the pseudonym Robert Franz (not the composer), was published in Paris, 1874. Its sequel, *Souvenirs d'un pianiste*, purporting to be the master's reply, also appeared in 1874.

35. G 3; R 478.

Rubinstein as conductor. I have been urged to conduct it; but I would sooner call off the performance than yield on this point.

I have still seen only very few people here and have been to only two concerts—that of Richter (now *Kapellmeister* at the Hungarian theater) and the concert of the Ullmann *Ménagerie*, of which Mme Monbelli is the principal lioness and the Florentine Quartet and Sivori are the elephants. I apologize for this silly remark, but by dint of hearing so many of them, I find myself repeating them.

In the course of this month we shall be having several evenings of classical music ("so irreproachable as to make me feel unworthy of them" as you charmingly put it) by M. Dorr [Door], pianist of the Grand Duchess Hélène, and of the Hellmesberger Quartet.

If the fear of catching a chill on the way does not make you abandon the idea of the trip to Jena, tell me about the *Beethoven Cantata*[36] in which you will again come across my stroll among the stars. Before and after the concert please give my warmest greetings to Gille. The "weakness of *l'ancienne*"[37] for L. dates from long ago. She was his major inspiration in one of the loveliest *Lieder* I know: *"In der Nacht"* – – –

> *O Herr! auf dunkel schwankend Meere,*
> *Fahr ich im schwachen Boot,*
> *Treu folgend deinem goldn'en Heere,*
> *Zum ew'gen Morgenroth.*[38]

FL

How is Clément?

Princess Hohenlohe has just lost her eldest son.

Princess Witt[genstein] will continue to live in Rome.

---

36. Probably G 68; R 538. Liszt composed his 2nd *Beethoven Cantata* (*Zur Säkularfeier Beethovens*) in honor of Beethoven's 100th birthday and conducted the world premiere in Weimar, May 29, 1870.

37. Unidentified.

38. "O Master, on dark and rolling sea,
    I ride in failing boat,
    Faithfully following thy golden host
    To the eternal dawn."

December 24, 71

Yesterday evening I hurried desperately to write to you and to send off my awful scrawl. I have just received your letter of the twenty-second. I'll send you Andrássy's photograph for your album from Vienna (the shops here being closed until Tuesday)—meanwhile here is a slightly insipid portrait of him from the prospectus of a new illustrated paper, which I am sending off together with this note.

The Grand Duke's idea of a Wagner Concert at Weimar is excellent. Provided that it should not be ruined by some meanness or other, or by too faint-hearted scruples!

I have been sent from Rome the little clipping enclosed herewith (from *La France*, I suppose) about "Lohengrinized" Italy! There is also talk of *Lohengrin*[39] being performed in Rome, as it has been in Florence, by the Bologna company.

Tuesday evening I shall be in Vienna at my cousin's at Schottenhof —en route there I shall continue reading *Dante et Goethe*, by D. Stern, which I thank you for having lent me.

I wrote to you yesterday that I shall be staying in Vienna until January 8.

Let me wish your children and yourself a most happy Christmas.

As ever yours,

FL

December 28, 71

Pest

Your comment on Pascal's "two kinds of men" seems to me very true and I pride myself somewhat on belonging to the third kind, the most numerous according to you, the "sinners who feel that they are

---

39. By Wagner; the world premiere conducted by Liszt on August 28, 1850, in Weimar.

sinners." Besides, one must not argue with Pascal about whether his thoughts are more, or less, true, but climb to the luminous gloom of his torments concerning the Infinite. Consequently, I stick to my mythological comparison of the "Phoenix," all the more so since the "Hydra" is an ugly monster which was dispatched by Lord Hercules. If you still find me too enigmatic in this I shall not contradict you further. Very humbly, thank you for striking this word from your letters.

Thanks to the news you gave me of the engagement of the grand-ducal heir,[40] I wrote, not too hastily, to Their Royal Highnesses three days before replying *subito* this morning to Mlle de Watz[dorf]. Mme de Helldorf, too, will denounce me in conversation with you; obviously I am a wretched and warped human being!

Notwithstanding this, I'll go to Vienna next Tuesday. Your host of the Via dei Due Macelli, Count Széchenyi, will come there too, he tells me, in order to hear my *Pifferari* [pipers][41] on December 31.—

Accept their humble homage, or even better, be present in heart at Jesus' crèche!

FL

Until January 6, write to Schottenhof, Wien—(my cousin Eduard L[iszt]. is kind enough to put me up).

---

40. Carl Augustus, son of Carl Alexander and Sophie of Saxe-Weimar.
41. The theme *Hirtengesang an der Krippe* (Shepherd's Song at the Manger), from the *Christmas Oratorio*; the first part of the *Christus* (G 3; R 478).

1872

January 2, 72
[Vienna]

Here is Count Andrássy's photograph. I saw him yesterday in his new quarters on the Ballplatz, once inhabited in stable times by Prince Clément Metternich. Heaven grant that Andrássy will live there as many years as did Metternich, to the honor and the glory of the monarchy.

My friends are pleased with my *Weihnachts Oratorium*, which was most intelligently conducted by Rubinstein and well received by the audience day before yesterday. As for me, you know that I like to declare myself satisfied with everything, save where I am concerned.

Last Thursday at an evening at Rubinstein's, I again saw your compatriots, M. de Novikoff and his sister-in-law Mme de Novikoff, born Kiréeff. I shall make a very humble call on them today, as well as on Mme de Dingelstedt, who is at home on Tuesdays.

Let me mention a very charming young lady, Countess Dönhoff (daughter of Mme Minghetti). She came to Weimar with Mme de Schleinitz in June 1870, and I often see her here.

Bülow arrives tomorrow, and I'll accompany him to Pest next Monday. I enclose the announcement of his concerts up to January 23. Perhaps I shall take advantage of the one on January 15 at Pressburg in order to pay my very affectionate homage to my octogenarian protectress, Countess Thérèse Apponyi (mother of the present ambassador in Paris).

34

Rubinstein cannot leave Vienna before the spring; he will come to Weimar in May and, at Whitsuntide, will direct the *Rheinische Musik-fest* (at Düsseldorf, I believe). In September he sails for America where he is to spend eight months, for which his impresario has guaranteed him $40,000 net, with all personal expenses of Rubinstein and his wife paid.

Your very humble and grateful reader,

FL

———

January 12, 72
Pest

After M. de Bülow's concert (Monday evening) I returned here with him. In Vienna as in Pest he is having a very considerable success. No other pianist commands admiring attention to the same degree and, I would even say, respect for the ability and talent so astonishingly combined in him. He has the most intimate insight into the music, as well as the nobility and perfection of beautiful style.

In about ten days he'll be playing at Gotha, and the following day at Erfurt. He will perhaps even be coming to Weimar, should M. de Loën show himself prepared to make amends for a previous misdeed by his predecessor. In any case I have informed Bülow of your kind intention to attend the Erfurt concert, and beg you to write him a note in order to facilitate the call he will be paying on you on my behalf.

Have you read his very witty dialogue (in No. 2, January, of *Signale*) on *Lohengrin* at Bologna?

I have taken the liberty of sending Princess Wittgenstein the passage in your last letter concerning the Tolstoys, whom I'll be very charmed to see again in Weimar. The Princess will probably send me her book for Tol[stoy], and you will be so kind as to tell me to what address I should mail it.

Speaking of books, my daughter speaks extremely highly of M. Nietzsche's *Die Geburt der Tragödie aus dem Geiste der Musik* [The birth of tragedy from the spirit of music], which she assures me is "the finest conquest of Wagnerian thought."

By the same mail you will receive my transcription, *Am stillen Herd*,[1] of which you heard a few bars at the Hofgärtnerei.

Thanks for your copies of *L'Univers*—and especially for your long-suffering indulgence and generous compassion toward your

FL

On the seventeenth, I shall see M. de Bülow again at Pressburg where I shall also see the Dénes Széchenyis and Countess Thérèse Apponyi— the very model of an ambassadress in Rome and Paris from 1825 to 1848!

Pressburg (Grüner Baum)
Saturday, January 20

On arriving here yesterday morning at five o'clock, I found your telegram. M. von Bülow, who had a few hours before played some fifteen pieces of Beethoven at the concert in Vienna, was sensibly in bed, and I only woke him up at ten o'clock in order to ask him what reply I should give you. He has heard nothing from Loën—save the enclosed note addressed to Bülow's secretary. The pressure of his concerts at Gotha, Leipzig, Dresden, etc., will make it difficult for him to stop off at Weimar, as the words "doubtful possibility" in my telegram pointed out. However, he promised me to do his best to please you. Kindly just let him know by postcard at what time he may call on you

1. G 448; R 281, transcription for piano solo, from Wagner's *Die Meistersinger von Nürnberg*.

at Erfurt, where you and he will probably be staying at the same hotel: Hotel Silber close to the railroad.

I am doubly grateful to you for your infinitely witty letter, for in addition to the intellectual pleasure it gave me, I seized the opportunity to broach again with Bülow the question of Weimar. As my most intimate and gallant friend, he was, of necessity, bound to suffer under the regime of the previous management; and the best proof that Bülow is able to judge matters clearly without harboring resentment lies in the fact that he did not prevent his secretary from listing the Weimar station among the stops on his concert itinerary. Moreover, his gentlemanly instincts enable him to understand perfectly well certain "subjectivities," and better still, yet another supreme "elegance": that which your letter reveals to me.

I have forwarded the Tolstoy paragraph to Rome. They have replied that you will hear directly.

Who put you on the track of the *Revue des cours littéraires*? I subscribed to it for two years in Rome and shall do so again, as I find this compilation most instructive and pleasantly useful. In the issue which you were kind enough to send me (and which will be returned to you) I read with interest several pages in addition to the remarkable and specious talk given in Munich by Father Hyacinthe. This time he remained skillfully moderate without losing any of his energy. Unfortunately Roman Catholics are obliged to treat him with the same "consideration" as he displays toward Protestants! Veuillot's article in the form of a Preface stunned me slightly. I don't feel up to contradicting him, being unable to grasp properly just what the "Holy Roman Democracy" could amount to as a posthumous product of the "Holy Roman Empire" and the "Holy Alliance." For me, the one bright point in this Vaticanist philippic is: "For the world to live, it needs the Eucharist."

This evening (after dining at the Dénes Széchenyis, whom you saw at the Babuino in Rome), I'll return to Pest.

Yours ever,

FL

Send me soon news of Bülow, who left again yesterday evening for Vienna. Your *entente cordiale* with *l'ancienne*[2] is highly congenial to me.

January 21

Pest

Your second little letter on the Loën case, written the same day as the first, arrived in Pest only after I had left for Pressburg. I found it this morning on my return, and hasten to express to you my admiration for your diplomatic sagacity, equal to your other superior qualities. You know already from my lines of yesterday that Bülow has not received a telegram from Loën. Consequently, your instinct of divination leads you to suspect that Loën deliberately refrained from sending it. However, it would not be "elegant" (as you very elegantly put it) to commit a little act of treachery, which would run a great risk of being misinterpreted and thus would do me a bad turn . . . but in order to fill in these little dots, I would have to go into details of certain matters which it is better to suppress, unless they interest you sufficiently to allow me to speak very frankly to you about them on some fine spring evening, while accompanying you from the Hofgärtnerei to the Karlsplatz. Meanwhile, I am sincerely grateful to you for the friendship you display to me concerning Bülow, and for your wish "that the same misunderstandings should not recur" . . . thank you from my heart for saying so in this way.

Today's mail brought me a letter from Fr[iedrich] Nietzsche, whom I do not have the advantage of knowing, a professor in Basel and author of the work about which I spoke to you recently. Forgive my seeming vanity in quoting to you the last paragraph of his letter: "When I look around me for the few people who have truly and instinctively grasped the phenomenon I have described, and which I call 'Dionysiac,' my eyes turn again and again primarily to you: you in particular must be

2. Unidentified.

familiar with the most recondite mysteries of that phenomenon to such a degree that I see in you one of its most remarkable exemplifications and have observed you time and again with the highest theoretical interest."

Nietzsche's work, *Die Geburt der Tragödie aus dem Gebiete* [sic] *der Musik,* was issued in Leipzig by Wagner's publisher, Fritzsch. I'll send you my copy as soon as I have read it.

When you see Gille please give him my greetings.

FL

January 31, 72
Pest

All you say about and concerning Bülow pleases and interests me. The favorable impression which his personality taken as a whole and in all respects made on you really gives me pleasure. As for Loën's evasiveness, it is fairly innocuous, even most understandable; but I protest against the sly tales, obviously very inaccurate (not to use a harsher term), spread by his predecessor, Dingelstedt. M. de Bülow could never have unburdened himself to him in the manner of the inept cruciform anecdote [sic] you told me about, and I sincerely regret that Their Royal Highnesses should have given the slightest credence to it.

When you have a chance, be so good as to tell the Grand Duchess that I have not forgotten the recommendation she deigned to make to me on the subject of artists worthy of real renown. Their number is very limited, whereas more or less clever mediocrities abound. Let them disport themselves where they please; I'll have nothing to do with them, and above all I shall not mention Weimar to them as a propitious stage for their glory and fortune. But, for exceptional artists—whether their reputation is already made, or whether they are striving to achieve it—it will always be an honor and a pleasure for me to assure them that at Weimar they will find an intelligent and flattering welcome, taste of a superior order, fine manners, and that *je ne sais quoi* which have attracted and held me there for a quarter of a century and more.

I have accordingly pressed Rubinstein to return there. His duties as Artistic Director of the *Musik Freunde* Society will keep him in Vienna until the end of April; but he has promised me that in May he will come to us, at the Erbprinz. As for M. de Bülow ("the Prussian nobleman"), I would certainly have wished that he not pass through Weimar without stopping there for a while. The *coup de Jarnac*[3] of Dingelstedt and Loën's cautious letter paralyzed my good intentions . . . speaking of which, I beg you never again to imagine that even the shadow of mockery enters into anything I say to you personally. If I used the word "friendship," this is because I know of no other which better conveys the sense of a certain noble soundness of outlook in matters of everyday life, and in making its practices agreeable and firm. Besides, your erroneous suspicions and your very scoldings are of so rare a quality that I bow in deep confusion before their magic.

You ask me for an explanation of *Duplicität des Apollinischen und des Dionysischen*? It is to be found on the first page of Nietzsche's book[4] (of which I have still read only two-thirds) in these terms: "In order to make those two impulses more accessible to us, let us envision them from the start as the separated artificial worlds of <u>dream</u> and of <u>ecstasy</u>; between which physiological apparitions a contradiction may be observed analogous to that between the Apollonian and the Dionysiac." Between ourselves it will be fairly hard for me to reply to the author so as to please him. His work is more brilliant than clear; and you justly note that many things in it run "counter to my feelings and to my manner of thinking and acting." The same holds for several articles in *L'Univers*, for sending which, with your underlinings and comments, I continue to thank you. I just cannot indulge in holy ranting and raving, though I have unlimited respect for those who do so with consuming zeal. Veuillot's diatribe against V[ictor] Hugo (very eloquent, be it noted) saddened me, and it already requires a certain effort for me to

---

3. In a duel in the 16th century, a certain Guy de Jarnac hamstrung his opponent; hence, the equivalent of a stab in the back.

4. *Die Geburt der Tragödie aus dem Geiste der Musik*, mentioned earlier in letters of January 12 and 21.

rise to the level of academic aloofness of Mgr Dupanloup, which, I am told, the *Revue des deux mondes* recently approved! My lukewarmness in this respect is such that it could not really heat up before the flames of the most fulminating preachers, whether lay or religious; but I beg you not to speak of this to anyone, for I almost reproach myself for this lukewarmness, and would be only too glad to rid myself of it, albeit rationally, the Catholic faith being above, but not contrary to, reason.

A Hungarian painter, M. Munkacsi [Munkácsy] (forgive me if I have maimed the spelling of his name), now settled in Weimar, has painted a strange picture[5] of a man under sentence of death at the moment of the last earthly pleasures being granted to him. Have you visited Munk[ácsy]'s studio? Tell me about it.

Yours ever,

FL

P.S. Allow me once again to give you an errand of the "Dionysiac" variety and kindly ask M. de Loën to purchase for me, at cost price, about twenty or more bottles of the same Marsala wine which he orders for himself, and which I would like to offer next spring to my guests at the Hofgärtnerei, beginning with Baron Loën and our friend Lassen.

I hope that Gottschalg too will derive more pleasure from it than he does from the lessons which are perhaps too much subject to your and Mme de Helldorf's strictures. Since falling out of favor with Your Excellencies he no longer writes to me. Do you know what has become of him? Was he given the job at the *Gymnasium* which he deserves, and for which Laukhardt [Lauckhard] had nominated him? I lack both space and the heart to tell you that I shall fail to carry out the epistolary duties which you are urging on me with regard to the. . . .

---

5. The painting in question, done 1868–69, was entitled "The Last Day of a Condemned Prisoner."

February 15, 72
Pest

How many things not to be said! Infinitely more than the famous dancer Vestris looked for in a minuet. I can imagine the merry dance you led Loën for his incongruity concerning your Wagnerian "foibles"; but his august master's minuet with Wagner surpasses all the Venusberg dances and even the *Walkürenritt*. To draw a parallel between the idea of the painting academy of Weimar and that of the "school" (?) of Wagner is superlatively bombastic. Humble mortals could not aspire to reach such heights and can only wish that those who feel comfortably installed there may go on congratulating themselves warmly.

It was indeed the Grand Duchess whom I asked you to tell, as the occasion arose, that I was not neglecting her artistic errand concerning the Court concerts which she deigns to pay for and to run with exemplary taste, which is also noted by the Russian, French, and other diplomats in Weimar.

Did you not forbid me ever to thank you, I would do so very sincerely for having sent me *L'Univers*, the *Débats*, etc. The independent approval of the academic withdrawal of Mgr Dupanloup may be read in the January 15, 1872, issue of the *Revue des deux mondes*, page 471, following the column by M. de Mazade.

And what about Canon and Vicar Michaud? He reached the point of opting for Greek Orthodoxy (*L'Univers* asserts) by virtue of Pascal's maxim, which I summarize as follows: man having failed to make justice power, power must be accepted as justice.

I take the liberty of begging you to continue writing to me and of assuring you that your letters shall never be treated on the same plane as others by your very humble servant,

FL

Tomorrow I'll be sending you a couple of lines which you will be good enough to pass on to Gille. Your impression of the *Beethoven Cantata* in Jena is my best absolution for the displeasure I cause my "critics."

1. Olga von Meyendorff (1838–1926)

2. Concert in honor of Franz Josef, Emperor of Austria, in Budapest, 18 March 1872 (see p. 47)

February 28, 72
Pest

You give me such persuasive reasons for your incorrigibility that, far from objecting to it at all, I can only praise you for it and ask you purely and simply to maintain this same incorrigibility, which is assuredly of the best and rarest kind.

If I remember rightly, I forgot to answer the musical question of your august conversation partner,[6] who is sometimes very disconcerting! I understand that he wants something extraordinary for the Wart-[burg],[7] but which will not change daily life or result in any excessive expense. If you will help me with your advice we shall probably find a fairly satisfactory formula, which it will be time enough to think about in April or May while strolling in the rose garden of the Hofgärtnerei.

Have you definitely settled on your residence in these surroundings? Will it be as convenient as the one you now occupy? When are you planning to move, and will you be living in the Helldorfs' home?

Your oscillations from enthusiasm to ill humor, and almost anger against Hy[acinthe] and Wag[ner] please me immensely, and I admire your retaining so much discernment in the course of your impassioned excursions amidst the precipitous peaks of intelligence and art.

As for me, I have only reached the stage of a kind of sad resignation regarding men and events, sometimes tempered and as though illumined by faith in divine providence, and invincible hope in Christ's redemption!

The *Weimarer Zeitung* is publishing extracts from Döllinger's speeches on the reuniting, or rather the unification, of the Christian churches. You are doubtless reading them and are also already familiar with the

6. A play on the common derivation of the two words *interlocuteur*, a person with whom one converses, and *interloquant*, a disconcerting remark or question.

7. A medieval castle located on a high hill near Eisenach in Saxe-Weimar. It dates from the early 12th century. Here Luther was brought for safety and completed his translation (1521–22) of the New Testament, and here for some time Elizabeth (later Saint) found a home. It was also the scene of the minstrels' contest in Wagner's *Tannhäuser*. Extensively restored by Carl Alexander, Grand Duke of Saxe-Weimar, it was one of his favorite residences.

Tagebuch vom Römischen Concil,[8] published by Friedrich, which it would ill become me to recommend to you, for I am far more grieved than diverted by it.

My time here is spent or wasted with no diversions other than a little reading now and then. People are most kind to me; I try my best to show appreciation for this, but the balance of my existence is upset due to being unable to work a couple of hours a day at my music. Lecture me sternly on my foolishness.

About mid-March there will be a charity concert sponsored by fine ladies and Princess Frédérique Auersperg, who entered the Order of St. Dominic seven or eight years ago, I think it was, and has assumed the name of Sister Raymondine. Perhaps you met her in Rome, where she came with the Duchess d'Arenberg.

I'll send you the program of this concert. Your very humble servant will perform there with a Beethoven sonata, some Chopin nocturnes, etc., which he would much rather hear you play, enhanced by your graceful touch.

Yours ever,

FL

The shipments of *L'Univers* and the *Débats* are always gratefully received.

———————

March 8, 72

Pest

The news about Mme Moukhanoff interests me very much. For many years she has inspired in me an enthusiasm at least equal to that which she professes for Wagner's works, and I remain faithfully enthralled by her. In former times she was often compared with Princess

8. *Tagebuch, während des Vaticanischen Concils*, J. Friedrich, pub. (Nordlingen, 1871).

Lieven which has never seemed to me flattering for her, for, to my mind, she has far more wit than her earlier predecessor and even than M. Thiers and M. Guizot put together; better still, an indefinable grace, musical, wonderfully nuanced, now measured, now *quasi fantasia*, but always enchanting. I hope that her new predilection for Gotha will not turn her away from Weimar, and that she will favor us with her presence this summer as she promised you. When you write to her, convince her that we await her and send her greetings.

Some time I will send you a page by Mme Mouk[hanoff] which she wrote to my daughter and which the latter copied out for me. It is a string of priceless pearls.

In the March 1 issue of the *Débats* you noticed the account of the interview in Antwerp between the French correspondent of *The Times* and the Count de Chambord.[9] The replies of Henry V are truly royal, of the highest loyalty and propriety, and confirm my long-standing respect for him in spite of my very pronounced "Napoleonism." Of all those who have been deprived of their throne, no one asserts with as much simplicity and faith, without any bragging or evasiveness, the principle of royalty, or upholds its cult as thoroughly. If it is true that kings are created for their people and not the people for kings, the result, in accordance with the theory of monarchy, is that the people suffer more harm by losing their kings than kings derive benefit from reconquering their people; in other words: France needs Henry V more than he needs her. The theory is perfectly plausible, but how is it to be reconciled with practice, and how are the French to be weaned from the all too familiar principles of '89 and from the ideas of the *Contrat Social*? Will the white flag make them succumb to the seduction of the colors? One may doubt this without being an unbeliever. Even in Germany, where feelings of respect and submissiveness are deeply rooted, and where ruling families are very closely identified with the spirit of the people, the principle of legitimacy of the monarchy would probably have suffered severe setbacks had it not been for the luster cast by

9. Bourbon claimant, as Henry V, to the French throne.

the definitive victories of the Holy Alliance over Napoleon I, and for the successes of the regular forces in '48–'49. All the more did monarchy wither away in France. Should it recover strength there, I think that it will hardly be able to do without the double formula: "by the grace of God and the national will," wisely employed formerly by Napoleon III.

Forgive me this "artist's" perhaps mistaken opinion. You know it from Rome, and it would now be very bad taste, to say the least, to repudiate my superlative attachment to Napoleon. As for Henry V, I have not seen him since 1826 or '27, when I had the honor of performing my little tricks as a little pianist at the house of the Duchess de Berry and of Mme de La Bouillerie.

I asked Princess Wittgenstein why she did not want to send her book to our very good friend Tolstoy. She replied that "it is not suitable reading matter for a sick room" and that she "preferred not to damage the book by unnecessary travel." Did she send you *L'Amitié des anges*?[10] If not, I think that you will give her pleasure by asking again for this edifying little book.

Yours ever,

FL

Don't be annoyed or worried if I don't write during the next two weeks.

March 20, 72

Pest

I thought I had told you long before I wrote to Mme de Helldorf and to Mme Merian that I shall be arriving in Weimar in the first half of

---

10. The second of the three volumes constituting *Entretiens pratiques à l'usage des femmes du monde* by the Princess Sayn-Wittgenstein. The first was *Réligion et monde*, the third *La Chapelle Sixtine*.

April. Since you are so extremely kind as to be willing once again to take care of the preparations for my settling in, may I beg you to request of Pauline that she have everything ready for Saturday, April 6. My little arrangements have been fixed as follows: Easter Monday I'll leave from here by the evening train. I spend three days in Vienna and if I can leave again on Thursday evening, I'll easily reach Weimar on Saturday. In any case, I'll write to you again from Vienna where I beg you to send me your Paschal letter, c/o my cousin (Schottenhof).

The complete fiasco of my political ramblings makes me feel quite sheepish; I promise you that I shall not again expose myself to a repetition.

Here is the program of day before yesterday's concert, on which the presence of His Majesty,[11] of the Archdukes and Archduchesses, shed extraordinary luster. It was the first time that the Emperor and T.I.H. [Their Imperial Highnesses] deigned thus to attend a concert in Pest, without being isolated from the audience by sitting in a box, etc. [fig. 2]. Speaking of boxes, I'll be very happy to subscribe to yours at Weimar, and am most grateful to you for having suggested it.

I still have nothing specific on the *Tonkünstler Versammlung*[12] at Cassel (essentially, it depends on the degree of good will of Monseigneur our Grand Duke); perhaps the idea will be abandoned, but there is no question of transferring it elsewhere.

Forgive these empty lines; today, I am extremely tired, and my room is never free of "interrupters."

A bientôt,

FL

---

11. The Emperor Franz Josef.
12. Meeting of the *Allgemeiner Deutscher Musikverein.*

June 4, 72
Weimar

Not knowing what to say was Brid'oison's mode of thinking. I'm just about at that stage myself, and on the verge of completely losing the use of words which correspond to my mode of thinking and feeling. Nevertheless, I wish punctually to discharge my duties of submissiveness; so keep up your compassionate indulgence, in view of the merit you acquire by putting up with me.

At Erfurt I bought an object of which I have often felt deprived at the Hofgärtnerei: a cross which now rests near my Roman books next to my bed.

I often repeat to myself the words of St. Paul: "We must place our glory in the Cross of Jesus Christ," and in Rome I used to repeat in St. Peter's Square this prayer: "*O crux, ave, spes unica* . . . grant to the just increasing grace, and to sinners forgiveness of their faults."

The performance of *Elisabeth*[13] at Erfurt was highly satisfactory. Your disgraced Gottschalg found a way to shine there once again by one of those inspired demonstrations of loyalty which are contrary to diplomatic usage, but which I deeply appreciate and will tell you about in this house.

The Helldorfs were particularly good to me yesterday. Not only did they place their coach at my disposal to go to Jena, but came there themselves with Adelheid[14] and your very humble servant. You can easily guess what our major topic of conversation was to be during the trip. Mme de Hell[dorf] found the music of Händel's *Athalie*[15] most accomplished, and Gille was wholeheartedly thrilled by the choirs, the orchestra, the six voices of the soloists, and the entranced audience. After the concert we had a convivial supper, not at The Bear, as last year, but at Gille's in the little garden room, hung with old family portraits; and by about half-past one we were back in Weimar.

An American came to invite me, at all costs, to the Boston Festival,

13. G 2; R 477.
14. Adelheid von Schorn.
15. Oratorio, first performed July 10, 1733, at Oxford.

to take place in June, and for which a colossal hall is being built with a capacity of nearly 100,000 people. They'll probably install an orchestra there consisting of cannons.

Besides the American, I received this morning three visits which it was impossible for me to refuse; and very much in spite of myself I am not quite punctual, for noon has struck.

The trees and flowers of the Hofgärtnerei greet you!

FL

Wednesday, October 9
Schillingsfürst[16]

As usual, your little letter from Eisenach (with Fre[dro]'s enclosure) arrived late. It was handed to me Monday morning just as I was leaving, and so I was unable to do the errand you were good enough to request of me. Fortunately I think it had already been taken care of, for on Sunday evening Fredro was spoken of at the Wartburg in very affectionate terms, and the Grand Duke told me he had obtained from your Emperor[17] in Berlin the kind of leave Fred[ro] is asking for.

Thus his quotation of the Psalm: *non confidere in principibus* [Put not your trust in princes] is not relevant in present circumstances, and I hope we'll have the pleasure of Fred[ro]'s pleasant and charming company in Weimar next year. A few words from you to the Grand Duke will facilitate our friend's final success.

The Grand Duchess asked me for news of you. I answered, like a simpleton, that you were well. During the evening Mme de Werthern shone very graciously. People told of some oddities and flights of poetic fancy of the King of Bavaria,[18] sailing about on the lake he has created

16. Home of the Cardinal and seat of the family von Hohenlohe-Schillingsfürst, near Rothenburg-ob-der-Tauber.
17. Probably the Russian Emperor while on a visit to Berlin.
18. Ludwig II.

in his winter garden at the castle, and planning the construction of a Vesuvius somewhere or other. This latter idea seems to me to have originated with others than the King, whose deeds and behavior I am in no way disposed to criticize in view of the extraordinary nobility of his feelings toward Wagner.

The latter has today sent me a telegram telling me that Cosima is well again. Tuesday or Wednesday I shall be at Bayreuth. The evening before, I'll probably accompany Cardinal H[ohenlohe] to Langenburg (four hours from here by coach). You are aware that Princess Feodora (the Duchess of Meiningen's mother) died recently.

The Cardinal displays the most affable affection toward me; our conversations roll and glide as at the Vatican. In addition to his religious virtues, which are very sincere, he possesses to a rare degree sound judgment, distinction, tact, and a princely mind, more complex and even more efficacious than that of M. de Voltaire. He leaves for Frankfurt this evening in order to meet there Duke George of Mecklenburg and his wife, the Grand Duchess Catherine, and will return day after tomorrow. Thus I find myself *padrone di casa* at Schillingsfürst, and will take advantage of this high station to remain alone in my rooms for forty-eight hours. My form of entertainment will be to write half a dozen letters, to be deducted from the twenty or so which I must send off before arriving at Szekszárd.

Thursday, 10th

Late yesterday evening I received your latest lines. You err in saying that sorrows do not make people kind. I am in love with yours, and being unable to rid you of them, I feel drawn to them and share them. If I could deliver homilies I would dedicate one to you on this text: "prosperity was the blessing of the Old Testament and affliction is that of the New."

You wrote down the name of the Galician author (Fachir Maroch?) of the novel *Le Legs de Cain*?[19] in such an ingenious manner that I was not really able to decipher either the name of the author or the title of

19. Unidentified.

the novel. Please be so kind as to have Peterle or Clément write both in fair hand in your next letter. My very affectionate compliments to Mimi on his successful examination. Besides, the "theme" of the novel, while not exactly false, seems to me taken from the usual half-truths of salons. There are numberless things which lie outside of and beyond the "war of the sexes" in love, and as far as I am concerned I do not accept the thesis that "to love is to be either the anvil or the hammer." Why the choice between these two very hard instruments? To love is to ascend into heaven.

The letter from the paragon of all beautiful, serious, charming, and meritorious qualities, Joseph, Prince of Chimay, embarrasses me. The welcome he extended to our first consignment places us under the gentle obligation of repeating it, and I shall send you a little manuscript for him from Pest.

For today, let me beg you once again not to worry about your "solitude studded with malevolence," but rather to have full confidence in the noble energies of your soul, on which I pray God that He shower His overflowing blessings.

FL

Since you ask me for errands, please ask Gross[e] to send me immediately to Bayreuth 200 Swiss cigars (you brought some back to me in former years from Geneva to Rome) of the same two kinds which he used always to get for me at Weimar.

P.S. At Schillingsfürst there is only one mail collection daily. Excuse the delay of these lines, and write to Bayreuth.

I am going to write a few words to Count Beust.

———

October 14
Schillingsfürst

My fault, and a very grave fault it is, is to displease you. I am sadly conscious of this, while aware that I could make no other travel arrangements, and that this was not my fault but that of the trip itself. You would perhaps spare yourself some unnecessary worry by having more confidence in my modest reasonableness.

C[ardina]l H[ohenlohe]'s excursion to Frankfurt (where he met Duke George of Mckl. [Mecklenburg]) kept me here two days longer than I had intended. The projected visit to Langenburg will not take place, Prince Herman being away, and tomorrow morning I leave for Bayreuth. Kindly send me newspapers and letters there until October 20.

The *Débats* announces a new edition, with additional posthumous notes, of Sainte-Beuve's fine work: *Chateaubriand et son groupe littéraire sous l'Empire* (two volumes in 18vo. [sic], 7 francs, published by Michel Lévy). I urge you to read it, as well as Sainte-Beuve's *Port-Royal*.

Thank you for your modest *Revue bleue*, which is most instructive and which I beg you to go on sending me. In the last issue I read forthwith the two pages on Ollivier, and am reserving for my journey Janet's course (*Les Origines de la société*).[20] This philosopher has just been very prominently mentioned in a long polemical letter by Doctor Sbarbaro, featured in the Italian press and which calls for *il Christianesmo* [sic] *razionale, quel Christianesmo* [sic] *di Kant, di Lessing, di Channing, dice il Janet nel suo recente libro sui 'Problemi del Secolo,' che sta per diventare la fede religiosa e morale di tutto il genere umano* [rational Christianity, that Christianity of Kant, Lessing, Channing, as Janet says in his recent work, *Problems of the Century*, which will become the religious and moral faith of all mankind].

As an antidote to perverse doctrines, I send you herewith the translation of an article from *L'Univers* describing the last audience of Cardinal Bonne[chose] with the Pope, and the present which His Holiness gave him of a work of art illustrating the caption: *Domine quo vadis?* This confirms the widely accepted opinion that the Pope will not leave Rome short of a situation of extremity. (The public ascribes to C[ar-

20. In a subsequent volume (*Les Origines du socialisme contemporain*) the foreword contained this statement: "Ce volume a pour origine un cours professé à l'Ecole des sciences politiques en 1872, et dont nous avons déjà publié une partie sous ce titre: Saint-Simon et les Saint-Simoniens."

dina]l Antonelli the thesis of the voluntary incarceration of the Pope in the Vatican.)

For his part, C[ardina]l Hoh[enlohe] does not intend to return there, and will also wait for a case of absolute necessity before leaving Schillingsfürst, his ancestors' castle.

I delivered your message to him and he once again sang your praises, to which I naturally added a "flowery counterpoint" (as professors of harmony say).

This has been a very peaceful week for me. I've been out only twice, in the morning to church (in the absence of the C[ardina]l, for on the other days I attended his mass in the castle chapel). I know the countryside only from the lovely panoramic view from the four windows of my drawing room, which rather resembles that from the terrace of the Villa d'Este save for the difference in vegetation and minus the dome of St. Peter's on the distant horizon.

The C[ardina]l's conversation is always most pleasant and interesting and in the best aristocratic tone, without stiffness or any awkwardness. As a result of his ambassadorial intermezzo in Berlin he has particularly favorable memories of the Emperor and of your out-of-favor Bismarck.

To amuse you, I quote a little dialogue between Princess Charles of Prussia and a wounded Frenchman in the Berlin hospital:

The Princess: Wouldn't you like some bouillon?

The patient: No, thanks, Your Royal Highness.

The Princess: Some soda water perhaps? Some lemonade?

The patient: No, thanks, Your Royal Highness.

The Princess: What, then? Don't hesitate to say.

The patient: Thank you, Your Royal Highness.

The Princess: Oh, please don't go on calling me Your Royal Highness, but just Sister Marie.

The patient: All right then, Sister Marie, run along (or, more accurately, get out of here!).

Yours ever,

FL

Send me news of Clément.

Sunday morning, October 20
Bayreuth

By good luck your last letter (addressed to Schill[ingsfürst]) did reach me at 1:00 A.M., Tuesday, in the railroad car at the Anspach station. It was a lovely nocturne, sadder and even more impassioned than that of Chopin (in C minor[21]) which I played for you at the Chimays in Rome. The minor motif of *l'amie* is properly emphasized in it. I only recommend that you play it with the soft pedal (*Verschiebung*) so as to leave a somewhat vague impression in the mind of *l'amie*. A quarrel with her would not be "elegant," and would greatly sadden me.

I entirely approve of your idea of asking the unfaithful Schöll for a professor who could teach you German in the manner which suits you. Should Schöll not succeed in finding one for you, you could still request the good offices of Bojanowski for the benefit of your Germanic studies. He will probably be able to suggest someone who isn't too much of a Philistine, and who will prove worthy of schooling you grammatically and of informing you on certain points unknown to "Russian princesses."

Having arrived here Tuesday after one o'clock, I'll be leaving again tomorrow for Ratisbon where I shall spend, <u>alone</u>, October 22, the sixty-first anniversary of my birth. For some twenty years this day was especially celebrated at the Altenburg and in Rome; also once in Munich at my daughter's, and in '70 at Szekszárd at the home of my most excellent friend Augusz. At the age of 61, my celebrations consist of . . . memories only. Ratisbon being on my way to Vienna I prefer to stop there. The cathedral is grandiose. In the past I dreamed there of a Music which I know not how to write. . . .

Wednesday I'll be in Vienna; write to Schottenhof, c/o Hofrath Ed. Liszt.

Although the stay of the W[agner]s at Dammallee is only temporary, Cosima has given proof there of her remarkable talents of Mistress of the House in the installation, the running, and the staffing of the house. No noise, no indecisiveness, nothing lacking . . . and, what is

21. Opus 48, No. 1.

more, "blue finger bowls," which gave me the opportunity to tell one of your judicious comments on the mores of the Germanic peoples.

Cosima told me she would write to you after my departure and I have passed on to her the errand of commenting to you wittily about my stay here, not having the talent to do so myself. I merely note that I imposed a musical evening on my hosts at which our <u>Isolde</u> from Weimar shone. A pity that M. Urspruch was not present.

Please ask Franz Servais to send my daughter as soon as possible the book by Saint-Victor, *Barbares et Bandits*,[22] which could be taken from the Hofgärtnerei if the question of keys were not too big a question. Ask Grosse if people dare risk opening my rooms in my absence. If the answer is in the affirmative, also tell him to send the full score of the *Messe de Gran*[23] to Bayreuth.

In any case Servais only has to write to his Brussels bookseller to obtain the book *Barbares* which I ask him to send to Cosima.

In the *Revue bleue* (Janet's course), there is an ingenious comparison between Descartes' system of whirlwinds and the paradoxes of Jean-Jacques' [Rousseau] discourse on inequality, etc. Thanks for having sent me the subsequent issues of this review, and the *Débats*. The <u>great</u> *Revue des deux mondes* ("*Reine Olga*"[23a]) will be returned to you from Ratisbon.

As for the "simple soldier" (popularly called *piou-piou*), whom Joinville would like to see placed atop the Vendôme column in lieu of the "little corporal in a gray frock coat," I hesitate a little to recognize him as the most "noble symbol of devotion to the fatherland." However, I would not like to contradict a prince of the royal blood, who has given proof of his courage and who takes pleasure in glorifying the "simple soldier."

Yours ever,

FL

---

22. *Barbares et Bandits; la Prusse et la Commune* (Paris, 1871).   23. G 9; R 484.

23a. Queen Olga, consort of Karl I, king of Württemberg, had little sympathy for Wagner or for the "music of the future." Liszt often used her name, or the initials *R.O.*, when referring to the special style and taste of the *Rev.d.d.m.*, which he identified with those of the Queen.

Did you make sure of mailing the letter to Mme de Schwarz [Schwartz]? And of the Swiss cigars for Bayreuth? I ask you once again very humbly to tell Grosse not to send anything to Szekszárd. My itinerary is changed; I am no longer going to Szekszárd this year, as Augusz is due to return to Buda at the end of October. Consequently, I'll pay my visit to the Széchenyis at Horpács (barely four hours away from Vienna) from October 26 to 29, and from there I go straight back to Pest.

———

Monday, October 28, 72
Vienna

I have always had the misfortune of hearing those I love best tell me that I did not love them much. In Geneva Mme d'A[goult] felt that the Conservatoire Helvétique (to the creation of which I had contributed a little) was closer to my heart than she; and she it was who was convinced of the absolute truth of the advice given her by one of my friends, never to count on me should any fad or an occasion to shine attract me elsewhere. Later, when I published the *Symphonische Dichtungen*, Princess W[ittgenstein] accused me of thinking only about Härtel, and now you sweetly insinuate that I write to you "as I do to Riedel." Very well then! Since Riedel has come up again I'll first of all tell you about the forthcoming concerts in Vienna and Pest: on November 2 and 8 (here), Bülow; the eighteenth, Bülow in Pest. In the course of the month, Mme Schumann and Mme Joachim together (without M. Joachim, they say). In December and January (in Pest) philharmonic concerts conducted by Richter, sessions of the Hellmesberger and possibly Florence Quartets, concerts by M. and Mme Jaëll, etc., etc.

Thank you for having so well succeeded in your Bayreuth errand. If you wish to crown your task and please me, send my daughter the two little books by Mey[24]: *Une Imprudence* and *Le Yacht*. I had promised them to her in Weimar and mentioned them to her again in Bayreuth, but I would rather not deprive myself of my own copies just

24. Not further identified.

now. Mme Dönhoff, of whom I see a great deal here, tells me that her mother has asked her many questions about you, and that Princess Czernitcheff [Czernicheff] (born Titoff) spoke of you with great affection and with a *schwärmerische Bewunderung* [rapturous admiration]. Furthermore, she asks me to tell you that she too desires to *schwärmen* by getting to know you more, and *moins en l'air* [less formally].

Makart is finishing an immense and very sensational picture: the homage of the Senate of Venice to Catherine Cornaro. In it, Mme Dönhoff's hair is a burnished blond, à la Titian. It seems that Makart has a marked predilection for this tint to the point that his wife has had her hair dyed, and from brunette has become auburn-haired.

Tomorrow evening I shall be at Horpács at the Széchenyis. They are in deep mourning because of the sudden death of their cousin, Countess Béla Széchenyi, born Erdődy. She and her sister (Countess Károly, wife of the Ambassador in Berlin) were called *die Götter Kinder* [the children of the gods] because of their beauty. Mme Béla Széchenyi died in childbirth two or three years after her marriage.

Write to: Pest, Palatingasse 20; I'll be back there next Saturday or Sunday. Be so kind as to tell Grosse to send me in Pest the Weimar newspapers and the case of books and music, etc.

Here, I spent my time talking with my cousin Eduard and seeing three or four people, making no other visits, neither writing nor working.

M[onsieur] K,[25] about whom you ask me for some information, has attracted attention through some distinguished articles of aesthetic criticism in the two Weimar newspapers. His opinions agree with those of M. Ruland—and of Queen Olga. Besides, he cuts a good figure and I think you will do well not to close your door to him.

Today I have nothing to add for Riedel, and I kiss your hands in most tender submissiveness.

FL

Doubtless you should write to Mme de Schleinitz about Fredro.

------

25. Probably Karl Kertbeny.

Wednesday, November 6, 72
Horpács – at Count Imre Széchenyi's

I'm staying here three or four days longer than I had planned, and will only arrive in Pest on Sunday. For more than a week (in Vienna), no news from you.

I spend my time catching up with very onerous arrears of correspondence. What servitude! All the harder for me in that I am completely unable to write with ease.

The tone of the Széchenyi household is of the finest, devoid both of stiffness and of larkiness. Of course I don't go out much, and restrict myself to looking at the park and the fine surrounding forest from my window. The chaplain (a distinguished, rather sickly man) says mass in the castle chapel every morning at half-past eight. We dine at seven o'clock, and in the evening I play four-hand with the Countess. Several of her husband's compositions grace our repertoire; they have both taste and spirit. In particular there are two or three books of very successful waltzes. I'll pass them on to you next spring, also a Hungarian march by the same author, which I am going to transcribe.[26]

Day before yesterday I paid a visit to my native village, Raiding, two hours from Horpács, with Széch[enyi] and Mihalovich (a serious composer and gentleman). On this occasion some aspects of my childhood came back to mind as well as the glorious prediction of the mid-wife to my mother in 1811: *Ach! der Franzi, der wird gewiss einmal im Gläser Wagen fahren!* [Ach! that Franzi will some day surely ride in a coach with glass windows!] In those times this was a quasi-miraculous destiny in this village, to which I have returned only twice, in 1840 and 1848, since my parents took me away in 1822.

The old peasants recognized me at once day before yesterday and rang the church bell in my honor.

I had indeed arrived in a four-in-hand coach, but without *Gläser*!

By the same mail, I am sending you in wrappers the October issue of the *Revue des deux mondes*, to which I add the new pamphlet which

26. G 573; R 261.

Wagner gave me: *Über Schauspieler und Sänger* [On Actors and Singers]. In it you will read without displeasure a few vigorous sallies on *les germains* and their highly debatable *theoretische Würdigkeit* [theoretical value] in Tartary. . . .

Yours ever,

FL

The cholera is causing some *Gastrollen* [guest appearances] in Buda, and even in Pest, but of an anodine nature, without *furore*.

Herewith a couple of words for Grosse to thank him for his congratulations on October 22 and to beg him to send me the cases and newspapers to Pest (Palatingasse 20).

November 13, 72
Pest

Once again, calm down, and let's speak no more of cholera, about which I worry not at all, neither in Pest nor in Buda. Try to give me better news soon about your eye trouble, and get rid of it as quickly as possible.

Tomorrow I'll send you Ollivier's opuscule: *Une visite à la chapelle des Médicis, Dialogue sur Michelange et Raphaël*. It's only about a hundred pages long. People query the opportuneness of the publication, but I don't indulge in finding fault with my friends even when I venture not to share their opinion.

Did I tell you the witticism following the postponement of Ollivier's appointment to the Academy: "Having had the nerve to elect him, the thirty-nine immortals will have the courage not to receive him"?

It now seems that good patriots and serious writers wax indignant that someone "who caused his country's loss should amuse himself by writing fine phrases on Michelangelo and Raphael."

The Grand Duke has replied with a most gracious and witty letter in which he reproaches me for not telling him about myself. That is a fault I have no desire to correct, being of the opinion that "myself," if not always "hateful," as Pascal used to say, is usually superfluous. Hence I would like to flatter myself that I am becoming even more of an impersonal individual. However, I still have far to go in this respect, for I am not devoid of jealousy as regards M. Eitner and M. Franz Servais, who have the good fortune of serving as your readers. . . . As for Beethoven's thirty-three Variations (on Diabelli's waltz[27]), I propose with all my heart to play them to you thirty-three times if this suits you, and without a trace of reminiscence of the scene at Schwerstedt.

Forgive me for having nothing of interest to tell you today, and for remaining quite foolishly, in sad but true humility,

Your,

FL

I have seen hardly anyone here, and keep busy only by tidying my rooms and sending off a few long overdue letters. Bülow is arriving in about ten days and will give three evenings of *Kammer Musik* (Dingelstedt used to say *Jammer Musik*) augmented by two ex-Weimarians: Singer and Cossman.

Thanks for having sent me the *Débats*, which keeps me company agreeably at dinner. I start by reading the passages marked in pencil, and this mark confers on them a hundredfold greater value for me.

When you have read Strauss' *Neue Glauben*,[28] send it to me. Your last letter but one was, exceptionally, sent to me at Horpács where I had not intended staying longer than four days.

---

27. Opus 120.
28. David Friedrich Strauss, *Der alte und der neue Glaube: Ein Bekenntnis* (Leipzig, 1872).

November 15
Pest

The childhood anecdotes about Raiding are accurate, and I myself told them at the time to Mihalovich, the author of the enclosed account of our village excursion.

I add an article on Wagnerian literature by Hanslick, a bigwig of our artistic world, and of major influence not only in Vienna, but even in St. Petersburg. I know that the Grand Duchess Hélène sets great store by his authority and his recommendations. Have you ever read his little book, *Über das Musikalisch Schöne?*[29] It is an almost perfect example of the style we call *"Reine Olga."*

Kindly return to me Hanslick's psychiatric article which I'll send off to Rome so that they should know there that if I sin out of excessive admiration for Wagner, it is not for lack of awareness of what his adversaries think. To them I would willingly say with M. de Maistre: "From the height to which one must rise in order to encompass the totality of things, one no longer sees anything of what you see; consequently I cannot answer you, unless you should take this as an answer."

Yours ever,

FL

I beg you to show Mihalovich's article to my friend Grosse who will read it with pleasure and show it to Gottschalg.

Keep it thereafter in our newspaper bag, which contains the Bayreuth articles, etc.

————

November 29, 72

The double photograph was sent off yesterday. Thank you for having asked <u>me</u> for it, and not one of the other persons in it. As a rule, requests for photographs, album leaves, autographs, etc., reflect idle curi-

29. *Vom Musikalisch-Schönen* [Of Beauty in Music] (Leipzig, 1854). One of the most important books on musical aesthetics of the 19th century, it is still attacked and defended today.

osity or arrogance. The celebrities to whom they are addressed have no cause to feel flattered by them; and they put up with them willy-nilly by tolerating the custom. I don't deny that there are exceptions, but unfortunately each one claims to be an exception, starting with Mlle Cruik[shank]. Now, I won't have you err like *tutti quanti*, and I consequently recommend that you increase your photographic collection only with deliberation, without idle curiosity or arrogance. Forgive me for what arrogance there may seem to be in this recommendation, which I send you in all humility of heart.

My fund of knowledge concerning the Knights of the Round Table barely equals your ignorance. Pending finding people who can inform me better I lay before you the erudition of Bouillet's *Dictionnaire* (22nd edition)[30] in which the article "Round Table (Knights of the)" tells me that "one owes to Monsieur La Villemarqué some interesting research on the Romances of Tristan de Léonais, Lancelot du Lac, Perceforest, and the Holy Grail, Merlin, Flore and Blanchefleur." Your Brussels bookseller will send you La Villemarqué's book, published in 1861, and when my daughter comes to Weimar, ask her for information on this subject which she knows by heart.

I suppose that you will also find in Bouillet's other *Dictionnaire* (*Science et beaux-arts*),[31] which I don't have by me but which is in your library, many pointers on the same Romances.

Several newspapers have reached me containing articles on Strauss's book (*Alte und neue Glaube*). Miska being in the habit of removing the wrappers (which I shall forbid him to do) before handing me the newspapers, I do not know if it is to you that I owe the three issues of the *National Zeitung* and one supplement of the *Allgemeine*. Please tell me whether this is so.

The article by St. René Taillandier on the German press and the interview between the three emperors is successful. The shadow it casts on M. de Bismarck will not trouble him much. Frederick the Great has been held up to general opprobrium as the "disturber of Europe"; how

30. *Dictionnaire universel d'histoire et de géographie* (Paris, ed. 1871).
31. *Dictionnaire universel des sciences, des lettres et des arts* (Paris, ed. 1872).

can one wonder that his heirs follow in his footsteps with no more scruples than he about disturbing?

I'll send back to you tomorrow the *Revue des deux mondes*, together with the *Revue bleue* in which you will find *Achille et Lancelot* and right next to it *La France et les français* (which you may not have read) by M. Karl Hillebrand. I introduced this writer to you in the summer of 1871, and I recall that we went for a drive with him and Mme Laussot through the Weimar park at the invitation, and in the company of Your Highness, to whose house we repaired that evening somewhat formally, in order to talk and have supper at the Tuileries, where you were then living.

A nice remark in Hillebrand's new book: "The Frenchman likes to pride himself on his feelings for equality: nowhere in the world is there a less well-founded pretension. This feeling exists indeed from bottom to top; each considers himself equal to the one above him, but from top to bottom, it's another matter."

Also read (still in the same November 9 issue of the same *Revue bleue*, which I insist on praising to you), the *Causerie littéraire* on Mme Récamier. For my part I admire this illustrious *maîtresse idéale de salon*, somewhat in the same way that I admire the sonatas and symphonies of Haydn—as long as I don't have to hear them often. M. Sach, to whom I'll be writing tomorrow, visited Mme Réc[amier]'s salon, and you will perhaps please him by telling him about the recent book by Mme Lenormant[32] and the intimate letters (trifles which are rather popular in society), which shed a new light on the goddess herself, "seductive as Venus and wise as Minerva," as well as on the circle of illustrious friends who formed the crown.

Finally, and somewhat as a contrast, I recommend that you read the letters from Joseph Mazzini to Daniel Stern,[33] "with an autograph letter"(!) 1864–1872, announced on the last blue page of our inevitable *Revue bleue*. Please send them to me after you're through. *Idem* Strauss,

---

32. *Mme Récamier, les amis de sa jeunesse, et sa correspondance intime* (Paris, 187.2)
33. *Lettres de Joseph Mazzini à Daniel Stern* (Paris, 1872).

and the *Chapelle des Médicis* by Ollivier. I'll settle my book accounts with you at Christmas.

Please reassure my friend Grosse on the fate of the large crate, which arrived last week in perfect condition.

What incongruity can Gottschalg have committed for you to erase four lines of your handwriting? Be so charitable as to write them again soon to your very affectionate Vassalet.[34]

FL

P.S. I have this minute received Gille's letter. Assure him of my old and true friendship.

———

December 12, 72

With all due deference to your omniscience, your triple argument is triply false. I receive your letters, I read them in their entirety, and do not forget their content. That goes without saying, although you claim to see it otherwise. Let's move on to details: I plead guilty to having received the *Revue bleue* of October 19 only three weeks later (because of my stay at Horpács), and to not having at first noticed in it the letters from Mazzini to Daniel Stern—perhaps as the fateful result of my old blunders with the author of *Nélida*.[35]

After your admonitory letter I looked for that issue of October 19, and in it I read with sympathy Mazzini's letter on the "Slavs" (September 29, 1864) and the following one (October 6, 1864) in which he speaks of Tacitus, of Lord Byron, and of the two series, "one of which descends from Homer through Shakespeare to Goethe," and the other "from Aeschylus through Dante to Byron." "My admiration does not choose between them," says Mazzini, "my love chooses the second one, that's all."

34. "Little vassal," a pet name for Liszt?
35. A novel published in 1846 under the pseudonym of Daniel Stern, in which Marie d'Agoult bitterly attacks Liszt.

If I sent back to you the issue of November 9, this was with the good intention of not hampering your studies on the Knights of the Round Table (in view of Moule's course: article *Achille et Lancelot*), and it is only as a minor point that I indicated to you Hillebrand's *Opinions allemandes sur la France*, and the chat about Mme Récamier.

Let us conclude: letters and newspapers with pencil marks will always be given very great and grateful attention and consideration. For the rest, do not go to the trouble of writing me "interesting things," and feel very sure that everything you write interests me. When you feel like writing trivialities to me it will give me extreme pleasure. Only one topic grieves me: that of your all too imaginary "disfavor." I don't understand your having false ideas, and that one is completely so, I assure you. What is more, it is insulting to me, and I am almost tempted to scold you for thus leading me into the temptation of getting into the forgiveness of insults with you, my very dear and dominating one. Therefore recover your good conscience entirely, and keep it always safe and sound.

I have not yet found a moment to write to M. Sacha, to whom I will venture to recommend a new tragedy (said to be remarkable) on the great historical issue of Henry IV and Gregory VII. You will oblige me by reading it and giving me your impression. The author is M. de Saar. I'll send you my copy shortly.

Strauss's book has not yet reached me, but there is no hurry. I have written (exceptionally, alas!) a few pages of music these last few days: a transcription, taking some liberties, of Széchenyi's *March*, and a new, very sad, Hungarian Rhapsody,[36] which I shall dedicate to Bülow, who has given very successful concerts in Lemberg, and is still engaged in doing so in southern Germany (Frankfurt, Mannheim, etc.). On December 17 he will be a witness at the second marriage of my old friend Richard Pohl at Baden-Baden, and toward mid-March Bülow will probably return to Vienna where he has signed up for *Kammer Musik Soireen* with Singer and Cossmann.

36. Probably G 163, 5; R 10e 5, "*Sunt lacrymae rerum*," en mode hongrois. The original manuscript is in the Library of Congress.

When are you leaving Weimar? Tell me where I can write to you.

Yours ever,

FL

Your comments on Walther's final song in *Die Meistersinger*[37] are much to my taste, and what you term, in an antiphrase, your "non-sense" seems to me very much more instructive than the critical rubbish officially recognized by Queen Olga and her numerous Court.

I am late in replying to Cosima and know nothing of her immediate plans. In Rome, the temperature has turned milder. Here, the cholera frightens no one any more, but as you wittily observe, my existence is still "poisoned and torn into shreds" by the epidemic known as epistolary.

———

December 18, 72
Pest

My best wishes for your trip. I would like to alter geography and place Geneva at Pressburg.

If you hear the bells:

let me know. I listened to them many times during the six or eight months I spent in Geneva by the "clear and placid Léman."

The Countess Maria Potocka (born Rzewuska [Rezewuzska]) was

37. First performed June 21, 1868, in Munich.

there then, and Balzac wrote to her: "May Geneva weigh lightly on you"! At her house I met the Countess Nesselrode, wife of the Grand Chancellor, to whom I was recommending one of my pupils, M. Pierre Wolff, who afterward had the signal honor of inhabiting the Nesselrode palace at St. Petersburg for five or six years, and of giving lessons there to the Grand Chancellor's daughters and to Mme Moukhanoff. The latter told me that Wolff used to bully her roundly in order to teach her to "introduce expression" in the right passages.

You will perhaps meet the aforementioned Wolff, a man of property and a prominent figure in Geneva and also the pianist-composer M. Lysberg, who ingeniously composed his name from that of Thalberg and my own. He prudently avoided the "szt." His father, Bovy, was a medallion maker of the highest merit. Acquire his large medallion of Calvin which is a masterpiece. He has also struck a very fine one of Napoleon I.

Neither Strauss's book nor Cos[ima]'s letter has arrived. Let me recommend that you write the address very legibly; and when you have something to mail to me, entrust it to Grosse.

Yours ever,

FL

––––––––

UNDATED NOTES OF 1871 OR 1872

Wednesday

1. May your awakening not be saddened because of me, and may a lovely day ever brighten your soul.

Forgive and erase anything I said that was odious yesterday. You could not deceive yourself as to the truthfulness of my sentiment. Understand it fully and simply.

Does it still suit you if I invite Fredro today at one o'clock? If so, kindly tell the bearer of the attached note to take it to him; otherwise throw it away.

> I lay at your feet my most humble pride.

> FL

———

2. I have been so crushed these last few days that it is becoming almost impossible for me to raise myself up a little. However, your words create in me a quiver—from Heaven—and I would like to gather more and more of them until eternity.

May the sobs of my soul fall again on yours as a dew of benediction, through the mercy of the Lord in whom we shall believe, and whom we shall love.

> [sic] † [38]

———

3. I shall have to do some musical work today, read and write a mass of notes, consequently *star al tavolino* [to be at one's desk].

With your permission I'll come to ask news of you tomorrow between noon and one o'clock.

> Yours ever,

> FL

———

4. This is just the right weather—for not budging.

Ergo, I'll come early, and we'll continue peacefully with the symphony *Im Walde*[39] in your Tuileries.

> FL

———

38. Liszt uses a cross as his signature.
39. By Joachim Raff, Opus 153.

Thursday

5. There's another rehearsal (in the church) this morning from 10:00 till 1:00, and this evening I shall make myself scarce.

Have you sent word to Bodenstedt to tell him when you will agree to receive him? He is staying at the Erbprinz, and will be leaving again Saturday.

I suppose you will not be going for a long walk today. Permit your *umilissimo servo* to come between five and six o'clock.

FL

6. The rehearsal will probably last until seven o'clock and a little later. I'll come immediately afterward to warm myself at your hearth—and if you have some tea to offer me, I accept.

Thank you for your kindness to Mme Mouk[hanoff], and even more for the "unforgivably conceited" sentiment. We'll talk about it this evening.

S[ervo] u[milissimo],

FL

7. I'm writing a note to Mme de Helldorf to warn her about our little non-diplomatic scheme.

In spite of the slightly unsettled weather, I hope that Schubert's *Rondo*[40] (a remarkable piece) and the *Hungarian Rhapsody*, with Köm-pel, will not bore you stiff. I will therefore be so bold as to reinvite you—and to await you at eleven o'clock.

In admiring homage,

FL

Sunday morning. Should you have the idea of bringing the *Rákóczy*[41] for four hands, we could play it for you with Schlözer.

40. Opus 70.
41. G 608; R 310.

8. Your young ones have derived greater profit from *L'Indép[endance] belge* than have most of its readers, and it really sets a good example of transforming newspaper articles into good men.

Thank you for Hy[acinthe]'s letter, the original of which I await and will bring you.

I invited myself to Mme de Helldorf's this evening, and tomorrow there is a meeting of Kömpel's *Orchester Verein*.

With a thousand respects,

FL

One can do without *L'Univers* for awhile.

----

9. The *Revue* will interest me infinitely more at <u>your</u> house than elsewhere, especially if you are so kind as to act as my elementary guide in this reading matter.

As for the small news item in *L'Indépendance* about my difficulty in acclimatizing myself in Hungary, and my "shaken resolve," it is more kind than accurate.

I'll try to call on you tomorrow between three and four and will bring you further news of Father Hyacinthe.

[unsigned]

Thursday

10. Today, I am devoting myself until about four o'clock to studying <u>ancient</u> history—very salutary at my old age. If you will permit me, I will come after my class to offer up to you my newly acquired erudition.

The Grand Duke told me yesterday that he will be going to the Tuileries this afternoon.

Umilissimo servo,

FL

Friday

11. On my way home yesterday evening, I was accusing myself of foolish vanity with regard to the <u>astronomical stroll</u> of the *Beethoven Cantata*. So as to compound my wrong, here is a piece by Saint-Saëns[42] on this same stroll.

Hoping that the heavens will be favorable to yours, tomorrow at four o'clock, I lay at your feet all the reproaches I owe to myself.

FL

Wednesday

12. Here is the piece on Moukhanoff from the *Allgemeine Zeitung*, which I wanted to bring you today. Several tiresome obligations prevent me from going out, but I ask your permission to come tomorrow after the performance of *Orpheus* (which ends early).

Umilissimo servo,

FL

Thursday

13. An extraordinary, solemn event is to take place at the Erbprinz this evening after the theatre.

Orpheus bids me be present, and I could not imitate the "specters, ghosts, and dreadful shades" by saying

Very much at your feet,

FL

42. *Improvisation sur la Beethoven–Cantate de Franz Liszt pour piano.*

14. A lovely day. The trees seem to be dreaming of some vague bliss. *Authorchsame Bäume* [obedient trees], says Lenau.

Between twelve and one, if you will permit, I shall come to call on you with our two tourists from Tiefurt, to whom you have been so exceptionally kind.

My homage to the "Muff,"

FL

Saturday

15. I got back only late yesterday evening from an improvised excursion to Tiefurt, to which I took with me the two volumes, enclosed herewith, with the intention of delivering them very humbly to you on my return. The hour was too late and I'll try to have better luck this evening—between eight and nine o'clock.

Mme de Moukhanoff writes me that you created "a deep impression" at Karlsruhe.

Yours ever,

FL

Tuesday

16. Twenty-four hours late (because of a visit to Halle, to a lyric poet of the rarest sort—Robert Franz). I ask your leave to come this evening toward nine o'clock in order to thank you for what you tell me and are thinking.

FL

Friday evening

17. I was a little put out by your telegram of this morning, and my letter of yesterday will explain to you that I am less guilty than you thought. Allow me to beg you to retain your entire certainty and security.

From Eisenach, I could no longer reply to you and my letter from here had to wait until the mail cart left for Ansbach, something which happens but once daily.

Tomorrow, when the Cardinal is back, I'll know where I stand with regard to the excursion to Langenburg planned for Monday. If it takes place, I shall arrive in Bayreuth only Wednesday evening or Thursday. In the meantime, I make so bold as to importune you with another errand which I entrust to your diplomatic skill.

I have an extensive epistolary debt of almost a year to settle with Mme de Schwartz. She writes to me "that the banker J. Elkan in Jena will forward my letter to her." I was hitherto unaware that there existed a banker Elkan in Jena and would almost suppose Mme S. to be mistaken. So please be so extremely kind as to clarify this matter and to have my enclosed letter forwarded to Mme S. by very sure hands, either through Gille, or Elkan, from Weimar.

You understand the problem with all its complications and will help me solve it, won't you?

I await a line of favorable reply and will write to you again on Sunday.

Umilissimo servo

FL

It would perhaps be a good idea to seal the letter for Mme S. with wax in view of the long trip from Weimar to Crete? So do add this final seal to your kindness.

Friday

18. Miska acts as a telegram.

I shall return tonight or early tomorrow morning, and between eleven o'clock and noon we'll draft our Erfurt plan, whose success depends on your gracious assistance.

Yours ever,

FL

---

19. It seems that logic rules and governs in the house you dwell in. Of this your note is a no less flagrant proof than is the <u>rosebush</u> of Mme Helldorf.

However, patience! This evening I shall come and teach you the true method of the ratiocinations "and the consequences extracted from the natural sense." I need only consult Gottschalg (now Professor of Philosophy—logic and moral—at the Seminary, whom your Asiatic instincts were prompting you to dismiss!); and armed with his knowledge I shall present myself at your door around eight o'clock in order to prove to you by all kinds of demonstrative and convincing reasons that I am . . . a great big old fool,

And your very obedient servant,

FL

1873

January 7, 73
Pest

I started the year with a bad cold which kept me in my room, more or less in bed, for several days. My friends here claim that among other faults I also have that of dressing too lightly in the winter, and they try to persuade me to wear fur coats. But my antipathy to this apparel is so strong that I am not going to resign myself to wearing one, and much prefer to catch cold and the grippe many times more. However, I appreciate fine furs when worn by the fair sex, or on fine costumes for grand ceremonies, Hungarian, Polish, Russian. There is a verse of Hugo which charms me and often comes back to my mind: *des vieux hetmans il ceindra la pelisse* [he will wear the pelisse of the ancient hetmans][1] (*Mazeppa*). It is in F major at the end of my *Mazeppa*,[2] which you have gloriously rendered with your ten fingers—untamed steeds.[3]

And my bells of Geneva?[4] The middle note (the third) is now "abolished or imperceptible" you tell me. Alas! time has wrought (figuratively speaking) the same ravages in me. My middle note, the one which tied me to life, has disappeared—there remain for me only the tonic and the dominant, which becomes a terrible dissonance when it rises to the augmented fifth.

Bülow writes that the Gewandhaus concert you mention will take

1. *Hetman*, related to the German *Hauptmann*, was the title of the chief of the Ukrainian Cossacks.
2. G 100; R 417, the 6th of Liszt's symphonic poems. It is also the 4th of his *Etudes d'exécution transcendante* (G 139, 4; R 2b4) for piano solo; the music is predominantly in D minor.
3. *On vous voit moins souvent, orgueilleux et sauvage, rendre docile au frein un coursier indompté*, Racine, *Phèdre* (Paris, 1677), I, 1.
4. G 156, 3; R 8, 3, *Les cloches de G. . . .*

75

place on February 6. I'll send you a line in Weimar for my old friend
David (*Conzertmeister*, and gentleman), who will get you tickets. You
will please me by writing a brief note to Bülow and by having a few
words with him in Leipzig. No other man in this world is as deeply
dear to me as he. Unfortunately I do not have the means of making this
as clear to him as I should like. He will perhaps speak to you about an
idea for Weimar (where, incidentally, he was most shabbily treated).
I very much want it to materialize, and that M. Sach not thumb his nose
at me on this occasion.[5]

As usual, you did wisely to read Tennyson's poem (on the legends of
the Round Table) and I thank you for having written to me about
them with so much charming erudition. If I am not mistaken Villemarqué has published two works on the cycle of the legends and poems
of the knights of the Round Table. In case they do not completely satisfy
your quest in this field, ask my daughter for further information. She
writes that she is going to start again on her peregrinations, beginning
with Berlin (next week) and she quotes a brilliant remark by Mme de
Moukhanoff, in reply to the King of Württemberg, who was upholding
the true and classic thesis that the husband is the wife's support: "Support—I protest—but package, full of precious things, doubtless of ines-
timable value," etc.

Yours ever

FL

Assuming that you have not read the last number of the *Revue bleue,*

5. The first complete performance of Liszt's oratorio, *Christus* (G 3; R 478), was
scheduled to take place in Weimar near the end of June, 1873. Bülow suggested a second
concert either to precede or to follow the choral evening. Liszt would conduct and
Bülow would be the soloist in a formidable program of Liszt's compositions. Liszt was
heartily in favor of the idea. But the oratorio evening was suddenly advanced to May 29
and the other concert failed to materialize. Moreover, the Grand Duke, whose presence
was deemed essential, was out of town. This letter offers one of the very rare instances of
Liszt expressing dissatisfaction (even tinged with vulgarity) with Carl Alexander. (Cf.
Briefwechsel zwischen Franz Liszt und Hans von Bülow [Leipzig, 1898], letters 178, 181.)
Did Liszt really conduct this performance of *Christus*? Most biographers assume so, but
in the 1968 edition of Raabe's *Liszts Leben*, on supplementary page 15, there is reference
to a statement by Apponyi that Lassen was the director.

I am sending it to you under separate cover. In it you will find a little letter from Hyacinthe.

If you do not yet know the impressions of Wagner's most recent journey (to Cologne, Karlsruhe, etc.) published in the *Musikalisches Wochenblatt* of Fritzsch (January 3rd issue), I'll send them to you.

January 22, 73
Buda Pest
(this is the
official name since
a few days ago)

You have certainly not been scolded; and I even beg you not to reprimand our excellent M. Sarring who has given me great pleasure by sending me your newspapers. It is only a matter of recommending that he have fewer scruples, and of not insuring this kind of mail shipment.

An old proverb says: "He who has land has war," and the very aged Job defined human life as "a perpetual war" (*Militia est vita hominis super terram*). I understand your sorrow, and your dislike of selling land linked to the memory of your husband, and on which you intended to install Mimi "of the bucolic tastes," who would have been as snug there as could be. However, M. de Bock's opinion seems to me decisive, and I feel as he does that the best thing a woman can do when she owns land, which she is unable to look after with concentration and continuity, is to sell it. It only remains to sell it as profitably as possible; and it is again M. de Bock who will be most helpful to you in this matter. As for me, I have never owned more than a few feet of land, in Bonn, in a street which, after the *Beethoven Fest*[6] in 1845, was to be named after me. I refrained from having the house built, and my cousin Eduard did me the service of selling the ground at not too great a loss. I am totally in-

6. The festival at which a monument to Beethoven was unveiled. Liszt had participated in the program, and contributed generously to its cost.

competent in such matters, but I will tell you of a delightful reply of Baron Rothschild (of Vienna) to Count Edmond Zichy. The latter asked the most illustrious Baron how it was that all Rothschild affairs prospered, while several of his were going less well: "The reason is simple; you have become a Jew with age and experience; as for me, I was born a Jew."

My very sincere thanks for the newspapers, and in particular for the delicate attention of the renewal of the subscription to the edition every other day of *L'Univers*. The articles by Veuillot (even those by Eugène) comfort me, and the numerous speeches of His Holiness edify me. I don't know whether you read in some German newspaper a commentary from Rome, not ill-intentioned toward me, published by *Deutschland* in Weimar, where it is stated that His Holiness, on hearing the news of my daughter's second marriage,[7] allegedly called me "Hans Wurst." I suppose this is a translation of "Bajazzo" or "Pulcinello." I have sent this piece to H. H. Princess Wittgenstein, adding that I in no way protested against it since, insofar as I know, "Bajazzi" and "Pulcinelli" are not excommunicated in Rome. Now all I want in this world is to attend mass regularly and, on the important feast days of the year, to go to confession in order to draw near to the sacrament of Communion in Jesus Christ our Lord.

The speech by Father Hyacinthe which you announced to me has not arrived.

From Rome I continue to receive the most excellent advice; and moreover people are so kind as to add more. If I come to a bad end, it will certainly not be for want of sound advice! I am indeed most grateful for this last, even should I find myself inclined to prefer a little more assistance to the finest sermons and arguments.

Your idea about the Gewandhaus in Leipzig seems good to me. I urge you to follow it up, and send you enclosed a card to David (*Conzertmeister*, etc.) who, over some thirty years, has always been very friendly and obliging toward me. His wife is Russian; and if I am not mistaken Wilhelmj married one of her nieces.

7. Cosima Liszt von Bülow's marriage to Richard Wagner, August 25, 1870.

Before going to Leipzig, send David this card and deign to send with it two lines in your illustrious handwriting. He will probably reply that your tickets are still safer than are Sarring's papers in the mail.

Don't worry about Bülow's incident in Weimar; talk it over with him *ad libitum*. I don't know whether you will be seeing Gille, even in Jena; consequently I shall no longer dare to burden you with my compliments for him. Take this as a scolding, and don't punish me for it with German squabbles, in the Byzantine—or *"Reine Olga"*—manner.

Yours ever

FL

———————

February 4, 73
Pest

Another little scolding today. Your imagination runs away with you when you attribute to me incongruous "desires" such as, among others, that Miss F. should play at court. Frankly this kind of remark and its correlatives coming from you (accept this compliment) make me impatient, for you must know, since Rome, that I practice abstention from desires. This has not prevented me from writing some pretty variations on Schubert's *Wiener Trauer Walzer*,[8] entitled in Paris *Le Désir* and attributed to Beethoven. I also know Tasso's graceful line *Bramo assai, poco spero, e nulla chiedo* [I wish for much, hope for little, and ask for nothing]. Young ladies in bouts of melancholy like to apply it to themselves, but for my part I retain only the last two words without concerning myself any more with the *bramare* and *sperare* in this world.

Thank you for your charming illustration of the fable "The wolf, the goat, and the cabbage," each one traveling separately for fear of an accident. You have more wit than M. de Voltaire himself; to me, this is clear, and everyone would be convinced of it were I to publish your letters.

8. G 427; R 252, No. 9 of his *Soirées de Vienne*. Liszt's holograph of the complete set is in the Library of Congress, Washington, D.C.

I cannot adequately convey to you how pleased and obliged to you I am for your kind and generous supplies of *L'Univers*, the *Débats*, and the *Revue bleue*. The book by Strauss has finally arrived. How wild he is, and what torments there are in this gloom! Cosima writes that M. Renan has announced the appearance this spring of *L'Antéchrist*, an interpretation of the Apocalypse, and of the history of Nero who is said to be the Antichrist of the Apocalypse. In Weimar I shall read *Les Vies de quatre grands chrétiens français* by Guizot. To combine St. Louis, Duplessis-Mornay, Calvin, and St. Vincent de Paul seems an even bolder undertaking than to attempt the fusion of the junior and senior branches of the Bourbon family (or even of the Prince Imperial), which is now so much the object of attention, and which will probably not have much success.

Even though you are not among the admirers of M. de Bismarck, let me quote a superb remark in his last speech (January 25): *So habe ich in Erfahrung gebracht, dass man einigermassen im Lande ermüdet, und seine Ohnmacht erkennt* [My experience has been that one grows somewhat tired in the country and recognizes one's weakness].

As for local events, which are scarcely diverting, I inform you that Mlle Hortense Vogt (of Weimar) has been staying in Pest for about two weeks. She had taken care to send me ardent telegrams ahead of time from Nice which I no more answered than her letters, which I never read any longer and only open by mistake when the address is in another hand—a subterfuge to which Mlle Hortense often has recourse, but without success.

On Sunday, February 23, I am arranging a musical evening *zu Ehren und Gunsten von Robert Franz* [to honor and benefit Robert Franz]. Afterward Richter's concerts will start again; the most illustrious Brahms will grace one of the programs; and toward the middle of March we expect Wagner. Have you read his three <u>cannonball</u> articles in Fritzsch's *Musikalisches Wochenblatt*? The fine tribute he pays to Normann (manager in Dessau) should stimulate our very honored friend Loën a little.

I have long been advising Servais to compete for the composition prize of the Brussels Conservatory. It's the most sensible thing for him to do (even should he win it only another time).

Have you seen Mme Moukhanoff again? How do things now stand with regard to your advantages and worries as a landowner and chatelaine? Let me know, and please convey my affectionate greetings to your "House Quartet," Peterle, Mimi, Clément, and the baby.

Yours ever from my heart

FL

———

February 11, 73

Pest

I hasten to give you my full approval and praise for your Berlin trip. It was judicious, opportune, in good taste, and perfectly logical. Moreover, it came off wonderfully well and I derive my own share of satisfaction from it, thanks to the charming, detailed account you give me.

Thank you particularly for the paragraph on Cosima (who wrote to me from Berlin in the last days of January, after the evening at the Schleinitzes with the reading of the *Götterdämmerung*⁹). I have always been encouraged by the favorable *andamento* of your relations with Mme de Schleinitz, and I applaud you for putting me in the right by recognizing her "precise tact" and a "worthy use of the advantages she possesses." On this last point, M. de Schleinitz is a great help to her— something few husbands are to their wives.

I am charmed by and grateful for what you tell me about the Russells, about the framed portrait of you on Lady Russell's table, and of the latter's delicious remark concerning us.

Once again you were completely right to go to Berlin at this time, and you could not reasonably doubt for one minute my full and entire approbation. Besides, it seems to me that you ought never to find it

9. The fourth part of Wagner's tetralogy, *Der Ring des Nibelungen*.

difficult to guess what pleases or displeases me. You know that I wholeheartedly detest meanness, platitudes, selfish and vulgar scheming. Consequently, all that is opposed to these comforts me.

With regard to M. de Bock, I am delighted with your new contract and I wish that you may keep your property forever without too heavy a burden. My confidence does not go so far as to accept as infallible forecasts even for the greatest fortunes based on land! It is merely a question of holding fast within the periphery of reasonable probabilities, and of not imitating the dog in the fable by letting go the piece one holds in order to chase after the reflection . . . in the river.

My modest opinions (which I do not recommend to anyone) also incline me to foretell a happy outcome for your Spaniards.

In spite of Janin's warm praise of the "thoughts of M. de Lagrange," I find in them the stamp of dilettantism for which I do not care. What is meant by: "the more wittily a good thought is defined the less it is true," or "the heart is more jealous than the mind," or "the great success of fools is their great hope"? etc. Even the thought which you underlined seems to me fairly equivocal: "Better withdraw confidence than measure it." In most affairs of this world, this is completely untrue, and even in the loftiest affections a noble and wide measure should not be excluded.

I would not wish to diminish the merit of the Marquis de Lagrange, but I confess that a good many of his thoughts quoted by Janin seem to me less pithy and original than the maxim of Baroness de Plötz (your compatriot): "There must be bounds to everything and limits to nothing" (forgive me if I have by chance put <u>bounds</u> in place of <u>limits,</u> and vice versa!).

I told you that the project of an Academy of Music[10] in Pest, rejected by parliament by a few votes last year, is to be put forward again this winter. It has just been voted unanimously (less three or four votes) and in the most extraordinarily flattering manner for me, for, although I have always stayed aloof from this project, my name has, as it were,

10. Two more years elapsed before the National Hungarian Royal Academy of Music was officially instituted on March 21, 1875. Liszt was appointed president.

become identified with it. This will place a very heavy load on me, and much burdensome detail – – – but I cannot decline the honor conferred on me by my compatriots without shirking my duty.

I enclose the little summary of the session on February 9.

Yours ever

FL

February 24, 73
Pest

It was a good and friendly idea of yours to send me the photograph of Napoleon[11] on his deathbed. It has been framed and placed near my writing desk in the little room in which I sleep, eat, and work, and spend all my time, except for that which is taken up by more formal visits and by pianists to be auditioned, for there is no piano in this little room, which is very crowded with furniture and books. Besides, you know that I don't have many portraits on display in my home. Here, as in Rome, I have only three: my mother, the Princess, Bülow (with the epigraph of *Die Ideale*[12]), and a red chalk sketch of my daughter Blandine, drawn by Etex who gave it to me in Rome.

My old feelings of deep admiration and humble attachment toward Napoleon III have not changed. The day after his death I wrote about this to the Princess, who tells me that she showed my letter to several members of the Bonaparte family. Since I am not at all involved in politics, I abstain from idle comments on topics too controversial, and simply confine myself to rendering privately unto Caesar things that are Caesar's.

What thunderbolts of eloquence has Reverend Father Hyacinthe hurled from the pulpit of the *Temple de l'Oratoire*, formerly Catholic,

11. Napoleon III, who died January 9, 1873.
12. G 106; R 423, symphonic poem.

now Protestant! To proclaim as truth "that we are perishing between two blasphemies, that which denies and that which affirms: on the one hand an idol, on the other a void!" seems to me terribly audacious for a "Catholic and priest"—two indelible roles which Hyacinthe claims he does not abjure. How can they be upheld against the Pope or without the Pope? Who will call up the "new heavens, the new earth, and the new human generation, born neither of blood nor of the will of the flesh, nor of the will of man, but of God, which the Apostles foretold?" Where is one to fix the central point of the "church of the future," "both Catholic and Protestant," which will, according to Hyacinthe's prediction, still be more Catholic than Protestant? In Our Lord Jesus Christ, doubtless, *omnis difficultatis solutio*, but this supreme solution of divine redemption is accepted only by believers of the Christian denominations, and even those, Roman Catholics excepted, are so divided on so many interpretations that, short of a great miracle, their "evangelical alliance" is not to be expected.

Being unable to allay them, I pass over in silence your worries about the cholera in Pest and in Pressburg, and your more legitimate ones (though exaggerated, I believe) with regard to the collapse of the *Gymnasium* in Weimar.

Your comments on the drawbacks of the atmosphere of idolatry, in which some persons of royal birth and a few men of rare genius bask, are infinitely wise. However, it would be dangerous to recommend to them a different climate, from which they would not derive the same benefits as ordinary men, and which would probably reduce the flow of their inspiration.

As for Cosima, she has spoken and written to me so firmly about her feelings of affection for you that no quarrel could occur. Recently she wrote to me: "You know through Mme de Meyendorff that she had the charming inspiration of going to Berlin for the concert. . . . Everything went splendidly this time and were it not for my fear of plagiarizing Schumann. . . ." (I shall convey to you orally these little dots which are very complimentary to you.) "I have become extremely attached to her, with the conviction that this attachment will be lasting—a feeling

I rarely experience, persuaded by and large as I am, first and foremost, that bonds between individuals are woven from illusions."

For the twentieth time thank you for *L'Univers*. The political scene is my principal recreation here and it goes without saying that the Holy Father's many speeches, the letters and instructions of bishops are for me a constant source of edification. Accordingly, in spite of the little time left over for reading, I read nearly every issue of *L'Univers* from cover to cover, as do conscientious provincial subscribers.

Yours ever

FL

Mme Moukhanoff is expected this week in Vienna. Mme Dönhoff leaves tomorrow for Rome with a Princess Obrenowich and Countess Marie Rossi, who sings charmingly. Should these ladies find themselves short of funds during their travels they can easily solve this problem by giving concerts.

March 6, 73
Pest

Just a line to tell you that I am not sick, but very envious of the "frightful reality" about which M. Franz moans after having "often" confessed it to you. May it please Heaven to grant me the "reality of being by myself"!

Brussels honors itself by applauding *Tannhäuser*.[13] For more than twenty years people have had the opportunity to know what to think of this great work, and I remember with pleasure having drawn attention to it[14] in Germany, and in the *Journal des débats* as early as the year

13. Conducted by Liszt in Weimar, February 16, 1849. Liszt was apparently confused in his dates.

14. In his *Gesammelte Schriften* (Leipzig, 1880–83), Band iii, ii. Abt., pp. 3–60.

'49, after the performance in Weimar on February 2, the Saint's day of Her Imperial Highness the Grand Duchess Maria Paulowna.

M. Franz's admission that he "would have understood," etc., reminds me of Marcelline Czartoryska repeating with success in Roman drawing rooms: "I would have understood Liszt if he had become a Carthusian or a Trappist; but why does he still come to my mother's house or to Princess Rospigliosi's?"

There is no need to worry about what this or that person is pleased to understand; for, in order to understand, it is not enough to talk nonsense.

Deign to believe that it is absolutely impossible for you to "displease" me and that I could never for a single moment imagine "being angry with you."

Yours ever

FL

March 19, 73

Pest

I think I told you that on the day after Napoleon's death I confidentially wrote my impressions of this event to Princess Wittgenstein. The publication of my letter in several French newspapers (first in *L'Ordre*), as well as German, surprised me slightly but in no way annoys me, for I did not violate the truth in predicting that when the day of justice comes, "France will bring back with glory the coffin of Napoleon III to place it next to that of Napoleon I." In reply I received yesterday the little anonymous note enclosed herewith which will amuse you. It is not "literature," but the author's conviction loses nothing in lacking stylistic embellishments. Besides, I have lived long enough to be used to the lavishness with which the titles of "ass, imbecile, fool, idiot"—and even worse—are conferred on those who deserve esteem and honor.

Your last letter reminds me of what I said in Rome to Chimay: "one would have to be a scoundrel . . . ," etc.; let me merely comment that I have already taken care to inform you precisely of my comings and goings.

I'll be here until March 31 and shall twice more expose myself to "articles" of the kind which displeased you, for good reasons. Therefore I shall play with *geistreichen Intentionen* [witty intent] day after tomorrow at a concert (presided over by Countess Anna Zichy) for the benefit of the *ungarische Hausfrauen*, and on March 31 for other charitable institutions. This is, for the moment, my humble tribute of respectful gratitude to Count Andrássy. . . .

On April 2 I'll be at my cousin's in Vienna (Hofrath E. J. v. Liszt, Schottenhof) where I shall be spending all of Holy Week. I shall perhaps stop off for one day at Ratisbon before returning to Weimar about April 20. Monseigneur the Grand Duke was so kind as to ask Gille affectionately for news of me; I'll answer Monseigneur directly from Vienna.

Day before yesterday, I had *eine herzliche tiefe Freude* [a deeply felt joy]. The Emperor of Germany deigned to pardon M. Schulz-Beuthen (a composer of rare talent, but militarily guilty!), in whose behalf I personally interceded—with no other recommendation—with His Majesty.

Forgive me for not writing longer. I am not sick and am doing almost nothing; nevertheless it is becoming sometimes rather difficult for me to continue living here below. . . . While this lasts, I beg you to grant me your indulgence and compassion.

Yours ever

FL

Thank you for what you say about *Parsifal*,[15] and Veuillot's *L'Honnête femme*. I'll send off the newspaper you request.

---

15. Wagner's last opera, first performed July 26, 1882, at Bayreuth.

March 26, 73

Here are some leaflets about the two concerts of Richter and the *Hausfrauen*. On Monday I shall be piano-strumming again for the benefit of other *Hausfrauen* and of several charitable institutions, and on Wednesday morning I'll be in Vienna: Schottenhof. Thanks for having sent me *L'Ordre*. I return it to you with the request that you keep it in our little file.

I'm very proud of your interest in the blue review, which M. Veuillot now honors with his attention.

What gibberish he quotes from the "Spanish Gambetta"! I still bet that your good Spaniards will stand fast.

A bientôt

FL

April 3, 73
Vienna (Schottenhof)

Newspapers sent in wrappers are often handed to me by Miska without wrappers. This will explain to you why I suspected you with regard to *L'Ordre*, and you encourage me brilliantly to continue by presenting me with the letter of Mme Sand. Several phrases and passages in it please me, although I don't have much success in distinguishing between the pure and the impure in politics in this world, and even go so far as to believe that we shall not know just what to think on this controversial point before Judgment Day—unless one accepts prompt success as the decisive *critérium* of "purity," which, I must admit, I find most repugnant.

I arrived here yesterday morning and spent the day correcting proofs (of music) and will continue until day after tomorrow.

Next week I'll have positive news of the *Messe de Gran* at Pressburg, where I shall probably go on Easter Sunday or Monday. N.B.: So long as a performance has not taken place, I continue to consider it doubtful.

If you will be kind enough to send *L'Univers* to Schottenhof until April 13, I will benefit from this and be sincerely grateful.

Yours ever

FL

April 24, 73

Notwithstanding my horror of writing I must this morning tell you with my pen, Madame, that your emotion of yesterday evening was—allow me this conceit—in harmony with my feelings. Do not regret it; and permit me, not to advise you nor prescribe rules for you, but to continue on my way passionately at your side.

†16

Monday, May 6

Your letter of yesterday had "la vertu des 'cinq heures,' "[17] and my silence dissolves before the "wholly Helvetian homesickness" which you arouse in me.

I'm sending you the *Débats* of May 4 in which you will find several pieces on the appointment of Cardinal H[ohenlohe] on which the press continues to comment. Once again I share the opinion of *L'Univers* in thinking that the Cardinal can "neither accept nor be approved" (by the Holy See, that is). It is only a "trial balloon" or, as I wrote at once to Princess W[ittgenstein], "a high-flying canard." Besides I incline to feel confident that His Eminence will rise yet higher.

Yesterday morning the Grand Duke gave me the pleasant surprise of coming to one of my Sunday musicals. There was more singing than usual: *Lieder* by Henschel (sung by the composer); *Lieder* by Franz

16. Again Liszt signs with a cross. See p. 68 note 38, "Undated Notes of 1871 or 1872."

17. An allusion to the innocence of tea-time in contrast to the hours *cinq à sept* when gentlemen sometimes found it convenient to call on ladies for purposes other than drinking tea. Liszt implicitly praises himself for not commenting on Olga's nostalgia for Switzerland which she has mentioned in a letter.

(sung by your non-protégé, Müller); some very pretty canons; and, as a crowning piece, *Lieder* by Lassen, to which Mme Merian gave wings. Verlat aspired to having yet another "dessert"; I sat on him, and helped myself in guise of a sweet course to three charming *Noveletten*[18] by Taubert (not the old and very eminent Taubert). I imagine that these pieces will please you and I'll introduce to you the composer who will probably be spending some weeks here.

Rubinstein wires me that family business prevents him from coming to Weimar before the Düsseldorf *Musikfest* and promises that he will visit here about May 25.

There is a rumor here that Mme de Bodenhausen has had to retire to a nursing home in Stuttgart. I would appreciate your giving me accurate news about this on your return.

I'll be going to Leipzig Wednesday morning, and probably to Altenburg the day after, and Friday morning I'll be back at the Hofgärtnerei, the better to nurse there my Helvetian affliction. Speaking of which, M. de Korff, who was also a non-paying member of the audience yesterday morning, paid me the compliment of assuring me that I didn't look well.

When "tea-time" comes again, such a compliment will no longer be appropriate with regard to

Your very humble and temporary Helvetian

FL

Lassen is working hard at <u>your</u> *Nibelungen* for four hands.

July 27, 73
Bayreuth

Three hours of sleep and the same period of reading and meditation enabled me to pass the time agreeably, waiting for the Eisenach train

18. His incidental music to Hebbel's drama.

which left only at 9:00 A.M. yesterday. Your precious handwriting, with specific departure times from Eisenach is of a poetical truth comparable with that of the *Sängerkrieg* at the Wartburg in Wagner's *Tannhäuser*.[19] Since the public does not have the advantage of your handwriting, I grant it preference over the score in order to equalize the merits.

I was in Bayreuth before four o'clock. Cosima had come as far as Neumarkt to meet me at noon, thinking that I would be arriving by the good train (which goes via Leipzig, not Eisenach). Not finding me at Neumarkt, she immediately came here and, being a sensible woman, went back to the station in Bayreuth together with Wagner to meet the 3:30 train.

She drove me right away to the Reichsadler (of glorious memory) where I have princely quarters.

At four o'clock yesterday, dinner at Wagner's (four of us, with Klindworth, professor at the Moscow conservatory, who wrote the three published piano scores of *Der Ring des Nibelungen*).

In the evening, a visit to Wagner's new house[20] about which I'll tell you; it will be ready next spring.

Yours ever

FL

August 2, 73
Bayreuth

I don't have Bülow's exact address in Baden, where he will perhaps return only after your departure. You'll please me by giving me news of him; ask Cossman where he is living, and also please get to know

19. First performed October 19, 1845, in Dresden, The *Sängerkrieg* is the song contest which occurs in Act II.
20. Wahnfried (free of delusion), Wagner's residence in Bayreuth, now the repository under government supervision of the Wagner archives.

personally my friend Richard Pohl, chief editor of the *Gazette* of Baden-Baden. He is one of the Weimarians from the active period—'49 to '59 —and I appreciate his remembering this. It is no fault of mine if my friends from those times (with the exception of Lassen) have had to try to settle elsewhere than Weimar.

While fundamentally resembling each other, the days in Bayreuth have great intellectual variety in their details. Wagner has the good sense to keep his door closed. We are nearly always two or three together. This is the best thing possible.

We have been on outings with the children to the Hermitage[21] and to Fantaisie.[22] M. de Voltaire appeared as an actor in the Hermitage theatre before Frederick the Great and his sister the Margravine, in a performance of his tragedy *Oedipe*. Now an entirely different performance is taking shape in a far more extraordinary theatre.

We shall attend it, I hope, in another two years; in spite of skeptical hornets, the faith of bees endures. . . .

This evening the workmen of the theatre of the Nibelungen are celebrating the completion of the roof, and will have a *Hebeschmaus*.[23] Wagner has written some charming verses for this occasion which I'll send you.

I leave Bayreuth Tuesday, spend the night at Nuremberg, and arrive Wednesday at Schillingsfürst. You know the address: per Ansbach, Bavaria.

Give the "quartet"[24] cordial messages from me, with *tacet* for the fourth one.

Yours ever

F. Liszt

21. The Eremitage; a castle with gardens, fountains, artificial ruins, theatre, etc., east of Bayreuth, erected by Margr. George William in 1715.

22. The Fantaisie, a château with gardens and park, built in 1758, west of Bayreuth.

23. The celebration observing completion of the framework of the *Festspielhaus*.

24. The Meyendorff children.

August 7, 73
Schillingsfürst

This time I'm going to say, like someone else we know: "I did nothing" to deserve a scolding; but this someone is a scold par excellence and on top of that a glutton for letters. Impossible to satisfy, and even more impossible to sate this someone.

I sent you c/o General Delivery, Baden, two Bayreuth newspapers with Wagner's new verses on the occasion of the workmen's celebration *Hebeschmaus*, and a little account of this festival which took place last Saturday. Cosima tells me that she wrote to you a second time (without my permission). Day before yesterday, Tuesday, she, Wagner, and the five children came with me from Bayreuth to Bamberg, whence they made a two-day excursion to Franconian Switzerland. I urged them strongly to visit, in Bamberg cathedral, the tomb of Clement II, about which one of his illustrious relatives recently deigned to pick a bone with me. At about four o'clock (Tuesday) I was in Nuremberg in order to spend the evening with Mlle Ramann, director of a school for piano, of very high repute, and author of several little books on musical literature. She thus combines the merits and advantages of the Misses Stahr and of Gottschalg, my Weimar patrons. Speaking of which, did I tell you that the Misses Stahr gave me the very agreeable surprise of coming to see me in Bayreuth? I showed and explained to them the marvels of the Nibelungen theatre, and I flatter myself that I converted them entirely to the good cause which R.O.[25] and other stars of wisdom take delight in scorning.

On arriving here yesterday (with the Cardinal [Hohenlohe], who was so extremely gracious as to come to fetch me at the Ansbach station) I found your letter from Wildbad. Thank you for the quotation from Renan. It is understandable that writers who persist in presenting Christianity as a historical fact, more or less complex but natural and devoid of any miracles, should find that St. Paul is not free of the faults which are shocking in sectarians, and that "his style is ponderous."

25. "*Reine Olga*," see p. 55 note 23a.

His role was not to sit "weary on the side of the road, or to waste his time in noting the vanity of established opinions." His faith in Our Lord Jesus Christ was not an "opinion"; he preached of Jesus crucified, resurrected, risen into Heaven; he fought the good fight and awaited "the crown of justice which Our Lord will confer in the full light of day on those who love his coming." Fine and great minds may understand nothing about all this; nevertheless millions of souls are illumined and fired by the words of St. Paul – – – – –

It will be a pleasure for me to give the Cardinal your message. He is very busy with the building and installation of a schoolhouse for some forty girls under the direction of a few Benedictine nuns (from Munich).

I am reading the two large volumes by Princess Wittgenstein: *Les causes intérieures des faiblesses extérieures de l'Eglise* [*Causes intérieures de la faiblesse extérieure de l'Eglise en 1870*],[26] and will soon tell you about them at Weimar, but not in writing.

Yours ever

FL

Write to Schillingsfürst per Ansbach until the 14th.

––––––––

Sunday, August 10, 73

This is only a telegram. On Wednesday I'll accompany the Cardinal to Langenburg where we'll be staying until Friday evening. Although Langenburg is but four hours away from Schillingsfürst, letters sometimes take three days to get there. Thus if you need to reach me, wire me here until Tuesday evening.

I shall not return to Schill[ingsfürst] after Langenburg, and expect to be back in Weimar Sunday morning.

26. The most important of the Princess' incessant literary production, in 24 substantial volumes. The work was placed on the Church's *Index librorum prohibitorum*.

Will you be so kind as to have Grosse told at once not to send me any more letters or newspapers.

No one has been here these four days. I dine alone with the Cardinal —and the evening passes in the same way—in the added company of newspapers which the mail delivers at eight o'clock. He is expecting the visit tomorrow of a learned and deserving Benedictine abbot. His sister Amélie will perhaps come too.

Yours ever

FL

———————

Wednesday, August 13 (5 o'clock)
Langenburg (Württemberg)

Your note like that of "the dove of the ark" was handed me this morning on the road from Schillingsfürst to Langenburg. Did you receive my note addressed to Stephanienbad, and the telegraphic message announcing my return on Sunday?

The slowness of communication between Schilling[sfürst] and Lang-[enburg] no longer permits me to receive either letters or newspapers here. I am staying until Friday (feast of the Assumption) and according to the information I have on trains, I can hardly be back in W[eimar] before Sunday. So please present my excuses to Loën as best you can.

You are aware that the *padrone* of this house is Prince H[ohenlohe] L[angenburg], brother of the late Duchess of Meiningen, and that his wife is a Princess of Baden.

The illustrious guests now at the castle are: the Cardinal, his sister, Princess Thérèse H[ohenlohe], his brother-in-law, Prince Salm, and the mitred Abbot (not crazy[27] like a certain little abbot whom we know) Birker, Superior of a Benedictine monastery in Switzerland.

I continue reading *Les causes intérieures des faiblesses extérieures* and am

27. A play on the words *toquet* (a visorless cap) and *toqué* (crazy).

correcting the proofs of the *Wartburg Lieder*.[28] In this latter occupation, I miss my principal corrector extremely. If the edition remains faulty, it is he who will have to be blamed.

Yours ever

FL

Wednesday morning, October 8, 73
Rome

I came straight through from Eisenach to Rome in sixty-four hours without incident. My telegram informed you that I am staying at: Vicolo de' Greci, 43.

From Saturday morning until yesterday evening, I went out only to go to mass and to see the Princess. Consequently I do not know whether or not Rome has changed, and am paying little attention to its ancient and modern marvels. The church where I hear mass (between six and seven o'clock in the morning) is that of "Gesù e Maria" on the Corso almost opposite your former home, the Russian embassy, now represented by Baron d'Üxkühl [Uexküll] (excuse me for not knowing exactly how he spells his name!).

I came across him yesterday evening at the Bobrinskis, to whom I gave lots of news of you while adding a few details concerning the progress of Peterle's and Mimi's studies and the ups and downs of Clément's health. Only the baby was forgotten, but I have it in mind, as the occasion offers, to talk about his instincts of pride, worthy of Alexander, with regard to the color of his soup.

Notwithstanding their acquisition of the Villa Malta the Bobrinskis continue to live in their old home: Casa Margherita. It will take more than a year and over 100,000 francs to arrange the Villa Malta to their

28. G 345; R 638; a group of seven compositions for solo voices and mixed chorus, written for the marriage of the Hereditary Grand Duke Carl Augustus of Saxe-Weimar to Princess Pauline; published with piano 1873, the orchestral version unpublished. First performed September 23, 1873, at the Wartburg.

taste. Several of the walls are even less solid than those of the *Gymnasium* at Weimar about which you had such deep misgivings. Tomorrow evening I dine at the Bobrin[skis]. Perhaps I will find there the "Gran Commendatore" and Baroness Visconti (still "courtier of misfortune" at the Vatican), and will not fail to express to him your very gracious remembrance.

It is still fairly uncertain whether the Tolstoys will be staying in Rome this winter, because of an element of vagueness which has emerged with respect to their finances. Nowadays the Italian capital offers no economic advantages whatever to foreigners.

The fall theatre season opened Saturday with Gounod's *Faust*[29] at the Apollo, and *Martha*[30] at the Polyteama theatre (on the other side of the Tiber).

Faust had been to all intents and purposes hooted off the stage when it was first produced here. This time it was fairly well received. However, I was told yesterday that as people were leaving, a connoisseur said, "*Per musica brutta, non è tanta brutta!*" [For bad music, it's not so bad!] May you pass a like judgment on your intolerable

umilissimo servo

FL

Please hand the enclosed note to friend Grosse. Do you have any news of Mme Moukhanoff?

———

October 9, 73
Rome

The best advice usually suffers from being quite useless. It comes either too late or too early, and any pretext serves not to follow it.

29. Opera, first performed March 19, 1859, in Paris.
30. Opera by Flotow, first performed November 25, 1847, in Vienna.

In your relations with the landlords of your present dwelling you must expect many an unpleasantness. Things have evolved in such a manner that it is becoming very difficult to reach a settlement; however, I still refuse to admit the probability of a breach of faith as flagrant as that which you apprehend. Your divinations have often misled you (at least, in certain details); I hope they are also misleading you now.

I don't know whether you are in the habit of paying your rent every three or six months, before or after it falls due. This time do as usual, without worrying unnecessarily. You no longer have the means of warding off boorish behavior which it would be "insulting" to anticipate, and you could hardly adopt a tone of amiable entreaty; thus all you can do is to be patient and dignified.

One should ignore comments by members of the household. It is better to suffer than to demean oneself.

It is only my submissiveness which prompts me to give you this advice; it is up to you to modify or spurn it according to your pleasure and your preferences which I refrain from discussing.

Yours ever

FL

————

October 18, 73
Rome

I haven't looked around much in Rome, and do not feel at all inclined to seek out its historical and artistic grandeurs and marvels. Most of my hours are spent in talking with Princess W[ittgenstein]; in addition, I see a few old friends: Hébert, the Bobrinskis, Mme Stroganoff (born Potocka), Sermoneta, his son, and the daughter who remembers you with affection and greatly appreciates your lack of insincere amiability.

To what I recently told you about the Villa Malta, I should add a small correction: the purchase price (with registration, etc.) exceeds five hundred thousand francs; the whole of the old building has already been pulled down, and only the tower will survive. The new building calls for several hundred thousand francs, and the Bob[rinskis] only expect to move in two years from now.

The Countess will be writing to you shortly, and Baron Visconti will thank you in his own hand for the compliments I conveyed to him, and with a paperweight which he is willing to entrust to me. Since assuming his new role of "courtier of misfortune" at the Vatican (where he regularly discharges his duties twice a week) his relations with the other bank of the Tiber have considerably diminished. One never sees him any more, either at the Bob[rinskis], or at Sermoneta's.

Last Sunday I was invited in my capacity of godfather of Teano's second son to the baptism of the third. The ceremony took place in the Caetani palace; the godfather was Prince Odescalchi (the father), from whom the newborn took the name of "Tito Livio," and the god-mother Countess Ersilia Lovatelli. She is entirely worthy of having a godson thus adorned with an ancient Latin name, for she herself writes Latin epistles of four pages in Ciceronian style.

I had asked to be admitted to an audience of the Holy Father. He was so gracious as to receive me alone Monday evening and to converse with me for more than a quarter of an hour. The persuasive charm of his words touched me deeply. There is something prodigious about his health and his spirits do not flag. While telling me about the present trials of the Church he developed admirably a text of St. Paul, the gist of which is that one can easily imprison, inflict suffering on, and even kill the body, but one cannot touch the free and immortal soul. More-over, those who suffer with Christ shall share in His Glory. The Holy Father also spoke to me about the visit to Rome, more than fifteen years ago, of M. and Mme Sach. I wrote yesterday to M. Sach to tell him Pius IX's comment on Mme S., while eliminating the first words. Here is the literal and complete text: "The Grand Duchess is short in stature, but her attitude and manners are regal."

At the Vatican, I saw again Cardinal Antonelli, Monseigneur de

Mérode, Monseigneur Pana. The Cardinal is in very good health and perfectly imperturbable in spirit. Neither he nor Pana has been outside the Vatican since September '70. Mérode and the others go out as they please. People assure me that Mérode is now expressing himself in a manner as little flattering and garrulous on the subject of the French legitimists as he formerly did about Goyon and Montebello. His cousin Mlle de Montalembert is marrying a certain Count Grün (who lives in Brussels). The newlyweds are to spend their honeymoon in Egypt.

For your amusement let me quote to you a new pronouncement attributed to Princess Sciarra (whom I met the other evening at the Bobrinskis): "Men are pigs looking for *tartuffes* (*truffles*)." Among other things, she had already invented the *fumier* [manure heap] (*fumoir*) [smoking room] of her son.

I have not received even the smallest snippet of an article from *L'Univers* but only an issue of the *Revue bleue* and two of your letters. Write to me at my cousin's: Eduard Liszt, Schottenhof, 3te Stiege, Vienna. I'll be there next Saturday. Please be so kind as to hand Mme Moukhanoff a note I will send you tomorrow.

Franz Servais arrived in splendor here day before yesterday. He is working on the piano score of his *Tasso*[31] which will soon be published in Paris.

Yours ever

FL

P.S. Why hasn't Grosse sent me the accounts I asked for?

Tuesday, October 28
Vienna

It was difficult for me to thank you for having sent me the Nietzsche pamphlet before receiving it. It only arrived the morning after I had sent off my last letter (from Rome) almost at the same time as Faxelles'

31. A cantata which won the Prix de Rome.

article on Daniel Stern. Thank you for having sent both, and also, in anticipation, for the numbers of *L'Univers* which you promise me in Pest. In order to allay your grief, I pray you to send me three together in the same wrapper, for this is material which I read attentively rather than hurriedly, the same for the *Débats*.

I suppose that, in Nietzsche, the philippic against the *Bildungsphilister*[32] is to your taste. He goes at it hard, and subjects the *Wir* of Strauss to the lashes of criticism and irony. Nevertheless, thanks to the sway of "mediocracy" and of the *Bildungsphilister*, editions of Strauss's book will grow in number and continue to enjoy success.

The copy of the Nietzsche pamphlet you sent me contains the name of Mme Moukhanoff. Before returning it I shall wait for the arrival in Pest of the owner, whom M. de Wardenegg [Wartenegg] saw as recently as yesterday in Dresden. He assures me that she will certainly come, and even assumes that you will not fail to attend the jubilee festival. I hardly dare suggest anything so inconvenient for you in view of the distance, the bad season, and other obstacles, which bid me remain entirely impersonal—for which you have already reproached me on other occasions, but wrongly it seems to me, since my impersonal attitude harms no one other than myself.

You run no risk at all of imitating *le Sieur* de Balzac, who "puffed himself up in a vacuum," but it does perhaps happen to you occasionally to write to me in a sharp and bitter tone, to which I find it hard to become accustomed. For example, with regard to Nietzsche's pamphlet and the portrait by Lenbach, since the photograph of this portrait is of a large and most awkward format, and since my sad face may not appear framed in your drawing room, I preferred to spare you the bother of a burdensome homage. All the same, if your heart is set on this photograph, I'll send it to you at the earliest opportunity together with Baron Visconti's paperweight. Have you written to him?

I saw Lenbach again yesterday evening at the home of Mme Dönhoff, who spoke to me of you in the most charming manner. She has met, I know not where, your friend Princess Czernicheff.

32. Cultural Philistine, a term coined by Nietzsche.

Mme Bobrinska and Servais are writing to you from Rome.

After tomorrow evening I'll be in Pest where rooms have been assigned to me at the Fischplatz.

With neither complaint nor recrimination, with all my heart,

Yours ever

FL

If you have not read Dumas' preface to *Faust*, I shall send it to you. I pretty well share his point of view which is somewhat biased and no doubt haughtily moral in tone, but not false. Even the strange title of "venerable rascal" which Dumas confers on "the auto-idolatrous" Goethe seems to me well enough justified by his amorous career.

Since my note to Grosse (which I felt sure I had sent you) has been mislaid, here once again are a couple of lines for him which I ask you to be so kind as to look after.

I am a big fool and a boor ever to say anything disagreeable to you, for — — —

F.L.

November 2 [1873?]
Pest

The few lines I received this morning suggest a letter, for which you almost apologize, and which has <u>not</u> reached me.

Once again I hardly dare give you advice on such a matter which concerns only my miserable self. Do please make up your mind and act accordingly. It would be too late to send you now an invitation from the Committee, but I am perfectly able to guarantee the decorum and the propriety of your stay here, without any "awkwardness" whatever.

Your

FL

Thanks for the papers.

Friday, November 21, 73
Pest

In spite of your sadness, you were well inspired to write to me. Your little letter moved me very much, my dearest one, and I would like to be able to tell you so better. Be indulgent toward my shortcomings and lapses in writing. It is not drought but fullness of heart which makes me silent. You are perhaps right in thinking that "only the selfish know how to love"; teach me to be more so and, till then, do not condemn me – – –

One would have to be a Petrarch, and I can only compare myself with a Servais, with the disadvantage of being three times his age. Like him, I risk displeasing you by telling you things which do not interest you much more than the *Tasso* cantata. All the same here is my little weekly report:

At Gran the Archbishop, Prince Primate of Hungary, was so gracious as to have me stay in his palace from Sunday morning until one o'clock Monday, and he put up with my company during his return here by coach (and four).

When I got back to my room I found there a pile of letters and a few delayed telegrams. Of about thirty to be answered I barely reached the fifth today!

Tomorrow at half-past two I'm going to Pressburg; Albert Apponyi is willing to accompany me, and we shall spend the evening together at the Dénes Széchenyis, whom you know from Rome. Sunday, in honor of St. Cecilia the *Messe de Gran* is being given in Pressburg cathedral; I'll be back Monday. Two or three weeks will be spent in letter writing and in calls in discharge of obligations.

I have received no news of the Vienna concert (December 2); perhaps there was no place for it in the program of the imperial festivities.

When you are so kind as to fetch the green blotter with the libretto of *St. Stanislaus*[33] from the Hofgärtnerei, please ask Pauline to give you the photograph of my portrait by Lenbach which I omitted bringing to

33. G 688; R 671, Liszt's unfinished oratorio.

you, out of discretion (not absentmindedness). The format is inconvenient and the subject not very attractive.

Thank you for offering to settle my accounts with Grosse; I accept, and am sending you (under separate cover) my bills for our dinners with Mme Moukhanoff at the Hôtel de Russie, and that of the binder and stationer, M. Heus: in all, 25 thalers.

As for the balance of the tailor's bill, M. Jahreis, please ask Grosse for it and send me the figure. I had not intended paying it right away, but since you are looking after the matter I'll take advantage of your good offices as soon as you have let me know what I owe Jahreis, without echoing M. de Talleyrand's famous reply to one of his creditors, who asked His Highness when he would deign to consider paying his debt: "You are indeed curious, Sir."

Do not be curious to know, I beg you, Madame, whether Pest does not seem even sadder to me than Weimar to you; and believe me to be

Your lovingly saddened

FL

When I return from Pressburg, I'll write to Mlle Gaul that she can call on your behalf on your sister and Mme Massenbach.

November 25, 73
Pest

Thank you for the charming good grace with which you are discharging your very good offices in favor of Mlle Gaul. She will do honor to them, I hope, being the very nice person and hard-working pianist that she is, and I wrote her yesterday evening that she should call with complete assurance of being well received, being recommended by you, on the ladies the Baronesses of Staal and Massenbach, and on Mme d'Adelung, to whom, over and above what you had promised, you were so kind as to write. When your sister has reported to you on Mlle Gaul, please drop me a line.

The performance of the *Messe de Gran* day before yesterday in Pressburg was wholly adequate. Countess Marietta Széchenyi graciously contributed to it by singing in the choruses, and that whole Sunday seemed like a last echo of the festival at Pest, save for the crowns and the *Fahnen* [banners], of which I think more than I should. If this is wrong of me, you will forgive me, won't you, dearest one?

In the train with Albert Apponyi I read the witty and instructive article by Alfred Pérot (in the *Revue bleue*) on the Count de Chambord, and I also reread on this occasion the reply of the Bishop of Orléans to Pressensé. Monseigneur Dupanloup is full of the monarchy's liberal promises. I don't know whether he has sufficiently taken the landlord into account, and am inclined to think that M. Thiers was well advised to say on November 29, '72: "I do not hesitate . . . were I to see before me the possibility of establishing the monarchy, were this possible . . . and could it be done, you must let me know, do you know what I would do? I would find a way of withdrawing from the scene, and I would give those capable of restoring the monarchy a free rein." Because of these memorable words quoted by Dupanloup, I am returning to you herewith his letter, in which the I and the we seem to me disproportionate to the existing state of affairs.

What a Court of *King Pétaud*[34] is this *Kunstschule* of Weimar! Fortunately people there are impervious to ridicule and, by saying his *quos ego*,[35] M. Sach will calm the fury of the waters.

I will convey your order for photographs to Mihalovich; should he delay fulfilling his promise, please send me a few friendly lines for him. N.B.: several of the photographs you ask for are not commercially available. As for Apponyi's toast, we must wait for it to be published.

Yours ever

FL

Tell Clément that *conter* is not written *compter* and that one remains in

34. Meaning disorganized and badly administered.

35. Virgil, *Aeneid*, I, line 135: *quos ego* — *!* These two words are uttered by Neptune in the scene in which he calms the storm.

suspens with an *s* and no *d*. As a matter of fact, great writers, M. de Lamartine at their head, don't bother much with spelling; so Clément can go ahead as he pleases.

December 3, 73

You have so well settled the accounts to my advantage, that I fear that you may be out of pocket. So as to ease my mind, please, my dearest one, check once again whether, after having paid so many bills, you in fact have 18 thalers in the till and, if so, keep them until I let you know what to do with them.

Last week's event in Budapest was the jubilee celebration of the twenty-five years' reign of His Imperial, Royal, and Apostolic Majesty.[36] Friday and Saturday morning there were receptions at the castle of Buda; on Friday, a gala evening at the theatre, and, on Saturday, a grand gathering at court (without ladies, except for the Queen and her ladies-in-waiting).

For the first time since I settled in Pest, I had the honor of being in the Emperor's company (at the Friday morning audience) and of expressing to him my very humble thanks and congratulations. Like the Holy Father, he spoke to me about the marriage of the hereditary Grand Duke of Weimar.

I enclose a spicy account by Jókai (the celebrated novelist and publicist, and Deputy of the opposition) of the Saturday gathering, after which I spent a couple more hours at Prince Constantine Hohenlohe's, where there were present Andrássy, Prince Paul Esterházy and about ten men, plus just one young unmarried woman, Countess Festetics, lady-in-waiting to the Queen. She came there with perverse intentions, which I hastened to satisfy by playing a few piano pieces, in particular the *Szózat* [manifesto],[37] dedicated to Andrássy who wrote me a very flattering note on the subject.

Did I tell you that Cardinal Hohenlohe sent me as a *Nachfeier* [extra

36. Franz Josef, Emperor of Austria and King of Hungary.
37. G 486; R 158.

celebration] for my jubilee anniversary a superb rug embroidered with roses, laurel branches, field flowers, and a red dahlia? In his letter His Eminence explains very graciously to me the symbolism of this embroidery, artistically executed. The rug is a little longer and wider than my bed, which it embellishes so well that I feel almost ashamed to have it removed in the evening.

Yesterday before going to sleep I read Viel-Castel's inauguration speech at the Academy—a perfectly suitable piece of literature, but nothing more. All the same, thanks for having sent it to me, for this sort of thing interests me even when of mediocre quality.

If I had the time, I would read the history of Russia by Philippe de Ségur, which Viel-Castel recommends in his speech, specifically by quoting the author himself. The book is probably in the Weimar Library, and as you devour a lot of books you will perhaps read that one and give me your opinion of it, which is for me very *massgebend* [authoritative].

Did you meet in Rome Count Anatole de Ségur (author of a volume of fables, and of two short poems: *St. François d'Assise* and *Ste. Cécile*)? I don't know whether he is Philippe's son, but unless I am much mistaken his mother is Russian and sister of the great Rostopchin. She has published some educational books.

Next week I'll be sending you a large sheet of photographs, on which appear the President and members of the Committee for my anniversary: Messeigneurs Haynald, Augusz, Széchenyi, Karácsonyi, Apponyi, Mihalovich, Huszár, Richter, Dunkl, and your very humble servant (at the piano). Ábrányi and Reményi are missing: the latter left Saturday for Lemberg and will not be back until spring; and Ábrányi, to my particular regret, was only told about the photographing session too late.

Did Pauline return to you the photograph of the portrait by Lenbach? Does Peterle approve of it? The expression is not gracious, as in the days of the *Fahnen Weihe* [consecration of the colors].

Yours ever

FL

I'm expecting a letter from Vienna which will settle the date of the concert for the benefit of the *Kaiser Franz Josef Stiftung* [Emperor Franz Josef Foundation]. It will probably take place toward the end of next week, and I'll spend only four or five days in Vienna.

Is Mme Moukhanoff back in Warsaw?

You will oblige me by telling the Grand Duke at an appropriate moment that I refrained from answering by telegram my anniversary telegrams, but that I shall have the honor of thanking him by letter shortly.

Alas! My good intentions of politeness with regard to my correspondence are only very slowly fulfilled because of the enormous quantity of obligations I face.

December 10, 73
Pest

It is only due to you yourself, dearest one, if my letters displease you less than before, since you left Pest. In such matters the homeopathic maxim *similia similibus* [things alike are cured by things alike to them] applies. You are not angry, and my natural mood, which is very ill at ease in anger but too much inclined toward the other extreme, has returned. The merit is yours; the gratitude—very humble and happy—mine.

This evening I am sending off to you the sheet of photographs of the Committee for my jubilee anniversary[38] in Pest. I am adding the names to it. That of Ábrányi is conspicuous by its absence. He is an object of suspicion because of his good will toward me, extended out of principle and frequently displayed over several years. In his noble quality as a Hungarian he will never alter course, and will hardly join other indulgent friends of mine who are concerned only with success as such.

38. The 50th anniversary of Liszt's career as a concert artist took place in Budapest November 8–11, 1873.

Accordingly, Ábrányi is in trouble, because of a matter of principle, but I thank you all the more for having a good opinion of him, and for telling me, like Scheherazade, who told stories so well, your little discussion about "the turned-down collar of Lord Byron," etc.

Thank you also for the Taine article on the *Lettres à une inconnue*[39] by Mérimée. In it I find several touches reminiscent of Olgha [sic], although she quite rightly points out that it is only through an excess of modesty and of condescension that she is able to admit to being like someone else, be it the Empress or the Queen of Sheba; others perhaps recall F.L.

You know to whom applies the "Memneso apistein" (remember to be distrustful) and the comment which follows: "By dint of turning the tapestry over, one ends by usually seeing the reverse side."

The blue underlinings are those of your pencil; the red—*ad libitum*. The letter, "in fairly good ink" to the Grand Duchess, charmed me.

I am sending back to you this number of the *Débats* with this marginal note: "To contradict oneself is to make man complete; and it is through contrasts that passions are harmonized."

Mme Mouk[hanoff] has returned to Vienna, and is staying at the hotel of the Roman Emperor [Hôtel Römischer Kaiser]. To my great regret I shall no longer find her there, for the concert at which I am to do some piano-strumming has been postponed to Sunday, January 11. Till then your FL will not stir from here.

———

December 12, 73
Pest

When I sent off the photograph of the Committee to you this morning, I added to it that of your lowliest servant, and beg you to have it delivered (by Grosse) to *Monsieur le Curé* of my parish, Hohmann. I am

39. Prosper Mérimée, *Lettres à une inconnue. Précédés d'une étude sur Mérimée*, par H. Taine (Paris, 1873). The "inconnue" has been identified as Mlle Jeanne Françoise Daquin (1811–95).

told that this very worthy priest would be pleased to have a picture of me, which I hasten to offer him, in memory of my respectful affection of some twenty years. Among his flock there is no one more grateful to him than I. Please decide whether this portrait should be framed and, if so, choose and order a simple and formal frame well suited to Hohmann's residence.

Just now I sent off to Kahnt the copy of Apponyi's toast which is to appear in the *Neue Zeitschrift für Musik*, and I will send it off to you at once.

I will find out whether there is some book "favorable to the Jesuits" which would make agreeable reading for you. Unfortunately, the counterpart of the *Provinciales*[40] was not so written as to offset the vogue and the literary reputation of the masterpiece you "detest."

As for works dealing with the lives of the saints, I recommend to you *Les Petits Bollandistes*[41] in twelve volumes, published by Monseigneur Guérin (already in its third edition). In it you will find for each day in the month the biography of the saints of the calendar written in good French, neither too verbose nor too condensed, and adequately buttressed by the most authoritative documents.

Furthermore these twelve volumes in octavo have the merit of being extremely well printed and of having very convenient notes and a separate index. The price of *Les Petits Bollandistes* is 60 to 70 francs at the most.

Yours ever

FL

Prince Paul Esterházy whom I mentioned to you recently is the grandson of Prince Paul who died several years ago and whom you met at the coronation of Emperor Alexander.

---

40. Blaise Pascal, *Les Lettres provinciales* (Paris, 1656–57).
41. *Les Petits Bollandistes. Vies des saints de l'Ancien et du Nouveau Testament, des martyrs, des pères, des auteurs sacrés et ecclésiastiques . . .* (Paris).

December 13, 73

I warmly support Loën. His personal manner here was noble and in good taste, and people also remember with great appreciation his two speeches at the matinée of the *Liszt-Cantata*[42] (Sunday) and at the banquet (Monday).

He could not have spoken or done better. I am particularly grateful to him for having properly emphasized three names with regard to my activity as a conductor: Schumann, Berlioz, Wagner; and three others with regard to my piano teaching: Bülow, Tausig, Klindworth.

The album *Weimars Gruss* with about a hundred signatures (among which figure the Mildes, the Ferenczys, Lassen, Count Beust, Alvine Frommann, and three Meyendorffs) is not a present from the Court, but a very flattering token of good will on the part of the signers, at the head of whom figure Baron and Mme la Baronne de Loën. To have talked about the Grand Duke on this occasion, and to have mentioned the payment for the trips of the manager and the *Kapellmeister* of Weimar, would have appeared odd in Pest, where the sentimental courtier is not much in fashion. So, *Éljen* [Long live] Loën; he discharged his mission perfectly, and I beg you to convey to him my thanks as a friend.

Yesterday, I started reading the *Lettres à une inconnue*, by Mérimée, which are very remarkable in style and thought, but oddly strained in feeling. What is the use of friendship or love if one is always looking for difficulties where there are none? The lady to whom these letters are written looked for difficulties even a mile away, or even two! I found again with pleasure in this volume, as a preface, the charming articles (in the *Débats*) by Taine, which you kindly sent me, and which are extremely to my taste except for the last two lines: "One is always being deceived by something, and it is perhaps better to resign oneself to this ahead of time." No, if you please; one need only live simply and in a Christian manner; never to be either a dupe or a rogue.

Yours ever

FL

42. By Henrik Gobbi, performed at the matinée on November 9, 1873.

I'm writing to Lassen tomorrow to recommend to him a singer of the Pest Theater, Mme Balazs (pronounce it Balasch).

The *Revue* [*des deux mondes*] of December 1 with the letters to the unknown lady has just this moment arrived. A thousand tender thanks from F.L., who would be happy to replace Franz Servais (even at the risk of being appreciated less and scolded more than the latter) in the role of reader to Your Highness.

For pity's sake, do not strain your dear eyes, of heavenly eloquence when they weep.

———

December 22, 73

Rarely has a letter given me as much trouble to draft as that which I have finally just sent off to M. Sach.

I wanted to write to him in sincere praise of Loën, whose personal manner here was perfect; then to talk to him about Gille and the *Deutsche allgemeine Musikverein* [sic][43] in order to fit in with a long letter from Gille which I received day before yesterday, concerning his recent discussion with M. Sach about the *Verein*. In addition I had to refresh the gracious master's memory on the matter of a little (silver!) bird, which should fly on the buttonhole of a most distinguished harpist, formerly applauded in Petersburg, now here, and long since decorated with the medal with ribbon, of Weimar. "How many things in an – – – epistolary – – – minuet"!

In any case, M. Sach handles his business in his own entirely sovereign manner. All things considered, he had no reason to be surprised by, still less complain of a shortage of letters from me. His was a reply to the one I wrote him from Rome (at the end of October), and it contained nothing which called for an early reply. As for the telegram on the occasion of my jubilee anniversary, I considered it more respectful to answer by mail. Now, you know how much I suffer from quantities

43. *Allgemeiner Deutscher Musikverein*, in which Liszt played a leading role from its beginning in 1859.

of telegrams and letters, and that it is absolutely impossible for me to deal with excesses of polite phrases so long as I remain subject to the ordinary necessities of food and sleep. Three days ago I wrote to Mme Sach, and this evening or tomorrow I shall write to the Hereditary Grand Duke.

I am very flattered, dearest one, that you should wish to keep the photograph from Vienna. When the opportunity arises, I'll send another one (from here) to *Monsieur le Curé*, for I fear that the Erfurt one is not sufficiently becoming to me.

Please do me the favor of putting into an envelope one of my little photographs from Weimar (in profile) which are to be found at the photographer's in the Schillerstrasse, the firm of Hardtmuth.

I enclose the Apponyi toast you asked for, and, in the same issue of the *N.Z.*,[44] Bodenstedt's poem. As a corrective I add Hanslick's kind remarks about my *Wartburg Lieder*.

Tomorrow I'll send back to you the *Revue des deux mondes*. After his article and Taine's preface on the *Lettres à une inconnue*, by Mérimée, I urge you to wait for the 3 francs a volume edition of these same letters, which are worth reading in their entirety, however astringent they may be. The world in which we have lived is treated in them with all the fine propriety of a studied contempt to which the worldly-wise aspire out of vanity.

To my knowledge Father Ravignan has published no work costing 50 francs. The brochure mentioned by Sainte-Beuve may have appeared as an introduction to another work. Copy out for me the exact title (according to your catalogue and to Sainte-Beuve), and I'll try to inform you precisely.

Count Bombelles sometimes used to ask: "Have you seen my wife's postures?" She shone in *tableaux vivants*.

I am unaware of the "impostures" of Mlle [sic] Jaëll, whom I hardly know, but it seems to me that I committed no blunder in mildly recommending her to Lassen and to Loën, with a concert at Weimar in

44. *Neue Zeitschrift für Musik.*

mind—nothing more. She had asked me for a personal letter to Mme Sach; imagine my terror!

Of the pianists of the fair sex, I have a friendly interest in only one: Sophie Menter (Mme Popper). If she comes through Weimar, I would appreciate your showing her some kindness.

Your

FL

———

1874

January 2, 74

The fact that certain polite customs are merely a convention does not prevent me from approving of them and even finding them sometimes very agreeable. So thank you, dearest one, for your New Year's wishes, which I fully reciprocate.

If I refrained from anticipating you, the fault for this lies with many others than myself. You know how harassed I am from all sides, and how absolutely impossible it is for me to set aside the minimum time I need. Besides, on Christmas day itself, O[lga] had shaken her little fists at me and made me feel her claws; this is hardly conducive to effusiveness.

Have you heard about the "magic inexhaustible ink well"? A new Parisian invention, of which I enclose the advertisement, with cut. I'm going to buy the thing, which costs only 5 francs.

Your Brussels bookseller will probably reply that it was by mistake that in the catalogue, the volume in 12mo *De l'existence et de l'institut des Jésuites* by Father Ravignan was listed at 50 francs. This kind of book sells for 3 francs 50 centimes, or 5 francs at the most. When you have read it please lend it to me. The article in the *Revue bleue* on Mérimée interested me and I firmly urge you to read through, later on, the *Lettres à une inconnue*. They are Mixed Pikles (excuse me if I've made a spelling mistake); one mustn't turn to them for nourishment, short of having invulnerable digestive powers. One of the underlined passages seems to me a massive and wicked piece of stupidity: "There is nothing I despise and even detest as much as mankind in general; but I would

115

like to be rich enough to rid myself of all individual suffering." What riches, good Lord, would be great enough for this? Contempt for mankind, if it is to be salutary, must, like well-ordered charity, begin at home. Otherwise it leads only to bragging and odious fibs. On the other hand, there are many noble thoughts in these letters, e.g., "Injustice sometimes revolts one to the point of imbecility."

Since you like Ségur's history of Russia,[1] you will perhaps also read with pleasure Mérimée's *Episode de l'histoire de Russie*.[2] I know it only from booksellers' announcements which state that the second edition, one volume in 12°, costs 3 francs 50 centimes (at Michel Lévy frères).

I doubt whether M. Sach is better pleased with my letter than with my silence. Alas! I must accept the fact that I lack charm, and I am too old to practice, with any chance of success, the difficult art of pleasing others.

Please thank Lassen for me for his very witty reply. He tells me that you are prudently withdrawing your protection from the author of *Schweden See*. There is nothing surprising in the fact that a second tour on that lake should have somewhat cooled your ardor. Your account of M. Sach's disappointment in not finding in M.E. a quarter of Rothschild, a half of Montmorency, and more than a Mozart combined amused me extremely. Besides, I will always maintain that it is both appropriate and a duty for the Weimar stage to offer new works from time to time, even should they topple over like ninepins one after the other.

Ábrányi's literary and musical evening (last Monday) was very successful. I enclose the most critical article on the subject (from the *Pester Lloyd*); the other papers are better disposed, even toward Gobbi, whose *Vorspiel* to my *Cantata* (now shortened by about a hundred bars) was warmly applauded.

I also applaud your methodical and zealous piano studies and kiss your hands.

FL

1. Count Philippe-Paul de Ségur, *Histoire de Russie et de Pierre-le-Grand* (Paris, 1829).
2. Published in Paris in 1853.

Thousands and thousands of thanks for your recommendations in behalf of Mlle Gaul, and for the good news of her you give me.

———

Tuesday, January 13, 74

I entirely share your liking for Mme Moukhanoff's letters; they are exquisite, and eminently graceful and intelligent.

Countess Coudenhoven [Coudenhove] told me yesterday that her mother had left for Warsaw after Christmas to spend a few days with M. de Moukhanoff, who will soon be going to Petersburg (for the wedding of the Grand Duchess, I believe). Like you, Mme Mouk[hanoff] is behindhand with a reply to me. I wrote her early in December, sending her the group photograph of the Pest Committee. Mme Coud[enhove] and Mme Dönhoff tell me they saw this photograph in her rooms at the [Hotel] "Roman Emperor" and I know also that my letter reached her there, though she has not yet replied.

It is impossible for me to write more. Thank you for sending me the newspapers, which I read with great pleasure when I take a cab.

Day after tomorrow evening I'll be at the Széchenyis' and expect to stay there two or three weeks.

The address is slightly complicated: Horpács, bei Oedenburg, Station Schützen, Hungary.

Herewith a short piece from the *Neue Freie Presse* which does not usually undertake to sing my praises.

The concert on Sunday was extremely successful in all respects.

The day after I arrive at Horpács I'll write you at length.

Yours ever

FL

I can't find the *Neue Freie Presse* and will send it off to you by this evening's mail.

———

Thursday,[3] January 21, 74
Horpács

Why hide from me your "varied, but equally depressing" sorrows
and worries? What other good quality will remain to me where you
are concerned if I am not to be a reasonably intelligent confidant, full
of tenderness toward your "aridness studded with nettles and thistles"?
Have I ever impressed you as an egoist, seeking pleasure in affection?
If so I would reply to you as did my friend Berlioz to an amateur who
asked him at a performance of one of Beethoven's last quartets: "Now,
Sir, does this really give you pleasure?" "For God's sake, who do you
think I am? Would I be listening to such music as this for my pleasure?"
(I've rendered the gist rather than the exact language, which ran: "Do
you think that I listen to music for pleasure?")

Let's speak of other things, since you refuse to speak frankly to me.
Veuillot's article (*L'Univers* of January 19) is superb and perfectly true.
I thank you for having sent it to me and take pleasure in copying out
the principal passage:

"Certain political figures have sensed and launched the device of
being a nobody in order to speak for everybody, of giving the impression of being inactive in order to be everywhere active, and of being
everywhere active in such a way that nothing gets done but leads them
somewhere; of taking a public position very briefly so as to live off it a
very long time; of folding their arms so as to stake out their future,
and finally of substituting themselves for all parties while withdrawing
from their own selves. Certainly this is an ingenious theory. We think
it is taken from natural history. It is the theory of the cuckoo which
lays its eggs in the nests of others. In short they have reached the point
of trying," etc.

This cuckoo and the following sally "Never be anything other than
a drawing-room soldier" are devastating.

There is nothing more typically governmental than to suspend
L'Univers after that; but in France it is difficult to suspend logic for long,

3. January 21, 1874, was a Wednesday.

in other words the march of events. Please also send me the issue of *L'Univers* with the pastoral letter of the Bishop of Périgueux, behind which the government prudently took cover in order to proceed with the suspension of the said periodical. I'll send the January 19 issue to Princess Witt[genstein] who, together with Princess Rospigliosi, does not in my humble opinion sufficiently appreciate the merit, and the moral and catholic superiority of Veuillot.

M. Sach has written me a charming letter; I'll answer it later – – – evasively.

FL

Friday

The return of the very gracious *padrona di casa*, Countess Alexandra Széchenyi, prevented me from sending off these lines yesterday evening. This morning I received your letter of January 20; it almost makes matters worse, for you reproach me with not reading your letters and ask me to reread them. In reply I return the sheet from which I quoted to you exactly two sentences. No less than the "just," "those who love"[4] live by faith. Where it is absent, all the wit of M. de Voltaire himself becomes superfluous. Now, it has been wittily said that M. de Voltaire had more than anyone of this wit, which is common to everyone.

January 31
Horpács

Napoleon I said to Larevellière-Lépeaux, the leader of the "Theo-Philanthropists": "You want something sublime, Sir; well, recite 'Our Father.' "

I follow this advice very humbly and recite every morning and evening: "Forgive us our trespasses as we forgive those who trespass against us."

4. A pun on the word *aimants* (magnets), or "those who love."

This prayer renders unnecessary much argumentation and redundancy.

Herewith the letter from Mme Betty Schott (wife, or very close relation of Schott the patrician publisher, almost the peer of Breitkopf and Härtel; and the Schotts even have the glory of having published, thanks to the subscription of the Emperor Alexander I of Russia, of King William III of Prussia, etc., Beethoven's Mass in D[5] and the Ninth Symphony!).[6]

Take thirty shares of the *Wagner Frauen Verein* at 10 gros per share, half of which I will ask you to register in my name. I have no Prussian currency on hand, but I'll send it to you immediately after my arrival in Pest. Also write Mme Betty Schott a few polite lines devoid of obsequiousness.

Weimar and its charms were poetically represented at Horpács today at the castle mass at half-past eight.

Mademoiselle Hortense Vogt (from the Aker Wand) appeared, very much unheralded. I took her immediately to the sacristy to entrust her to the care of the ecclesiastic, while excusing myself for not being able, in such circumstances of major absurdity, to attend mass. The said demoiselle won't give up the idea that she has the vocation of bringing about my matrimonial happiness in spite of myself!

I forget who it was who defined happiness as: "A blow which has more or less healed."

Alas! Mine must forego these correctives.

Thank you for Taillandier's and Nisard's speeches. I read them with great interest, recalling Father Gratry.

Your

FL

---

5. Opus 123.
6. Opus 125, dedicated to Friedrich Wilhelm III.

Sunday, February 8, 74
Horpács

Is it not possible to suffer without abusing and insulting others? And what but this are you doing in ringing the changes on the absurd theme you have invented: "I count for nothing in your life," to which you even add the blasphemy: "I am certain that neither God nor man will count my tears" – – – Dear Olga, in what sinister chimera are you indulging? What a frightful condemnation for me not to have been able to snatch you from its claws! Ah, believe me, I beseech you, we must kill the hateful ego within ourselves; and then divine mercy and its truth will shine once again within us when we ask Him to "forgive us our trespasses as we forgive those who trespass against us."

To begin with, I dare to forgive you for having misunderstood the sentiment of humble contrition which prompted me to write to you recently that verse of the *Pater*. Your misfortune is that you want to be too wise, too shrewd; mine, that I remain too dull.

Let us return to the Jesuits (who have perhaps sinned, heroically, as you have) and to Father Ravignan. Send me his brochure—book. You mention an apologia of the Jesuits by Mai[s]tre in his history of the Gallican Church(?). Who is this author? Could it be the great Joseph de Maistre?[7] If so, I cannot allow you to misspell his name, if only out of literary decorum.

In Joseph de Maistre's letters I find, among many others, a fine retort in reply to an ill-advised adversary who was very sure of his knowledge: "From the vantage point to which one must rise in order to see things, one no longer sees anything of what you see; consequently, I cannot answer you, unless you should take this for an answer." (I quote from memory, but the sense is accurate.)

La Chute des Jésuites,[8] by Saint-Priest, was preceded by many years by d'Alembert's arrogant and sly memoir on their "abolition" under Clément XIV. Once involved in this kind of reading, d'Alembert's

7. Joseph-Marie de Maistre, Count, *De l'Eglise gallicane dans son rapport avec le souverain Pontife* . . . (Lyon–Paris, 1821).
8. *Histoire de la chute des Jésuites au XVIIIe siècle, 1750–1782* . . . (Paris, 1844).

memoir (perhaps there is another title for this text?) should not be overlooked. It has been published and re-edited with the corresponding texts for 25 centimes. Ask your Brussels bookseller for it, for I do not know where the copies, at 25, or at most 50 centimes, which I used to own, have disappeared to.

Next Thursday: concert at Oedenburg, sponsored by Princess Esterházy, wife of Prince Paul, great-grandson of Prince Nicolas Esterházy (whom my father served with integrity) and *Obergespann*, a title which is pompously translated in French after the Latin as "Supreme Count" of the County of Oedenburg (where I had the misfortune to be born).

The Széchenyis are also sponsoring this concert, and I'll have the pleasure of accompanying them Thursday to Oedenburg.

On Ash Wednesday, February 18, I'll be back in Pest.

The "charms" of Weimar, in the person of Mlle Hortense Vogt, spent four or five days at Horpács, and menace me in Pest. As a consolation, please send me the *Revue bleue* which you forgot.

Apponyi asks me to convey to you his excuses for not having sent you the jubilee medallion, which is not yet on sale. He won't be the one who is late—and I am too early, alas, for the jubilee – – –

No less yours

[unsigned]

P.S. I reopen this letter, having just received yours. You are not going to be scolded for having exceeded my little instructions concerning the *Damen Wagner Verein*; but neither would I want to encourage [you] in this too costly and inconvenient method.

Forgive me for having forgotten that you still had a few thalers of mine; why do you balk at making use of the 5 thalers which I mentioned to you for this *Verein*? Please do me the favor of asking at Seitz's for the exact price of the History of Music[9] by Ambros, published by Leuckhard [Leuckart] (Leipzig), and of sending me Seitz's bill, without yet buying the work. Three volumes have, I believe, appeared; imagine: the Vienna bookseller asked Mme Széchenyi 19 florins for the first two

9. *Geschichte der Musik*, issued in several volumes over a period of several years.

volumes! I pointed out to her that this was either an error or a swindle.

Thank you for Veuillot's letter. I shall note this statement, which applies to situations other than his: "On the roads which faith opens up for us accidents, misfortunes, and pain are neither pain, nor misfortunes, nor accidents. One's inner feelings alter the meaning of words and the nature of things."

I am swamped by my epistolary task, which grows daily. If things go on like this, and I receive fifty to sixty letters a week, not counting manuscripts, I don't know what will become of me.

Your comments on Mlle Vogt are, as usual, most judicious. It could indeed be that behind her formal role, carried to the point of scandal, of being my imaginary and hostile wife, she may be discharging other and less exalted functions. Fortunately I am entirely blameless in this whole too laughable and odious affair. I shall avoid calling in the police as long as possible; but in Pest it will probably be necessary to have recourse to this; and already at Horpács, Széchenyi had to do so in order to restrain Mlle Vogt from prowling around his house more than four days.

I learned yesterday in a letter from Pest that having been evicted at my request from the Hotel Frohner, she brazenly camped at the Hotel Hungaria; that she called on the Catholic priest and on the Protestant pastor, and that she parades everywhere as my wife, whose wedding, in church or before the mayor, has unfortunately been hitherto delayed by intrigues of the blackest hue.

Did you see that Gablenz has died? I knew him in Como (in '38) as a lieutenant, and have always had for him feelings of sincere affection and high esteem. The manner of his suicide was most noble and military.

January [February]¹⁰ 21, 74
Pest

Your friend and neighbor at Klein Roop, Mme Tiesenhausen, has written to you about our meeting at Oedenburg, which was very agreeable to me.

10. Liszt dated this letter "January" in error.

I trust that she will not have blackened me in your eyes. Two days after the Oedenburg concert I returned to Horpács with the Széchenyis, Mme Dönhoff, Apponyi, Mihalovich, Lenbach, and Wartenegg, who at once started looking around in the park for an elm tree under which to await, and meditate comfortably on the favors of – – – –.

Mme Dönhoff stayed only one day at Horpács, and, as for me, I came back here on Ash Wednesday morning in the company of Mihalovich and Apponyi. That same evening my two traveling companions prevailed on me to go and admire Rossi, an Italian actor very much in vogue in Vienna and Pest. They were giving *King Lear* (in Italian): sublime and upsetting.

Since my return I have left my room only to go to mass and to call on Monseigneur Haynald, who has only just recovered from a bad spell of sickness which kept him in bed for several days. I spent all my time yesterday and the day before putting into final form one of my old compositions: *L'Hymne de l'enfant à son réveil*[11] (by Lamartine) for chorus of female voices. This required much erasing and patching up in order to achieve a kind of simplicity free of silliness. I am dedicating it to the *Liszt Verein* which will sing it shortly, after which I will publish it. The two charity concerts, at which I am to strum on the piano are fixed for Wednesday, March 4, and Monday, March 23. The *Coronation Mass*[12] is to be given (in the church of Pest) on the Sunday of mid-Lent; and a Palestrina mass on St. Joseph's day in Buda. I shall probably be conducting both.

Thanks for having sent me the articles by Cuv[illier-]Fleury, *Le Revers de la médaille,* and the little book by Ravignan. Fleury is not very charitable toward "the correct attitude, the latent sensitivity and the selfishness [sic]" of Mérimée. He is even less partial toward *L'Inconnue.* I forget who told me that Mme Montijo, mother of the Empress Eugénie, hides behind this title. This seems to me fantastic, although there was some gossip in former years of Mérimée's intimacy with the

11. G 19; R 508, for women's chorus with harmonium (or piano) and harp ad lib.
12. G 11; R 487.

illustrious mother, whose acute displeasure I was so unfortunate as to incur in Madrid—almost as much as that of the late Princess Metternich and of various others. During my stay in Madrid in '44, Mme Montijo, on grand occasions, used to do the honors of the salon of Marshal Narvaez; she recommended me so warmly to His Excellency that my modest successes turned into disgrace. If you have more information on *L'Inconnue*, let me know.

Your underlinings in Ravignan's book indicate to me that you lean toward the Jesuits. I have no intention of arguing with you about this. The Holy Father,[13] his predecessors, the great majority of the cardinals and bishops are of the opinion that the Jesuits excel in virtue and knowledge. The hatred which they and their Order inspire excites the respect of noble hearts; they struggle heroically, and apostolize. Will they triumph, or must they go under? That is the question! [sic], whose solution rests with divine wisdom. What seems certain to me is that their cause is intimately linked to the triumph or the defeat of Catholicism as established by the Council of Trent. Will transformations follow? Will heretics and heterodoxy, protestantism, and the Greek Church return to the bosom of the Catholic, Apostolic, and Roman Church? My limited mind prohibits my coping with these immense and formidable problems. I feel qualified neither for theology nor politics, nor for business in general—and remain a very humble musician, who recites his "Our Father . . . hallowed be thy name, thy will be done. . . ."

Yours ever

FL

If it is not a nuisance for you to send me the *Revue des deux mondes*, I shall gratefully accept it.

Your letter has just come. The kindnesses of the H., which the Chief of Police appropriately terms *Gemeinheiten*, come as no surprise; they

13. Pius IX.

are merely consequences. Tell me what is that monstrous carrot which hangs from your ear?[14]

Perhaps you will add to your copious reading matter for and against the Jesuits the volume by Quinet and Michelet,[15] whose title I forget, and which I know only from hearsay. The names of the two authors gave it prominence when it appeared. I assume that a 3 fr 50 edition of it has come out since then. Your Brussels bookseller can tell you. Thank you for the telegram from Seitz.

Mlle H[ortense] V[ogt], my wife, is going to have a little trouble with the Pest police in spite of all my efforts to prevent this scandal.

March 3, 74

The fear that you should get wind of my reply to your landlord induced me to write you a line or two yesterday. Today, one is enough to solve the question of your letter which has just arrived. No, and again No! There must be no *Elisabeth* at Weimar, with or without costumes; and I beg my friends on the banks of the Ilm to think of me as dead. This will inconvenience no one and will be a relief to me.

Yours ever

FL

March 22, 74

My only excuse is that I mean well. My heart hears what you tell me and what you do not tell me. I will perhaps have the chance of replying to this at greater length – – – – As for the related woes, let's speak no more of them.

14. The French expression *tirer une carotte de longueur à quelqu'un* means to spin a long yarn to someone, and FL alludes here to the length of his letter, which goes on and on after he has signed it.

15. Jules Michelet and Edgar Quinet, *Les Jésuites* (1843).

I have to play the piano in public again two or three times in order to wind up the season: tomorrow here (at a benefit for the Sisters of Charity); next week in Vienna (at the salon of Princess Wilhelmina Auersperg; that evening will perhaps be postponed to Easter Monday?); finally, Sunday April 12 or 19 at Pressburg. Herewith the announcement of the performance next Wednesday of the *Coronation Mass* at the parish church of Pest. My visit to Mgr Haynald at Kalocsa depends on the instructions he will give me. I will probably spend a few days of the Easter fortnight with him. They say that Mgr Dupanloup is coming to Gran after Easter and will also be going to Kalocsa.

The concert agitation here will peak with Adelina Patti on Easter Sunday and Monday.

The Marquise de Caux will get more than twenty thousand florins out of it, which will in no way bother her spouse.

Do you still correspond with your Brussels bookseller? If it is not too much of a nuisance, I'll be obliged if you will have a copy (for which I will pay) of the *Dictionnaire universel*,[16] by Boiste, 15th edition (if there is no more recent one), "revised and corrected in 1866," sent to Count Albert Apponyi, Hochstrasse No. 14, at Pest.

His aunt, Thérèse Apponyi, the type and model of an ambassadress, died this week, aged eighty-three, at Pressburg where I saw her again last winter, still in perfect freshness and grace of mind.

Yours ever

FL

A thousand thanks for the *Revues* and *Débats*, which I'll return to you tomorrow.

Lassen has sent me his charming arrangements for wind instruments of the three pieces from my *Années de Pèlerinage*; please convey to him my very friendly thanks.

---

16. *Dictionnaire universel de la langue française* . . . first published in Paris in 1804; there are many subsequent editions.

March 30, 74
Pest

Were you to sin, it would be through excess of wit and shrewdness. Here below, no one gains from rising too high: even "double eagles"[17] do not always soar, and M. Prudhomme[18] used to note wisely that to withdraw man (or woman) from the world means isolation. And so no isolation, unless it be to enter the Carthusian Order, where isolation would still be lacking, for the Brothers repeat "one must die." If the truth be told, it seems to me more difficult to live with the *modus vivendi*.

I am returning the *Revues* to you by this mail, and am keeping back Ravignan's brochure in order to lend it to Apponyi, one of the best and most sympathetic examples of the excellent and venerable education of the Reverend Fathers of the Company of Jesus.

I am adding Ollivier's little book with the preface and notes of his speech at the Academy, as well as the report on the national award for Lamartine (in 1867) which remains a glorious achievement of Ollivier.

Please return this little book to me in Vienna, Schottenhof, where I shall be tomorrow evening. From there I will write to tell you about my arrangements for the month of April, embellished by a concert at Pressburg and a trip to Kalocsa, which I shall make with gratitude. In May, I shut myself up in the Villa d'Este; if people make my stay there uncomfortable, I shall think about shutting myself up elsewhere.

Yours ever

FL

Tuesday, April 7, 74

Your recent letters moved me deeply. At this time I am hardly in a state to write with any coherence. Various minor tasks preoccupy and

17. An allusion to the imperial coat of arms.
18. Joseph Prudhomme, a fictional character created by the writer and draftsman Henri Monnier (1805–77), as a caricature of bourgeois conformism and smug pomposity.

disturb me all the time. I need still another month before I can fully turn into my sad self again.

I go back to Pest this evening, taking with me the same heavy cold that I brought from there last Wednesday – – – – I need to spend two or three days in my room. Don't let this worry you, for I indulge in this little superstition of fancying that to speak of illnesses brings them nearer. That is why I exclude this trivial subject from my conversations and correspondence.

Tuesday or Wednesday I will probably pay a visit to Mgr Haynald at Kalocsa; on the eighteenth I arrive at Pressburg where, on Sunday the nineteenth, I play at a concert of the *Kirchen Musikverein*. Countess Rossi will sing, and Sophie Menter is giving me the pleasure of playing the *Concerto Pathétique*[19] and the *Walkürenritt*[20] with me! It will be my last pianistic feat of the year.

On the twentieth I come back again to Pest for about a fortnight in order to take care of a crushing backlog of letters and manuscripts before going to Rome.

You are suffering more from moral sciatica, for which science has not yet found an effective cure. There do exist some palliatives, but for them to be even slightly efficacious there must be an adequate measure of good will on the part of the patient.

I continue to want to be one of these palliatives for you, and I love you from my heart.

FL

Write to Pest. Do you still subscribe to *L'Univers*? Tell me about your new lodgings, and give me the name of the street and the number of the house. In such matters I push pedantry to the point of the ridiculous.

19. G 258; R 356. FL dedicated this 2-piano version to Mme de Bronsart.
20. From *Die Walküre*, by Wagner.

Friday morning, April 10, 74
Pest

On arriving here day before yesterday morning I immediately took to my bed and stayed there some fifty hours. Naturally I am not sick and do not allow people to talk to me at all about my health, as I retain my long-standing superstition (which I told you about) on this subject. A medical oracle in Geneva used to say to me: "Health is the basis of all progress," and since then I have come across important people who solemnly repeated: "Health above everything!" I have never been of their opinion, and consider many other things to be greatly preferable to health which is but a relative, secondary, and most of the time trifling blessing.

Your two last letters, sent to Vienna, reached me here. I thank you for them, briefly, from my heart and beg you to feel assured that they have in no way "annoyed" me. Always write as though you were speaking to me, without any Byzantine subtleties, and all will be well. It is hardly necessary to set your mind at rest with regard to my indiscretions; no one will ever know anything of the contents of your letters, except for trifles about the Weimar theatre and other matters of the same stripe: and even here you know that I am not guilty of indiscreet confidences.

Your Bayreuth idea is excellent. I urge you to carry it out around May 22 and to stay there a few days. As for me, I cannot go this time, but will arrange to meet you there another time. Before doing so it seems to me proper that you should pay a visit there on your own, unless a serious obstacle should arise, and the date of Wagner's birthday[21] would be a good choice. I am going to write to my daughter that I have to give up all thought of seeing her again this year. It is not a period of rustication that I seek at the Villa d'Este; I need to have several lengthy talks with Princess W[ittgenstein] on matters relating to my will, of which she is to be the executrix, and on two other no less serious topics. This cannot be done effectively short of a stay of six or eight months,

21. May 22, 1813.

which it is my duty not to postpone or quibble over. If my straight-forward intentions succeed, I shall regain my former influence over the Princess' mind. It never has weighed on her and I even dare to say that it has lightened for her the heavy burden of her long afflictions and trials before and since she was condemned to loss of all civil rights by the Russian government. Since then, something more sacred has merged with my deep love for and inexpressible gratitude to her. She has re-vived my conscience and kept alive the few good qualities with which I have been endowed – – – –

I, and only I, know her feelings toward Cosima; the forms these have assumed have sometimes been so strange and awkward that it is better now for them not to see or write to each other; but I maintain that what really lies within is truly beautiful and worthy of a great heart. Cosima will think so too one day, for she is after all my very dear and very beloved daughter. Any falling out between us is impossible.

As I have already written you from Vienna, continue writing to me in spite of Kalocsa and Pressburg.

Yours ever

F. Liszt

Wednesday, April 15, 74

Pest

In order to cut short the insipid and forbidden topic of health, I'll tell you right away that I am off to Kalocsa today at noon. The trip there takes five hours, and the return seven to eight. Mgr Haynald is taking the same boat; I'll have the honor of accompanying him and of spending a day in his fine house. I'll be back here Friday morning, and on Satur-day afternoon at Pressburg, from which I'll return Monday to spend another fifteen to twenty days here in order to take care of a crushing backlog of letters (which I don't want to drag with me to Italy) as well as of a few minor local matters. In addition, I have to correct proofs and copies of music (henceforth unimportant for me since the manuscripts are completed) such as the orchestra scores of half a dozen of my Hungarian Rhapsodies, the choruses of *Prometheus*,[22] and the second edition of the volumes of Weber and Schubert with my annotations, published by Cotta, who was already pressing me for them in the month of January!

Toward May 12 or 15 I shall go directly to Rome without even passing through Vienna. At Pragerhof (six or eight hours from Pest) I shall catch the train from Vienna to Mestre, Padua, etc.

Impossible for me now to stop over in Germany; major reasons, before which I bow, militate absolutely against this. In my last letter (which was perhaps a little unclear, for I felt fairly ill that day) I indicated the principal point of my activities, which would take a bad turn were I to delay. There are moral sufferings which call for more radical treatment than physical illness. To swerve off course at the key point means losing all.

Have confidence, dear Olga; I hope that you will be better pleased with me than you imagine.

M. Sach persists in the erroneous opinion that the fiftieth anniversary of my little deeds and doings as a pianist falls on April 13, '74. He was so kind as to send me on that date a telegram of "sympathetic remembrance," with which the Grand Duchess and her august family deign to associate themselves. I replied yesterday with a letter of thanks, in which I made the comment that a biographical slip concerning me is a matter of complete indifference, but that in fact my name already appeared on concert posters (of which several were kept and recently republished) in the winter and spring in Vienna and in Pest in 1823; later on in the fall of the same year in Munich and in Stuttgart when I was on my way to Paris and London where I performed my tricks as an infant prodigy in 1824. The Jubilee Committee in Pest wisely kept to the date 1823, the year of my concerts in Vienna and Pest, although I had played in public at Oedenburg one year before *als elfjähriger Knabe* [as an eleven-year-old boy], but in fact it is from the time of the subsidy which six

22. G 69; R 539.

Hungarian grandees granted to my father in '22 or '23 for six years, in order to provide for my musical education, that my strange musical career dates.

Excuse these details which are as accurate as they are superfluous; they simply show that if I had accepted the Weimar invitation to a jubilee festival in 1874, I would have involved the town in a very obvious biographical error which people elsewhere would not have failed to pick up.

Ever yours with all my heart

FL

A friendly attention for which I thank you: the renewal of the subscription to the *Revue bleue.*

Thank you also for *L'Univers* which I continue to read passionately. While I was sick, I read the three volumes of '93[23] by Victor Hugo.

─────────

April 22, 74
Pest

What miseries within the Church, free or not; within the State, powerless or not! The little enclosed note bears witness to this and demonstrates to me once more how important it is to read *L'Univers* if one is interested in Roman debates. Hence my repeated thanks for sending it.

On my return from Pressburg day before yesterday, I was hoping to find a certain blue envelope. It has not arrived, and I am waiting for it.

I at once replied to M. Sach's very kind telegram for April 13 (a wrong date, as I explained to you) and to his letter which was accompanied by evidence of gracious favor which, confidentially speaking, facilitates my return to Weimar, not at this time when I must think only of Rome and of my major duty (about which I don't much consult others), but next winter.

23. *Quatrevingt-treize,* 1874.

Mazzini's last piece on Renan's book: *La Réforme intellectuelle et morale de la France* (published in the last issue of the *Revue bleue* which I will return to you) exalts the sentiment of duty and sacrifice. I embrace it while remaining firmly attached to the Cross of Jesus, our eternal salvation.

Yours ever

FL

April 27
Pest

I had to send off several urgent business letters, and have been unable to write any others these last few days. Besides my cold continues to bother me; I cough a good deal, don't go out much, and when the evening comes I feel so tired that I am barely able to concentrate on reading for an hour.

No less than you, and with much more reason, I feel totally discouraged "when faced with ink and paper." However, I would like to be able to use up enough today to make you correct your erroneous opinion on a crucial and dominant issue in my life. Although you have several times told me that, basically, no one had a decisive influence over me, you seem now to allow that the Princess[24] exerts a kind of pressure. That is not so and shall not be so. Of course I have often sought her council and advice, all the more so since she has nobly helped me in circumstances which it was hard to settle satisfactorily; however, I have never either understood or indulged in smug or surly subjection where love is concerned, and except for the dogmas of the Church, I retain my complete independence.

In fact it was my opinion which triumphed in the major decisions of the Princess for twenty-seven years. This was so in the matter of her stay in Weimar (from '47 to '60) and in Rome (from '60 until today)

24. Princess Carolyne von Sayn-Wittgenstein.

with all that flowed therefrom. People almost blamed her for my having entered the Vatican, of which she had no suspicion, and which I simply announced to her, one month before, as settled. On this and other matters the falsest views on the Princess have gone the rounds; I could not prevent, and only rarely contradicted them to the extent that it seemed appropriate to me to do so, knowing the superlative degree of deafness of those who do not wish to hear! So I have not been able to "defend her against her enemies" who are too powerful. Don't speak of the "same old story," if the wound you inflicted on me by such a reproach has not healed. Woe to me if a shadow of cowardice should darken my life!

Are you also aware of the real pain which Their Royal Highnesses have caused me—perhaps unconsciously?—during my three last stays in Weimar? They have never once mentioned the Princess to me. The opportunity frequently arose, especially at the time of the wedding of the Hereditary Grand Duke, for the Princess had written a letter to the Grand Duchess, the draft of which was known to me and which I found dignified and respectful – – – –

You are the first person to whom I have mentioned this pain which it does not behoove me to spread about. "To complain is miserable; to arouse pity, ridiculous." Besides it is now some thirty years that I have been proclaiming sincere and forthright gratitude toward the House of Weimar. You may be sure that I shall never fail in this, and in all fairness, please take my word for it when I tell you that in the present situation it is absolutely my duty to go to Rome, and that it is entirely of my own accord, without anyone else "prescribing" it, that I go there. Later, after my return, if you ask me to do so I shall explain to you in detail the complicated matters to which I must attend without delay.

What you tell me of the Grand Duke's conversation with Odo Russell touches me very much, and I desire only that you yourself share the good opinion of me which H.R.H. is willing to entertain. His last letter reveals this in the most affectionate manner.

I am cutting out a little page from Cosima's last letter; her feelings toward Mme Mouk[hanoff] are very close to mine. The idea of not seeing her again oppresses me – – – –

Cosima has presented me with Nietzsche's latest pamphlet; I'll return your copy with the Ravignan book, which I took the liberty of lending to Albert Apponyi, a paragon of the Reverend Jesuit Fathers education. He returns tomorrow from Nice, where his sister Georgina (who spent a few years at the Sacred Heart in preparation for taking the final vows) became engaged to Prince Paul Sanguszko, widower of a very agreeable and pretty woman.

Fancy: not only have I read *'93* of Victor Hugo, but I am driving myself silly by reading Flaubert's *La Tentation de St. Antoine*—prodigiously colorful and erudite. They say the author spent more than twenty-five years working on this book, which is steeped in the substance of several hundred other volumes. Berlioz would have enjoyed more than I these saturnalia of the mind through centuries, superstitions and beliefs. The issue of the *Revue bleue* I sent back to you this morning will give you a brief analysis of the work. Should you happen to fancy the idea of reading it, I'll send it off to you.

To your sorrows I could, alas! only reply with my own, which are better left unexpressed. Inertia and despair are false remedies, and too pagan; let us scorn them.

Your

[unsigned]

I shall be here for another couple of weeks. Return the page from Cosima's letter.

———

May 6, 74

Pest

I must not answer the key point in your last letters, for were I to do so it would probably be in a most unreasonable manner; so let us continue to talk about minor matters; all together they make up roughly two-thirds of life; to neglect them is a fault which does harm.

For me, Bayreuth is the main thing, but your visit there remains a detail *ad libitum*. However I am rather of the opinion that you should go there in the course of the summer at the most convenient time for you, either before or after your journey of filial piety. I had at first mentioned May 20–22, thinking that there would perhaps be at that time some festivity in Bayreuth which would interest you.

I noticed with pleasure in your lines from Berlin that the splendors of the theater in the capital of Germany had not dazzled you to the point of causing you to disparage the merits and the distinction of the one in Weimar. It does not too often suffer from comparison with larger ones, and even boasts several advantages. So long as I was active there I liked to hold its little flag on high in other towns, to the surprise of various people who fancied themselves important. If I am not mistaken it is the diplomats accredited to Weimar who have contributed most to running down elsewhere its laudable aspects: most of them, considering their assignment merely as a transition—sometimes too long—like to retaliate later by making cheap gibes.

Thank you for having sent me M. de Moukhanoff's letter. In returning it to you I take the liberty of correcting a very pardonable spelling mistake. Instead of *paillatifs* one should write *palliatifs*.

Do you have any news of the Tolstoys?

In spite of my injunctions, prayers, and prohibitions you hark back to the topic of my health which I am resolved to ban from all my conversations and correspondence, for it is only a waste of time and ink. Once again: I am not sick; my heavy and tenacious cold is at last showing signs of clearing up and I shall be going out in three or four days. Meanwhile I have read Nietzsche; I find his impassioned and flashing tone sympathetic. Since he strikes without intermittence, he often hits the nail on the head, and his campaign against the *Bildungs-Philisterium* [narrow-minded intellectualism] is as courageous as it is justified (*berechtigt*).

Speaking of reading matter, let us make a sensible little arrangement.

I gratefully accept the *Revue bleue* as well as your sending me from time to time an article from the *Journal des débats*; but with regard to *L'Univers* I absolutely protest. You read it only to be obliging; whereas I cannot do without it. So I will renew my subscription in Rome on June 1 to *L'Univers* and to the *Allgemeine* (Augsburger) *Zeitung* (in which the *Bildungs-Philisterium* plays a prominent role; but there are some sly fellows on the editorial staff; and, of the German newspapers, it is the one I prefer to read—thereby imitating Beethoven!). When I come across articles in one or the other of them which seem to me worthy of your attention or apt to entertain you, I'll send them to you.

From my heart
Your

[unsigned]

Mihalovich will send you his new album of *Lieder* dedicated to Countess Dönhoff. She is going to Bayreuth around May 15 and then to Franzensbad.

Sunday evening, May 17, 74

Having to write harasses me. And now, at the last moment the crushing blow has fallen on me of the Brunswick *Musikfest*, where they are determined not to dispense with my uselessness even though I had already written very clearly in mid-March that I shall not be coming to Germany this year. This crusher coming on top of a number of other, more or less precious, stones is driving me out of my mind – – –

I leave in one hour and will be in Florence Tuesday evening, where I shall spend a day with my very dear old friend Mme Laussot, and hope to see Bülow.

As soon as I reach Rome I will write to you.

Let me kiss your hands with my tenderest respect.

FL

My train goes from Buda to Pragerhof straight through to Italy, without a detour to Vienna.

May 22, 74
Rome (Vicolo de' Greci, no. 43)

Having arrived yesterday morning, I was in the evening handed your latest lines, addressed to Pest. If you could manage to avoid mentioning my health to me, or worries about me, any more, you would infinitely oblige me. You have long known how I dislike this very superfluous topic. On the other hand I am interested in your health and in that of your children. Whatever news you send on this subject is important to me.

Your idea of having Peterle and Mimi spend a few months in their country seems sound and reasonable to me; I therefore approve of it unreservedly. There is every reason to entertain high hopes for their future. They inherited intelligence from birth and will make their way fairly easily under your guidance. It is one of your real merits that you have so far brought them up so well. Every merit exacts a price, but I hope that this one will also bring you returns and rewards in this world, and I pray God that He grant them to you.

My daughter had an inspiration dear to my heart in proposing to Mme Moukhanoff that she go and see her in Warsaw. For a number of years, I have felt more than in harmony with Cosima—quasi-identical —and when she happens to take an initiative, it is always with the best and most constructive intentions.

In Florence I spent a day with Mme Laussot. She is expecting Bülow in a few days, and I hope to see him again at the Villa d'Este. He attended the first performance of Glinka's opera: *A Life for the Tsar*,[25]

25. First performed December 9, 1836, in St. Petersburg.

in Milan; and will publish an article on this work which the late Grand Duke Michael (in '42) praised in this curious manner: "When I have to punish one of my officers, I send him to Glinka's opera." His Imperial Highness thus showed himself more kindly disposed toward his officers than toward the most famous Russian composer.

I have still left the house only to go to the Babuino. Next week I'll pay calls on the Bobrinskis, Sermoneta, Teano, Lovatelli, and Mesdames Minghetti, Helbig, etc.; and in the first days of June I shall move into the Villa d'Este.

I accept *L'Univers* gratefully until the end of June; but thereafter allow me to renew my subscription to it; and also allow me to send you any remarkable article—as a form of revenge. The one by St. René Taillandier (in the *Revue des deux mondes*) on *La Tentation de St. Antoine* is an execution. M. de Pontmartin (in *Le Correspondant*) had preceded it with a slashing attack. In spite of this, I'm not much convinced that Flaubert's work is nothing but "the caricature of poetry and falsification of history."

Yours ever, with all my heart

FL

I want to reread here Ravignan's little book on the Jesuits, after which I will return it to you.

———

June 2, 74
Rome
(43 Vicolo de' Greci)

I'm very happy to make a little contribution to Mme de Schleinitz' Bayreuth lottery. Thank you for your good idea (on what to do with the painting I happened to win at the lottery of the Weimar *Kunstschule*).

So please give me the pleasure of becoming the owner of this picture, and of sending it, as coming from you, to Mme de Schleinitz.

The whole subject of the Bayreuth theatre remains a case apart for me; but I hope that next year I will be able to make my participation public. Meanwhile since you assure me that you have always benefited from my rare recommendations, I recommend that you keep up your propaganda in support of Wagner's *Nibelungen*.[26] Countess Bobrinska does not display much zeal because she has her own "Bayreuth" to build in the Villa Malta, as she was telling me yesterday while joking about the fact that she had not yet sent you the 50 thalers she had promised, with which she hopes to win a *Patronatschein*!

People are maliciously reproaching a prelate whom you know for being less *ultramontain* than *ultramondain*.[27] Much in spite of myself, I fall into the same error in Rome, where I am obliged to pay more calls than elsewhere.

The Holy Father has been unwell for two days; on the third day he took his usual walk in the company of Baron Visconti, etc. Yesterday, he was said to be again unwell; nonetheless I have had my name put down for the next audience.

The people I see most often are: Mme Minghetti, the Teanos, and M. de Keudell who is also, by a superabundance of merits, a most serious and distinguished musician. He promised to let me hear this evening his arrangement for piano of the Schubert Quartet, which Sgambati and others praise highly.

Princess Julie Bonaparte (Rocca-Giovine [sic]) has sung your praises to me, and has kept a few letters from M. de Meyendorff, among which is one which states very clearly that M. Thiers' eloquence would lead France to her ruin. It's a little like the story of the young lady dying of love—and of a pulmonary disease.

You know that your friend Mme Czernicheff (born Titoff) is suffering severely from an – – – unspecified nervous ailment.

26. *Der Ring des Nibelungen*, Wagner's tetralogy, first performed in its entirety on August 13, 14, 16, and 17 in 1876, at Bayreuth.

27. A play on words: *ultramontain* (faithful to Vatican precepts), *ultramondain* (ultra-worldly).

Next Saturday I plan to move into the Villa d'Este. Write to: Tivoli, via Rome. As soon as my head is rested I'll write at greater length.

Yours ever

FL

Herewith a couple of lines which authorize you to remove the picture from the Hofgärtnerei.

I have just written to M. de Moukhanoff.

Saturday, June 13, 74

Villa d'Este

After arriving here Sunday evening I stayed alone in my rooms without stirring, except to go to the Franciscan church adjoining the Villa d'Este. I hope to continue this mode of life, which I greatly enjoy, during the summer and fall. Until now I have not even been down to the garden; the long terrace (with a superb view of the Roman Campagna) serves both as my dining room and a promenade.

Bülow writes from Florence that he will come to see me here Monday next. You have read his two dazzling articles in the *Allgemeine Zeitung* (May 28 and 31) on Glinka's opera *A Life for the Tsar*, and Verdi's *Festival Requiem*[28] in Milan. Many Italian newspapers rail and storm against Bülow; among other amiable things they call him "Khan" ("Gran Can") of Tartary because of his ardent praise of Glinka and of Russian music—in particular that of Tchaikovsky, whom Mme Moukhanoff alone appreciated among the group of the new Muscovite composers. Sgambati and I played four hands his *Romeo and Juliet Overture* which is highly colored and robust. The love aria has charm and is somewhat analogous to Raff's tender inspiration. In order to pursue my

---

28. A tribute to Alessandro Manzoni, who died on May 22, 1873. The first performance of the Requiem occurred on May 22, 1874, in Milan.

Tartar culture which is already fairly well advanced, I am going to acquire Glinka's two operas which particularly pleased me at St. Petersburg, but of which I have only a vague recollection. The publisher Fürstner in Berlin has published their piano scores with the texts translated into German. Had this translation appeared some fifteen years earlier I would certainly not have failed to conduct *A Life for the Tsar* at the Weimar theatre. One might, given the opportunity, consider performing there this work, which is popular and a classic in Russia, and on which Bülow's pen has just conferred a European luster. It seems that in Milan it is Mme Gortschakoff who more than anyone helped to get it performed. Is she by any chance a relation of yours? Don't be angry at this very harmless question.

How can we settle the form which your pious and sympathetic idea of honoring the memory of Mme Moukhanoff musically should take? It will suggest itself, I hope at Weimar, next year if not before, in the month of May on the anniversary of the death of our incomparable and unforgettable friend.

What can I tell you about my fortnight in Rome? The Holy Father deigned to grant me an audience (last Saturday). I paid a call at the Vatican on Cardinal Antonelli, on Mgr de Mérode (edifying to listen to on the subject of the destructions by the Barbarians—Italians in Rome!), and on Reverend Father Theiner. On the other bank of the Tiber I frequently saw Mme Minghetti, the Teanos, M. de Keudell (a very serious and excellent musician; he has transcribed a Schubert Quartet in perfect style, and plays it likewise), and my dear Sgambati (who has published a second album of charming Italian *Lieder*, dedicated to Mme Minghetti).

At a matinée at the house of her sister, Countess Proruoli, Princess Julie asked me for news of you and praised you in expressive terms. She has kept several letters from M. de Meyendorff, notably the one in which he predicted to her that the spirit and policy of M. Thiers would end by dragging France to her ruin.

I forbear from answering two lines in your last letter, for I would not be able to comment on them without paining you; but ask yourself whether such bouts of wrongheadedness to which, unfortunately, you are frequently prone, can count as signs of affection? If so it would be of a baroque nature which I prefer to ignore.

Assuming that Mme de Schleinitz is coming to Weimar for *Tristan*,[29] please convey to her my most affectionate respects. Won't you hint to M. de Loën that it would be proper to send an invitation to Wagner in the name of the Grand Duke, to attend the performance of *Tristan*?

Uninterruptedly, yours ever

FL

All the issues of the *Revue bleue* have arrived, but none of *L'Univers* for more than a fortnight. The last I received contained two remarkable articles on *l'enfouissement civil* by Veuillot, and by Daltonsher [d'Alton Shée], a hereditary peer of France under Louis Philippe, thereafter ultrademocratic; also the reply and the notes to the long letter of the Vicar of Monseigneur d'Orleans.

———

June 22, 74
Villa d'Este

Your emotions and enjoyment of *Tristan und Isolde* are not very pleasing to me. You pen superb indictments against me in a fine style, but of these there have been too many examples both before and after Cicero. The guilty party is never sufficiently accused; in dealing severely with him one is still being too indulgent, for beneath his visible crimes there are certainly others hidden which deserve harsher punishments.

In this noble zeal, Princess, Daniel Stern anticipated you by more than a quarter of a century. Her novel of indictment, *Nélida*, condemns me to loss of civil rights for possessing only "sham" lofty sentiments and even genius. Consequently, I should be relegated to the company of the menials of Princes, and "dine" with the scullions and broomsweeps

29. *Tristan und Isolde*, first produced in Munich, June 10, 1865.

who, contrary to the holy Christian law, are quite wrongly despised, in the servants' hall of Monseigneur the Grand Duke of Saxony.

Shall I complain of such a fate, decreed by noble ladies who are over-prodigal in sacrifices? Not at all. I have, thanks to this, tested the truth of the well-known maxim: "Judging by its effect, love is closer to hate than to kindly and helpful friendship."

F. Liszt[30]

June 24, 74
(Villa d'Este)

Your last letter makes it again possible for me to write to you. So let us together celebrate the fifty-sixth anniversary of the birth of the Grand Duke of Saxony. June 24 is moreover a great Catholic feast day: that of St. John the Baptist of whom Our Lord said, "Among the children of men there has been none greater."[31] It used to be the custom in Italy to celebrate this feast with magnificent fireworks. If this is still the case, I shall today burn there in my mind the whole file of my crimes together with that of your worries, torments, sacrifices, objurgations, and minatory ukases. For pity's sake, do not ask that I become an epistolary poodle – – –

You know that letter-writing is a punishment for me, often a very harsh one. My pen knows not how to flow, and easily becomes petrified. I absolutely must have the stimulus of *viva voce* talk for my modest wits to have running room. So why force me to adopt phraseologies which are extremely antipathetic to my nature? "Let us not strain our talents," nor that of others – – – Besides, even when I happen to be living alone, as here, I am always short of time because it is impossible for me to take care of a hundred letters and other matters which never cease bothering me.

30. FL dispenses with his usual *Bien à vous*, and signs his family name, which he does rarely in these letters.

31. "For I say unto you, Among those that are born of women there is not a greater prophet than John the Baptist: but he that is least in the kingdom of God is greater than he." Luke 7:28. King James version.

I wrote to M. Sach on his birthday and will speak to him later about Glinka's opera, and recommend that it be performed at the Weimar theatre next season. Help me to this end by using your influence as the opportunity offers. Metzdorff is right to consider you a power, and to pay assiduous court to you, but his opera,[32] well composed though it is, and even containing some brilliant passages, will have difficulty breaking into the theatre circuit in view of the general prejudice (fairly well justified by experience) against new works not signed by names already made known by preceding successes, and above all against those in a serious historical vein with lofty pretensions. Pleasing and unassuming composers still have a slightly better chance of winning a few performances here and there.

With regard to the lottery tickets of Countess Bobrinska, it seems to me better to stick to what you had offered her first (Mme Schott's tickets) unless it is easier for you to send her those of Mme de Schleinitz which are no doubt much more noble (as you would do well to point out to Mme Bobrinska), but lack the prospect of acquiring a *Patronatschein*, which appealed particularly to your friend.

I have no idea who can be the "Dame Cosaque," author of the two little books *Souvenirs de Robert Franz*.[33] I would be obliged if you would send them to me.

By this same mail I am sending you *L'Italie*, which has an account of the "manifestation" of the *Société des intérêts catholiques* in St. Peter's Square day before yesterday.

It is more than a month since I received any issue of *L'Univers*.

Saturday evening I'll be in Rome and shall stay there till Monday, the feast day of SS. Peter and Paul. The day after, I come back here into my shell.

Yours ever

FL

Bülow, who must already have arrived at Salzungen and intends to

32. *Rosamunde*, given in Weimar in 1875.
33. See p. 30 note 34, letter of December 1, 1871.

spend at least six weeks there, has told me of an eccentricity of our friend M. Loën.

When I see Mme Bobrinska again I will urge her to buy tickets for both lotteries at once; hence to send you another 50 thalers.

———

July 8, 74
(Villa d'Este)

I felt moved to write a sheet of music in memory of Mme Moukhanoff. It is a simple *Schlummer Lied im Grabe*,[34] without any pretensions – – – and more for dreaming than for playing. Here it is, copied out for you in my least bad handwriting; have it recopied with large notes so as not to tire your aching eyes. Should you try out the *Schlummer Lied*, and assuming that you do not find it too displeasing, will you please accommodate the two rhythms, triplets and quavers, for the right and the left hands, differentiating them for the thirty-two bars of the first page:

and <u>don't</u> play:

34. G 196; R 76, *Slumber Song in the Grave*, his first *Elegy* in memory of Mme Marie von Moukhanoff-Kalergis, who had recently died.

I have written a second version of this melody for cello, piano, harp, and harmonium;[35] it can thus figure in the program of our commemorative evening for Mme Moukhanoff on May 22 next year at Weimar.

In the last ten days or so I have been working at a rather strange composition, whose text you will find at the head of the volume of poetry by Longfellow, *The Golden Legend* (*Les Cloches de la cathédrale de Strasbourg*,[36] with Lucifer and his cohorts mounting an attack on the cathedral and trying to destroy it). My composition is for chorus, solo for bass voice (Lucifer), and orchestra; there is a prelude of some thirty bars, entitled *Excelsior*. Longfellow has also written a poem with this title. I do not go into details of the story and only attempt to express the epigraph in musical terms.

The whole thing will last a full quarter of an hour; the rough draft is entirely finished, but I need another week for the instrumentation.

Yesterday Loën wired to ask if I thought it suitable that "Lassen be appointed to the position of Court Conductor." I at once replied, "Very suitable assuming that it suits all concerned."

I avoid as much as possible involving myself in such matters, for my way of looking at them is not everyone's. Thus I have a high regard for rewards, honors, decorations, while feeling that those who deserve them must well and cheerfully be able to do without them. They are not a goal in themselves but an accompaniment *quasi ad libitum*.

At this particular time it seems to me that it is the bird that hangs from the neck which is luring Lassen. The title which is proposed for him will perhaps entice the bird down from his tree later on. No one wishes for Lassen more than I the honors and satisfactions which he so well deserves – – – I only urge him to adjust to the custom prevailing at Weimar where, as B—— commented to you, the Cross of Commander does not now correspond to the position held by Lassen. Had I attended the performance of *Tristan* I would probably have taken the liberty of

35. G 130; R 471.

36. G 6; R 482. Liszt's holograph letter offering the dedication to Longfellow is in the Library of Congress.

The correct title of the Prologue to the poem to which Liszt here refers is "The Spire of Strasburg Cathedral."

drawing the attention of the Grand Duchess to the appropriateness of distributing some presents to the notables of the theatre, starting with the Musical Director.

As for Loën, his situation is more complex and much more favorable; I would very much regret his leaving Weimar. We would all miss him keenly and it would also be a loss for the theatre, for as managers go I know very few to equal him and, all things considered, he fits in better than anyone else with the Court and the town to which we are attached and in which we are, as it were, rooted.

You did right in recommending Mlle Brandt to Cosima; one should not press further; let things be without heeding the gossip of this or that "character" – – –

What horrors has the "Cosaque" then written? Were it not for my total lack of curiosity with regard to low deeds, what you tell of the slander by the "Cosaque" (whom I did not suspect at all of sporting this pseudonym) would almost make me want to read it.

Send me news of Peterle and convey to him my compliments on his success as a pianist at Berka.

Yours ever

FL

Saturday, I'll be again dining at the Bobrinskis who leave the following day. Monday evening I'll be back here.

July 20, 74

I had understood that you would not be leaving before the fourteenth (at the earliest), and my little sheet of music went off on the ninth. Fortunately Sarring has put everything back in good order. I hope this is already the case with the theatre at Weimar. Lassen having for a number of years been conducting the small and large Court concerts, the title of *Hofkapellmeister* was so clearly appropriate for him that I thought it had been firmly conferred on him long since.

Their Royal Highnesses are most favorably disposed toward him and I have no doubt that they will take pleasure in making this even clearer to him on some appropriate occasion. That provided by *Tristan* was a little premature—except for the title (conferred late, unbeknownst to me) or for a gift *de sentiment*, as they say at Court.

Your comment to Loën is most judicious and will probably make him decide to stay on the job for which he is so perfectly suited. In actual fact a period at the Leipzig theatre would remove him from the "distinguished hierarchy of managers," a drawback which would not be offset by him for two or three thousand thalers more a year.

As for Hülsen's succession, it is subject to so many shifts of fortune that it is prudent not to covet it. First of all, Hülsen doesn't look much as though he were going to resign, and has no reason for doing so; then, when it will be a matter of replacing him the competitors will jostle each other as hard as they can – – – and the choice will be made on the basis of the factors favorable at that time.

You are preaching to the already converted with regard to the difficulties which are slowing up the progress of the *Deutscher Musikverein* in many cities, including Stuttgart. However, as there is a prosperous and active music school there, as well as other factors to be taken into consideration, I had thought that one could, without too much temerity, risk taking a highly discreet step with the object of obtaining from the Court grants like those we received for the *Tonkünstler Versammlungen* at Karlsruhe, Meiningen, Cassel, etc. Several people had encouraged me a little in this opinion: should it prove unfounded I will not persist in it, and will nonetheless continue to admire from a distance the sovereign graces and the perfection of Queen Olga.

My existence here suits me very well, thanks to its complete monotony. I hardly leave my room and see almost no one. Since Bülow I have had only two visitors (not of the fair sex)—they stayed a couple of hours and left as smoothly as they arrived. Yesterday I finished the instrumentation of the *Cloches*: you will find Longfellow's poem in the volume of his *Légende dorée* [*The Golden Legend*] (I forget the spelling of the English title), whose prologue, pages one to three, *Les cloches* [sic] *de la cathédrale de Strasbourg* [see p. 148 note 36], served as a text for my composition, which is preceded by a prelude of some thirty bars entitled *Excelsior*, after another poem by Longfellow (whom I occasionally saw in Rome [*frontispiece*]). *Excelsior* is synonymous with the *Sursum Corda*; we repeat it daily at mass, and the faithful reply: *Habemus ad Dominum!*

Yours ever

FL

July 27 [1874?]

First of all I answer the postscript of your last letter. Please ask me all the questions you wish without any embarrassment or oratorical hedging whatsoever. My answer will be straight and true. I have nothing to hide from anyone and sometimes commit the error of making this too clear.

Do not fear that I shall ask for the Cosaque book: the summary you have been good enough to make for me is amply sufficient, and I shall certainly do nothing to prevent you from "disinfecting" your library of that "fabulous flower from Brazil," which blooms only every hundred years. Besides, people have written to me about it from Paris and from Rome. Should you happen to be curious about the nature of my reply I shall try to remember it and write it down once again for you [see Appendix at end of 1874 letters].

Cosima greatly appreciated your letter about *Tristan*; she also sent me the telegram from M. Sach which seems to me in good taste.

The preliminary rehearsals with piano of the *Nibelungen* are getting under way at Bayreuth. Speaking of which, I have mentioned Mlle Brandt's name once again to Cosima, while assuring her that with regard to recommendations I observed the same most wise reservations as she does herself.

It is not to Calixtus III (Borgia from Spain), but to Gelasius II from

Gaeta (†1119) that the Gaetani go back. In this they are more modest by nearly a century than the Meyendorffs, with Clement II the Saxon (†1047).

I hold Gregorovius in too high esteem to imagine that he worries much about being invited to salons. What one usually learns there would almost be worth not learning at all.

You missed the *versöhnender Schluss* [conciliatory ending] of Longfellow's prologue; it is not Lucifer who could express it, but the bells do so in the final stanza:

> *Nocte surgentes*
> *Laudeamus Deum verum.*

Be so gracious as to excuse my incurable brachylogical [few words] infirmity, and do not punish me for it with shorter letters. Even perissologies [redundance] charm[s]

Your

FL

———

Tuesday, July 30

Rome

If you go on like this, you will end by turning me into a letter-writer. The proof is that, instead of going out this morning as I had intended, I am dispatching these lines to you; but don't start grumbling again and being morose to me.

I have just spent two days here without seeing anyone in the social world except Countess Bobrinska, at whose house I dined yesterday evening. She spoke to me of your letter, of your raptures over *Tristan*, and of the new Bayreuth lottery tickets (the object and advantages of which I explained to her). Your excellent rule of not chaffing people, even in order to give them a fleeting pleasure, has borne fruit for you here; and Mme Bobri[nska] took pleasure in emphasizing yesterday evening to Mgr Lichnowsky, much in your praise, that at first sight it could happen that one did not find you extremely agreeable, but that in getting to know you better one could not but appreciate you more. Thus, said she, when the Mey[endorffs] arrived in Rome, everyone liked to say: he is charming, amiable, full of wit; and after their departure, everybody missed Mme Mey[endorff]. Loën would lose nothing by following your method a little. He is pretty much a first cousin of Proteus which, incidentally, does not harm his quarterings of nobility; and in the end I hope he will go so far as to perform our Proteus— and perhaps even the opera by Metzdorff who will, thanks to you, be reasonable concerning the *ritardandos* of certain promises by friends of ours.

Bülow is not one of these; he is quasi-heroically in a class by himself.

If you are returning to the Wartburg you might perhaps stop off for a half day at Salzungen in honor of the most valiant of my friends, Bülow. He is to spend at least six weeks there. His last publication is a Dante sonnet[37] which he has dedicated to young Countess Masetti on the occasion of her wedding to Count Durazzo-Pallavicini, who is said to have a fortune of 18 million francs. Mlle Masetti has a dowry of one million and there had been some talk in Florence of her marrying Bülow.

Your trip to Holland will do both your health and your morale good. While there read Daniel Stern's *Histoire de Hollande*,[38] the only book by Cosima's mother which Cosima praises highly. Also read *Lucrezia Borgia*[39] by Gregorovius, very properly praised, touted, and admired. This work is already a huge success, which time will only confirm: let us say, in our private jargon, that it is completely "*Reine Olga*," perfect in its perfection, not boring. Mme d'Usedom could also win acclaim in her own style as another Queen Olga; I found the way she illustrated by "pantomime" her complaints about the seats of the Weimar theatre

37. Liszt arranged this sonnet for piano solo, G 479; R 144. His original manuscript is in the Library of Congress.
38. *Histoire des commencements de la République aux Pays-Bas, 1581–1625* (Paris, 1872).
39. *Lucrezia Borgia. Nach Urkunden und Correspondenzen ihrer eigenen Zeit* (1874).

vastly entertaining. When the hall was renovated, certain people[40] (as well as Loën) worried more about the box office than about the right size and comfort of the seats – – – –

I am delighted that my very favorable hunch concerning the Hereditary Grand Duchess is being vindicated.

You might have written to M. de Moukhanoff, but I almost approve your having abstained from doing so. The conciliatory *mezzo termine* will be to have your sister in Warsaw convey your message to him.

Whereupon I will do my utmost to pamper and coddle you – – –

FL

I am told that Gregorovius will follow up his *Lucrezia* with a *Beatrice Cenci*. I have predicted that *Lucrezia* will run to at least fifteen editions.

(Forgive me for having transposed the popes; I promise not to do this again.)

August 6, 74
(Villa d'Este)

The question about my "contentment" made me smile sadly. Short of wishing to be a nincompoop, one must be displeased only with one's self, and restrict to this intimate and salutary purpose the dose of discontent inherent in human nature.

Thank you for the Petrarch letter of Victor Hugo. I am all the more glad to read it again in that it found its way back to me through you. The last twenty lines please me extremely: "Petrarch is a kind of Plato of poetry . . . but he is a stranger to misfortune . . . ," etc. The part preceding this strikes me as bombastic and false; and so, in spite of my profound admiration for V. Hugo's genius and his astonishing accomplishments, I refuse to follow him in his demagogic aberrations. No, and again No, the *Marseillaise* is not the "voice of the future." "The

40. *L'on* in the text presumably alludes to the Grand Duke and Grand Duchess.

ferocious foreigner" has no *raison d'être* any more; innkeepers and manufacturers protest with reason against this epithet. People don't cut the
throats of sons and wives in the countryside, and to "irrigate the fur-
rows with impure blood" isn't going to benefit the harvest. It is at the
frontier that defense must be effective; after that it's too late. Enthu-
siasms and machinations born of hatred are condemned to impotence.

Forgive this digression and let us come back to Weimar, which is
peaceful and devoid of impure blood, for people there suffer rather
from mild and sickly anemia.

Loën has written me a cordial letter to which I replied this morning,
letting him know that several weeks ago I had conveyed my humble
opinion on the pending, not hanging, matter[41] which will be solved
amicably on the basis of the status quo.

Which history of Maria Theresa, "male-female," have you read "in
French or in German"? The one by Arneth?[42] He has also published
the correspondence between Maria Theresa and Marie Antoinette[43]
and other respected works on the same period.

An ingenious invention of the celebrated Paris clockmaker, M.
Haas: the calendar-watch! Have you seen one?

My Longfellow bells are now completely cast. I shall probably set
them tolling next winter at Pest. They will not soothe the ears of the
critics any better than other compositions of mine.

Yours ever

FL

---

41. FL puns: *cas pendant, non pendable*
42. *Geschichte Maria Theresia's* . . . (Vienna, 1863–76). When completed this work ran
to ten volumes.
43. *Maria Theresia und Marie Antoinette. Ihr Briefwechsel.*

September 7, 74

You have sometimes teased me about your "<u>crimes</u>"; but it seems I have committed some which are no longer a matter for levity.

You have not written to me in the last fortnight. In view of the maxim "To complain is ridiculous, to solicit pity, miserable," I dare not complain. However, a little commiseration would be charitable – – –

Yours ever

FL

Rome, September 15, 74

My last lines told you (too drily, doubtless, according to my deplorable habit), that I was conscious of the lack of letters from you. Thank you from my heart for what you have written since then, and especially for the <u>adorable</u> letter I received this morning. It finds me in a state of deep depression, and although I refuse to let myself worry, I feel nonetheless overwhelmed.

When I moved into the Villa d'Este, at the beginning of June, I agreed with Princess Wittgenstein that I would come back here for a day or two every two weeks. This has been the case up till now; but day before yesterday her painful condition, which is very usual with her and is due to arduous and excessive work combined with far too sedentary a life, for she has not stirred from Rome in the last fourteen years and leaves her room only to make a few calls <u>in her carriage</u> without ever going out on foot—this painful condition, which is closely linked to two or three grave illnesses she had in Germany, lingers on and is now dangerously aggravated by Roman fever – – – – The doctors don't reassure me much and advise a change of air, which is impossible now, and I even doubt whether she would resign herself to this later on, given her total dislike of any change in the mode of living she has devised.

I shall stay in Rome this week, and the post office will deliver all my letters to me here without first forwarding them to Tivoli.

The incident which has created the loudest repercussions of late in the religious world is the posthumous publication of Father Theiner's letters to Professor Friederich. I am sending you a French translation of them, just as they appeared in the newspaper *L'Italie*. The *Allgemeine Zeitung* of Augsburg has published two or three more, which *L'Italie* omitted. If you like, I'll send them to you; but as one of them contains a few highly spiteful words (unjustly, I consider) against Mgr Haynald, I am reluctant to disseminate them for fear of even a shadow of connivance in denigrating persons for whom I feel affection and gratitude. Not being able to defend them often, as I would wish to do, I at least avoid participating even tacitly in attacks against them. For pity's sake, do not take this as an allusion; and believe me to be absolutely free of all spitefulness or of dredging up old tales.

Have you heard of a young Russian sculptor, Mark Antokolsky, who settled here three years ago? People here and elsewhere praise highly his (seated) statue of Ivan the Terrible, and another more recent one of Christ. Someone very knowledgeable in the field of art has told me that the Ivan has character and inspiration, but that the Christ "is a downcast Jew, wretched and crestfallen," in spite of all the praise lavished on his Hebraic cast of features, which is original, and in keeping with the "Son of Man." It is modeled on Lessing's John Huss, which is very superior in terms of the artist's talent.

I kiss your hands

FL

September 23, 74
Duino (near the Austro–Italian frontier)
c/o Princess Thurn–Hohenlohe

Don't be surprised if today I don't answer some question you may perhaps have included in your last letter.

I spent all last week in Rome because of worry over the physical condition of Princess Wittgenstein who, in addition to other ills, has caught the Roman fever. Without her knowledge (for she thinks me back at the Villa d'Este), I left Rome Sunday evening in order to come straight here where her daughter now is, whose advice on several points I wanted to seek.

I arrived here yesterday morning and leave again this evening for Rome; and as soon as Princess Wittgenstein is on the road to convalescence I'll return to my lodgings at the Villa d'Este.

The castle of Duino, built on a rock, backs onto an old Roman tower, surrounded by the Adriatic. Under my window is a little rock to which are linked the memory and name of Dante, who wandered for some time in these regions. A short distance away one can see Miramar and Trieste. I came here in '67 or '68 to visit Princess Thérèse Hohenlohe (widow, born Countess Thurn) whom I had formerly seen fairly often in Rome. She is a friend of the Countess de Chambord, and was pleased by the graciousness shown her by Her Royal Highness when she came to Duino this spring.

Yours ever

FL

October 5, 74
Rome

On my return from Duino I did not find the patient improved; so I stayed on here, and shall only return to the Villa d'Este in another week or so. On top of everything, I felt unwell, but recovered rapidly after having had to spend a day in bed.

I would like to find the word which exactly expresses my feelings on what you are pleased to call crimes; it is not forgetfulness, nor is it forgiveness, unless one links to this word a connotation of something sad, sweet, and very humble—which one hardly feels authorized to forgive —in other words a certain feeling, fairly vague if you will, but which I seem not to have found in others. If it is an illusion, it forms part of the innermost fibres of my being, and sometimes expands during prayer and at the peak of artistic experience. However this may be, you have no reason to complain of it, and you can be very sure of receiving more than you ask for.

Speaking of crimes, an anonymous man of letters (whose name is entirely unknown to me) has me confessing in public in my own name to one of my crimes and to my "immeasurable pride"! This in a lugubrious tone of lamentation (in the manner of Claude Frollo in *Notre-Dame de Paris*), in a small book entitled *Souvenirs d'un pianiste en réponse aux souvenirs d'une Cosaque*.[44]

I can only be grateful to the author for his kind and edifying intentions toward me, while admitting that until now I had no more discovered moral resemblance within myself to Claude Frollo than physical resemblance to Quasimodo; and that in the circumstances in question, I consider myself to be much more silly than criminal – – – –

As for my immeasurable pride, it reaches the point of believing that people have often been mistaken with regard to me, and of not feeling in the slightest obliged to subscribe to opinions and judgments which seem to me false.

The Bobrinskis will only return later. In a railroad station, on my trip back from Duino, I came across M. de Chevicz, who was on his way to Milan to pay a visit to Princess Czernicheff (your friend), who is still very ill, and at another station, M. de Moukhanoff, who came to see me here, one hour before leaving for Naples. From there he returns

44. See p. 30 note 34, letter of December 1, 1871.

to Warsaw via Munich and Weimar (for he has to go to Jena because of the young man whom Mme Moukhanoff placed there). We spoke of you with Chevicz and Moukhanoff, whom you will see again in Weimar. Sgambati has kept a copy of my *Schlummer Lied im Grabe* (written in memory of Mme Moukhanoff) and intends to perform it this winter in Rome at one of his concerts. I also told Moukhanoff about your intention regarding a commemorative musical evening in Weimar, next May, with which I associate myself with all my heart.

Yours ever

FL

October 17, 74
Rome

Not having been back at the Villa d'Este since my return from Duino, your letters have been somewhat delayed, all the more since communications between Tivoli and Rome are fairly lackadaisical. Thus I received your letter, in which you spoke of seeing Cosima again in Leipzig on the twelfth of this month, only the evening before, and I had no time to reply; but once and for all it goes without saying that your friendly relations with Cosima please me very much, and that I approve in advance everything which sustains them and draws them closer. For her part, she has always spoken to me of you in a manner which convinced me that she fully understood me. Again recently, with regard to Chimay, she was praising your sustained zeal, devoid of false pretensions, in favor of propaganda for Bayreuth, and on every occasion she has the gift of telling me specifically and exclusively those things I like to hear.

The patient is on the mend but still bedridden.

In ten days or so I shall go back to the Villa d'Este; till then write to Vicolo de' Greci, 43 Rome.

Thank you for having remembered Pohl to whom I remain much attached although we never write to each other. Under the pseudonym of Hoplit, Pohl was one of the first champions of the good cause which we continue to defend. His pamphlet *Das Karlsruher Musikfest* dates from '54, I think – – – Nohl only came some ten years later. People find fault with him a great deal, but so far as I'm concerned this is a reason for drawing closer to him. I'll try to be of some use to him and to lighten the burdens of his excessive paternal bliss, attested to by six or seven children! As in the case of the military, marriage should be forbidden to artists and men of letters so long as their income cannot provide regular sustenance for their wives and children.

You speak to me of Mme Chérémétieff, the daughter-in-law of Mme Chérémétieff, who is quasi-Roman and owns the Villa del Drago, near the Gate of San Lorenzo. It is through Princess W[ittgenstein] that I came to know slightly this young and pretty woman, when I arrived here in May. She plays the piano most agreeably and composes certain *œuvres choisies*, of which she has published a graceful *Minuet* which she very graciously dedicated to me.

Speaking of compositions, I've hardly been able to attend to mine in more than six weeks. However, I have not been idle and I devote several hours daily to the arrangement for four hands of the *Symphonische Dichtungen*, for which Härtel has asked me; furthermore I am revising, correcting, and recasting a number of transcriptions of the *Lieder* of Beethoven, Mendelssohn, Franz, as well as six old pieces taken from Wagner's operas, which will appear in 8º (second edition) at Härtel's during the winter. You will consider this work very superfluous and not very important. I agree; but for want of something better I am devoting myself to it with a kind of conscientious passion, and I fancy that I succeed better in improving myself musically than in other ways.

Kömpel has asked for my Steinway piano for a concert of the *Orchester Verein*. Willingly; tell me if you have room enough to house this piano for the winter. You could put it at the disposal of the more or less well-known pianists who pass through Weimar? If my question seems to you preposterous, let's drop the matter.

Moukhanoff did not give me the date of his passage through Wei-mar. As he is soon to return to Warsaw I suppose he will be seeing you before the end of October.

Yours ever

FL

I'll be sending you tomorrow two curious articles by Gregorovius (in the *Allgemeine* of Augsburg) on Lucera and the Sarrasin colony of Frederick II (in Apulia).

Émile Ollivier came here yesterday evening to see me with his wife whom I had not met. He is going to spend three weeks in Rome, incognito, and will not be making any calls.

If I meet Princess Barat. [Bariatinska], "who has one-third of the *Patronatschein*," I'll do your errand.

No railroad between Tivoli and Rome. The ramshackle carriage takes four hours, more or less, for the trip, during which I read.

The winter here is extremely mild; not a single snowflake.

Thursday, October 29, 74

(Villa d'Este)

Saturday I came back here; and next week I go again to Rome for the feast of St. Charles (November 4), after which I hope to find time here for several weeks' work.

Did I tell you that Émile Ollivier and his wife have been in Rome since mid-October? I took them to the Villa Mellini (Monte Mario) of vivid memory—to the palace of the Caesars, where Commander and Senator Rosa was so kind as to explain eloquently to us some archaeological mysteries—and to the basilica of St. Paul. Notwithstanding the widely accepted criticisms leveled against the reconstruction of this church, it harmonizes more with my own personal feelings of worship than any other in Rome excepting Santa Maria degli Angeli.

The tall columns of the nave of Simplon stone are impressive; and the columns of the high altar which were donated by the Viceroy of Egypt do not mar them. Even the malachite altars, a gift of the Emperor Nicholas, (disparaged by many visitors) seem to me to produce a fine effect there, solemn and not at all loud.

Were my lodgings not so far away, I would frequent St. Paul, and Santa Maria degli Angeli which Michelangelo was unfortunately unable to finish; but in order to economize the morning hours I usually hear mass at the church of Gesù e Maria (on the Corso between the Chimay house and the Russian palace – – – on the other side), or at San Carlo al Corso.

I have been told that the Bobrinskis are back. I'll see them again next week; item [*idem*] the Malatestas, the Teanos, Mme Helbig and Mme Minghetti, and M. de Keudell, who are very kind to me. Sgambati has rehearsed my *Schlummer Lied im Grabe* for Mme Moukhanoff with Pinner (my American pupil), Turino (cello), and Miss Sargana (harp). They will be playing it at a concert in the near future. If you answer these lines at once, write to 43 Vicolo de' Greci where I shall be until Saturday, November 7.

Did you read in the latest issue (October 15) of the *Revue des deux mondes* the article signed <u>Robert Frantz</u> [Franz] on gypsy music? I only know the title through a summary of the *Revue* inserted in my daily newspaper *L'Italie*, and I wonder if the "Cosaque" has managed to raise herself to the heights (eminently *"Reine Olga"*) of the famous *Revue*, which, incidentally, has always been most harsh on Berlioz, Wagner, and their poor follower, your very humble servant? I recall an interview in 1850 or '51 with Baron Blaze de Bury, brother-in-law of Berlioz and Director of the *Revue*. At that time he deigned to grant me his protection to the extent of proposing to slip an article by me into his Olympus of the *rue des beaux-arts*. I accepted naively on condition that this article should be entirely devoted to the praise of Berlioz and Wagner, but the Baron scowled at this neat ploy[45] and consequently

45. *Fit mauvaise mine à très beau jeu.* FL reverses the usual *fit bonne mine à mauvais jeu*: to smile in the face of adversity.

I remained one of the lowly outcasts—a very little <u>Jean</u>[46] as before, at Weimar. Happily this doesn't prevent me from enjoying the fine literature of the <u>Dominations</u> of the *Revue des deux mondes*.

Please be so good as to explain the enclosed note to Kömpel, who should know that I don't want to take back anything whatever (neither book, nor music, nor any object) from the storeroom of the Altenburg, since all my belongings are mixed up with the very much more valuable ones belonging to Princess Wittgenstein. Otherwise the personal furniture of the Grand Duke at the Hofgärtnerei would make no sense. Thus it is mere parochial stupidity to ask me for "one of my pianos," other than the Steinway piano which has remained at the Hofgärtnerei and which I invite Kömpel to utilize at the concerts of his *Orchester Verein*. <u>You</u> will tell me later what was done with it, without any further correspondence with Kömpel.

Princess Wittgenstein will probably come back, at last, to Weimar next June for a few days in order to settle, as the owner, the final destination of her furniture, works of art, etc., which are still as of now under the care of Mme Pickel in a house opposite the *Kunstschule*. By agreement with the Princess, I will attend to the disposal of my stock of books, music, pianos, etc.

For more than thirty years by now, I flatter myself that I have served the ruling House of Weimar faithfully and punctiliously; even were it to make it difficult to continue, I would not be untrue to my Spanish motto "Pundonoroso."[47]

Au revoir perhaps in Vienna or Pest—in February—for I will only leave here after the carnival.

Yours ever with all my heart

F. Liszt

46. FL puns phonetically on *gens* and *Jean*.

47. In a letter to the Grand Duke Carl Alexander from Cadiz, dated January 1, 1845, Liszt explains the Spanish term *pundonoroso* as an "admirable expression in the Spanish language, which indicates the practical application of a point of honor." *Correspondance entre Franz Liszt et Charles Alexandre, grand-duc de Saxe; pub. par La Mara (pseud.)* (Leipzig, 1909).

I am writing by this mail to Lassen in reply to a letter which he transmitted to me.

———

November 11, 74
Villa d'Este

On my return here yesterday evening I found your two letters of November 3 and 5. You already know through Gust[chen] that I spent two days in Florence (Nov. 6, 7), and your charming friend will have reassured you on my state of health, about which there is never any cause for worry. M. S[ach] started off by speaking to me about you, and in a wholly convincing manner. I am truly grateful to him for this and I hope he will not fail to convey to you my deep homage, to which Gust[chen] will add a more tender commentary.

Now for the most urgent matter: Pest. Before leaving I warned my friends that this time I will not be coming back there as in previous years in early winter, but only in time for Ash Wednesday. Already last winter, I had freed myself from the pleasures of the Carnival at Pest by spending three or four weeks in the country at the Széchenyis. Henceforth I shall always arrange matters, one way or the other, so as no longer to find myself in Pest in the season of balls and masquerades. I have made this point with my friends too often for me to attempt to go back suddenly on my word. Besides, at carnival time music is an hors-d'œuvre; great concerts are given only during Advent or Lent, and I suppose that Richter has informed Wagner accordingly. Consequently, I count not only on finding W[agner] in Pest, but on waiting for him there already on Ash Wednesday – – – – If he had made other commitments and were to arrive in January, I would have to reconsider. Doubtless W[agner] is sure of getting what people call a full house, whatever the time of year; but it seems to me that the season of Lent will suit him better.

It is now several weeks that I have been wanting to write to Cosima;

unfortunately I can no longer hold a pen in the evening, and I don't really spend my days as I would like to. Do not ask me to explain; to go on living is enough – – – without any further explanation.

What a strange scruple to tell me that you will not be using my Steinway piano. I do beg you to do the opposite and to be willing to use and abuse this possession of mine. If the *Dante*[48] doesn't seem to you too baroque and boring, practice it with Lassen. Perhaps there will be an opportunity to hear it at your house next spring with the little final chorus (of women's voices). The *St. Cecilia*,[49] of which you ask me for news, was composed here, after a poem by Mme de Girardin—some forty to fifty verses long, which please me. So long as I am engaged in composing music, it absorbs me passionately; then, when it is a matter of performing it, of publishing it, etc., I have to make an effort to re-involve myself even slightly in it, and generally I prefer to forget it completely.

M. Sach will speak to you about a young man of twenty-five whom good connoisseurs declare to be the foremost contemporary sculptor. He is the son of Professor Hildebrand of Jena; his two medium-sized statues—an adolescent asleep, and another drinking—caused a sensation at the art exhibition in Vienna and are considered works of genius. Dr. Fidler in Leipzig is their fortunate owner. Hildebrand is now finishing (for the Leipzig museum) an Adam with the apple; we admired it together with M. S[ach] in the studio in Florence where there was also a magnificent bust of Heyse (the poet's uncle, formerly known in Weimar as *der junge Goethe*).

Ask M. S[ach] to lend you an important publication to which he took out a subscription in my presence: *Italia*. It is to appear quarterly at Hartung's (Leipzig) under the guidance of M. Karl Hillebrand (with one *l* more and one *d* less than the sculptor), whom I introduced to you in Weimar in the company of my excellent friend Mme Laussot. During the two days I spent in Florence, I stayed as usual with Mme Laussot, Lungarno. The first issue of *Italia* (October 15) has a long article by

48. Probably the arrangement for 2 pianos: G 648; R 370.
49. G 5; R 480.

Bonghi (now Minister of Public Education) on Church matters, another on Leonardo da Vinci by Hess; Grimm, etc.

Speaking of Jesuits, people are talking a great deal about Father Curci's latest pamphlet. I think it serves as introduction to a work of several volumes: *Commentaires sur l'Evangile.*[50] I have not yet read it and don't even know its exact title; but people have assured me, *horresco referens!* [I shudder to say it!], that Father Curci has had no scruples in making short shrift of the Pope's temporal power. This, coming from a Reverend Father of the Company of Jesus is, to say the least, surprising, given the no less categorical than repeated statements by the Holy Father. I completely fail to understand what it's all about, and I also feel too ignorant to understand much of Nietzsche, who dazzles me with his fine style much more than he enlightens me. I agree that this is really my fault and in no way Nietzsche's; but how can I become converted to the man created by Schopenhauer (*der Schopenhauer'sche Mensch!*), or to the man of Goethe and of Rousseau, whereas I adore our *bon Dieu*, the creator, and call upon him as "Our Father" who is in Heaven?—Ah! believe me, dear beloved soul, let us leave to others more learned than we the perilous paths of thought, and let us remain united in heart to our heavenly Father and to His Son Jesus Christ our Savior!—

Just these last few days, Pius IX was repeating St. Paul's word: *Sic state in Domino!* We will breathe more easily there, and be better comforted than in Schopenhauer or Goethe, without diminishing ourselves or depreciating the higher intellects which are drawn to an ideal other than that, infinitely sublime and practical, of humility and Christian charity. Alas, eighteen centuries of Christianity have still imbued us very little with its truth and its invigorating spirit! ————

I will soon return Nietzsche together with the October 15 issue of the *Revue des d. m.* Over and above the irridescent botany and the fragrant flora of the Rákospalota landscape (!), the pseudo Robert Franz discourses as an initiate on the gypsies' music. One must not expect ac-

---

50. *Lezioni esegetiche e morali sopra i quattro evangeli* . . . (Florence, 1874–76) (5 vols.).

curacy from him, but just follow his inspirations through the zigzags—
of the Puszta "slumbering in the warmth of a haze as white as an ermine
cloak" up to "the cleaning-brush of Baron Rosty's flute." On the way
one comes across charming witticisms—such as this one: "There are
times when the friendship I feel for people is combined with the pleasure of being rid of them."

You told me about your "insane" compatriot Lazareff, who formerly
accused me of scheming against him to withdraw from him the support
of the late Grand Duchess![51] I regret that you did not deign to attend
his concert and tell me about it. In terms of absurdity devoid of talent,
Lazareff reaches the zenith, and I hardly know of anyone other than a
certain Maestro Cimosa (at Trieste) who could claim to compete with
him. He has also composed and published a *Last Judgment* compared
with which that of Michelangelo is only a bashful mediocrity; but
Lazareff far surpasses both Michelangelo and Cimosa. Please keep the
program of this memorable work; it will serve for our aesthetic entertainment.

From the ridiculous to the sublime – – – there is more than one step.
However, I must again bring up the matter of the *Patronatscheine* of
the Bobrinskis. You will perhaps succeed in softening up the Countess
to the point of enriching her with one of these precious coupons; she
seemed fairly favorably inclined to this day before yesterday; and her
brother-in-law has made her understand that the Bayreuth lottery
ticket which she owns confers on her the right to acquire now, for a
pretty penny, a *Patronatschein*.

The Bob[rinskis] arrived in Rome in early October, but I saw them
again only the day before yesterday for dinner. The Count is busying
himself actively with the work at the Villa Malta which requires another
year (at least) and more money than would be needed for the Bayreuth
theatre and its first twenty performances.

Yours ever

FL

51. Very probably Maria Paulowna (1786–1859).

I have just this minute been handed your letter of the seventh. The newspaper story about the Conservatory at Pest is just a canard; I have received no official or unofficial information on this subject, and things will long remain in a dilatory or even negative state which I explained to you. As for my return to Pest, I repeat that I had six months ago fixed it for the end of the next Carnival, in February. That is why I wrote you this date which will, I hope, coincide with Wagner's trip. This afternoon I'll write to Cosima. She has not said a word to me about the concerts announced in the press for the near future, with W[agner] as conductor and my active participation as pianist. In my view this combination, natural though it may be, would not be to the advantage of the Bayreuth project where the question of money has priority over sentiment, without any doubt. Now, since concerts with Wagner alone inevitably produce a full house, and mine are not unattended, it is better to give them separately in Pest, save in exceptional cases, when I shall be in a position to extend to W[agner], so to speak, the honors of the city and, as an extra gesture, to contribute my little talent as a pianist to his program.

I no longer dare beg you not to alarm yourself, but I await from your heart confidences and communications free of all restraint. So always write to me at great length; I'll try so to answer you that you won't have to reproach me for leaving you in a state of uncertainty.

November 22

You were right to convey to Cosima the details in my last letter. The reply from Bayreuth will probably not affect the date of the Pest concert in February.

Are your eyes still bothering you? Can you read without tiring them too much? If the Jesuit controversy interests you, you must read *Gesuita moderno*[52] by Gioberti (the Italian edition in eight volumes—reduced to

52. *Il Gesuita moderno* . . . , orig. ed. (Lausanne, 1846–47).

three in the German) and Quinet's book on the Jesuits.[53] Pious erudites distinguish between a good Jesuit and a Jesuit who is a good man, by establishing two corresponding categories: the Ignatians (who follow St. Ignatius of Loyola) and the Xavierians (for whom St. Francis Xavier serves as a model).

Be so kind as to write me legibly the name of the author Tomache, Lomache, or Jomache (?), the spelling of which I was unable to decipher in the enclosed learned scrawl.

With regard to the *Exercices de St. Ignace* which I read recently, someone said to me: "It's an infernal machine for sanctification."—

FL

November 22, feast day of St. Cecilia, patron saint of music. In her honor I have composed music for the verses by Mme de Girardin:

> "All the arts pay homage to her
> She dictates pious songs," etc.

—————

December 2, 74
Villa d'Este

Cosima will already have told you that our reunion in Pest holds for the month of February. You must therefore cease sounding the alarm bell, but I hope that other bells will start ringing. I shall be installed again in Pest (Fischplatz), on Ash Wednesday, and will be staying there until Easter week. The news about me in the press is always *ad libitum.* It seems that I was recently made to say, I forget what, in Venice where I have not been in many years.

No one has officially informed me about my honorary presidency[54] (in Pest) which incidentally would in no way obligate me to an extra

53. See above, note 15.
54. Of the Royal Conservatory of Music.

curtsy in Vienna, a town which I do not intend to frequent this winter. At the most I shall spend a few days there without giving any concert before returning to Weimar.

Since you are pleased to ask my advice with regard to the *Patro*[*nats*] *Sch*[*ein*] of the Hereditary Grand Duchess, I urge you not to expose yourself to the point of personally acquiring them; this would be risky, and might cause you some embarrassment later on, but the idea of the Christmas present is a good one; stick to it and try to carry it out with the help of Gustchen—and of Loën whom, it seems to me, it would not be proper to leave out of this scheme. No matter whether he, for his part, has taken back or not taken back his own *Pat*[*ronats*] *Sch*[*ein*]. He remains the natural master in Weimar of the Bayerisches Theatre and the most agreeably obliging intermediary with Their Highnesses. When you have informed him of the favorable attitude of the Hereditary Grand Duchess, he will certainly waste no time in following up on this, and you will no longer have much trouble in concluding the business according to our wishes.

At the same time, if you are of a different opinion, act upon it without paying the least attention to mine; for I cannot flatter myself that I am skillful at Court, nor that I am able to judge from a distance little things which can only be properly seen close to. In the advice which you are so modest as to ask of me I concern myself chiefly with the major point— to spare you subsequent unpleasantness. Now since your relations with Loën are good, I would fear impairing them by advising you to betray a kind of mistrust toward him and to act secretly. If, contrary to all likelihood, he were to declare himself opposed to your intentions, you would still be in a position to undertake your task loyally and quietly.

These lines were written yesterday morning in Rome. On my arrival here in the evening, Ercole told me that he had sent off several letters, amongst them a *carta turchina* [blue notepaper], which will come back to me tomorrow.

Mme Bobrinska had already carried out your errand for Kopf before I mentioned it. He cannot ship marble to you; it's too expensive, and as for plaster, the choice becomes difficult. No doubt the effect of the bust of Queen Olga would be magnificent, but the august original is so little in favor of affairs at Bayreuth that I would not dare exhibit her lovely likeness among the objects in Mme de Schl[einitz]'s lottery. I shall probably invite Kopf to present to this lottery the medallion of our Grand Duke and his son, and perhaps in addition, as a very humble accompanying piece, the one of me which he will complete before Christmas. Let me know by what date the prizes must be in Berlin. As for discovering other artists in Rome disposed to contribute gifts to Mme de Schleinitz's lottery, there's not much chance of this (at least, within my reach).

Father Curci's pamphlet was sent off to you yesterday morning. I have not read it, and you will do me a favor by giving me your impression of it.

Herewith the program of the third concert of the Orchestra Society conducted by Pinelli. He has been most successful, and the success of the fourth and sixth concerts will be *crescendo*.

Don't worry about the temperature at the Villa d'Este; Cardinal Hohenlohe has had two chimneys installed in my lodging.

Yours ever

FL

December 12, 74
Villa d'Este

Alas! There is only sad news about the continuing illness of Princess Czernicheff. Hannstein, the incomparable factotum of Mme Mouk[hanoff], now in the service of Mme Czer[nicheff], told me last week that she could neither read nor write and sleeps hardly at all. The crises are frequent and lengthy; she sees no one, and Countess Bobrinska restricts herself to calls on your friend's housemaid.

Illnesses of the body benefit the soul, the *gran poverello di Dio* St.

Francis used to say. Let us pray to the God of Mercy that he shed his grace on the pains of the body and of the soul of his frail creatures.

Your Byzantinism persists with regard to the Jesuits. You ask for works which support the illustrious and much decried company: the *Provinciales* of Pascal and other indictments worry you – – – – Indeed, spirit, brilliance, passion, and even eloquence are far more often to be found on the side of the Jesuits' enemies than of their apologists. So do be satisfied with the excellent and sound pamphlet by Father Ravignan, and above all lift up your soul to the noble spectacle of a few thousand men who practice the most difficult virtues and the hardest abnegations; who are resigned to outrages and tribulations, firm and persevering in serving the Catholic Church and thereby glorifying the holy name and the Cross of Our Lord Jesus!

The modest *Revue bleue*, still not admitted to the Court of Queen Olga, prospers. I read with interest the articles on Bourdaloue, and the one by Franz on the limits to German autocracy, not much now disposed to submit to restraint. The preface to the new French translation of the Bible[55] by Reuss, a professor at Strasbourg University, has inspired in me the desire of acquiring the entire work. Will you ask your bookseller the price of the volumes and whether several of them have already appeared?

I should in my turn reproach you for treating me like a kind of Riedel. Is it necessary to go on bringing up certain matters which are entirely clear? My daughter has perfectly understood: on February 10 I'll be in Pest and I beg you to feel entirely convinced once and for all of everything which is self-explanatory concerning

Your very humble

FL

When you see our Grand Duke again please convey to him my very faithful homage.

Don't forget to compliment Clément for me on his gifts as a drafts-

55. *La Bible. Traduction nouvelle avec introductions et commentaires* . . . (Paris, 1874–81) (16 vols.).

man. It will be a great pleasure for me to get to know his work personally – – – and to thank him for the care he takes in drawing pictures of me.

Your reply concerning the Kopf medallion has not yet arrived. I hesitate to send such a meager offering—which, in spite of the simplicity of my good intentions, might seem pretentious—to the lottery of Mme de Schleinitz.

———

December 18
(Villa d'Este)

Pinner's concert (of which I enclose the program) obliges me to return this evening to Rome. I'll stay there until December 26—in the same lodging which they let me rent by the day—Vicolo de' Greci, 43. If you are writing to me right away send your letter there.

Adelheid arrived Sunday (December 6). I'll tell you about her at greater length on another occasion. Please tell Lassen that she is staying at Piazza di Spagna, 51, Casa Tellenbach. Her stay in Rome will probably be prolonged until the end of May. May this fact not encourage Lassen to postpone to the Greek Calends his promised and awaited letter.

I'm glad that my advice on the negotiations on the *Pat[ronat]scheine* for the Hereditary Grand Duchess does not conflict with yours; and since you insist, I shall henceforth dispense with all forms of politeness when you ask me for any advice. To tell you the truth I consider you to be very superior to your very simple FL in prudence, behavior, and ability. Even what I call your "Byzantinism" confers on you advantages to which I could not aspire, since I succeed in getting along only by dint of naïveté.

In your talks with Loën about Metzdorff, I do not at all feel that you pushed caution to excess and I would have, like you, suggested to Metz[dorff] that he obtain a "confirmation in writing" of the copying costs.

Thank you for having remembered *Proteus*; we will perhaps end by seeing it appear this spring on our illustrious stage. In Rome, the season at the Apollo opens on December 26 with *Aida*. In the fall, they gave *Le Comte Ory*[56] and *Dinorah*[57] at L'Argentina. I have not been to the theatre since Pest.

You give me very wise information on Curci's pamphlet which I have not yet read. *Italia* is a quarterly review. So the next issue will only appear in January.

Miska is pressing me about packing.

Yours ever with all my heart

FL

December 30, 74
Villa d'Este

Olgh. [sic] remains very much on her high horse. She is almost angry at the title of "Byzantine" which, so far as I am concerned, was entirely laudatory. In order to punish her I am not going to get angry, and since she claims to be neither ingenious nor subtle nor in any way refined, I will simply take her word for it – – – as I have been doing for a number of years. Besides, what I termed "Byzantinism" corresponds to embellishments in music. I relish them very much in Rossini and others. I employ them more or less clumsily on the piano and even with orchestra (particularly in the Hungarian rhapsodies), and only recently I spent several hours looking for some of a certain kind which seem to me pleasant. Beethoven and Chopin didn't turn up their noses at them, far from it – – –

So no tantrums on this matter, and may Olgh. be fully convinced that any intention of hurting her feelings could <u>never</u> enter my mind.

56. By Rossini, first performed August 20, 1828, in Paris.
57. By Meyerbeer, first performed April 4, 1859, in Paris.

Your friend Princess Czer[nicheff] has let me know through Hann-stein that she was greatly touched by, and grateful for your remembrance. Her illness is not getting worse; rather, it is abating. She still can see no one, nor read nor write, but there is a fairly good sign: appetite. Should you wish for more detailed news, write to Monsieur Hannstein, c/o Mme la Princesse Czer[nicheff], Casa Serny, 20 Piazza di Spagna (next to the Hôtel d'Angleterre).

You know that it was with Hannstein that I corresponded during Mme Moukhanoff's last illness. It is also through him that I have just received the first news of something which moved me to tears. He showed me a letter from M. de Moukhanoff inquiring to whom he should remit the 2000 thalers left by his wife to the *Allgemeiner Deutscher Musikverein* and to the *Liszt-Beethoven Stiftung* (it is thus that she names this foundation, which was founded in 1870 thanks to a bequest of 3,000 to 4,000 thalers from poor Pflughaupt). What an admirable gesture on the part of our incomparable friend, and all the more admirable in that it springs quite spontaneously from the heart, with no previous hint or request from anyone! On the contrary, I used to tell her that she had already done almost too much for us poor devils of musicians by doubling the 24 thalers of her dues, with which she associated her husband.

I'll take care that her 2,000 thalers are put to good use, and that they will contribute to perpetuating her memory in music and among musicians. To start with you had the excellent idea of a commemorative matinée or evening: help me to bring it about next May at Weimar. I hope that the Grand Duchess and her daughter-in-law will deign to favor with their presence our pious concert, whose program I will try to put together in a way which our dear departed would approve!

Meanwhile, don't let your lack of success in the matter of the *Patronatscheine* trouble you; but be patient and persevere in the right path.

The only failure which it was hard for me to bear was M. Sach's withdrawal from Wagner's *Nibelungen* (in 1860—more than a year before my arrival in Rome). Not only was it possible to perform it in Weimar, but also it would have cost little, then. Let's speak no more of it. Wagner greatly benefited from my failure and I must, though regretfully, sacrifice Weimar's and my own pride to him.

Since you read music journals, I recommend to you the articles on Cornelius in the last issues of the *Neue Zeitschrift für Musik*. I don't know who wrote them, but it is obviously one of my friends, and I will thank him as soon as I know his name.

The *Briefe eines ästhetischen Ketzers* are by Hillebrand who spoke to me about them last month in Florence. He is now publishing a three-volume work by his father: *Deutsche Litteratur-Geschichte*[58]—which he has annotated and completed. I have urged Hillebrand to send M. Sach these volumes.

I am correcting myself and will no longer say the "lottery" but the "sale" of Mme de Schleinitz. Do the same yourself and don't write "loterie" with two t's, nor "aristocratie" with a c any more.

Yours ever

FL

Mme de Sch[leinitz]'s sale being over, I will pose for Kopf only toward the end of January.

Please tell Clément that the only thing about my sorry features which interests me is his drawing.

---

58. First appeared in 1845–46 as *Die deutsche Nationalliteratur* . . . and there were subsequent editions.

APPENDIX

(See letter of July 27 [1874?], p. 151)

Here is the extract from my two letters about *la Cosaque*.

"I have not yet read the *Souvenirs* in question; but from what I have heard about them the writer delights in making me look both ridiculous and odious. She and her friends are free to behave according to their good or evil pleasure. To certain scandals, I can only oppose decent silence, which does not sink into the mire and leaves to others the responsibility for their debasement. That *la Cosaque* should excel in decrying me and flaying me with the learned *Nélida* is none of my business. Each of them has in the past written me numerous impassioned letters on the nobility of my character and the uprightness of my feelings. In this I shall not contradict them, and will continue to prize sincerely their remarkable and brilliant talents as artists, writers, and inventors, while regretting that they should turn them so energetically against my poor self. The last volume will serve as a final warning against my mistake in tolerating the artificial excitement of artists in the art of contraband and the blaze of intrusive passion – – –"

Having read the above: "*la Cosaque*, like *Nélida* an interloper, but an incendiary, prowled for whole nights around my lodgings in Rome. My great wrong lies in my having let myself finally be taken in by her make-believe eccentric heroism, by her babble which is not devoid of wit nor of a disconcerting kind of eloquence. She has, moreover, astonishing energy in her work and very rare talent as a pianist. Assuredly, I should have sent her packing immediately after her first avowal and not have yielded to the silly temptation of imagining that I could be of use to her in any way. Little snakes of this kind can only be tamed by riding in coaches with powdered footmen and by flaunting their shame in lodgings adorned with fantastic furniture and tropical plants. Their ideal of happiness is to preen themselves in boxes at the theatre and at orgies in the private rooms of restaurants – – – –

"*Vade retro me, Satana: quoniam non sapis quae Dei sunt*—On such occasions one must resolutely and right away follow the edifying example of St. Thomas Aquinas who, in the castle of St. John, put a woman to flight 'with an incandescent ember.' Unfortunately, my modest Thomist knowledge was not up to the occasion. However, if it were a matter of explaining my conduct before a Court of Honor, even one composed of people prejudiced against me, I would not find it in the least embarrassing to clear myself by correcting, in accordance with the truth, facts and dates repeatedly attested to by the adversary party itself."

I add that the real Robert Franz has written to me in the most decorous manner, asking me to authorize him to protest in the press against the abusive use of his name by the pseudo Franz. I replied that the respectable public would certainly never confuse the author of the lovely *Lieder* and *Gesänge* with the croakings of *la Cosaque*, and that, for my part, I was so enthralled by the former that the Cossack dissonances hardly reached my ears and disturbed them not at all.

January 10
(Villa d'Este)

I am not guilty, though always somewhat under suspicion. A long letter went off from here, on December 29,[1] to Olgh. in which I wrote of Princess Czernicheff, of the admirable bequest by Mme Moukhanoff, of Mme de Schleinitz's "sale," etc., etc. If I omitted the topic of Pest, this is because it has been too much in my thoughts.

We certainly must go ahead with the celebration of the Metzdorff soirée—and twice would be better than once. Make up the program with him ahead of time. Besides the opera, a piece from his symphony (for four hands) and a few of his *Lieder* could figure to advantage at the Carl Alexander Platz, in the presence of Carl Alexander.

You won't be expected at all to "confirm your zeal by laudatory comments." Your reserve will even contribute to the importance of the evening. When the opera is given, we'll be able to indulge together in greater enthusiasm.

Please thank the Grand Duke for having conveyed to me through you the news of Preller's portrait, which was requested for the Gallery in Florence. It will find itself in distinguished company there, and it is an honor for Weimar's artistic renown that one of its most worthy representatives should be there.

I find Lassen's new uniform almost disconcerting, but if it gives him pleasure, I'll put up with it. Meanwhile, I'll pass on the photograph to Adelheid.

1. Actually December 30, not 29, 1874.

Did you see Count Wilczek and attend the lecture on the North Pole expedition?

In one hour I have to leave again for Rome, where Miska is a cause of concern to me. His illness is not very serious, but very painful. He is in despair, weeps and cries. I will perhaps have to go to Pest without him, which will be rather inconvenient for me.

I have just written a few lines to Cosima, asking her to let me know what she has arranged in the way of concerts in Vienna and elsewhere.

I shall in any case be in Pest on February 10.

Yours ever

FL

The weather is so fine that my dinner is served on the terrace.

———

January 15, 75
Villa d'Este

I have had to put Miska in the San Giacomo hospital, and I would very much like to spend a long time there myself. Illness would spare me the bitter pain of causing you distress, dear beloved soul – – – but I must make up my mind to fulfill my duty; it commands me imperiously to suffer for making you suffer, and to say to you, with a grieving heart: stay in Weimar until I return there (in early April). Otherwise, your stay in this town would be aggravated by many sorrows, perplexities, and tribulations against which I could not defend you, nor could I find a remedy for them. Unfortunately, I am well informed on this, and it is not lightly that I brace myself to give you a loyal piece of advice, so much against my wishes, and which makes me feel deeply downcast.

I kiss your hands, and truly remain

Your

FL

———

January 26, 75
(Vicolo de' Greci 43,
until February 8)

I have told you the "why." Don't look for any other than my loyal and devoted solicitude for your peaceful existence, which I beg you not to endanger. Not being able to "defend" you, I want to spare you sordid struggles which sometimes cause the collapse of the strongest characters. If, after several years of intimacy between us of heart and mind, you still entertain any doubt as to the complete purity of my wishes, how can I convince you now? And what words could I find in order to "defend" myself against you yourself? – – –

On February 8 I leave for Pest, where I arrive on the tenth. Cosima writes that Wagner's concert is set there for the twenty-first and in Vienna for March 1.

Yours ever

FL

Your two letters of the nineteenth and twentieth reached me almost together yesterday. I reject your gloomy forecasts, which will not materialize; but you will be generous and help me to fight them.

Sunday, February 7, 75
Rome

I leave here day after tomorrow morning, and expect to arrive in Pest Thursday evening at the latest. The agitation and entertainments of these last two weeks have slightly addled me; like Wolf von Goethe: *stehe ich vor dem Capitol, und weiss nicht was ich sagen soll* ["I stand before the capitol and don't know what to say"].[2] Those I have very much en-

2. In his book of autograph draft letters of 1874 (in the Library of Congress) Liszt quotes this phrase and attributes it to "Wolf. von Goethe, junior," grandson of the poet Johann Wolfgang von Goethe.

joyed seeing frequently are Mmes Minghetti, Bobrinska, Helbig, Chérémétieff (the young and well-known pianist–composer) and M. de Keudell with whom we used to make music in earnest at the Caffarelli palace and elsewhere.

I have promised Princess Bariatinska (Cocona) to play for her this evening the *Vorspiel* and the last pages from *Tristan*[3] – – –

All this doesn't interest you much, and I do wish I could talk to you about the only relevant subject; but, fearing lest I touch this wound clumsily, I forbear—not without sadness and sorrow. Certain sorrows are made worse by thinking about them; one must, as much as possible, resign oneself to bearing them in silence.

Your friend, Princess Czernicheff, asked me again yesterday, through Hannstein, to be sure to convey to you her affectionate thoughts. She is still in the same deplorable crisis condition you know about, and can neither read nor write, nor engage in any form of activity. Princess Cocona goes to see her every day; she is the only person admitted, but without conversation, asserts Hannstein.

In silence too, yours ever from the heart

FL

Miska faces another three or four weeks in the hospital, and will return to Pest only when he has fully recovered. However, I have found both here and at the Villa d'Este people who look after me very well.

Don't worry about my trip. I'll write to you on arrival.

———

February 13, 75
Pest (Fischplatz 4)

A new phase—or rather eclipse. Wagner will very probably go neither to Vienna nor to Pest. After I had wired you yesterday, a letter from Cosima told me of the postponement of the Pest concert until

3. G 447; R 280.

after that of Vienna; but I hear from a good source that both have been postponed until next year. The reason for this postponement is said to be that they dare not guarantee W[agner] a net sum of 10,000 florins in Vienna, and of 5,000 in Pest, as the costs total more than 5,000 or 6,000 florins. However, it may be that in Pest we'll overcome the difficulty, a new formula having emerged. If it succeeds as I wish, I'll wire again in a few days. In the meantime: no unnecessary words, and even less any "defense" whatever!

On my arrival here, I had the surprise of finding the locks of several closets smashed in, and the silver and linen, etc., gone. The thieves are under lock and key, and the police assure me that part of the objects will be restored to me. The only thing I really want back is a fine, solid laurel wreath (made of silver) from Holland, because of the Dutch inscription, the translation of which is as follows: *Dem Helden der Tonkunst, deren Verehrer* [To the Hero of Music, from its admirers]. It was presented to me in Amsterdam in 1866, after a performance of the *Messe de Gran* and of *Psalm 13*, by kind friends previously unknown to me.

As for Miska, he is still in San Giacomo hospital in Rome, too innocent of the robbery committed by one of his habitual cronies here, to whom he liked to show the pretty things which we owned. He may perhaps even have asked him to look after the key of the cupboards.

More soon

FL

If you get on well with Cosima, no more need be said. No other explanations needed.

———

Saturday, February 20, 75
Pest

I'll be arriving April 6 or 7—
Your letter of February 18 has just been handed to me. You stand

once again guilty of Byzantinism; Cosima is perfectly right in telling you that there's no reason for your going to such trouble to look for difficulties where there are none, and I hope that you will understand very simply the telegram which will shortly reach you.

More soon, not in writing

FL

Please tell Grosse that I would like him to keep my money, and to hand it back to me in Weimar.

Thank you for the speeches in the Academy and for the articles on Sainte-Beuve.

———

Tuesday, March 16, 75
Budapest

After your first stay in Pest you were not unhappy with my letters; if I knew how to write in accordance with my heart, you would be even more pleased this time. Truly I am indebted to you for a lovely beam of light. It will never leave me.

The (horn) lorgnette was found in the Hungaria—and will be able to continue to defy all the *Fernröhre* [opera glasses].

Cosima writes that she'll be in Bayreuth tomorrow. The second Vienna concert was a magnificent success; a third will follow toward mid-April. Between Vienna and Pest the total of the net receipts amounts to about 12,000 thalers.

Joseph Rubinstein is going back to Bayreuth and is settling down there permanently until the performance of the *Nibelungen*. People are doing me the honor of assuring me that I have contributed to perfecting both his powerful talent as a pianist, and his comportment.

Herewith the program of the little concert yesterday evening, where Olgh: inspired the *Vortrag* [performance] of Weber's Sonata, played much better by A. Rubinstein. See where vanity likes to lurk! and condone my sadness—at being alive.

Tomorrow I shall write to M. S[ach], and ask you to convey to him my deep attachment.

Yesterday evening, Count Zichy told me that the Duke of Ossuna used to send birthday greeting telegrams of more than two hundred words to his father-in-law (Count Karácsonyi). In contrast, I am so boorish as to be barely able to entrust more than a couple of lines to the mail.

Your

FL

Your letter reached me yesterday evening.

March 23, 75

Budapest

The postscript of your last letter follows wonderfully the magic thread of the little speech which moved me so much here. From it hang FL's dreams and his *intimate* music.

The *Walküre-Wallfahrt* (ohne Ritt!) [The *Walküre* Pilgrimage (without the Ride)] at Gotha was entirely appropriate. Likewise the prompt dispatch of the fur-lined cap with the dedication message in French. When the next opportunity arises, it will be the turn of the third of the *Patronatschein* for Peterle. How did it happen that the *Walküren Abend* was not given in Weimar? Is Loën nodding like the good Homer?

Day before yesterday I wrote to M. Sach to thank him for his message and for the messenger. She will scold me for arriving too late at the Hofgärtnerei – – – but I can't arrange things otherwise in spite of my strong desire to do so. Instead of going straight from Vienna to Weimar as I had intended, I shall have to go via Munich and spend four or five days there because of the performance of the *Christus Oratorium* set for

Monday, April 12. Please assure Mme Merian that I insisted as much as my customary reserve in such cases permits, that she and M. and Mme Milde should be asked to sing the *soli*.

From April 1 to 7 I shall be in Vienna (Schottenhof); from the eighth to the thirteenth, in Munich, when FL will be scolded *viva voce* for all his misdeeds and shortcomings.

I spent several hours with Rubinstein yesterday and today. This morning he rehearsed his Fifth Concerto,[4] and his new dramatic Symphony[5] which has been performed at Petersburg, Leipzig, and Vienna, and is published by Senff in Leipzig. These will be performed tomorrow at the Richter concert, when Mihalovich will also present his *Ballade Symphonique: Sello*. On Thursday, Rubinstein is giving a piano concert; I enclose both programs herewith. The performance of Rubinstein's *Les Macchabées*[6] has been announced in Berlin for April 15. The text of the libretto follows the tragedy of Otto Ludwig. Read it; it is worthwhile. In the second act, there is a pagan love lesson (a duet). The gentleman ardently supports the theory of practical happiness advocated by the lady; the music is graceful, persuasive, even elegant, but quite naturally happiness collapses promptly (in the third act), and the gentleman, in order to extricate himself honorably, has no other recourse than to burn himself alive, without the lady, The main female role—not that of the professor of erotic love, but that of the mother, whose stern tenderness defies the stake and whose stern example draws her son to it, is to be sung by Mlle Brandt; Judas Maccabeus by Bey.

Before the end of April, Rubinstein, who will be conducting the performance of *Les Macchabées* in Berlin, will go to Paris to conduct his Oratorio (or Biblical Opera), *Le Tour de Babel*,[7] twice at the Théâtre Italien. Thereafter he returns to Peterhof, where his American trip has provided him with a property worth 200,000 francs. His wife and children live there, and he will this summer compose, in the bosom of his

---

4. Opus 94.
5. Opus 95.
6. A sacred opera, first performed April 17, 1875, in Berlin.
7. Opus 80.

family, his new opera *Néron*,[8] the French text of which was furnished to him by Barbier.

Rubinstein very ingeniously explained to me Chopin's first sonata (in B flat minor)[9] by Heine's *Tragödie*.[10] I'll tell you about this soon—after having been scolded.

Your

FL

April 3, 75
Vienna

I am more put out than you think at postponing Weimar for a week. Instead of arriving on the seventh—for the birthday of the G[rand] D[uchess]—I'll only be there on the fifteenth—and you will give me a double scolding right away, for I have to go to Hanover on April 23 in honor of my old friend Bronsart (I'll explain the rest to you by word of mouth), and on May 2 I am due at Loo castle.[11] So many displacements are doubtless not suitable at my age. When someone has shown me how to remain quiet honorably, I'll take advantage of this at once with total satisfaction and gratitude.

Cosima writes that because of the King's illness, the audition of extracts from the *Nibelungen* (in Munich) has been postponed, as well as the performance of *Tristan*. Thus Wagner will not be coming to Munich now; Cosima is taking her two elder daughters to Dresden on April 8. She will enter them there for two or three years in a *Stift* [educational institution], whose name escapes me. A few days later she accompanies Wagner to Berlin, where his concert is set for April 24.

Thank you for the *Débats* with the speech by Hugo, and Reyer's arti-

8. First performed November 1, 1879, in Hamburg.
9. Actually his second, Opus 35.
10. *Tragödien, nebst einem lyrischen Intermezzo* (Berlin, 1823).
11. Residence of Willem III, king of the Netherlands.

cle on Massenet's *Eve*,[12] César Franck's *La Rédemption*,[13] and Pfeiffer's *Agar*.[14] When the time comes, we shall give ourselves the pleasure of playing four hands one or the other of these works.

Don't remove the Steinway from the Carl Alexander Platz. I have no use for it at the Hofgärtnerei, and will ask Bechstein to send me as usual one of his *Flügel* [grand pianos].

In Victor Hugo's speech at Quinet's funeral, we read: "In our time, human thought has many peaks; among these peaks Quinet was a summit"!

FL has no such ambitions and would be very happy if you would be willing to consider him as the very docile sheep of your valley.

FL

I will give Metzdorff your very reassuring little message.
On the evening of April 8 (Thursday), I go to Munich.

———

Thursday, April 8, 75
Vienna

I have had no word from Steinway, and your telegram surprised me a little. As the piano is already back at the Hofgärtnerei, the only thing to do is to leave it there (in view of the trouble of moving it on those stairs), but I would have preferred it to remain quietly with you, and could very well have done without a piano for the first week. Should the Bechstein arrive before me, please be so good as to request of Grosse that it <u>not</u> be unpacked; two grand pianos clutter up my apartment. We'll decide how to arrange matters when I'm back; so long as the Bechstein is not a nuisance to you, I very humbly offer it to you. In all matters, I try to simplify, not complicate things.

12. An oratorio or sacred drama, 1875.
13. A choral work for voices and orchestra, the first version first performed April 10, 1873, in Paris.
14. An oratorio.

Tomorrow morning I'll be in Munich, Hôtel Marienbad. You will please me by writing to tell me how the festivities on April 8 went off!

Is the Grand Duchess in good health? Was there a large reception? Did they give Götz's *Widerspänstige*,[15] which I heard here? It is really good music, entirely to be recommended as such, but in my humble opinion this comedy by Shakespeare scarcely lends itself to operatic treatment. The sparkling wit of the dialogue is lost in the music, and the scenes themselves are of little interest. Furthermore, in spite of the musical talent of the composer, the work seems to drag and verges on the boring. I'm well aware that people are at their wits' end where to turn for a libretto, but is it really so essential to write scores for the stage? Couldn't young and old musicians find a better way to spend their time?

I saw Metzdorff again here; he conducted *The Merry Wives of Windsor*[16] and *Lohengrin* quite successfully, and his chances of being appointed *Kapellmeister* seem good—unless the new Director, chosen in order to put an end to the current theatrical crisis, has someone else up his sleeve.

Herewith a brief passage excerpted from your last letter but one, which almost confused me. Fortunately all will be cleared up at the Hofgärtnerei in a week's time, and to our mutual satisfaction, I hope.

Yours ever

FL

If possible, I'll arrive Wednesday next—at the latest, Thursday.

15. *Der Widerspänstigen Zähmung* (*The Taming of the Shrew*), opera, first performed October 11, 1874, in Mannheim.
16. *Die lustigen Weiber von Windsor*, opera by Otto Nicolai, first performed March 9, 1849, in Berlin.

April 27, 75
(Hanover)

Friday, my route went through Sondershausen—of happy and peaceful memory, in spite of the too long-drawn-out conversations of our friend Gille. A lovely echo of those hours lives on in my heart; and the turret of Sond[ershausen] castle turned my mind gently to Klein R[oop]. Keep the watercolor of it in your room so as to show it to me more often after my return.

Here, I am staying with Bronsart, whom I have esteemed highly and been fond of for many a year. His character is of the finest temper. The ill-bred accuse him of haughtiness, a fitting reproach from those who willingly do without dignity and distinction.

The sight of *L'Univers* is always pleasing to me, and I thank you for supplying it to me, even in Hanover. Did you see the article with cutting praise of the Princes of Orléans?

The illustration of the umbrella, the omnibuses, and hackney carriages utilized by the Orléans Princes of today is not without grandeur. Whatever one's opinion may be—and mine unfortunately differs markedly from that of Veuillot—fairness commands that one admire a great talent at the service of a cause which could be lost only by the behavior of those representing it. Speaking of which, you may recall our conversations in Rome, and my deep respect for the Count de Chambord, steadfastly loyal to his faith in the divine right of kings – – –.

In the preceding article by Veuillot there is, among others, a witty phrase: "The Devil too has his martyrology, which is very long and very bitter." It was Pascal who said: "So many people damn themselves so stupidly"!

The *Elisabeth* was even more applauded here (Saturday evening) than in Cassel. Several people assure me that such a success is very rare indeed in Hanover. Tomorrow is the concert for the monument to Bach. Herewith the program.

On May 2 I shall be at Loo castle—near Arnhem, Holland. There will be no lack of "phonetics." Among the guests will be: Ambroise

Thomas, Gevaert, Wieniawski, and the painters Portaels, Hamman, Rochussen, ten Kate, and Hemmschenk.

Please give me news of Mme and M. Sach, and of our Weimar.

Yours ever with all my heart

FL

Briefe aus Rom[17] tell me of the stay there of an *âme de roses et de lys* [a soul of roses and lilies] whom you have not entirely considered to be such.

Monday, May 3, Loo Castle

You will greatly oblige me by continuing to discharge zealously and accurately your important functions of impresario for the Moukhanoff concert. With this in mind, please get together with Lassen, Mme Merian, Mlle Dotter, and the prima donna who will be doing us the favor of singing the trio of *Le Réveil de l'enfant*. Also please settle now the date of the concert, between the two performances of *Tristan*, in full agreement with Loën, Count Beust, or Count Wedel—and, after having made all arrangements with Their Excellencies, have the Grand Duke agree to, and confirm them. The day after my return we will settle together the contents of the program, which will have to be printed. Mme Milde is always extremely pleasant toward me, but I don't know whether it will suit her to put herself out for something as slight as a portion of the trio; and since Mme Merian has agreed to sing a few *Lieder* by Lassen and Mihalovich, the program includes no other *Lieder* for soprano. Lassen will be so kind as to remind M. de Milde that he promised me to recruit in my behalf Bouhers, the second tenor, and the second bass for the first piece of my *Requiem*.[18] Immediately after my return we shall rehearse with these gentlemen and ladies.

17. *Briefe aus Rom über die Aufklärung von Zakharia, päpstlichen Geheimschreiber an seine geistlichen Freunde. Hrsg. von einem Protestanten* (Frankfurt-Leipzig, 1785).
18. G 12; R 488.

Is there an adequate harmonium to be found in Weimar, or will we have to obtain one elsewhere?

Thank you for having already provided Mme Kovachi with the part for harp of the hymn. Please add to it that of the *Elégie*,[19] as soon as the music arrives from Rome.

I'm most comfortably settled here since yesterday morning. The King received me most graciously. He is remarkably well informed on matters of music and painting. The dinner conversation (no ladies present) was very lively indeed, and filled with racy Parisian anecdotes by Ambroise Thomas, Portaels, Hamman, and others, which I'll tell you about another time. Gevaert is expected. This evening, there will be the first of the concerts, for which His Majesty's pensioners provide the programs. These subsidies and concerts set a fine example and deserve to be imitated more elsewhere. Few sovereigns have the good taste to indulge in little pleasures of such a noble kind.

I thank you for the Porges article and await *L'Univers* and the *Débats*, thanks to your munificence, at Loo, where there are only English and Dutch newspapers. The local *Beust* (Baron Fugel) kindly informed me yesterday that the matter of my forthcoming departure should not be taken up with the King – – – –

Could not Loën or Wedel invite Wagner for the *Tristan*? In any case tell Cosima that I wish her to attend the Moukhanoff concert.

Your

FL

I am writing to M. Sach and sending him Hillebrand's letter.

At Alexander Platz I will tell you about a very gracious gesture toward me by the King yesterday morning. Short of being boorish, this places me under an obligation.

———

19. G 130; R 471.

May 7, 75
Loo

Being very convinced that your ideas are always the best, I beg of you to follow them up completely for the benefit of the program of our matinée in commemoration of Mme Moukhanoff.

We'll talk about this in full agreement, Tuesday or Wednesday next, at the Alexander Platz.

For today, I only dare ask of you that you wire me (exceptionally!) which is the shortest road from Loo (Arnhem) to Weimar? People here have been able to give only rather vague information.

Do please have someone ask kind M. Marshall what, in order to arrive quickly, will have to be done by

Your very eager servant

FL

Herewith the first program of the daily, very brilliant performances at Loo.

M. S[ach] was good enough to recall me by telegram.

July 27, 75
Wilhelmsthal

Berlioz used to take offense when people assumed that he listened to Beethoven's sublime last quartets "for his own pleasure." Nor is it for the sake of pleasure that one goes on living. However, Frederick, the Great seems to have found the clue to the riddle when he said: "One must find one's pleasure in doing one's duty." One can philosophize and quibble about this; for, if duty is easy to define in the case of tradesmen, innkeepers, and the man in the street, it sometimes becomes hard to define within ourselves, since it also implies rights. Now this equilibrium between rights and duties remains the philosopher's stone of the human species, which only the catechism leads to heavenly salvation, and to relative rest, in this earthly life.

Wilhelmsthal was most animated this weekend. Mlle de Watzdorf will give you details. Day before yesterday we celebrated here and at the Wartburg the twenty-third anniversary of the birth of the Hereditary Grand Duchess. She and her husband, her sisters-in-law, and the Grand Duke leave today for Ostend and Blankenberghe. Mme S[ach] is to spend the month of August at Heinrichsau.

I am reading with great interest the first volume of Schuré's *Drame musical*,[20] which contains one hundred eloquent and impassioned dithyrambic pages on Greece. On page sixty-one is this little passage: "For us, no doubt, the man Jesus is the necessary complement to the god Apollo. What Greece did not yet know is the principle of human sympathy pushed to the point of effacement of self. The highest civilization of which the human mind can dream today would be that in which Apollo and Jesus could join hands, in which Beauty and Love could together hold sway."

I leave it to Capnisz to convey this kind of thing to Rome.

Day after tomorrow, I'll stop off briefly at Liebenstein at the Stahrs and once again express my grateful homage to the Duke of Saxe-Meiningen. Herewith the postscript of the last note from F. L. Stahr. Count Wedel, whom I am pleased to appreciate better because of our similar sentiments with regard to Bayreuth (including Schuré's book), will come with me as far as Liebenstein.

Sunday I stop in Nuremberg, in honor of my valiant and earnest biographer, Mlle Lina Ramann. The following day I'll be in Bayreuth, where I ask you to write to me until August 15.

I still have not received a letter from Hillebrand. Almost a scolding (for O.) for the absence of an address on the letter from M. Sach to Tolstoy, which was returned and handed back to its illustrious author.

Always very humbly

Your

FL

20. *Le Drame musical* (Paris, 1875).

My cordial affection to Peterle and Mimi, and my recommendations to Clément and Sachi that they sketch properly the lovely landscapes at Rippoldsau.

———

August 3, 75
Bayreuth

M. Sach left Wilhelmsthal for Ostend last Wednesday; his daughters and the heirs preceded him at Blankenberghe by twenty-four hours.

My poor self arrived here Thursday (my appointments at Liebenstein and at Nuremberg having fallen through because of Stahr having caught a cold which kept him in bed); soon after, at five o'clock, an enthusiastic rehearsal of the gods and goddesses, heroes and heroines, mythical and human personages represented by Betz (Wotan), Mme Grün (Frika), Unger (Siegfried), Scaria (Hagen), Mme Materna (Brunhilde), etc., etc.

Friday, continuation of vocal rehearsals with piano accompaniment by Joseph Rubinstein, in the same spacious and glorious halls of Wahnfried.

Wagner has had inscribed high up on his house the distych:

Hier, wo mein Wähnen Frieden fand,
Wahnfried sei dies Haus von mir benannt.[21]

Saturday morning, rest, and at five o'clock in the *Halle* (vestibule) of the drawing room where rehearsals take place, a grand feast, to which were invited Wotan, Frika, Brunhilde, and their consorts, totaling more than twenty seats at table.

Sunday, five o'clock, solemn inauguration of the orchestra rehearsals in the new theatre. As Wagner enters, Wotan's sublime melody resounds. Richter is conducting. Wilhelmj leads the violins. My old friend Grosse distinguishes himself (even though invisible) with an F and an E flat, in the low bass:

21. "Here, where my madness found peace, / Let this house be named by me Wahnfried."

 on the bass trombone.

Until August 15 there will be two rehearsals daily, and I shall stay through the last chord. Mme de Schleinitz has similar intentions. She arrived Monday, and is staying at the castle. This is creating a sensation in town, for this castle has not been inhabited in many years. Rumor has it that King Ludwig will come here before the rehearsals are over. This would be a glorious event, but Cosima knows nothing about it and doesn't think it very likely.

I immediately put to Mme de Schleinitz the question about Tolstoy's address. She doesn't know it. Fortunately Mme Eckert, who is here with her husband, is willing to help me. She has just been spending several weeks at Karlsbad with Tolstoy, and yesterday wired to a friend of hers, who promises to send her the desired address. Herewith her friend's telegram, and tomorrow I'll send you the final outcome of our efforts.

Hillebrand's letter to Your Highness reached me, and I think I returned it to you. Furthermore, Hill[ebrand] has written to me favorably about our concert idea at Weimar; only he postpones its fruition until next year. M. and Mme Sach will decide.

The portrait which M. Sach mentioned to you is of Mme Moukhanoff, of which a photograph was recently taken at Weimar from the admirable painting by Lenbach, which shone on our musical commemoration at the *Tempelherrnhaus*. The photograph is remarkably successful, and I urge you to thank M. S[ach] for it, and to place it, framed, in your Carl Alexander Platz turret.

Cosima tells me that you saw last year the graceful drawing room (now adorned with many works of art and souvenirs) which I occupy at Wahnfried. Spiridion exclaims thus: *Questo è veramente re[g]ale* [This is truly regal].

The sight of the *Débats* and *L'Univers* gladdened me, and I hope soon to take up again their perusal in your company—very selfishly.

I'll bring back to you the piano version of *Gretchen*,[22] which I wrote yesterday morning.

With all my heart, your

FL

Saturday, August 30, 75
Hanover

The publisher of the *Hymne de l'enfant à son réveil* and of *St. François de Paule*[23] writes that these two pieces have been sent off to Weimar. Have you received them? Will you be so kind as to confer with Lassen and Mme Merian about the distribution of the three parts? I fear that Mme Spohr may find this hymn too slight, but I will be all the more grateful to her for embellishing it with her voice, and beg our friend Lassen to ask this kindness of her in my behalf, as well as Mlle Dotter, who will probably take the third part (the lowest). As soon as I'm back I shall hasten to thank the three obliging singers, and to rehearse with them.

The Rome music is on its way and may have already arrived at your house.

Hillebrand has replied in the most friendly and charming manner. I will send his letter to M. Sach day after tomorrow, and will add to it a couple of lines from Loo castle. The train which leaves tonight will deliver me at Arnhem tomorrow at nine in the morning; from there it takes another three hours by carriage to reach His Majesty's residence.

Hillebrand's new book *Zeiten, Völker und Menschen*[24] will keep me company en route most agreeably. I will soon bring it back to you and think that you will find much in it to your taste.

There is nothing more ingeniously phrased than the savage attack on

22. The 2nd movement of his *Faust* symphony, G 513; R 180.
23. G 175, 2; R 17, 2.
24. (Berlin, 1875–86) (7 vols.).

the *Revue bleue*, "pure, solemn, and suffering," by Veuillot. However, FL would not swear that he is completely free of "garotinisme" (see the explanation of this neologism by Veuillot, in La Fontaine's fable of the pumpkin).[25] Sometimes acorns well prepared by modern science seem to him to be nourishing food; and pumpkins high up on oak trees would not spoil the landscape. The only thing is not to stick out one's nose as they fall.

Even more than Veuillot, Olgh. excels in the way she depicts "roses and lilies" and in the delicate philosophical analysis of the "sweet impression" created by associating with such lovely flowers grouped together. Olgh. has written an entrancing page on the subject; it amply makes up for the ill-temper of the double flowers, whose perfume asphyxiates.

Your favorable forecasts for the Bach Concert were fulfilled; Bronsart will tomorrow send somewhat more than 2,000 thalers to the Bach Monument Committee at Eisenach.

Impossible to write more today.

Till soon

FL

I hardly dare ask Cosima to come to our Moukhanoff matinée; but wish she would. Write her to this effect, and ask them to put up with *Tristan* at Weimar.

———

Thursday morning, September 16, 75
Nuremberg

One of my old friends, Ferdinand David, has composed a symphony on Goethe's poem: *Verschiedene Empfindungen an einem Platz*. Although I have forgotten this poem I was perfectly prepared to compose it anew, and more, day before yesterday evening at Leipzig, and yesterday as I passed through Lichtenfels.

25. *Le Gland et la Citrouille* (The Acorn and the Pumpkin).

One hour after your departure, I attended the performance of the *Folkunger*[26] in the director's box of M. Hase—a box which has on various occasions been favored with the presence of M. Sach and of his Gotha and Meiningen cousins. The Leipzig audience, exceptionally, took pleasure in applauding the *Folkunger* very loudly, and in giving a curtain call after each act to the singers and to the composer M. Kretschmer, to whom someone also threw a laurel wreath.

The work has already been performed some fifteen times at Dresden, and I am told that fifteen theatres are planning to give it. Nonetheless, I greatly doubt that it will have a real success, for neither the libretto (very unsuccessful, in my opinion) nor the score is powerful enough to sustain it. The poet and the musician have attempted to decoct and amalgamate Meyerbeer's *Le Prophète*[27] and Wagner's *Lohengrin*. It's a waste of labor. It would have been easier to achieve the fusion of the younger and the elder branches of the Bourbons. Moreover, the *Kapellmeister* at Leipzig, Gustav Schmidt (a native of Weimar, where two of his operas have been performed) once said to me naïvely: "Aside from Wagner, no one achieves success at the theatre any more."

The *Folkunger* will probably soon be resting next to *Golo*,[28] which was so much appreciated at Weimar and Nuremberg; but it does not follow that one should give up performing new works. Quite the contrary, and I insist on contemporary composers being granted their share in a spirit of intelligent generosity. So please recommend once again Metzdorff's *Rosamunde* and Saint-Saëns' *Samson*[29] to M. de Loën, at the risk of neither of them achieving the hoped-for success. Above all, one must guard against inertia in the theatre and elsewhere.

Leaving here tomorrow, your FL will arrive in Rome Sunday evening or Monday morning.

Send me news of your "quartet."

26. *Die Folkunger*, opera by Edmund Kretschmer, first performed March 21, 1874, in Dresden.
27. This opera was first performed April 16, 1849, in Paris.
28. Opera by Bernhard Scholz, first performed April 4, 1875, in Nuremberg.
29. *Samson et Dalila*, first performed December 2, 1877, in Weimar.

Friday, September 24, 75
Rome

Nuremberg to Munich takes five hours. Spiridion being rather unwell, I spent last Friday night at the Hôtel Marienbad, haunted by Mme
Moukhanoff's ghost. Next day, having attended mass at the basilica of
St. Boniface (which I am fond of because of its restful and harmonious
architecture), I took the train again at nine in the morning and arrived
here Sunday evening at six-thirty. This thirty-three-hour trip was free
of incidents. A pamphlet, which I recommend to you, was excellent
company: Goethe's *Unterhaltungen mit dem Kanzler Friedrich von Müller,
herausgegeben von C. A. H. Burckhardt* [Conversations with Chancellor
Friedrich von Müller, edited by C. A. H. Burckhardt] (at this moment
still in Weimar).

I have never been an excessive admirer of the conventional image of
Goethe: an idol, whose worship has become far too convenient for
slackers; but Napoleon I was right to call the real Goethe "a great man
in his own land," and to honor him by showing him attention.

Many thoughts in these *Unterhaltungen* are pertinent and will please
you; among others this one from the year 1830, June 6: *Weimar war gerade nur dadurch interessant, dass nirgends ein Centrum war. Es lebten be-
deutende Menschen hier, die sich nicht miteinander vertrugen; das war das Be-
lebenste aller Verhältnisse, regte an und erhielt jedem seine Freiheit. Jetzt fin-
den wir hier kaum 6 Menschen, die zusammen in einen geselligen Kreis passten
und sich unterhalten könnten, ohne einander zu stören.*[30] (Page 141.)

Other good maxims: *Mit Briefantworten muss man nolens volens Banke-
rott machen, und nur unter der Hand diesen oder jenen Creditor befriedigen.*[31]

---

30. "Weimar was only interesting because it lacked a center. Important persons were
living here who disagreed with one another; it was the most invigorating of all relation-
ships, it stimulated and preserved for each his freedom. Now we find here scarcely six
persons who would be congenial in a social circle and who could converse without annoying each other."

31. One must willy-nilly declare bankruptcy as regards replies to letters and quietly
satisfy this or that creditor.

Auch den Verdruss muss man sich zu Nutze machen, denn er ist ja ein Theil und zwar ein grosses des Lebens.[32]

In 1823 a Polish lady, Mme Szymanowska, a charming pianist whom I often used to see and hear at the Erard house in Paris (in '24 or '25), made a great impression on Goethe. You will find details of this on page seventy-three.

Here is another saying which pleased me particularly: *Byron allein lasse ich neben mir gelten! Walter Scott ist nichts neben ihm.*[33]

Goethe often comes back, with an accent of exceptional admiration, to Byron, who dedicated his *Sardanapalus* to him (unless I am mistaken) as the homage of a "vassal to his sovereign lord."

Thank you for the Chateaubriand article which Veuillot has superbly carved in the rock of St. Peter.

N.B. Since your subscription to *L'Univers* lapses now, please renew it only next April; but when there is some article under *Variétés* in the *Débats* which you think to my taste, send it to me.

Princess W[ittgenstein] is in fairly good health, and much absorbed in a huge work in five or six volumes, of nearly one thousand pages each.

With all my heart, your

FL

I'll be spending another week here. Please write to 43 Vicolo de' Greci; and, at Baden-Baden, don't forget the academic (in the sense of Cl. Antonelli) conversation with Nohl and Pohl. I await hearing from you about it.

None of my fashionable acquaintances are in Rome at this time.

---

32. One must also turn vexation to one's advantage, for it is a part, indeed a great part of life.

33. Only Byron do I consider as being on my level! In comparison to him Walter Scott is nothing.

Monday, September 27, 75
Rome

Your telegram of yesterday is an admonition. Having received it only about three o'clock, I fear that the reply will no longer have reached you in Weimar, and the letter I sent off Friday probably also runs the risk of reaching you only at Baden. I am a little to blame in all this, I agree, but not much. My impressions of Rome do not make me very loquacious: I always need a few days to settle down again to my usual state of mind.

Fortunately I found Princess W[ittgenstein] in fairly good health, and almost in good spirits. She spends all her time at her work, which is expanding indefinitely, and grows yearly in length, breadth, height, and depth. A few printed pages (in proof) which she passed on to me seem to me very remarkable.

Her daughter will perhaps turn up unexpectedly during my stay here.

On Thursday, or Saturday at the latest, I'll return to the Villa d'Este, where I hope no longer to deserve reproaches for being a lazy correspondent.

As for news, I have but one sad thing to tell you today: Mlle Wenzel, who arrived with Mlle Rielke two days after me, is in a very alarming condition: she coughs up blood increasingly, and if this goes on, one will have to take the step of having her cared for in the German nursing home (on the Capitol), for in her small lodging she would suffer too much from a lack of things an invalid needs, and from excessive expenses.

Moreover, she has the idea that she is about to die, and in moments of crisis calls frantically on death to come as soon as possible.

The drawing room crowd returns to Rome only in October or November. My present company is limited to Zarembski (who has a room next to mine), Pinelli, Blum, and Sgambati. The latter has written three charming French songs on poems by Mme Hugo, the great Victor's niece, who has quarreled with her husband and has been living in Rome since last winter. Sgambati has also composed a second Grand Quintet[34] for piano and stringed instruments. I have asked him to let me hear it, as well as the first one which has been played several times, and of which I think almost as highly as of the Symphony[35] by Borodin, of tender recollection.

By the way, I have written to Riedel (but without throwing my arms around him!) to say that I particularly want one or two orchestral works by the new Russian composers—Rimsky, Tchaikovsky, Cui, Borodin—to figure on the program of the *Musikfest* at Altenburg next May. Should they fail to please at the first hearing, we will play them again—until people understand and applaud them.

Truly yours

FL

Tell me about Metzdorff and Nohl; write to 43 Vicolo de' Greci: it's quickest, even for the Villa d'Este.

October 7 [1875?]
Villa d'Este

You did not catch the (somewhat subtle) point of my recent quotations from His Excellency Goethe. It was a way of keeping Weimar alive, the *Fahnen Weihen*, the *Walkürenritt*, the Borodin symphonies, and other pieces we read. May your very understanding view of life forgive me for thus lingering on, and for these ties with the past. One could argue about this, but "to love is to understand."

Since Saturday evening, here I am settled down again in solitude at the Villa d'Este. This spot pleases me above others, and I am deeply grateful to Cardinal Hohenlohe for having put me here—like the solitary sparrow in the psalm. Music, the most communicative of the arts,

34. Opus 5.
35. No. 1, in E flat major.

is also the most lonely for those who plumb its depths. Beethoven tells us this sublimely in his last years.

Did I tell you about Tolstoy's ballad, translated by Mme Pawloff [Pavlova]: *Der blinde Sänger?*[36] He sings, thinking that people are listening to him, but the king and his suite were somewhere else, enjoying themselves. He was singing, what matter whether he was being listened to? I am writing an accompaniment to this ballad (in the manner of that of *Leonore* [*Lenore*][37] and of *Der traurige Mönch*).[38] Should Tolstoy return to Weimar I shall ask him if he will recite his ballad at your house, and will take the liberty of accompanying him myself.

So, in the near future *Rosamunde* by Metzdorff (who would be well advised not to draw too much attention to himself by speaking Russian) and in April *Samson* by Saint-Saëns—projects possibly doomed to failure, as part of activity necessary to the theatre.

Thank you for the *Revue*: Russia, *Elvira*, Italy, *Zerlina*, and Austria, *Donna Anna* (page 452) are well met in the arms of Don Juan Bismarck.

Thank you also for the *Débats* with the articles on Vinet and Hyacinthe. To compare Vinet with Pascal seems to me somewhat excessive in spite of the alleged very fine thoughts. As for Hyacinthe who, without his Carmelite habit, impressed you merely as a mediocrity, Princess Wittgenstein told me recently that he has only drawn back the better to leap, and to return at the propitious time, with greater effect, to the fold of the Holy Roman Church, in which, without a bleat, remains that timid and peaceful sheep,

Your very humble

FL

Being very confident of your almost pedantic conscientiousness with regard to Nohl and Pohl, I accept your good offices and call for them in the event – – – of my not succeeding.

---

36. Liszt set this poem as a recitation with piano: G 350; R 658.
37. G 346; R 654.
38. G 348; R 656.

October 17, 75
Rome

I approve entirely of all your arrangements and entertainments (including the races) at Baden. There is nothing more appropriate than to mingle with that high society to which you belong. Its faults and failings are not basically different from those of other levels of society. They come from human nature, which is everywhere much the same and imperfect. A little girl from a bourgeois family could have been just as astonished as was the daughter of Louis XVI at the fact that her maid had, like her, five fingers on her hand. The seven cardinal sins apply no less to democracy than to aristocracy; but the latter retains many advantages in status, form, and attitude, which it would be unseemly not to admit. It washes itself, clothes itself, disguises itself, feeds itself, houses itself, walks and dances better than do people who have to make greater effort than merely being born in order to make their way.

As in the case of great thoughts, true nobility springs from the heart. Aristocrats have not been found wanting in this, and their glory will now be to follow the road of the great examples of gallantry and intelligence of their ancestors.

So it is not exactly due to boorishness that I sometimes permit myself to make certain comments to you (concerning the too facile praise of the *Le Barbier de Séville*[39] or *Don Giovanni*,[40] and the too banal desire to see Prince Bismarck – – –).

Certain conversational phrases used even in very high circles strike me as the equivalent of repeated sneezes, which one should rather apologize for than indulge in.

I am pleased that you saw M. Sach again at Baden without any unnecessary fuss. No one appreciates his superior and charming qualities more than I.

An Italian newspaper (of yesterday evening) announces the marriage

39. Opera by Rossini, first performed (as *Almaviva*) February 20, 1816, in Rome.
40. Opera by Mozart, first performed (as *Il Dissoluto punito, o sia Il D. Giovanni*) October, 29 1787, in Prague.

of Princess Marie of Saxe-Weimar with Prince Reuss, German ambassador at Petersburg. Do you know anything about this? Despite a few small problems of etiquette, it should be a well-matched marriage.

Having spent a couple of weeks at the Villa d'Este (and having just about completed Tolstoy's ballad), I returned here yesterday and will be staying until October 23.

Thank you for the *Débats* and the *Revue*. The article on Catholic Congresses with the quotations from Montalembert certainly interests me very much. If "liberal Catholicism" is looked upon in Rome like the snows of yesteryear, it nevertheless does not seem to be losing ground elsewhere, and I know some extremely intelligent people who are convinced of its ultimate victory—which I hardly flatter myself that I shall see in my lifetime.

I'm sending off to you an issue of *Le Figaro* with the article on Fanny Lear,[41] the great current scandal. You may perhaps be tempted to order from Brussels Fanny Lear's book, now banned in Paris; they say the author has been expelled. Also, Alexandre Dumas' letter, *Tuez les* [Tue-la!], which is, to say the least, most curious.

Your own

FL

The Bobrinskis are back; I shall see them tomorrow.

October 24, 75
V. d'Este

Owing to the negligence of the post office or of my excellent Ercole (custodian of the Villa d'Este) the pleasure of receiving your very charming letter of October 13 was delayed until yesterday evening,

41. Pseudonym of Mrs. Harriet Ely Blackford. *Le Roman d'une Américaine en Russie, accompagné de lettres originales* (Brussels, 1875), recounts her romance with the Grand Duke Nicholas of Russia. Cf. *The Scandalous Mrs. Blackford*, by Harnett Thomas Kane with Victor Leclerc (New York, 1951).

whereas those of the 17th and 18th had reached me in Rome. Your reply has anticipated my question concerning the marriage of Princess Marie; it seems to me a happy one, and properly in keeping with the conventions of our times, though the House of Weimar is a good deal like that of the Bourbons, of which M. de Talleyrand used to say that it could marry only beneath itself. Do you already know the date of the wedding? Please tell me, and I will send my very humble and sincere congratulations to the Grand Duchess. Like you, I think that the daily life of an ambassador's wife provides more pleasure than being the ruler of a small country.

What sad news! While I was composing his ballad, *Der blinde Sänger*, our friend Tolstoy was breathing his last!

A letter to Princess W[ittgenstein] from a niece of Countess Tolstoy says that death in no way disfigured the features of the noble poet and generous human being whom we loved. As he was being placed in his coffin, his face was radiant with the calmness of eternity; it expressed a celestial satisfaction and seemed to be bidding those present to share in the peace of Our Lord.

When I get back to Rome (November 3) I'll ask Mme Bobrinska for the Russian title of Tolstoy's ballad; and if it is published, I'll send it to you. My accompaniment was written for a German translation (a copy) by Mme Pavlova. It has probably been printed, but I don't know where.

Allow me to scold you a little for being persistently unfair to yourself. In spite of your assertions, I don't much believe in your total lack of kindness, since I am aware of many proofs of your good will, obligingness, and even willingness to help. It's only that, contrary to the common herd which affects qualities it does not possess, you pride yourself on a fault which you lack. Let's settle things amicably, and say that you detest twaddle and falseness; also perhaps that your nose likes to exaggerate its natural propensity toward higher things. However, at heart your individuality remains very deeply stamped with good will, which reveals itself in good company by unfeigned kindness. Even more than cleanliness, kindness is a duty.

Since you have confidence in my recommendations, I renew the one pertaining to the Litanies of Mgr Isoard's book of prayers.[42] Repeat them from time to time with me in mind.

[unsigned]

———

[October 1875?]

Isoard will be preaching, this Lent [i.e., 1876], at the church of St. Louis des Français, at Rome. I have just read a little book by him: *La Vie chrétienne*,[43] which I do not urge you to acquire, however praiseworthy it may be. The Bishop of Nancy wrote to the author: "The respect you have for the public, and that which the subject deserves, have conferred on your approach a solemnity and fullness which will be noted by careful readers, and will make them go back to what they have read, and know how to linger there to let it sink in more deeply."

Formerly you were interested in the endless question of the Jesuits, and you used to ask me to suggest a work to you which encompassed the whole range of the ideas and practices of the illustrious "Company of Jesus." I am reading one now (published this year in Paris—two volumes costing 7 francs, by Sandoz and Fischbacher, 33 rue de Seine), entitled *The Jesuits*,[44] by J. Huber (professor of Catholic theology at the University of Munich), translated by Alfred Marchand. The spirit of this book is certainly strongly opposed to the Jesuits and to Catholicism as it is taught *ex cathedra* in Rome, for already on page fifty-nine of the first volume, we learn that "the Catholic Church of today betrays in its entirety the stamp of Jesuitism, which is nothing but papism carried to its extreme consequences"; and shortly thereafter one reads, on page 65: "Just like the Roman Church, the Society of Jesus is on its way to slow but certain death" (!!).

42. *Prières recueillies et mises en ordre* (Paris, 1873).
43. Paris, 1871.
44. *Les Jésuites*, tr. by Alfred Marchand, 3rd ed. (Paris, 1875). Originally *Der Jesuiten-Orden nach seiner Verfassung und Doctrin, Wirksamkeit und Geschichte* (Berlin, 1873).

Under the Restoration, M. Cousin made this sally: "Catholicism is three hundred years old; I take my hat off to it"! A lot more hats will have to be taken off to it, and still more and better things will happen than that!!

To go back to Huber, his book contains many facts and data which do not seem false—and the French translation (slightly pruned of Germanic pedantry, too indigestible for the ignorant) is as easy to read as the *Variétés* articles in the journal the *Débats*. I'll send you the two volumes if you are at all interested.

I have taken out one month's subscription to *Le Figaro*, whose advantages, in its little tiff with *L'Univers*, are merely "fictitious"—or a joke.

Our *Figaros* crossed each other.

And Messire Bury de Blaze, or Blaze de Bury, goes on cutting and thrusting at Bayreuth! Queen Olga will congratulate herself on having from the first so well sized up this mad enterprise.

If it is really no trouble to you, keep on sending the *Revue des deux mondes* to your very humble serf at heart

FL

P.S. I have just been handed your letter of October 20 with the envelope for Mme Tolstoy, for which I thank you. I'll write to her tomorrow.

———

November 9, 75
Villa d'Este

Having spent three days in Rome (to celebrate St. Charles's Day), I returned here day before yesterday evening and found a very kind letter from M. Sach, which I answered at length yesterday. M. B. de Bury's article, which you were good enough to send me, contributed to making this reply lengthier: it was impossible for me not to protest, vis-à-vis Monseigneur (who knows B. de B. and reads the *Revue des d. m.*), against the disgusting and impudent attack on one of Mme Moukhanoff's most graceful and noble remarks: "One loves oneself in Him." As for the title which B. confers on me on this occasion: "the most imperturbable mountebank of the notorious gang," I deserve the adjective and leave to those cleverer than myself, B. included, the profession of mountebanking, a profession which is often lucrative, and confers importance on those who follow it. They don't impress me much, and I would not wish to stray into their bigoted company.

Saturday evening, Baron de Keudell, to whom I am very sincerely grateful for his amiable and kindly ways, invited me to dinner at the Palazzo Caffarelli, where I became slightly acquainted with Princess Frederick Charles of Prussia, and her two daughters. We made conversation and music. Zarembski ("a pianist of the first order") played one of Chopin's last *Nocturnes* superbly, the *Pilgrims' March* from *Tannhäuser*, and the tempestuous *Prélude*,[45] the twenty-fourth, of Chopin. I also—as a sexagenarian—joined in the game; and Schubert's *Reiter Marsch*[46] (6/8) for four hands sparkled under the very keen and well-trained fingers of Mme Helbig.

Did I tell you that on October 22 she made me a princely gift of a dozen handkerchiefs decorated with a number of angels playing all kinds of instruments, drawn with pen and ink by Mme Helbig?

The Bobrinskis, whom I have seen two or three times, are having many troubles—in the worst sense of the word. Bad crops this year, aggravated by a loss of 800,000 francs in a Moscow bank. In Rome they moved out of their old home (rented by Princess Lopuchin who is not coming because of the bad year which has affected her husband's finances); then a temporary stay of six weeks in the Via Sistina, with a distraction in the form of a little fire, put out by firemen who played their hoses down nearby chimneys; and finally, last Sunday, a precipitate move to their Villa Malta due to the fact that Lady Morton is arriving and taking over the fire-damaged apartment in the Via Sistina.

45. Opus 28, No. 24.
46. Probably from G 632; R 354.

For the time being, they are installed on the ground floor, which is still without doors. I commented to the Countess that this meant that no one could literally be thrown out of the door. She said to me: "At the Villa Malta we will, like Raphaël, have three styles: the first on the ground floor, the second on the second floor (in the years '76–'77), and last of all, the third, with three floors, and the doors open or closed."

In view of such vicissitudes, I took the liberty of offering the Bobrinskis the hospitality of the Villa d'Este; but they would rather take a *Patronatschein* at Bayreuth in the company of Princess Cocona Bariatinska.

Your friend Princess Czernicheff has arrived. I suppose she has kept Hannstein; he'll give news of her, which I'll relay to you at the end of November.

Spiridion assures me that he did in fact send off *Le Figaro*, and *L'Italie* with Dumas' letter *Tue-le* [sic], or let us kill ourselves. This issue of *Le Figaro* had a cut of the coat of arms of Fanny Lear drawn by the Grand Duke, and bearing the device "Take all."

According to the same *Le Figaro*, Victor Hugo is said to have favored a dentist with an autograph of the following device: *Dieu aidant* (in the vernacular: *Dieux et dents*). Tell this to our friend Lassen and send me news of the *Goethe Vorstellungen* [Goethe presentations] which began on November 6 at Weimar, and will conclude with Lassen's *Faust*, according to M. Sach.

No formal ending but indeed with all my heart,

Your

FL

Will you please hand the enclosed note to Grosse, and ask him to get Burghardt to ship promptly to me the spirits I have listed.

Sunday, November 14
(Villa d'Este)

Your telegram of yesterday strikes me as somewhat exaggerated. There cannot have elapsed eighteen days, not even fifteen, between my letter of October and the one which went off last Tuesday, with five seals on it (in spite of my dislike of this form of distrust) so as to make sure of its delivery. It probably reached you shortly before my telegraphic reply, for five days in transit between here and Weimar would be abnormal—and I recall having several times made this trip in three days.

I hope that M. Sach will not be unhappy at my reply to his very gracious and friendly letter. Please tell me more about the theatrical performances in honor of the Weimar jubilee of Goethe. Did Lassen's *Faust* figure among them?

When are Metzdorff's *Rosamunde* and Saint-Saëns' *Samson* to be performed? The press announces Saint-Saëns' arrival in St. Petersburg. I hold him in sincere esteem and friendship, and wish him success everywhere, in keeping with his great talents: particularly in Weimar for his *Samson* this spring.

Methinks you should not economize by canceling your subscription to the *Revue des deux mondes*. To borrow instead of lending hardly becomes you; so, by order of Queen Olga, continue both the *Débats* and the *Revue*.

Adelheid, who will be accompanying her aunt (Frau Pröpstin von Stein) back to Germany in a couple of weeks, will bring back to you the two issues of the *Revue des deux mondes*, a pamphlet by Nietzsche, and two or four books, as well as the *Débats* article on our noble friend Tolstoy. Because of him, please file this article (of mediocre style) in the folder of our souvenir printed matter.

I continue to be victimized by the mails. They burden me daily with more than half-a-dozen tiresome letters which disturb the little musical work which I would like to pursue here. Deign to compensate for these numerous troubles by writing a few lines (free of worry)

To your very humble

FL

November 20, 75
Villa d'Este

You scold me so gently that I could not complain without adding to my very unintentional faults.

For the last couple of weeks I have been gloomily writing quantities of letters. I get nearly fifty a week, not counting shipments of manuscripts, pamphlets, books, dedications, and all kinds of music. The time required to peruse them, even casually, deprives me of the time needed to answer them.

Up till now it has been impossible for me to concentrate steadily on my musical work because of this too flattering and steady harassment by my correspondents in various countries. Some ask for concerts, for advice, for recommendations; others for money, for jobs, for decorations, etc., etc.

I don't know what will become of me in such a purgatory.

However, since you are so kind as to concern yourself with my musical work, to which I would prefer to attend, without expatiating on it, here is my little balance from October 2 to November 20, consisting of: a new version of the *Marche Hongroise* (*Sturmmarsch*)[47] for orchestra, also arranged for piano for two and four hands; an arrangement for four hands of the second edition of the *Tscherkessen Marsch*[48] by Glinka; a revision of the score of *St. Cecilia* (for I had to correct the copy, set it up for printing, provide the three texts in three languages— French, Italian, and German, etc.); a similar revision of the dramatic scene from *Jeanne d'Arc*[49] (a poem by Alex[andre] Dumas).

(These tasks were urgent, for I had promised to get the material promptly into the hands of the publishers.)

In addition, Tolstoy's ballad, about which I've told you—and which I still have to adjust to the spoken text so that the music should not be just an *hors d'œuvre*—this ballad will be published at St. Petersburg (with the Russian text, of course).

47. G 119; R 437. G 524; R 54b. G 610; R 305.
48. G 629; R 351.
49. G 373; R 646.

As soon as the outside world gives me a little rest, I shall write a series of short and simple piano pieces, to be published under the collective title *Weihnachtsbaum* [The Christmas Tree].[50] Please be so good as <u>not</u> to mention this title.

Later on, I'll go ahead with the composition of *Via Crucis*,[51]— which I started at the Colosseum, when I lived very close by, at Santa Francesca Romana.

The instrumental introduction and the two first scenes of the *St. Stanislaus* Oratorio are written. Metzdorff has probably seen or heard them; but in order to finish this work, I must make several modifications in the text, to which I must still give some thought and attention; hence: delays.

Let Olgh. graciously forgive me these trifling, most superfluous details, of which she is herself the cause because of her worrying.

She also shows herself as most unjust toward a certain "Majesty," and I will always be so bold as to beg Olgh. to observe a proper measure of good will toward those rulers who deign to show some to me. Queen Olga herself would not blame me for this.

"One cannot help feeling that the Sultan is beginning to become interesting," as John Lemoinne so excellently puts it. Thank you for having sent me this article, preceded by the one I had read (in German translation in the *Allgemeine*) beginning with the words: "Turkey follows the market value of her bonds—the trend is definitely down, even for her faithful believers." The comment that "for the first time England has adopted a Russian tone of voice" is entirely timely.

The last issue of the *Revue des deux mondes* (with the articles by Caro, Réville, etc.) argues in favor of my recommendation that the subscription be renewed.

Adelheid will give you the issues of the *Revue* together with the relevant volumes.

Your

FL

50. G 186; R 71.
51. G 53; R 534.

Herewith a conundrum. Please write the word out for me clearly.

Although the Luciani litigation is only of local interest, I'm sending you the summary in *L'Italie.*

———————

Monday, November 22, 75
(Rome)

A letter from Baron Snoukaert, sent to Weimar, and which reached me yesterday (after a detour via Leipzig and in an envelope of Kahnt), informed me of H[is] M[ajesty]'s renewed munificence. I was about to write to ask you to dispose as you please of this royal cask of *Bière-Princesse,* which is very comforting and of exquisite taste. You were perfectly right to regale my friends Grosse and Gottschalg with it, together with the other members of the Weimar orchestra; only I would have liked you not to forget the extraordinary and intimate quartet (to whom I had promised that they would taste this liquid): Peterle, Mimi, Clément, and Sachi – – – I hope that Grosse will have made up for your forgetfulness by offering you first access to the cask, and that the most illustrious quartet will thus not be cheated of my promise.

Please have Grosse or Gottschalg drop me a couple of lines about the evening of quaffing (to which Lassen was probably invited). The Elefant [Hotel] could not compete with my master's non-small beer. In the rush to get my last letter off to you (day before yesterday), I forgot to enclose the conundrum; here it is: write out clearly for me the word which I was unable to decipher. I am also awaiting the "simple" solution of the Eastern question by the Byzantine genius of my very beloved autocrat – – –

Lemoinne's articles on this question are excellently written, although they give neither the direction to be followed nor the conclusion—which, I agree, would be premature. There will have to be many sinuous lines in diplomatic documents before people reach the point of – – – failing to reach agreement, and cutting each other's throats.

Thank you for von Arnim's letters, which are studded with true and subtle comments; there is only one thing wrong with them, or maybe two: their publication at this time, and the fact that they were formerly secret (behind the back of the boss, Bismarck). As I retain sincerely affectionate feelings toward von Arnim, I fear that this publication, however interesting it may be for the public, will scarcely be to his personal advantage.

I came back here yesterday evening and will return to the Villa d'Este Thursday at the latest.

This evening I am dining at Baron de Keudell's with M. de Radowitz and his wife (born Ozeroff) whom I do not yet have the advantage of knowing. Radowitz is leaving day after tomorrow for his post in Greece. Zarembski has been made most welcome in your former home (with the double eagle) and Mme d'Uexküll is willing to take piano lessons with my first-class pianist – – –

Your very humble

FL

December 2, 75
(Villa d'Este)

The matter of the concerts of the Weimar orchestra is hardly my business. For a dozen years I've not been even nominally the director of this orchestra (which boasts three *Kapellmeister*), and if people still wish to turn to me for this or that matter concerning it, this is only for the sake of formal courtesy. For the rest, speaking academically (in accordance with Cardinal Antonelli's famous Italianism), I see no objection to Kömpel conducting next winter's concerts, unless Müller-Hartung should claim them. In this case, Müller would have priority, since he conducts the *Singverein* excellently, and as *Kapellmeister* he outranks the *Conzertmeister*. As for our friend Lassen, urge him to complete his *Faust* and not to worry about any pettiness around him.

What a baroque idea to perform the *Danse Macabre*[52] at the Court concert on New Year's Day! To change its title would be silly. It would be more appropriate to perform Saint-Saëns' *Danse Macabre*[53] at one of the orchestral concerts in the theatre; and if you have any influence on their programs, please recommend specifically the *Vier Charakterstücke* (1, Allegro risoluto, 2, Notturno, etc.) by Hans von Bülow (*persona non grata* at Court—which does not impair his merit).

These four *Charakterstücke* have been published by the *Hofmusikalienhandlung* of Robert Seitz at Weimar in score, orchestra parts, and for four hands—in which form you will enjoy playing them with Lassen.

I shall certainly guard against taking literally your promise not to ask me questions without rhyme or reason. So, quick, here is a reply to the last one, so as to encourage you to continue.

The Polish text of the oratorio *St. Stanislaus* is by M. Siemienski. He published it in a Polish periodical a year or two before you moved into the Carlsplatz. My dear and deeply lamented friend Cornelius did the German translation in which substantial cuts and changes seemed to me necessary. Cornelius undertook these without too much success, for my taste, and died a few weeks later. In the summer of '74 I composed here roughly a quarter of this oratorio. In order to continue I absolutely must have the changes in the text which I can obtain only from a poet whose ideas are in perfect harmony with mine. I am still looking for him and will perhaps find him in Vienna next spring. Meanwhile I have laid my composition aside and hope not to return to it before the fall of '76. Its completion calls for four or five months of hard work. How shall I find them?

Adelheid has undertaken to send you in the near future Ozanam's book, *Poètes franciscains*,[54] the work on the Jesuits (which, in spite of his anti–Roman Catholic point of view, is not without interest, and even a certain sincerity); one of Nietzsche's pamphlets (unfortunately,

52. G 126; R 457.
53. Opus 40.
54. *Les Poètes franciscains en Italie au treizième siècle avec un choix des petites fleurs de Saint François* (Paris, 1852).

I am unable to find the preceding one: *Die Wiedergeburt* [sic] *der Tra-gödie*);[55] and an issue of the *Revue des deux mondes*. The subsequent issues, which I thank you for having sent me, will be returned to you honestly, for I take leave once again to recommend that you have them bound, and keep the collection of the *Revue*.

You have already heard of the brilliant success in Vienna of the new staging, under Wagner's direction (with additions from Paris and Munich and a few variants), of *Tannhäuser*. One would do well in Weimar to follow this good example, notwithstanding the too facile objections and the formidable – – – expense. Willy-nilly, M. von Hülsen and M. Jauner have finally understood that Wagner represents something other than the ordinary theory and practice of art. Why should those at Weimar, where we had the glory of realizing this from the start, be slow in recognizing this fact? – – – But I should keep quiet on this subject—and I remain with all my heart

Your

FL

Sunday, December 12, 75

Rome

Day before yesterday, Friday evening, I climbed the stairs of the Russian Legation again for the first time since our Roman farewell (in '65). I did not know the first floor, where a brilliant evening was taking place, brilliantly enhanced by Zarembski playing several piano pieces. The audience was admirably selected: the Princesses Teano, Gortschakoff (born Stourza), Wolkonska (born Lvoff—a famous beauty), Baron de Keudell, and Mme Minghetti, etc., etc. The Uexkülls showed good taste in leaving it to Zarembski alone to do the musical honors that evening, without mixing other artists with him. *L'Omnivorie* (forgive

---

55. *Die Geburt der Tragödie aus dem Geiste der Musik.*

this neologism, invented by Gregorovius) is getting to be bourgeois, even among phony Russian princesses.

On the second floor of the same palace, yesterday, there was a small dinner at the Uexkülls – – – afterward Mme Uexküll came (without "Lindeman") to the Jaëlls' concert, of which I enclose the program, together with two others.

I wanted to go back to the Villa d'Este this morning, but shall be staying here until Christmas.

Your very humble

FL

I'm sending off this very hasty word so that you shouldn't grumble.

December 20, 75

Rome

Turning first to the most urgent matters, I send you herewith a few lines for Mme Schirmer, which kindly pass on to her. To write directly to Bülow under the guise of making a recommendation in Schirmer's little publishing matter seems to me inappropriate. It will easily be settled in New York between Schirmer and Bülow, without my involving myself otherwise than by the enclosed lines.

Another errand: do please ask Count Beust in my behalf to recommend M. Hiller, one of my most conspicuous adversaries (in music) for some twenty years, to the Grand Duchess.

Formerly, when I was still in charge of programs of concerts at the Weimar Court, M. Hiller figured in these, and I recall having conducted, at a concert in the theatre, one of his best works: the symphony entitled *Es muss doch Frühling werden* [Spring Must Come]. As a title for being recommended locally at Weimar, Hiller has that of being a pupil of Hummel; consequently, in his youthful years, he dined, more or less badly, at the Erbprinz and at the Elefant. (N.B. –

The Hôtel de Russie did not, it seems to me, exist before 1830)—and I will be happy to invite him there again now, should I have the good fortune of finding myself at Weimar with him.

Zarembski played superbly day before yesterday at his concert (of which I sent you the program): Princess Marguerite deigned to attend and to applaud. On this occasion, your very humble servant had the honor of being introduced by Mme Minghetti to Her Royal Highness. Mme d'Uexküll very graciously sponsored Zarembski's concert. He also has the advantage of giving piano lessons to your cousin, Constantine Gortschakoff, to whose house I am going this evening.

In great haste
Your

FL

Have you received the Lesseps and Gortschakoff articles from *Le Figaro*, which were sent off day before yesterday?

Thursday, I'll be back at the Villa d'Este.

———

December 28, 75
(Villa d'Este)

I have just written to M.S. recommending that Saint-Saëns' *Samson* ("Simson" or "Schimeschen") be performed next April. Lassen and Loën will, I hope, take care to see to it that my very humble recommendation is successful.

Speaking of recommendations, I was afraid of spoiling everything by asking Bülow directly to reach agreement with Schirmer on the American edition of I don't know what piece. The matter will be very naturally settled at the right time and place, after a concert by Bülow in New York.

Did you forward my note to Madame Schirmer? When is the first performance of Metzdorff's *Rosamunde*? Does it really last four and a half hours? Please send me specific information about it, and also about the Court concert of January 1. Lassen has probably abandoned the wild idea of having the *Danse Macabre* played then as a New Year's present – – –

Another question: was my Hiller-message (which I wrote to you last week) well received, first by you, and then at the castle? When Hiller comes to Weimar, please do him the honor of being kind to him, and tell him that I am sorry not to be at the Hofgärtnerei, where it would have been most pleasant to me to have seen him again without causing him the slightest embarrassment.

As have several other old friends of mine (Joachim at their head), Hill[er] thought it better to ignore, even to bury me, after a fashion, under criticism. Far from resenting this, I am almost tempted to praise their prudence, which has never prevented me from frankly recognizing their talents, nor from deriving pleasure from their works – – – to the extent that they made them available to me.

After about a couple of weeks of social activity (dinners, soirées, and concerts) in Rome, I returned here on December 23, and shall stay until mid-January in meditation and prayer, and always as your

Very humble

FL

Herewith the last but one chapter in the Bauffremont affair. The court will give its decision today.

I have been invited to go to Vienna for the performance of the *Elisabeth* on January 6. I replied by sending my regrets.

December 29, 75
(V. d'E.)

My letter of yesterday was interrupted by the visit of my young Tiburtine friend, Deacon Colomba Fausti. He takes after a dove rather than after the German Faust, while being extremely fond of German music, which has become most fashionable, quasi *R.O.* in the last few years in Italy.

Therefore, to all that I was telling you yesterday I add:

A) A note for Gille, which you will be so kind as to hand him, asking him please to remind Riedel that I attach <u>great</u> importance to one or two <u>Russian</u> symphonic works being played at the Altenburg Musikfest. In my opinion, one would do well to pick Rimsky's *Sadko*,[56] and Borodin's symphony. As Secretary of the *Allgemeiner Deutscher Musik Verein*, Gille is just the person to take up once more with President Riedel my oral and written recommendation on this subject.

B) Propaganda in favor of Russian music at Weimar calls for a certain circumspection. I doubt whether Loën and Lassen will exert themselves much to perform this winter one of the three opera scores sent by His Majesty the Emperor of Russia. Do you know the titles of these scores? Probably the two by Glinka; and the third – – – ?

C) Your idea of recommending Pinner for a Court concert seems to me excellent, and I urge you to follow it up.

Pinner's recent concert in Berlin was a great success and he now ranks with the *comme il faut* pianists, of whom there are not very many.

Incidentally, Mlle Gaul tried my patience Sunday by asking for a letter of recommendation to Mme de Schleinitz – – – She will perhaps ask me for another with the object of calling on Princess Hohenlohe in Vienna, since the patronage of these two gracious ladies has become an absolute must for all concert-givers, composers, etc., of both sexes.

I receive each year more than fifty requests similar to that of Mlle Gaul. When I am back in Pest and Weimar, I shall put up a little notice on my door: "It is forbidden here to talk about letters of recommendation for Baroness de Schleinitz, and Princess Hohenlohe."

I enclose a letter from Princess Georges Bibesco to M. de Villemes-

56. The orchestral work known as *Episode from the Legend of Sadko*, Opus 5 (originally Opus 7).

sant, head of *Le Figaro* and arbiter of opinion in the field of morals in France and elsewhere.

Because of her brother, Princess Bibesco is of interest to <u>us</u>.

Yours ever

FL

Did you receive my reply to Mme Schirmer? Did Adelheid have the books delivered to you?

I was unable to make out the name of Saint-Saëns' <u>macabre</u> instrument. Please write it out clearly for me.

It goes without saying that you will lend <u>our</u> piano to Hiller, if it suits him to make use of it either at the theatre or elsewhere.

———

1876

January 12, 76
(V. d'Este)

I deserve at least a week's punishment on bread and water, with a "xylophone" accompaniment as sole entertainment, for my great blunder in having attributed to Lassen the diplomatic stroke of the change of title of Saint-Saëns' *Danse Macabre*. I was extremely embarrassed to learn that the idea of this change came from such high places, and it only remains for me to crave your mercy for the offensive word "nonsense," intended <u>solely</u> for Lassen, and for no one above him.

When I last wrote to the G[rand] D[uke], I was not aware of Hiller's arrival at W[eimar]; thus could not combine my renewed recommendation of *Samson* by Saint-Saëns with one by my ex-friend H[iller]; but I thank you for having so well understood and carried out without delay my intentions, which I had taken the liberty of expressing to you clearly. It was right that H[iller] should be well received at Weimar. The meanness of cliques and spitefulness must not take root there (in music, at least). Let us leave to larger cities the spurious advantages of certain intrigues. As for us, let us frankly remain human beings *comme il faut*, even *grands seigneurs* now and then, and let us only exclude that which is positively stupid and hateful.

Now Hiller deserves to be treated as a musical figure; he has been enormously industrious and has produced a quantity of works of all kinds: operas, oratorios, symphonies, *Lieder, Kammer-Musik* (somewhat lacking in spirit at times[1]), etc.; as a polygraph he could be ranked with Raff and Rubinstein; but each one of these three composers cares little for a common link and would prefer being ranked with Beethoven, or at least with Meyerbeer and Mendelssohn combined.

Was the "lecture" on Rossini taken from one of the volumes published by Hiller? Or from a new manuscript?

If you can find the program of the New Year's Day concert and of those in which H[iller] figures at W[eimar] and Jena, please send them to me.

Regarding illusions as to the success of a new work, many composers are alike. Metz[dorff] recalls to me an old friend who, on the day after the first performance of his opera at Weimar, said to me pompously: "All the same, what a pleasure to see everyone now looking at me and saluting me with admiration!" Only he was conscious of this, whereas the thought had entered no one else's mind!

Since you take care of my humble messages flawlessly, I am so bold as to entrust another one to you for M. de Loën. It is not up to me to write and thank him for *Rosamunde*, but I wish you would tell him that I am most grateful to him for his friendly gesture, in which I encouraged him without malice, and simply in view of the commendable custom of German theatres to produce one or two new operas each year.

This time, *Rosamunde* seemed to me from several points of view to deserve being selected, since the *Prophètes [Le Prophète]*, and the *Africaines [L'Africaine]*[2] of the year 1876 do not yet seem inclined to fall, like roast quail, from the heavens of art into the box offices of the theatres.

On another matter, the news from M. de L[oën] with regard to the setback of the singers at Bayreuth is somewhat out of date—and has already been refuted. It is better not to talk about such incidents.

1. In the original: *un peu en robe de chambre, parfois.* Liszt here puns on *Kammermusik (musique de chambre).*
2. Opera by Meyerbeer, first performed April 28, 1865, in Paris.

Thank you for the *Débats*, with the article on Pictet, Montalembert, and the J's.

[unsigned]

Tomorrow, I'll send you Pinner's exact address, which Zarembski has promised me. But the simplest thing would be to write to Bechstein.

January 16, 76
(Villa d'Este)

A Weimar publisher, whose name is an antiphrasis[3] asks me to contribute to a *Tanz Album* to be published in honor of Princess Marie. I don't care much for *Albums*, or for dancing either. However, I would not wish to abstain from paying homage to Princess Marie on this festive occasion.

Here is a *Polonaise*;[4] please try it out with Lassen. If it seems all right to you I will offer it to the Princess. Forgive me for sending it in my poor handwriting, but there is no copyist here, and to save time I am sending you the manuscript as is.

Should you give me any encouragement I'll orchestrate (barbaric word) this *Polonaise*; the second theme (E major—a wee bit *R.O.*) would lend itself to a prettily colored combination of stringed instruments, clarinet, and horn—which Lassen would blend together better than I could, but I dare not ask him to devote several hours to giving me the pleasure of orchestrating my little work – – –

These three pages of *Polonaise* may perhaps contribute to your soirée of Russian and Samsonic music.

Mlle Brandt would be highly desirable for Delilah. M. de Loën, I

3. A figure of speech by which words are used in a sense opposite to their proper meaning.
4. *Festpolonaise*, for piano duet, G 255; R 296. The original manuscript is in the Library of Congress.

trust, shares my opinion, and will be willing to contribute his good offices for the success of Saint-Saëns' *Samson*.

More soon—

and as ever your very humble

FL

Zarembski has not sent me Pinner's address. Bechstein will see to it that the letter reaches him.

January 25, 76
(Villa d'Este)

Your two last letters enchant me. The *fioriture* of song, in the guise of "maternal illusions" (before a harsh audience which feels no need of being compensated for the singer's sterility), are extremely entertaining! I also greatly praise your cleverness in the diplomatic negotiation of the *Patronatscheine*, and would like to refute even more your apprehensions with regard to the "realm of ideal realism." To be sure, people have raised their tone on the subject to a very high, but not therefore false, pitch. Speaking of *Patronatscheine*, the Imre Széchenyis have taken some, on the recommendation of Apponyi and Mihalovich. On my way back to Pest (mid-February), I'll lengthen my trip by one hour, so as to spend a day in Venice with the Széchenyis. The two brothers, Imre and Dénes, and their very amiable spouses are spending the winter there. I'll probably leave Rome on February 10, and stop for a few hours in Florence, at Mme Laussot's, and at Lamporecchio at Princess Rospigliosi's, who has kindly invited me in the most gracious manner. I am still most grateful to her for her affectionate attitude in the years '65–'70.

Tell me quite frankly whether you find my *Polonaise* (for the wedding of Princess Marie) adequate or not. I wrote it with a Weimar Court festival, or a *Fackel Zug* [torchlight parade] in mind. The melody in E major (♯♯ ♯♯) is in homage to the Grand Duchess – – – I have already hinted to you that Lassen would please me greatly if he would orchestrate this *Polonaise*, assuming that your Most Serene Criticism is not unfavorable to me.

Forgive my having bothered you with my request for the concert programs. I retain the bourgeois taste for printed matter which contributes to accuracy of information. M. S[ach] was so kind as to send me recently the one for January 1, and to inform me of the element of personal good will toward me in the welcome extended to Hiller.

Has the symphony characterizing *die bedeutendsten Theaterspiele* [the principal stage categories]: *Tragödie, Comödie, Drama, Ballet und Oper* been published? If Hiller has succeeded in characterizing symphonically in a single work these multiple and multiform species, he can boast of having outdone the illustrious Jean Marie Farina, the inventor of Eau de Cologne—and even out-topped the whole Cologne cathedral.

Please send me the weekly edition of *Le Figaro*. Does it give the complete text of the lecture by Legouvé on Lamartine? Did you notice this verse:

> *Car mon âme est un feu qui brûle et qui parfume,*
> *Ce qu'on jette pour la ternir.*[5]

Now let's turn directly to the Danicheffs. Just think: Princess W[ittgenstein] <u>at one time</u> interested herself very much in their fate. I'll tell you how.

In atonement for my inexcusable absentmindedness, I sign twice today

your
very humble

FL FL

I'm staying here until February 2 with no other company, good or bad, than myself—and with my daydreams.

---

5. For my soul is a fire which consumes and perfumes / That which others throw to sully it.

February 4, 76
(Villa d'Este)

Yesterday, I was on the point of returning to Rome when Cardinal Hohenlohe's chamberlain came to inform me that His Eminence was arriving here. Not having received any letters from Rome in several days, I knew nothing about the Cardinal's ultramontane journey nor about his audience (Tuesday) with the Holy Father. He is in perfect health, both physically and mentally (save for a slight pain in his foot) and he intends to spend a few months in Rome, where he has rented an apartment, Via Gregoriana. Tomorrow evening I'll be in Rome and will stay there until February 9 or 10 at the latest. On the thirteenth I'll stop over with the Széchenyis in Venice. Please drop me a line there in care of general delivery.

My last days here have been spent in concocting tedious letters and in revising the manuscript of the big catalogue of my poor compositions,[6] to be published by Härtel this summer. The same publisher will soon print your Nocturne.[7] My *Via Crucis* is barely sketched, and is still more in my head than on paper. I'll pick it up again later; meanwhile I have written some ten little piano pieces (for two and four hands). Their collective title will be: *Arbre de Noël*.[8]

If my *Polonaise* for Princess Marie is well received at Weimar, this will give me great pleasure; Olg. has finally guessed correctly with what end in view I had, out of politeness, sent her this piece. To tell the truth, I have an increasingly poor opinion of my things, and it is only through my reaction to the indulgence of others that I manage to find them acceptable. On the other hand, I greatly enjoy many of the compositions of my colleagues and masters. They amply repay me for the tediousness and shortcomings of my own.

Tell me soon about Lassen's *Faust*, which I hope we will hear to-

6. *Thematisches Verzeichnis der Werke, Bearbeitungen und Transcriptionen von F. Liszt. Neue vervollständigte Ausgabe* (Leipzig: Druck und Verlag von Breitkopf & Härtel). A facsimile reprint was issued in 1965 by H. Baron, London.

7. A version of his *Impromptu*, G 191; R 59. The original manuscript is in the Library of Congress.

8. G 186 and 613; R 71 and 307.

gether at Weimar. I can hardly return there before April 8, for I'll need at least six weeks to settle my presidency of the Musical Academy at Budapest, and discharge my most pressing obligations there. In this matter your opinions are no doubt very flattering for me but too mildly patriotic; and if I am not to disgrace myself, I shall henceforth have to spend more time in Hungary.

I hear from Pest that H.M. the King deigned to ask Minister Trefort "why" I was not there – – –

Cardinal Hohenlohe met Prince Ourousoff (who is at this time replacing Capnisz in Rome) at Ragaz, and speaks most highly of him.

Zarembski continues to flourish in Rome – – – and Mlle Wenzel leaves for Cairo tomorrow. Adelheid asks me for news of Mlle Wenzel, in whom Mme de Pirch is good enough to take interest. I will answer her tomorrow (from Rome) after obtaining the most accurate information.

Yours ever

FL

Please be so kind as to tell Grosse to have Burghardt at Erfurt send me promptly (by express) to Budapest, Fischplatz 4, a case like the one which arrived in Rome, containing some Nordhäuser and some Aromatic. On February 16 I'll arrive at B. Pest.

Sunday, February 13, 76

Venice (Grand Hotel)

You please me greatly by assuring me that my *Polonaise* made a good impression. When I get back to Weimar I'll have it copied and printed.

The press seems to know more about Cardinal Hoh[enlohe]'s mission than he does himself. I hardly touched on this subject in my long conversations with him at the Villa d'Este where we were once again alone as of yore, for two days. The Holy Father welcomed him warmly, and his colleagues of the Sacred College are all of one mind concerning him (with varying degrees of emphasis). Whatever the situation concerning his "mission," I am very glad that the Cardinal decided to return to Rome at this time. In addition to other great qualities, he is very tactful and resourceful; thus he will know how to protect himself against misadventures, and will not err through excess of zeal.

I spent Thursday at Mme Laussot's in Florence, and the following day at Princess Rospigliosi's at Lamporecchio—a superb castle built by Bernini for Pope Clement Rospigliosi. Together with Hillebrand (who still kindly lets me have his room in Florence) we talked about Weimar. He'll probably be passing through there this summer. If Their Royal Highnesses are still favorably disposed toward him, there could be agreement. I'll let you know orally how the solution of this problem could be facilitated. Hill[ebrand] is working hard on his history of France[9] from 1830 to 1870, and is to go to Berlin for research in the Archives.

It would almost have been an act of ingratitude on my part, not to have called on Count von Arnim, for he has often been affable and forthcoming to me in Rome. At this time, he is struck, above all, by the total absence of moral sense in Europe. *Pro nihilo*[10] lives up to its title, he said to me, and will be worthless. To my comment that in certain cases it was chiefly a matter of knowing how to let a certain amount of time pass, he replied, "It's no pastime."

Someone recently assured me that Arnim's father and grandfather had committed suicide. Is this true? He, though sick and beset by troubles, still retains his aristocratic style and correspondingly fine manners.

Princess Rospigliosi seems to have fairly well recovered from her long and serious illness. The elegance of her mind has not diminished. She went to Bologna expressly for the performances of *Lohengrin* ('72?) [sic], and might be very much tempted to show up in Bayreuth.

9. *Geschichte Frankreichs von der Thronbesteigung Louis Philipp's bis zum Falle Napoleon's III* (Gotha, 1877–98). A projected third volume, to cover the period from 1848 to 1870, was never completed.

10. *Pro nihilo. Les Antécédents du Procès d'Arnim* (Paris, 1876). (Also published in German.)

Meanwhile, she lives in retirement, not devoid of *grandezza*, at Lamporrechio, and is building a school near her castle for young ladies, etc. – – – The *Revue des deux mondes* and the *Revue des questions historiques*, which Rayneval used to lend you, are both on her table. But she remains strongly hostile to *L'Univers*, to which I had formerly urged her to subscribe, and very much prefers *Le Figaro*, which she receives and claims to read assiduously.

On Thursday, the quasi-homonym of Hillebrand, Hildebrand (the very famous young sculptor), was present at dinner at Mme Laussot's. Imagine that he has had the good luck of buying the whole lovely convent of San Francesco in Florence for the modest sum of 29,000 francs! Since M. Sach is interested in Hild[ebrand], please pass this detail on to him. Please also be so kind as to convey my very sincere congratulations to Count Wedel. I would willingly send them by letter, were it not for my increasing clumsiness in this art.

Here, I shall be seeing only the Széchenyis, in whose honor I have come, and will be making only one other call – – – on Countess Cholmeley. Her second husband, M. Bermani, is *Consigliere di Prefettura* in Venice.

Tomorrow I the take train again and will be arriving in Budapest Tuesday evening.

Yours ever,

FL

Before leaving Rome, I sent off to you your two issues of the *Revue des deux mondes*. Tell me whether they reached you, and also please urge Grosse to have Burghardt's spirits shipped off to me right away.

———

Sunday, February 20, 76
Budapest

Without pushing "discretion" to the point of exaggeration, I make it a rule that one must never gossip critically about others, whatever their social position may be. Arnim did not have to argue either for or against his participation in the pamphlet *Pro nihilo*, insofar as I am concerned. Obviously the supporting documents were not published fortuitously. Several people I know attribute the final version of the pamphlet to Arnim's son. However it may be, this son acted nobly, and I permitted myself to congratulate the father on having such a valiant heir. In critical circumstances, children do not have the right to sin by being impartial, but must resolutely follow God's Fourth Commandment: "Thou shalt honor thy father and mother," as H. von Arnim is doing.

Prudence being the first of the cardinal virtues, His Eminence Hoh[enlohe] will not fail to observe it. Besides he knows too well the Vatican's *andamento* [practice] to imagine that any other advice is taken there than that of the Holy Ghost, of whom the Holy Father remains the supreme and infallible confidant. Only the Sacred College has the prerogatives of submission closer to the pontifical throne – – –

I have been asked several times in Rome why H[ohenlohe] didn't return there. According to the social status, and the nature of the curiosity of those asking this question, I replied: (a) that His Eminence's position was most unusual; (b) that his name was Hoh[enlohe]-Schillingsfürst; (c) that Schillingsfürst is a small town in Germany famed for a castle of the Hohenlohe princes; (d) that the Holy Father did not disapprove of the Cardinal's prolonged retreat in his own home; (e) that the Cardinal is building schools there and is busying himself in an exemplary manner with pious works; (f) that he had no diocese to administer, and no congregations elsewhere over which to preside; etc., etc., and only recently I somewhat shook the composure of a rather ill-intentioned questioner by firing back at him the question: "Do you find that there is a noticeable lack of cardinals in Rome?"

Hoh[enlohe]'s lodging, Via Gregoriana 34, is extremely simple and inexpensive, but not uncomfortable. Hitherto, no cardinal had lived in this quarter. He has rented it for six months and will probably go back to Germany after the feast of St. Peter (end of June).

Let us return to our topic – – – of pianos. You did wisely to decline the offer of the <u>Vice</u>-Steinway from Brunswick.[11] Please persevere. I am not in a position to pay back certain presents; I therefore ask to be excused for not accepting them.

If Bechstein is, as usual, obliging enough to send me a piano to the Hofgärtnerei on April 8, I'll be grateful to him for this. Please in any case keep the Steinway with you, and do with it as you please until I arrive. There is no hurry to remove it before then, and I will even be very pleased not to see a piano at Weimar for a few days. Do you remember the name of the manufacturer in Brunswick? If so, the quickest thing would be to ask Lassen to send him a few polite lines, explaining that the exiguity of my lodgings does not permit me to take advantage of his kind offer, and thanking him in my behalf.

Several people from Berlin have informed me that Pinner's second concert was a brilliant success. The press reviews were also very favorable to my young "first-class" pianist who has just written to me, and this time gives me his address: Marienstrasse, 4, Berlin.

I arrived here Tuesday evening and have left the house only to go to mass. Some twenty letters to be answered will confine me to my room all week, except for half a dozen indispensable calls. On March 2 I shall start my course of piano lessons with eight or ten pupils of both sexes. On this date Wagner is conducting *Lohengrin* in Vienna (as a benefit for the members of the choruses). I regret I cannot be there, and will not see Cosima again before the summer. I shall spend a couple of days in Vienna on my way back to Weimar at the beginning of April, and will not fail to go and congratulate Dingelstedt on his new title of Baron, as much deserved as hoped for. That of Excellency will soon follow and suits Dingelstedt perfectly.

M. S[ach] has very kindly wired me. I'll reply tomorrow—as well as to Count Wedel's announcement.

Invariably

Your

FL

---

11. In 1876 the Steinway plant in Brunswick was in the hands of Steinway partners. The Steinways were settled and successfully manufacturing in New York.

(Ash) Wednesday, March 1, 76
Pest

Last week there were disastrous floods of the Danube in Hungary! Komorn, Gran, Neu-Pest, Alt-Ofen, etc., have been devastated, and Pest is gravely threatened. More than fifteen thousand people, it is said, are now seeking refuge here and have abandoned their houses and possessions to the waters.

The King and Queen, all the ecclesiastical, military, and civilian authorities are acting with generous charity to aid the flood victims. The poor Franciscans and Capuchins have given shelter in their monasteries to some one hundred families which have been reduced to misery. Hungary has not experienced such a calamity since 1838.

Olgh. was quite right to lend the Steinway to the concerts at the Therns' Erholung and to the theatre. Please be so kind as to convey my very affectionate compliments to the Therns and to ask them whether they intend to prolong their stay in Germany, or perhaps even to reside elsewhere than in Pest? Papa Thern has, among other things, made an excellent arrangement for two pianos of the Sonata in B flat (Opus 106) of Beethoven, and of the forty-eight fugues and preludes of Bach's *The Well-tempered Clavier.*

I recommend that you learn his arrangements. They will provide you with a better use of your time than geography lessons to Müller-Hartung. People are not unaware that the distance between Düsseldorf and Arnhem is less than that between Weimar and Düsseldorf; and if FL planned things badly, Olgh. might well charitably imagine that there was some good little decisive reason for this. All his life this poor FL has constantly been scolded, lectured, counseled, reprimanded, denounced. Sick persons have, on many occasions, proved to him that he was neglecting his health, though he was well; and people who were ruining themselves have triumphantly demonstrated to him that he understood nothing about his business interests, even though he has never owed a penny to anyone. He has, willy-nilly, had to learn that most of the time the best arguments are superfluous, and that of all faults, that of being right is the least excusable. May Olgh. deign to forgive this sally, which your very humble FL hopes to rectify by his very modest return to Weimar.

Your very humble

FL

Thank you for the articles on the St. Joseph Psalter, and on the new works on linguistics—very interesting.

I entirely share your opinion on the propriety of the *Patronatschein* for Lassen, and foresee no difficulty there, when the appropriate moment comes. Up till now, not a single *Pat. Sch.* has been issued to those not paying. They will do well to await their turn, and I have no doubt that Lassen will figure among the first on the list of the elect. Pass on to me any news he gives you of the *Tristan* in Berlin.

I have written to Cosima how very much I regret not being able to go to Vienna or to hear *Lohengrin* conducted by Wagner, tomorrow.

───────

March 15, 76

Budapest

Do I have to calm you once again concerning the ravages of the Danube, my very dear curious one?

My friend Ábrányi's insistence led me into temptation: I spent a night in Albert Apponyi's room; but on the following day, half-ashamed of this superfluous concession, I proudly declared that no one, not even His Eminence the Lord Danube, will ever make me move for one minute from No. 4 Fischplatz.

Herewith the program of the concert for the flood victims, next Monday. After that, I hope never to play the piano again in public.

As last year, I'll spend April 2 at my cousin's in Vienna, and will let you know from there when I am to arrive in Weimar. Please be so kind as to tell Pauline that my rooms must be ready for Friday, April 7. Also, please renew, as from April 1, a subscription of three or six months to the semiweekly edition of *L'Univers*, which is becoming completely indispensable reading for me because of the papal speeches and briefs, the instructions and pastoral letters of the bishops, etc., etc. Now *L'Univers* is the only French publication which prints regularly and *in extenso* all the pieces, to which the seasoning of the commentaries of L. Veuillot and several of his colleagues is excellently suited.

Have you heard people speak of Father Monsabré (Dominican)? He has, for several years, held the prestigious chair of Notre Dame, which does not look to the *Revue des deux mondes* for guidance.

Thank you for the Academy speech of Cuvillier-Fleury. If you still have that of John Lemoinne, please send it to me. In the *Revue* I read the abominable lawsuit against Queen Caroline of England, and the article which followed on King Leopold and Capo d'Istria. People are singing the praises of *Le Fiancé de Mlle Saint-Maur* by Cherbuliez,[12] but being totally devoid of romantic feeling, I avoid reading anything which calls for it.

You did well to write to Cosima after her mother's death. As for me, the only thing to do is to keep quiet and to bury in silence the strange behavior of Mme d'A[goult] toward her children – – – It is a consolation to me that even in the most difficult circumstances, Cosima should have nobly observed the Fourth Commandment of the Decalogue. She will certainly make this same observance more easy and more pleasant for her children. God bless her!

I have just this minute received from Rome the little enclosed printed matter.

And so, there will soon be the lessons of geography, topography, hygiene, music, and above all astronomy, which your very humble FL will be so happy to receive and to follow.

---

12. The second edition was published in Paris in 1876.

March 24, 76
Budapest

M. FL will try to follow the recommendation of the most illustrious Olgh. and will do all he can to become as *"gentil"* as a little sheep. If he hasn't been very successful hitherto, this is not for want of exhortation and scolding. In this area one is extremely openhanded; as a result, I am quite dazed and non-plussed – – – I send you herewith a copy of a recent Roman letter which will interest you. In my reply I allude to the Abbé de Saint-Pierre's little work entitled *Un Projet pour rendre les sermons plus utiles*,[13] and I intend to ponder it zealously.

Have I already asked you to renew my subscription to the semi-weekly edition of *L'Univers* for three or six months, beginning April 1? Also please get me a book which has been heavily censured by the Chapter of the Canons of Orléans, and formally disapproved of by His Eminence Cardinal Guibert, archbishop of Paris. In spite of this, *L'Univers* announces the sale of the sixth printing of this book, whose title is: *Monseigneur Dupanloup – épisode de l'histoire contemporaine, 1845–1875*, by Monseigneur Victor Pelletier, canon of the church of Orléans, Honorary Chaplain of His Holiness Pius IX (one volume in 8vo, price 3 francs, at René Haton publisher, 33 rue Bonaparte, Paris). Without having the least taste for scandals (and Mgr Pelletier is accused of having caused some), I am interested in knowing the sum total of the objections to the activities of Mgr Dupanloup from 1845 to 1875, as defined by a canon of the church of Orléans. So that you should be informed on this incident, I'm sending you the two printed letters of Cardinal Guibert and Mgr Dupanloup.

An astonishing piece of news! Dingelstedt claims and advocates the use of the Bayreuth theatre for the performances of his master stroke in dramatic art: the adaptation of Goethe's *Faust*. On this subject, he has given several lectures at the Concordia in Vienna which were very warmly applauded.

He will probably publish them in pamphlet form. In the meantime,

13. In vol. II of his *Œuvres diverses* (Paris, 1730).

here is the little summary from the *Fremden Blatt*. Assuming that Mgr le Grand Duc is interested in this new staging of *Faust*, kindly pass on to him the *Fremden Blatt* articles.

This time, I'll go and see Dingelstedt in Vienna in order to compliment him very sincerely on his title of Baron, which is fully deserved. That of Excellency will follow. People say that he has devised his coat of arms as follows: one white rose and one red rose, plus thistles—and the motto, "No rose without thorns."

I look forward eagerly to hearing Lassen's *Faust* at Weimar, and hope that permission to accompany you to the rehearsals will be graciously granted to

Your very humble

FL

I arrive in Vienna (Schottenhof) on April 2, and will stay there three or four days.

May 4, 76

Hanover

Rehearsals and concerts, visits, dinners, and suppers have occupied so much of my time these three days at Düsseldorf, that it was hardly possible for me to write. The two concerts (whose programs I enclose) were a complete success. Ratzenberger deserves all praise for this; he conducted in a remarkable manner, with perfect understanding and assurance, the choruses of *Prometheus*, and the *Messe de Gran*, etc. – – –

At the rehearsal on Sunday morning, Hiller came up to me. I spared him beating about the bush by saying right away: "I'm sorry I was not in Weimar when you were there this winter." He complimented me on my indestructible – – – youth! Mme Clara Schumann paid me more or less the same compliment.

To harbor a grudge seems to me mean and unworthy. Not to do as others have done, or might do, suits me better; and without bragging too much, I maintain complete personal objectivity toward my friends or my enemies. To serve well is the main thing in this world—while awaiting a better one.

Day before yesterday we had a most pleasant dinner at Hiller's. There was no lack of spice in the anecdotes. They are the equivalent, in culinary language, of *les chaudsfroids* [cold jellied chicken].

Mme de Loë (born Hatzfeldt), whom you met in Pest, and I have spent these three days in the same hotel (Europäischer Hof). Two of her daughters were with her, and are charming. Mme de Loë wears the watch (of lapis lazuli, I believe) which Mme Moukhanoff left to her husband.

Tell me about Lassen's *Faust*. Bronsart assures me that the glorious Weimar management is announcing the postponement of the first performance—till when?

The Bayreuthian Concert will take place here, Tuesday next, May 9. Before then, please send me *L'Univers* and the *Débats* to Hanover.

Your very humble and grieving

FL

May 11, 76
Hanover

I just missed coming to Weimar to hear *Faust*, yesterday evening – – – but I did not succeed, in spite of all my good intentions. I will write this evening to M. Sach to convey my regrets; please pass them on to Lassen. Thanks for the article from the *Weimarer Zeitung*, and still more for your commentary which we will pursue quietly together, while reading Lassen's score at the piano at your home. With the *Faust* performances Devrient has firmly declared his candidacy for the position of Artistic Director of some theatre more affluent than that of Weimar. I hope that Lassen has not labored for nothing *pour le roi de*

Prusse[14]—a proverb which is no longer topical, and against which I have already protested in 1842 under the late King William IV, who possessed in the highest degree the sense of royal largesse. Among musicians, Mendelssohn and Meyerbeer, whom he called to and settled in Berlin, together with Cornelius and Kaulbach, testify to the fact that "to work for the king of Prussia" was a happy task.

Dingelstedt's first lecture (*Vorlesung*) at the Concordia in Vienna has appeared in the latest issue, May 8, Berlin, of the *Deutsche Rundschau* (the Germanic *Revue des deux mondes*). I urge you to read this brilliant impromptu, drafted at leisure, for it is at least some fifteen years since Dingelstedt conceived the idea of installing in his own manner the two *Fausts* in German theatres. Otto Devrient anticipated him, but Ding-[elstedt] is a man capable of seizing the opportunity to move in ahead of the cleverest, and the publication of his *Vorlesungen* in the *Rundschau* at the very time of the *Faust* performances at Weimar does not lack pertinence.

Do you know anything about the four-volume novel[15] which Loën is going to publish? Countess Wedel spoke to me about it on Sunday at dinner at Count Eulenburg's.

If you have Gédroie's [Giedroyc]'s piece on the two [illegible], please send it to me at Loo Castle (by Arnhem-Holland). I'll be spending about ten days there from May 15 to 25. I expect to arrive at Weimar on the twenty-sixth and at Altenburg on the following day.

Mme de Schleinitz and Mme de Loë came here for day before yesterday's concert. FL feels stupidly melancholic.

Yours ever

FL

---

14. A popular expression meaning to work for nothing.
15. *Verloren und nie besessen. Roman* (Hanover, 1876).

May 13, 76

Hanover

I don't know how to commit to paper the delicate reason which prevented my Faustian excursion to Weimar; but when I tell you, you will not be wholly displeased.

Please be so good as to invite Kömpel and his quartet for Friday, May 26; I'll be there punctually.

Olgh. is guilty of slight inattention, which I beg her to correct quickly, by sending me at Loo No. II (two) of the articles by *l'Anc.* on *Faust.* I received only Nos. I and III.

Day after tomorrow, Monday morning, your very humble and saddened FL will be at Loo.

Yesterday I sent M. Sach my apologies.

May 18, 76

Loo Castle

I already asked you, from Hanover, to keep your quartet together on Friday, May 26. I'll arrive (by the night train) about ten hours before the first stroke of the bow; and the next day we'll go to Altenburg. Please find out whether some new railroad might enable us to avoid passing through Leipzig.

Loo provides no fewer pleasures this year than last. The King is really most charmingly gracious toward the famous artists, painters, and musicians whom he has deigned to assemble here. Here are their names: Gérome, Cabanel, Bouguereau, ten Kate, Heemskerck, Rochussen, Gevaert, Vieuxtemps, Batta, Hartog. Thomas and Saint-Saëns are expected.

No awkwardness in conversation, but always very good form with great liveliness. Gérome, Cabanel, and Gevaert talk, and tell very witty stories. A strong desire to please the King animates and inspires the entire company. The King's prerogatives do not suffer much. He upholds them with perfect assurance without letting them become oppressive.

Twice a day, we number between fifteen and twenty members of the ugly sex at table; at noon, lunch; at 5 o'clock, dinner. The menus and the wine are plentiful and excellent. At meals, the fair sex is conspicuous by its absence, and only appears in the form of a few selected examples in the evening at the theater, where the same fifteen or twenty guests foregather in order to attend the daily auditions by His Majesty's pensioners. Here is yesterday evening's program. Mlle Gaetana (not a pensioner) was the star singer. She has frequently sung with success in London and is returning there.

The large Malibran Medal which the King ordered to be struck as an award for one of his female pensioners has an intrinsic gold value of 800 florins. The costumes of the four or five young ladies, whose task it is every evening to perform a few scenes from comedies, tragedies, or operas, are magnificent and very artistically designed. M. de Loën could not attempt to compete in this field with the theatre of Loo!

Please tell our friend Loën (who is no less absentminded than overworked) that I count on his promise to reply affirmatively to Saint-Saëns (168, rue du Faubourg Saint-Honoré, Paris) with regard to the performance of *Dalila* at Weimar, in the course of the next theatrical season.

If the performance of the *Fausts* were repeated after Altenburg, I would be much interested in this. Prince Teano has sent me a friendly letter with his regrets, which I am forwarding by this mail to the Grand Duke.

Very humbly your

FL

I hope not to find Riedel still at Weimar on the morning of the twenty-sixth.

September 27, 76
Hanover

It is something of an effort for me to live through certain hours and days. Sometimes sadness envelops my soul like a shroud. This was the case last Saturday from morn till eve.

Later: to find Bülow in such a state of suffering distressed me. He feels at the end of his tether, and thinks that he is done for. However, his doctor, who is most experienced and able, has a more cheerful opinion and assures me that recovery is not only possible but probable, on condition that there be several months' treatment and rest.

Bronsart showed himself to be a true friend; he practically forced Bülow to stay with him until October 1: Bülow will then move into his new lodging, which is convenient and agreeable, and quite near Bronsart's house.

I don't know how the rumor spread that Bülow had lost his mind; several people have written me about this, but nothing is more false. The fact is that his mind remains most markedly lucid, and he retains that great nobility of character with a heroic touch, which I admire and love in him. In order to satisfy your taste for specific information (which I share), I'll tell you that Bülow's mistake has been to ignore a (fairly light) stroke, which he suddenly suffered in London last year, shortly before leaving for America. For many long years he has been habitually overdoing it and exceeding the limit in work and fatigue; witness the excessive programs which he put together for his concerts in Germany: at least a dozen pieces, among which several sonatas or suites, each with three or four movements, and which he played in 140 concerts during six or eight months in America. At this rate, Fasolt[16] and Fafner[17] would have killed themselves, without any other assistance or ceremony. A. Rubinstein, who has followed Bülow's excessive programs, and the young matadors of the piano, Zarembski, et al., will be hard put to it to adapt their muscular and nervous systems to the task of *pantagruelizing* musically in this fashion.

16. In *Das Rheingold.*
17. In *Das Rheingold* and *Siegfried.*

If you are so kind as to write, mail letters to Nuremberg (Bavaria) where, all next week, will be

Your much distressed

FL

Just in case, don't forget Nohl's recommendation. His dedication in the latest volume of the biography of Beethoven touched me to the core. Thank you for *L'Univers* and the *Débats*. In the September 23 issue (of the *Débats*, I mean) you will read a remarkable article by Renan on M. Athanase Coquerel the younger. Father Hyacinthe is well characterized in it by references to "secret worries," etc.

October 5, 76
Hanover

I stayed here a few days longer: M. de Bülow's illness is serious and the worst of his condition is his lack of confidence in his recovery, which the doctor is trying to effect – – – and for which I still hope.

Tomorrow morning I'll be in Nuremberg.

Please convey my loyal friendship to Pohl and thank him cordially for having quoted my lines on *Rheingold* (written in 1855) in his *Bayreuther Erinnerungen* (*Neue Zeitschrift für Musik*, September 22).

Yours ever

FL

My next address: bei Herrn General Procurator Liszt, Schottenhof, Wien, where I expect to spend three days next week before returning to Hungary.

Monday, October 9, 76
Nuremberg

May this note express once again to you in Baden my grief at not having found you in Weimar. My sorrow comes from my not being able to arrange matters according to my wishes, or those of Lo.[18]

The precept of Horace and Boileau, "Make haste slowly," does not please me much; however, I have to follow it in practice, including my travels. I only arrived here on the sixth; in a few hours I'll be in Ratisbon, and on Thursday in Vienna, where I hope to find a letter from Lo. If she will deign to write again at once (still to my cousin's address in Vienna), this will be charming. Give me news of the quartet, in which Rubens plays the viola, and Sachi first violin; by right of seniority the cello falls to Peterle; and the four gentlemen will no doubt have made their mark in Baden.

During these three days I have done nothing but talk music with Mlle Ramann, who is very intelligent, hard-working, and of a rare and noble cast of character.

Yours ever

FL

I expect to arrive in Budapest next Sunday or Monday (Fischplatz).

October 12, 76
Vienna

Banish the gloomy mood of Weimar. You have to spend a certain amount of time there for your children's sake, and hence to put up with local boredom, which is fairly benign, while reflecting that the essence of human life is nothing but inexorable boredom. Bossuet, the eagle of Meaux, expressed this most eloquently from his episcopal

18. Russian diminutive, or nickname, for Olga.

throne; and many centuries before him, Master Job asked the Lord: "Why hast thou set me as a mark against thee, so that I am a burden to myself?"!

What business have Bossuet and Job in Madame Pellet's [Pelet-Narbonne][19] house? If you tax me with being preposterous, I'll keep quiet.

I wrote to Cosima from Hanover, c/o general delivery, Bologna, as she requested. My letter will probably have reached her after yours.

Bayreuth in 1877 seems to me a quasi-necessity. However, I shall take care not to involve myself inappropriately in matters which only Wagner can decide.

Let's turn to minor matters. The semisuccess or failure of Martha R[emmert] at Baden doesn't much surprise me. You were right to support her; artists of greater stature than she have had to endure harsher trials over a period of years; witness Bülow, Rubinstein, Tausig – – – Nowadays, for one's name to become well known, one has to work hard, be patient, and endure.

If Martha wants to practice in Pest for a few months more, I'll try to be helpful to her. She will find two or three rivals there who will be less of a bother than useful. She can count on my sincere affection. Tell her that she need only come to Pest, without writing to me ahead of time, and that I will welcome her warmly. Vera Timanoff seems to be well on her way to fame: she is to play at one of the Philharmonic Concerts in Vienna this winter, and has been signed up for a series of concerts in the Austrian monarchy (Bohemia, Moravia, Styria, Galicia, Hungary, etc.). Sophie Menter–Popper will make another tour to the north as far as St. Petersburg. Mlle Essipoff is going to America (they say) where Mlle Mehlig has blossomed so well and borne fruit. Mlle Krebs (who spent a few days in Weimar at the House of the Double Eagle, inhabited formerly by Maltitz, and now by Toll), Mlle Krebs, whose name I must repeat after that long parenthesis, is not gaining in renown, and is almost fading away on the horizon of female pianistic celebrities. Mlles Gaul and Martha Remmert will soon shine; but, as

19. Liszt's short piano piece *Carrousel* (1879?) is a description of Mme Pelet-Narbonne riding on a merry-go-round. The original manuscript is in the Library of Congress.

Baron Dingelstedt well put it: "Concerts are a superfluous evil. The necessary evil is the theater."

Our friend Tolstoy's ballad, *Der blinde Sänger*, has deep significance. Courts and cities are not interested in listening to poets and musicians.

The most recent news of Bülow is moderately good. In Florence he became enamored of Leopardi and is translating his prose writings into German. Leopardi was a noble pessimist; among other thoughts of the same stamp, he wrote: "The rarest thing in this world is someone who is at all times bearable." My ambition is to become this rarity for you, and I beg you to put up with my unbearableness, while remaining with all my heart

Your

FL

Sunday evening I'll be in Budapest.

Saint-Saëns wrote me a charming letter in response to my sending him his *Danse Macabre*. From Hanover I also sent off Tolstoy's ballad to the publisher Bessel (Saint Petersburg).

October 26, 76
Szegszard [Szekszárd]

I was saddened and worried at not having received word from you at Pest. Because of the slowness of communications with Szekszárd, your letter of October 20 reached me only yesterday. Next Tuesday I go to Kalocsa and will spend All Saints' Day and All Souls' Day (November 1 and 2) at Monseigneur Haynald's. The next day I'll be back in Pest for the whole winter.

Thanks for having sent me the *bien pensant* (*gut gesinnt*) article by Schuré on Bayreuth, written in good French. He also wittily depicts Wagner's genius as an impresario, which constitutes an addition, not something superfluous, to his genius as poet-musician (*Wort-Ton Dichter* as King Ludwig of Bavaria writes).

As for the idea of founding in France a theatre on the model of that of Bayreuth in order to present accomplished productions of the works of Gluck, Spontini, *Les Troyens*[20] by Berlioz, etc., it is unlikely that it will be carried out in the near future: it will be hard for the French, with all their rare, brilliant, and superior qualities, to decide to take their musical pleasures really seriously. Nevertheless, Schuré is right to advise them to do so, and to suggest the project of a model theatre in Paris or Versailles. Ábrányi is translating and publishing in Hungarian several passages from Schuré's article.

In Vienna I bought Wolzogen's pamphlet *Tragödie und Satyrspiel.* I like the title; but up till now I have only read some thirty pages without quite understanding how "the impropriety of situations" in a drama brings out its basic morality, and I beg the very learned and adorable Lo to give me some explanation of this secret. Spiridion having forgotten to pack W[olzogen]'s pamphlet, I shall only be able to finish reading it in Pest, next week. I hope that Lo will not refuse to provide FL with the *Leitfaden* [guiding thread] he needs, and the latter promises to be as gentle as a lamb.

Cosima has wired me from Sorrento. Also, I hear from Rome that *Lohengrin* is to be given there in the near future in Wagner's presence. Why not? Bologna, Florence, and Milan have already, in this matter, followed the example of German, Russian, English theatres, and it remains to Weimar's honor that it should have taken the initiative in 1850, on August 28, the anniversary of Goethe's birth. It is not my fault that this initiative did not bear more fruit; pettiness in the city of Weimar would not have prevented this had there not been certain other great and highly placed pettiness. In addition to ordinary (non-symbolic) animals, the "Double Eagle" was against me – – – and the gods decided otherwise (*Dis aliter visum*). What will they decide in the case of the Turks and the Serbs? I await the great oriental inspiration of Uncle Gortschakoff, while wishing that it not be too much out of har-

---

20. Opera in two parts by Berlioz; Part II was produced first. II: *Les Troyens à Carthage* first performed November 4, 1863, in Paris; I: *La Prise de Troie* first performed (in German) December 6, 1890, in Karlsruhe.

mony with the style and manner of Andrássy, who must know best how matters stand within the Austro-Hungarian monarchy. In Pest, he is accused of not being sufficiently forthcoming toward the Turks, and to be leaning toward Russia. Some even more important figures than he in Vienna seem to be leaning in the same direction, so that And[rássy] would only have to give up his ministry, which would be for the new incumbent a heap of troubles and headaches. In the <u>Concert of Europe</u>, the normal pitch is lacking, and the physicians who presume to cure the "sick man," Turkey, don't much agree on which treatment to apply. Some prescribe a series of amputations; the others, strangulation without more ado.

Yours ever

FL

Write to Budapest (Hungary).

November 3, 76

Budapest

On top of everything, I was also worried at not hearing from Lo and last week wrote you so from Szekszárd. This letter will have reached you at long last – – – but in certain regions of Hungary postal communication is often impeded by various accidents; at this time, in the region of Szekszárd, wolves are devouring both the livestock and the shepherds, and in the vicinity of Kalocsa brigands are active, just like their notorious Sicilian cousins. During the two days I just spent with Monseigneur Haynald at Kalocsa, the Pest and Vienna newspapers did not arrive – – – Lo is more cruel than the wolves and the brigands in imagining FL to be committing impossible misdeeds. How am I to plead innocent before such a tribunal? Nonetheless, FL is not in the least at fault and remains humbly, and dumbly if need be, what you know him to be.

On my return here this morning I found your telegram and the anxious note. Lo is respectfully requested to entertain a higher opinion of herself and of FL. Granting a sentiment to be noble, let us simply abide by it.

What will <u>Uncle</u>'s great inspiration be? Its time seems to have come, and the war over the old Eastern question will soon be settled, no longer by the pen of diplomats, but by guns.

In Hungary people are very much pro-Turk, and reproach Andrássy for compromising too much with <u>Uncle</u>. However, Andrássy is no dullard—and *fin contre fin n'est bon à faire doublure*; and Sancho Panza would go on being more of a pirate than ever; and *de corsaire à corsaire n'y pend que barriques rompues*![21] – – – Besides, the Austro-Hungarian monarchy also has its Double Eagle. Will fate deprive it of a beak and talons in the Concert of Europe, which has for more than thirty years been singing the litanies of the dying to the sick man of Constantinople?

In all Slavic countries, Russia has obvious and continuing advantages. It is up to her to know how to benefit from these, shamelessly or not. Her natural role in the Eastern question is that of *prima donna assoluta*, aside from certain husky tones and lack of responsiveness on the part of the orchestra in which Bismarck and d'Israeli are now playing first violin and trombone.

Thanks for the *Revue* with the article on Doudan. Send me the Hebbelian *Nibelungen* (for four hands) by Lassen, who still owes me his *Faust*.

Yours ever

FL

Mme Schirmer has written me a nice letter of thanks for your Bayreuthian kindness.

P.S. I don't know how you can reproach me for having written

---

21. The uncle is Olga von Meyendorff's uncle, the Russian Chancellor, Prince Gortschakoff. The proverb (*fin contre fin* . . .) literally means that a thin, light cloth does not make a good lining for a lightweight garment, implying that Gortschakoff and Andrássy, being both able men, are not likely to make concessions, or give anything away to each other. Like Sancho Panza, they would try to outwit, and gain advantage over each other, as when corsairs, fighting among themselves, smash each other's barrels to pieces.

"solemnly." My want of wit does not go to the point of lacking heart, where required. If I express myself poorly, it's my fault, my very great fault; but Lo might show more understanding, and not abuse me more harshly than she does Gottschalg and Müller-Hartung.

———

November 16, 76
Budapest

Loën's fine zeal for next year's performances at Bayreuth is no doubt most praiseworthy; but Lassen won't have to take the trouble of writing about it, and I strongly advise against his asking Wagner for copies of music. The latter might think it strange to be thus disturbed.

You seem to forget that the four scores of the *Ring des Nibelungen*, not only the *Clavier Auszüge* [piano-vocal scores], appeared in their entirety before being performed at Bayreuth. Lassen saw them at my house: the most illustrious and very dear Lo deigned to thumb through them several times, and Peterle was diligently studying their instrumental effects while I was playing the *Clavier Auszüge* for you. So if arrangements have to be made (in the orchestral and vocal parts, etc.), it is Schott, the Mainz publisher, who should be approached, not Wagner.

Simply write to Cosima about Loën's general good intentions. She will let you know whether the *Wagner Vereine* are pursuing their activity in 1877. If so, it would be perfectly proper for Loën, Lassen, Wedel, Bojanowski, etc., to set up a *Wagner Verein* at Weimar, with which one will immediately associate our friend Gille and his followers at Jena, as well as a few prominent people from Eisenach. I recommend that Loën not prune off Müller-Hartung and Baron Unruh. It will be an easy matter to obtain the necessary information through M. Heckel, the promoter of these *Vereine*, in Mannheim.

As for the Bayreuthian concert which Loën has in mind, the program listed in your letter of yesterday seems to me very well composed.

Your little shipments of newspapers please me greatly. Pasdeloup's[22] letter only half pleases me because of its bragging tone. The final argument that "music must be listened to before being hissed" is reasonable. I go even further and consider that hisses are poor company: silence suffices for a well-brought-up audience to express its disapproval – – – and M. Pasdeloup should have particularly refrained from uttering a coarse insult such as: "Today it is as a man that M. Wagner is judged." – – – By whom, in what way, if you please? – – –

M. Doudan was fulfilling the role of a decent man when he wrote: "Let us not concede to anyone that our friends are inferior on any point whatever. Mean people abuse this . . . I'll always fire on those who want to attack a single tent of the camp in which I live . . . He who tells me, outside the circle of my personal friends, that M. de Rémusat, M. de Lasteyrie, or M. Guizot, etc., have this or that fault will have me to contend with." The article in the *Débats* (on the young Mecklenburger dismissed from the École des Beaux-Arts the same week that Siegfried's Funeral March[23] was being hissed) cuts a far better figure than the <u>attitudes</u> of the *fier à bras* [braggart] Pasdeloup. You know that I like fine French style and literary manners, which the *Débats* respects better than other publications.

The kind parcel from Mme Judith Gauthier [Gautier] has arrived. It consists of two volumes by her entitled *L'Usurpateur; épisode de l'histoire japonaise, –1615*. One of the works by the same author now in press is called *Les Cruautés de l'amour*.

I am awaiting proofs of *Der blinde Sänger* by Tolstoy. Postpone the evening's recital with Lehfeld until the ballad has been published.

If you still have Ehrlich's pamphlet[24] (which I have not read) please send it to your

FL

---

22. FL writes *Pas de loup*, breaking down the name into three words meaning "wolf's step," or "no wolf."
23. *Die Götterdämmerung*, Act III.
24. *Für den Ring des Nibelungen, gegen das "Festspiel zu Bayreuth"* (Berlin, 1876).

You are right to sacrifice Metzdorff on the altar of the Bayreuthian "saw." Only, use kind terms shorn of any exaggeration.

Thanks again for Lassen's *Nibelungen* which I replayed for the sake of pleasant memories and of good friendship. Mihalovich and Végh are my usual partners for pieces for four hands.

There is no dearth of concerts in Pest. In less than two weeks we have had five or six, with Saint-Saëns' *Danse Macabre* (enthusiastically received and encored), some Schumann and Mozart symphonies, Turkish airs, Verdi's *Requiem* (performed better here than in Weimar), as well as the Florentine Quartet, which played the Verdi quartet perfectly, a more attractive piece than many renowned classical compositions, and just as carefully composed.

At the theatre I again saw Goldmark's *Die Königin von Saba*;[25] it continues to draw the public in Vienna and Pest: here it has been performed at least a dozen or so times this year. I prefer Metzdorff's *Rosamunde* for which I would wish an equal success, which is not very likely, for Metzd[orff] does not have the firm support which Goldmark enjoys.

I have also heard Bizet's *Carmen*:[26] the music is by no means boring, and is even polished, but of a kind which is most successful in Paris.

The happy times when the *opéras comiques* of Scribe-Auber flourished on German stages are over, and the success of the successors is uncertain.

———

December 2, 76
Budapest

Your maternal worries are fairly well justified just now. You have heavy duties to perform, but God has given you the required intelligence and heart for you to discharge them well. Place your hopes in

25. First performed March 10, 1875, in Vienna.
26. First performed March 3, 1875, in Paris.

Him, and pray with confidence and humility. I have told you several times: you are an excellent and admirable mother; hitherto, God has blessed your task; pursue it by keeping your worries within the limits of reason.

No doubt there is a threat of war; how could it be otherwise with the system of standing armies and the perfecting of engines of destruction? Fierce beasts serve as emblems to the most highly civilized great powers: eagles, lions, leopards, etc. Napoleon I tried to introduce *bees* – – – they have worked well in French domestic affairs, but in the foreign field the eagle had to prevail – – – and to succumb to others. The double eagle of Russia (which originated in Byzantium, if I am not mistaken), keeps its double beak; pacific assurances can only be considered as temporary prudence: in the end, it will have to bite. However apocryphal Peter the Great's famous testament may be, it contains the outline of Russian policy followed by Catherine, Alexander, and Nicholas; and Uncle Gortschakoff's inspiration, which I am awaiting, will not be a contradiction—at the most a respite. My wish is that Andrássy, who represents another double eagle, will also be inspired by his role. In this old question of the East there is a huge difficulty and a great obstacle. The difficulty is how to be as thick as thieves when it comes to sharing the spoils. The obstacle is that the Christian powers are not so Christian that the Turks can take them at their word and trust them, under penalty of being crushed by them.

The diplomatic crusade of the d'Israelis, Decazes, and their colleagues seems understandably suspect to "the sick man."

If I'm talking nonsense, it is only to reply politely to the very judicious points in your last letter on the Eastern question; for you know that a pianist such as I has no business with politics.

As always, thanks for the newspapers which you so kindly send me, and which I read with the priority due to the stamp of Weimar. Herewith an article from *L'Italie* on a soirée at the Palazzo Caffarelli of Germany. My daughter writes that Wagner is very pleased with Sgambati and will recommend that Schott publish his quintet. In Rome, she came across Lord Lindsay (President of the London *Wagner Verein*), and established good relations with Teano, Mme Helbig, etc. We must hold the line for Bayreuth next year, and you did entirely the proper thing in writing to Feustel.

This letter has already twice been interrupted by callers. In order not to delay further I am sending it off to you while craving all your indulgence.

Yours ever

FL

Cosima is staying at the Hôtel d'Amérique, Via del Babuino, in Rome.

―――――――

December 4, 76
Budapest

The good La Fontaine well said: "Absence is the worst of evils." Lo indulges in nonsense when she dreams up the most completely impossible "grudges" – – – and she should make due amends for this. If I sometimes utter a harsh word, please do believe that its real meaning applies only to me, not to others, and least of all to you.

Although you subscribe to the *Neue Zeitschrift*, I am sending you a copy of Pohl's latest article on Bayreuth, which you have probably not read. It indicates fairly well the role of the *Wagner Verein* and their continuing importance. In my opinion, *Der Ring des Nibelungen* still belongs to Bayreuth for the year '77, and must be presented there exclusively (with no admixture of Mozart, Gluck, or Weber). I assume that Wagner will not contradict me in this, and that his friends will understand that before creating a National Theatre at Bayreuth, the Wagner Theatre must first be firmly established. That is the question.[27]

I telegraphed right away to Gille that he merely had to follow your instructions for Tolstoy's ballad [*Der blinde Sänger*]. You know my habit of not involving myself in the performance of my works (which

27. Liszt wrote this in English.

are always too long, even when they consist only of two or three pages) and of urging my friends to ignore them entirely.

Recently, I again had to write a few letters in this vein to Vienna and Berlin. It is not a question of spite—but, rather, of wise and slightly condescending resignation on the part

of your very humble

FL

December 11, 76
Budapest

Like all good ideas, that of the Wagner Concert at Weimar must be well carried out. Frankly, the first request on this subject, "how to obtain the scores" (published more than a year ago by Schott), wasn't very encouraging to me for the negotiations to follow. Without in any way reproaching Lassen or Loën for their absentmindedness, you must admit that they would have cut a very strange figure had they turned to Wagner in order to obtain bundles of music which can be easily obtained from his publisher at Mainz – – –

So, organize properly the Wagner Concert and the *Wagner Verein* in Weimar. In my view there would be an advantage in having the concert precede the *Verein*, for which Feustel's basic ideas must be followed, and in associating with it Jena and Eisenach, perhaps even Apolda if there are men of good will there. I'll soon write about this to the Grand Duke, whose support is necessary unless people enjoy going to a lot of trouble for nothing.

It seems to me that you exaggerate the possible receipts from the concert; but no matter: let's stick to the essential, which is to affirm the continuity of the work of a great genius, which the Weimar theatre had the honor of recognizing and publicizing at a time when other theatres were prevented from so doing – – –

The conclusion of Ehrlich's witty pamphlet is a trap, if not a substantial, so-called national, piece of nonsense. To turn Bayreuth into a Baden-Baden, or the living Valhalla of great German art, cannot be undertaken either by the town of Bayreuth or by Wagner, so long as the German nation, through its representatives in the two parliaments of Munich and Berlin, has not voted the necessary funds. Were such an event to occur, I would be delighted, but would request that no works other than those of Wagner be performed in the Bayreuth theatre during the first three years.

Do you know the pamphlet *Die Bühnenfestspiele in Bayreuth* by Martin Plüddeman (published at Colberg)? It pleases me, and is not a repeat of Wolzogen, though it is similar. A biting and witty Bayreuthian dictionary[28] by Tappert has been announced.

Let us not belittle those who are not accredited to the *"Reines Olgas"* and to the illustrious *Revue des deux mondes*. They have some preposterous sides to them; well and good, but don't ambassadors, Excellencies, and Highnesses in the highest sense of the word have theirs, too?

Be indulgent toward my legendary Gottschalg, who has merit, notwithstanding his preposterous behavior. Among other things, his little articles on Bayreuth were worth more than the ill-tempered pieces on aesthetics (in the tone of Lübke, Hanslick, etc.) in the *Weimarer Zeitung*. – – –

When one keeps a salon, only Highnesses, Excellencies, etc., must be admitted; they have the advantage of having been, in general, well brought up, and even their nonsense or impertinence has a certain, much sought after, flavor. However, as mistress of the house, one may add a few current or recent celebrities; but with great moderation, for there is always something of the commoner in these newcomers, who usually don't know what prudent degree of modesty they should observe so as to please others without appearing too servile.

Excuse this silly digression. I sent off to you yesterday the second volume of Lamartine's *Voyage en Orient*, with the "political summary"

---

28. Wilhelm Tappert, *Ein Wagner-Lexikon* (Leipzig, 1877).

written in 1833. Naturally, this summary may seem to be poetry only to the real political leaders; their formula is not to jump, but to make others, the silly rabble of musicians, poets, hack writers, and those of this ilk, dance but not at too great a cost.

Yours ever

FL

December 14, 76
Budapest

Lo is manifestly unjust to the heroic Gille. He has to yield to the enthusiasm of the Jena public, which would never forgive him for depriving it of the Funeral March from *Götterdämmerung*, of the *Walkürenritt*, etc., which are no less admired in Vienna and Berlin than at Gera and Hilburgshausen.

Between you and me, it is fairly absurd to play certain richly instrumented masterpieces in small halls such as the "Rose," but Queen Olga's maxim prevails: "Achieve great things on a small scale" (*Im Kleinem Grosses leisten*), and in this our friend Gille is prodigious. So don't spoil for him his *Nibelungen* Concert at Jena, either before or after the one at Weimar. Loën might well refuse him his musicians, and Mudoli (I forget the spelling of the name of the ex-Governor) might call for a ukase from Emperor Alexander to prohibit completely all concerts at Jena. Only Gottschalg would be left to save the honor of Castile with some well-turned article in *Deutschland* – – – –

Joking aside, I urge you not to interfere with Gille's enthusiasm; his Wagner Concert will help more than it will harm that of Weimar; this is FL's very humble opinion.

So concentrate all your efforts on what you yourself are doing for the concert and the *Wagner Verein*.

The little column of the Paris Stock Exchange (in the *Débats*) strikes me as highly intelligent. I am also very much of your opinion on the utopia of an amicable agreement in the matter of the partition of the East. This would require too great a consumption of the famous vinegar of the four (or six) thieves.

Pedantically, I'm sending off to you today the first volume of Lamartine's *Voyage*, while thanking you for the warm welcome you extended to the second.

Varzin's *Psychologue* has good reason for abstaining from giving friendly advice, the least of whose faults is its uselessness.

Mme de Stockhausen (born Beulwitz) arrived here some two weeks ago, followed by Martha Remmert who will harvest applause, and a little money (I hope).

Yours ever

FL

December 27, 76

Budapest

As for "imbecility" I could spot you many points, as they say in billiards, with this added difference, that, where you are concerned, it is only accidentally caused by migraine headaches, or by some physical indisposition, whereas it is permanently lodged in my brain. You have had many proofs of this, and in particular last week at the time of our polemics on the misdeeds of "your peers" (an expression I don't much approve of) and the transcendent virtues of Gottschalg and Müller-Hartung! – – – Forgive me the silly things I said; I wanted to say other things which you know better than I, but I lacked the time to develop them to my advantage, and you disconcerted me royally by suddenly unfurling the banner of your "peers" – – – And so I was unable even to utter, just like a certain person who, presenting his credentials to Louis Philippe, could find no other words than: "Sire, my august Master – – – your august Majesty, – – – the lofty throne on which you are seated – – – my august Sovereign – – –" and thereupon pulled out his pocket handkerchief in order to wipe the tears of his indescribable emotion.

Besides, for my recent imbecility I would also have the excuse of an accident, which I only mention today so as not to hear it mentioned again, for the little publicity about it in a few newspapers has already resulted in my receiving several letters and telegrams full of that concern which I absolutely refuse to accept at its worth. Yes, I fell in getting out of a cab at the Hotel Hungaria; from this fall I still have a little discomfort in my right arm, nothing more. Short of a relapse I'll be back in good shape before New Year's day. *Basta così.*

Tell me about the Court concert next Monday with Sarasate (whom I do not know). Talk with him a little, and tell him that I will have the pleasure of hearing him in Pest: Bösendorfer told me that he'll be coming here in the month of February – – – Tell me about the Spanish opera with which M. Sach seems to be very pleased.

My gracious master sent me a very friendly reply to the three points in my last letter: a monument to Bach (to be carved by Dondorff [Donndorff]); the *Wagner Verein* and concert; and, in the near future, a performance (in which please take an interest) of a drama by M. de Saar, a fine gentleman and distinguished author.

The Wagner Concert seems to me in no way embarrassing for Weimar. Similar ones are given everywhere without any problem; herewith an announcement of the one at Düsseldorf, conducted by Ratzenberger.

If I am guilty of not having answered explicitly one of your questions on the *Verein* or the Wagner Concert, please repeat it to me, and in general, when questions of this kind arise again, please be so kind as to mark them with a + in red pencil.

Yours ever
with all my heart

FL

1877

January 3, 77
Budapest

Now that you have so well launched the business of the *Wag[ner]* *Ver[ein]* and the concert, take a little rest and leave things to Loën, Lassen—and M. S[ach]. The assurance that Mme S[ach] is not against the idea pleases me very much. For my part I am always ready to do all I can; but this is very limited, due to various obligations and considerations of propriety, which do not permit me at this time to involve myself in a Wagner concert. I have also had to refrain from doing so in Pest for two years, until the opportune moment came for the concert you attended. When a comparable occasion arises at Weimar, I'll willingly offer my humble services. It's first of all a matter of launching the *Verein* there with a concert, and Lassen as the conductor. Schott's authorization presents no problem. Last week Mme Materna once again sang the last scene of *Götterdämmerung* magnificently at a concert here of the Philharmonic Society. Wagner concerts, consisting of excerpts from the *Nibelungen*, are announced for Düsseldorf and other towns. Thus to do likewise at Weimar seems to me to be neither a labor of Hercules, nor an annex to the diplomatic conference at Constantinople.

Albert Apponyi (who is to spend part of the winter in the country at his father's place at Eberhard, near Pressburg) has just sent Mihalovich a printed handbill from Bayreuth about making up the deficit for the year 1876, to which the sponsors are invited to contribute. This handbill is only a prelude and I think Wagner will shortly let people know his intentions and wishes – – – then the sponsors will have to ponder the matter and comply with good grace.

Several passages in Legouvé's academic speech in reply to that of the new immortal, M. Boissier, please me. First of all, with regard to Cicero: "Ah, believe me, Sir, when one comes across such men in history, one must not depreciate their greatness because of their shortcomings, but rather absorb their shortcomings within their greatness," etc. Then, on Juvenal: "Why demonstrate to us with your impeccable erudition and your implacable observation that this very Juvenal, so eloquently called by Victor Hugo the ancient, free, soul of the defunct republics, cared neither for the republic nor for freedom? Victor Hugo is nonetheless right!" etc. I am sending back Legouvé's entire speech for you to reread these two passages.

Yesterday I received the two operas in vogue in Paris: *Piccolino*[1] by Guiraud and *Paul et Virginie*[2] by Victor Massé. Both of them seem pretty thin. By comparison, *Carmen*[3] and *Der Widerspänstigen [Zähmung]* by Götz are masterpieces.

Rubinstein has just published (by Senff, Leipzig) his last two grand operas simultaneously: *Néron* and *Le Démon*.[4] I have not yet read them; but no one wishes Rubinstein complete and lasting success more than I, for he certainly has far more musical quality than his rivals, with the exception of two or three.

Lassen has forgotten to send me his *Faust*. Please don't mention this to him; rather lend me your copy for a week or so. I'll be sure to return it to you, and with it I'll send you a copy of the *Revue des deux mondes* (for July) which you instructed me to put aside.

Yours ever

FL

1. First performed April 11, 1876, in Paris.
2. First performed November 15, 1876, in Paris.
3. By Bizet, first performed March 3, 1875, in Paris.
4. First performed January 25, 1875, in St. Petersburg.

January 9, 77
Budapest

Berlioz sometimes used to amuse himself by rewording proverbs, and ranked among the virtuosi of this not very distinguished art. Among others, he produced the brilliant variation: "One should beat one's <u>brother</u> while he is hot"[5]—an excellent practice in which Lo will excel without effort. Not only do I grant her full latitude, but I will gladly offer her both cheeks in honor of art and of Castile. So try to beat the "brothers" Loën and Lassen so soundly that they will set the date for the Wagner concert and move ahead promptly as they should. For the *Wagner Verein*, one must await the next announcement promised by Bayreuth. Should it prove desirable for me to associate myself with the subsequent proceedings, my zeal will not be wanting; but the first thing to do is to give the concert (with Lassen as conductor) and to set up the *Verein* under the protective support of the Grand Duke.

The motto of the Order of the House of Weimar being *Vigilando ascendimus*, I recently ventured to solicit the Grand Duke's interest for the Bach monument at Eisenach. This business has been dragging along for some ten years; the gentlemen on the committee are asleep, while writing a lot of letters. This is not enough and does not look good, for before begging right and left, one should oneself first contribute a substantial sum if one does not wish to look like a beggar; and as the Bach monument must belong to Eisenach, it is only fair that there be substantial local contributions.

M. d'Eichel is no doubt a man of great weight, but he seems hitherto to have applied his weight too much – – – in a vacuum.

You are completely and absolutely right to save me from my friends. My excellent and legendary Gottschalg has his pockets full of such brickbats, but I am fond of him and grateful to him for the many hours of comfort I owe him during my tribulations in the years '54 to '65, and I thank you from my heart for the watchchain and the briefcase (*Briefmappe*) which you gave him for Christmas and of which

5. A pun: *frère* (brother), instead of *fer* (iron).

he writes effusively in his last letter. As for his idea of my pressing
harder to have some of my compositions performed, I am categori-
cally opposed to it. The attention they receive at Weimar and here and
there elsewhere is completely satisfactory to me; I find this already
more than enough and protest against any excess – – –

Give me news of Ratzenberger's concert. I consider him one of my
best pupils and see only one fault in him: his not very elegant name. In
fact, names of more than three syllables are an obstacle to fame—except
for Napoleon! If Ratz[enberger] is still at Weimar, invite him cordially, and tell him that he will soon be receiving a letter from me.

Yours ever

FL

Your letter of January 7 has just arrived. It sums up the Bayreuth
situation perfectly, with that superior lucidity of fair and lofty good
sense which I have long admired in you.

I had noticed Veuillot's praise of Doctor Frédault's book: *Forme et
matière*,[6] and wrote to Rome about it. The reply states that *L'Univers*
knows nothing about either form or matter: and that Frédault is only
a superfluous phrase-maker, who ought to start by learning the ABC
of Saint Thomas' *Summa*. In short, people treat his knowledge of philosophy much as I treated the pianistic talent of Mlle de Jagwitz.

Martha Remmert wrote you about her success here, to which a
kindly Maecenas, Mme Földvari contributed effectively.

You reproached me at Weimar for not appreciating Mme de Stockhausen sufficiently. She has studied well at Stuttgart, and comes twice
a week to my piano class. Yesterday she played two of Chopin's late
nocturnes with distinction.

------

6. Paris, 1876.

January 28, 77
B.P. [Budapest]

Let us, very dear Lo, strike the word "displeasure" entirely from the vocabulary of our intimate conversation. I have too many reasons for being displeased with myself to find room for others, especially those I love. So long as Lo is not too displeased with her very humble FL, the latter will always be very happy with the indulgence she grants him.

Your recent letters are all excellent, and what you write about Bayreuth and my daughter fits in perfectly with my own views which, I imagine, do not conflict with good sense. After Wagner's recent announcement, the non-millionaires must wait a while so as to become conscious of their duties, and the corresponding form of activity. The proposal to the *Reichsrath* is nothing new: M. de Radowitz spoke to me about it in Rome (before last year's Bayreuth performances) and he thought there would be some chance of success – – – (??).

Whatever happens, Lo and FL will firmly hold aloft the banner of Bayreuth.

The mourning of Their Royal Highnesses postpones the Wagner concert and *Verein* at Weimar; nevertheless you did well to keep your shoulder to the wheel while it could turn.

In memory of kind attentions from his late sister, Princess Charles, I have sent M. S[ach] a couple of lines of condolence. Besides, writing is becoming more and more onerous and sometimes odious for me. Banalities repel me no less than affectations. It is indeed difficult for me to make my way between them with my pen. So long as there is work to be done, I still feel relaxed and in fairly good form. For the rest, I am overcome by indescribable depression and have reached the point where Carthusians and Trappists often seem garrulous to me.

From Rome I receive nothing but superb admonitions in the finest style. I answer these by an increasing devotion to the repentant thief; his cross was close to that of Our Lord Jesus—may all hearts bless him!—and the repentant thief administered justice to himself with the words: "I deserved my punishment." This confession earned him the divine promise, in which I have complete faith. *Das Unbeschreibliche hier ist's gethan!* [The indescribable has here been done!][7]

Please thank Lassen very much for having sent me his *Faust*, and hand him the enclosed note.

Your

FL

I'll be here until March 10; then I spend a week in Vienna and will play at the concert for the Beethoven monument which, people say, is a remarkable sculpture by Zumbusch.

Thanks for the witty and slightly sarcastic article in the *Débats* on the *Mémoires d'une idéaliste*.[8] In the same issue, John Lemoinne puts it well: "In political sweeps of the broom there is only one truth: be on the same end as the handle."

—————

February 12, 77
Budapest

You often reproach me for not giving you my opinion: in this you are mistaken and wrong me. It is simply that when I share your opinion I can give you no other. Fortunately our opinions on most things are usually alike; we play the same themes, but our instruments differ. You don't care much for the flute, nor I for the trumpet or the trombone. My normal register is that of alto (viola or *Bratsche*); I like mutes when it's a matter of giving advice: they do not impair accuracy of pitch, and, save for exceptional cases, it is better to be restrained rather than noisy.

Yet again I repeat that you were right to prod Loën and Lassen on the Wagner concert and the *Verein* at Weimar; and I thank you for

7. The close of Goethe's *Faust*, Part 2.
8. Malwida von Meysenbug, *Memoiren einer Idealistin* (Stuttgart, 1875).

having thus acted to some extent on my behalf. Carry on; success will come in its own time – – – if it is delayed, this is no reason for relaxing our effort. The kindly assurances of M. de Zedlitz sincerely pleased me.

To explain the method *der Auswahl der Würdigen, und würdig den Weg zu einer Verbindung mit den obersten Reichsbehörden aufzufinden* [for selecting the dignitaries and how to find a dignified approach to a relationship with the highest government officials] far exceeds my feeble capacity. However, I retain my faith; and the road already covered at Bayreuth in spite of so many obstacles makes me confident that we will finally succeed. Besides, there is something greatly comforting in the alleged exaggerations of men of great genius like Wagner; far from laughing at them, which is not difficult and may even seem almost reasonable, I attempt to rise to the height required for one not to misjudge things belonging to the higher order of inspiration. In the midst of so many theatrical indignities and filth why should it be forbidden to speak of the dignity of art? Do we have ears only for mountebanks? – – –

Omnis anima potestatibus sublimioribus subdita sit ("Let every person be subordinated to the higher powers"), said St. Paul to the Romans.[9] Now, in the sublime procession of men of genius down the centuries before and since Homer, Wagner has his place. So greetings and glory to Bayreuth.

I'll write to my daughter tomorrow. She has always understood me well, and knows that I love her without my having to explain or beat about the bush.

This is a very mild winter, but I am suffering physically and mentally. I beg you not to tell anyone, and believe me for ever to be

Your very humble

FL

I will return Cosima's letter to you tomorrow.

On the matter of the Bayreuth "dignitaries," we can relax: Lo and

9. "Let every soul be subject unto the higher powers." Romans xiii:1. King James version.

FL are to be admitted to the ranks of the *Würdigen*. Assure those of your friends who tend to have doubts about the efficacy of the "political functions" of the *Reichsrath* of this.

––––

February 15, 77
Budapest

I wrote to Cosima this morning and, alluding to the *Würdigen*, told her:

"One must count on Wagner's great and propitious star shining on the *Patronat Verein*, in which I shall shortly have the honor of playing an active role." In my humble opinion people were wrong to be shocked by the triple accent, grave, acute, and circumflex, which Wagner places on the *Würdigen*, and the *Würdigung* of his grand design and of his sublime work. Let those who have been led astray by the common practice of theaters find it impractical that a man of extraordinary genius should speak seriously of the dignity of dramatic art, should ponder it and propose its achievement.

Those who have a dignified conception of art will help Wagner to overcome obstacles – – –

Your

FL

––––

February 23, 77
Budapest

I don't know who said: "Were it not for me, I would be in very good health." Were it not for the *moi*, which Pascal denounced as hateful, and which to me seems to be chiefly a nuisance to each of us, one would also be fairly happy in this world of ours. Without philosophizing, I thank Lo with all my heart for her very affectionate letters, and renew to her my old prayer not to worry about me. At the same time, I accuse myself of having betrayed a rash confidence to you:

don't misinterpret it, and rest assured that my health is adequate, my nerves and my mood are holding their own fairly well, and that I would be an arch idiot not to recognize the fact that Providence has placed me among the most favored.

In reply to your questions:

A) I have no concert in view for the *Patronat Verein*; this could come about. In the meantime I am resolved simply to serve Wagner *und seine Kunst* at Bayreuth as much as I am able to, everywhere and always.

(Cosima writes that Wagner will probably be going to England this spring and that there will be no performances at Bayreuth in 1877 – – – We'll discuss the situation at Weimar in early April –).

B) Vera Timanoff spent a week here. She is on a concert tour with Mlle d'Orgeny, daughter of an Austrian Field Marshal, and an excellent pupil of Mme Viardot, and with Mlle Haft (a seventeen-year-old violinist). These three young ladies are now charming audiences in Hungary, Galicia, Bohemia – – – Vera is an artist of rare talent; furthermore, I think she enjoys fairly good protection from the direction of St. Petersburg. If the person who spoke to you about her wishes to write to her, say that the letter should be sent to M. L. Bösendorfer, piano maker to Their Majesties, 6 Herrengasse, Vienna. Vera is perhaps already back in Vienna where, she told me, I'll see her again on March 16 at the concert for the Beethoven monument. In Vienna she played Rubinstein's Third Concerto (in G),[10] as well as other pieces, with success. If she goes on like this, she will shortly become an accepted and established celebrity – – –

Martha Remmert is succeeding beyond my expectations (for she has no impresario), and her concerts at Klausenburg, Debreczin [Debrecen], Grosswardein were productive. Her next goal is Vienna. There, Sophie Menter, who is in my opinion the greatest of the pianists of the fair sex in Germany or anywhere, not excepting Mme Essipoff, nor even Mme Jaëll, the <u>impassioned</u> French Alsatian virtuoso and scintil-

10. Opus 45.

lating composer – – – where am I with all my admirations? with Sophie Menter; her presence at Vienna will not contribute to Martha Remmert's success, which will also be challenged by Vera Timanoff's fingers of steel and seductive Slavic personality.

Pursuing the chapter on pianists: you were to be a patroness of Schlözer in memory of our admirable friend, Mme Moukhanoff. He has in him more the stuff of a sound professor than of a dashing virtuoso, and would be just right for some well-known conservatory or even the Berlin *Hochschule*, where the *hochnäsigen Professoren* [arrogant professors] know no more than he does about the piano, and are inferior to him as concert pianists.

Altra cosa for my "first-class" pianists. Zarembski is quite ready for the famous baptism of celebrity in Paris; and Pinner (who is in Warsaw) will not fall short. Item [*idem*], two other lads: one Dutch, the other a Hanoverian, whom I will introduce to you at Weimar. This winter, they are thundering and storming on my pianos at the *Fischplatz*.

Mihalovich is composing *Wieland*[11] (the Blacksmith) and has already completed the first act. He tells me he read a remarkable article in the *Revue des deux mondes* on Shelley, by Schuré. When you have read it, speak of it to

Your very humble

FL

If you are still in touch with your Brussels bookseller, I'll ask you to get him to send off a few books, whose titles I'll provide.

Your claim that you resemble the composer Metzdorff, *der immer zu breit wird* [who is steadily becoming too broad], is completely unjustifiable.

Don't scold me if I write a little tardily. Fifteen or so letters which absolutely must be answered languish on my table, and my pen is unwell.

---

11. *Wieland der Schmied*, 1876–78.

Monday, March 12, 77
Vienna
(Schottenhof)

Last Monday I conducted *The Legend of St. Elisabeth* in Pest, and day before yesterday there was a charity concert, to which I had the pleasure of contributing by playing two pieces for two pianos with Mme Sophie Menter-Popper (*La Fée des Alpes*[11a] by Schumann-Reinecke, and the *Walkürenritt*).

On my arrival here this morning, I was fairly tired. My stay in Vienna won't afford me much rest, for the Friday concert for the Beethoven monument is combined with an extraordinary and very profitable dress rehearsal, in order to satisfy the many people who cannot get tickets for the concert. The rehearsal too is already sold out, people assure me. I cannot account for such a crowd.

Next Tuesday (March 20) I'll go to Bayreuth from here, and will probably stay there until Easter Tuesday; thereafter we shall be deprived of letters and telegrams for some time.

From Pest I returned to you Montalembert's remarkable letters, as well as an old issue of the *Revue des deux mondes*. If you have at hand Reyer's article on the *Timbre d'argent*,[12] please send it to me. You know that Saint-Saëns had a brilliant success in Paris with this *Timbre*. Is Weimar still thinking of performing *Dalila*? Several people have repeated to me the press rumor that Loën is accepting the position of manager at Frankfurt, and that Rudolph Gottschall (not A. W. Gottschalg) will replace him in our town.

Do you have any harder information than gossip?

At Bayreuth I'll learn exactly what the real situation is with regard to the business of the *Wagner Verein*, and will at once give you an oral report.

I suppose you have already ordered Rémusat's drama, *Abélard*, and I'll ask you to lend it to me when I am back at the Hofgärtnerei.

11a. Probably from Schumann's *Manfred*, Opus 115.
12. Opera by Saint-Saëns, first performed February 23, 1877, in Paris.

The opening line of the new series of the *Légende des siècles*,[13] "The father has slapped his son" – – – even surpasses the lion saying to the bear: "That's very fine, imbecile." So long as the very dear Lo says as much to her poor FL, the latter will always be very happy.

FL

Mme Dönhoff informs me that Mme Coudenhove died day before yesterday at one of her castles in Bohemia.

—————

March 17, 77
Vienna

Will be here until Thursday morning.
Will write tomorrow.
Am sending you the *Tageblatt* which reprints a letter about Copenhagen written thirty-five years ago.

Your

FL

Keep the Steinway at your home; it would be a nuisance to me at the Hofgärtnerei.
Yesterday evening's concert was a great success.

—————

March 24, 77
Amberg
(Waiting Room)

I'm being held up here by a railroad breakdown, with no harm to the passengers other than a few hours' delay, of which I take advantage

13. Ser. 2, *Le cycle pyrénéen*, III: *La paternité* (Paris, 1877), by Victor Hugo.

to tell you that it was almost impossible to write to Lo from Vienna. When I had an hour or two free from outside obligations, I spent them with my cousin who, as you know, has been my most intimate friend for a quarter of a century. His talents and sound qualities have gained him general esteem, and I know of but one fault in him: that of thinking too highly of me. This is no reason why we should squabble.

This time, the Vienna public was <u>extremely</u> responsive, to the point of causing my modesty (which few people are aware of but which, I am so bold as to admit, is nonetheless sincere) extraordinary embarrassment. It will find itself more at ease again and, so to speak, wearing slippers too long and too wide on many other occasions – – –

I've seen the *Walküre* again; the Court and the city are enthusiastic about it. The Emperor attended three or four performances; Princess Metternich states that after this one cannot listen to operas other than those by Wagner and, in particular, the three other dramas of *Der Ring des Nibelungen* which the Director, Jauner, is trying to obtain. He has requested me to negotiate to this end with Wagner; but I doubt that it will succeed, at least for the present.

Instead of arriving at Bayreuth at half past one (having left Nuremberg this morning at eight o'clock), I will only get there after eleven o'clock in the evening, if no further hitch occurs.

I hope to find a letter from you at Wahnfried.

Your

FL

Bayreuth
Sunday morning
Arrived here safe and sound yesterday before midnight. I am expecting your letter.

In the train I read an article (which I'll send you) on V. Hugo's *La Légende des siècles*.

Easter Sunday, April 1, 77
Bayreuth

You will scold me for my laziness in writing; however, I am not as delinquent as you think. Holy Week church services have claimed several hours a day since last Sunday. Besides which I have had to get through proofs, which were rather a lot of trouble to correct. Finally, long conversations with W[agner] and my daughter have prevented me from writing. Fortunately, in another three days pens will no longer be needed.

Mme de Heldburg having very kindly invited me, I'll stop at Meiningen on Tuesday, and will be at Weimar the following evening (fairly late). Please be so good as to have Pauline notified of my arrival on Wednesday evening.

Your recollection of the Litanies in Mgr Isoard's book touched me deeply.

Thank you for the information about Loën, which conforms to my prior assumptions.

Indeed, I had someone in mind should Loën have left Weimar.

If the train does not arrive too late Wednesday evening, I'll come straightaway to welcome myself at your home.

Yours ever

FL

If necessary, wire me at Meiningen Tuesday evening or Wednesday morning (early).

———

Sunday, May 20, 77
Hanover

Spiridion is becoming a complete courtier. Imagine that he has been practicing tying his necktie according to the latest fashion, like those which Lo wears. He pointed this out to me yesterday, with that satisfaction peculiar to artists who cater to the taste of the public, so I rewarded him by urging him to embellish my appearance with these same knots for the duration of the *Musikfest* at Hanover.

Gille tells me that he (on his own) sent you the schedule of the concerts. Mlle Brandt is being so kind as to sing the part of the Landgräfin Sophie in the *Elisabeth* this evening, and on Tuesday, the *St. Cecilia*, to which you granted your support at the Tempelherrenhaus at Weimar.

Last Thursday, Prince and Princess Albrecht spent the evening at the Bronsarts. I played several piano pieces for them—starting with the Fugue and Prelude in A minor for organ,[14] long ago transcribed for piano,[15] by your very humble servant:

[16]

Mme Schumann having in the past been so kind as to play this transcription in public, it has been accepted as tolerable, even in the conservatories of the pure conservatories (*Hochschulen*) where my name is excluded, and is considered an insult to sound doctrine.

Molière was well aware of how things stand when he wrote: *Le monde, chère Agnès, est une étrange chose.*

Without any strangeness, I remain

Yours ever

FL

Monday morning

The *Musikfest* seems to have a fair chance of success, although the *Kapellmeister* (Bott) who conducted the *Elisabeth* yesterday evening, literally fell from his stand onto the floor—fortunately without hurting himself—just before the end of the work. Thereupon, fright, compas-

14. By J. S. Bach, Schmieder 543.
15. G 462, 1; R 119, 1.
16. Liszt copied this incorrectly.

sion, and comments. Tell this incident to Lassen, who will personally cut a *cattiva figura* [poor figure] if he does not come here.

People having already noted that since Monseigneur the Grand Duke of Weimar is the protector of the *Allgemeiner Deutscher Musikverein*, it would be appropriate if someone were sent (let's say Loën) to represent His Royal Highness.

————

Sunday, May 27, 77
Hanover

All went well at this *Musikfest*. One can rejoice at the artistic and financial success, for which I give credit chiefly to my friend Bronsart. He has once again given proof of those rare qualities called tact, good taste, real obligingness, firmness, and administrative competence. If our *Verein* had three people of Bronsart's stamp, the musical situation in Germany would be different and better. Mme de Bronsart played the Saint-Saëns *Variations* and the *Concerto Pathétique*[16a] like a first-class pianist. The performances of Berlioz' *Symphonie Fantastique*,[17] of the ballad *Des Sängers Fluch*[18] by Bülow, of the *Scherzo* by Dräseke, of the first movement of the *Symphonie Tragique* by Metzdorff, and of the *Andante* and *Finale* of Tchaikovsky's Second Symphony (well received by the audience—which pleased me, as I had more or less imposed this work on the program) were more than satisfactory. I was able to say in good conscience that these orchestra performances were on a par with those of the more famous Leipzig, Vienna, Paris. Berlioz would not differ on this point. Marianne Brandt sang admirably the *Legend of St. Cecilia* and the Landgräfin Sophie in the *Elisabeth*.

Thursday evening there was a performance of the *Barber of Bagdad*.[19]

16a. *See* p. 129 note 19.
17. Opus 14.
18. Opus 16.
19. Opera by Peter Cornelius, first performed December 15, 1858, in Weimar, conducted by Liszt. The hostility of the audience was responsible for Liszt's resignation as Court conductor. Cornelius himself provided the libretto.

You are one of the very few people whose taste is refined and educated enough to appreciate the high musical quality of this work. Though very witty, the libretto is a failure, as it lacks stage action. Nothing happens, and the public cannot do without that which is indispensable to it at the theatre, where even the most charming music is not enough. Nevertheless, I think there will be a way to preserve the *Barber of Bagdad* because of its musical quality, but on condition that it be shortened by at least one-quarter, and that the opera be reduced to a single act. Besides, the audience last Thursday did not follow that of Weimar; there was much applause, especially from the musically knowledgeable.

With all due respect to M. de Loën and Otto Devrient, the performance here of *Faust* (of which I saw the first part yesterday evening) seems to me far superior to that at Weimar. Lassen's music also impressed me more favorably than it did at home.

Gille, who left day before yesterday, will give you a detailed report on the *Musikfest*; and the last issue of the *Neue Zeitschrift* contains an introductory article by Pohl.

Next Thursday I'll be back

and as ever your

FL

Your letter and the *Débats* have just this moment been handed to me. Till Thursday.

Cosima writes that the Wagner concerts in London are going well. In spite of costs amounting to 9,000 pounds sterling, the surplus receipts will cover the Bayreuth deficit.

———

August 1, 77
Weimar

Clément (Rubens) is perfectly right, and Lo even more so. I counted on being at Wilhelmsthal yesterday for the birthday of S^t,[20] but I have

20. Unidentified.

not packed or arranged anything here, and it would be too silly to return to Weimar just after having left. Cosima stayed with me till Monday, and has no Bayreuthian plot in mind. She read me *Parsifal* Sunday evening. In the third act there is a sublime religious page. I don't know whether it's possible to stage this miraculous work. No matter; Wagner's genius overcomes even the impossible.

You know that the King of Bavaria constantly addresses his letters to Wagner: *dem Wort und Ton Dichter, Meister R.W.* [to the poet of word and sound, Master R.W.].

Sunday morning I showed Cosima the castle, its paintings, drawings, and furniture. At about five o'clock, Zarembski played his *Fantaisie* for us. Lo's most judicious correction was pointed out to the composer.

Cosima accompanied her daughter, Isolde, back to Altenburg. Unfortunately, the latter will have to stay there even longer; her mother will be back at Bayreuth today.

I have received very distressing news from Rome. In the latest decree of the Sacred Congregation of the Index, published July 17 in Rome, several works have been condemned and, finally, the nine volumes entitled *Les Causes intérieures de la faiblesse extérieure de l'Eglise* as well. The author's name is omitted in the decree, for it did not appear on the title page of the work which, though not yet publicly available, was, it appears, already circulating in proof in Italy, Austria, Poland, etc.

The Roman acts of kindness to Princess Wittgenstein are rather like those of St. Petersburg, with this difference, that in Rome it can no longer be a matter of governmental brutality, such as confiscation and loss of civil rights under false pretexts! Governments which still have recourse to these abominable measures should be scorned and spurned by European civilization.

This is the humble opinion of a more or less famous pianist, who is both a strong *russophile* and very humbly with all his heart, your

FL

I shall probably only go to Wilhelmsthal next Sunday or Monday. Write to Weimar.

From August 12 to 14, I'll be at Schillingsfürst, and soon thereafter in Rome.

August 3, 77
Weimar

In honor of the new Rubens, Clément de Meyendorff, I'm sending you the very kind invitation from our friend Verlat to the brilliant festivities at Antwerp for the three hundredth anniversary of Rubens' birth. Don't take umbrage at "*l'aimable Baronne*" – – –

This morning I made my call on Brehme [Brehmer] in Zarembski's behalf. I might have consulted the doctor about my own physical condition; my nerves are seriously out of order.

Gille is coming to dine with me today; I'm postponing my departure. The trunks are not ready, nor have the parcels been sent off. Depending on when I wake up Sunday, I'll go to Wilhelmsthal in the afternoon, or postpone it one more day.

Sarring is so good as to bring me the *Débats* and *L'Univers* for which I thank you, as this reading matter distracts me from my somber thoughts—all the more somber in that I am conscious of their total sterility.

The July 29 issue of *L'Univers* contains the decree of the Sacred Congregation of the Index which condemns the work you know about.

Your

FL

Write to me here.

Saturday, August 4, 77

W[eimar]

When I received Verlat's letter yesterday morning, I answered it at once. His intentions are of the best and I regret my mood is no longer very festive. Send him a friendly line or two as well on your own account. When Verlat returns to Weimar he will perhaps be so obliging as to direct Clément Rubens' studies a little.

Zarembski has already received his certificate from Brehmer, and will be writing to you about it tomorrow morning. He has just played Chopin's First Sonata[21] for me admirably. As he will probably stay here until Lassen's return and the reopening of the theatre, please ask Lassen to grant him a rehearsal with orchestra for the *Fantaisie* of which he has just completed the instrumentation. In my opinion, it should be slightly altered and in particular toned down; but the work is remarkable, original, vigorous, and refined in character—and worthy of your support. It would not be advisable for Zarembski to risk performing this *Fantaisie* with orchestra in public before it has been tried out in private. At the time of my musical activities at Weimar I used to make it easy for young composers to hear their own works in rehearsals and to correct them; one would do well to follow the precedent of my erring ways. We only have to set rules here for them to become the rule elsewhere, by setting good examples. If Borodin had come to W[eimar] before the orchestra went on leave, I would immediately have asked our artists to hold a rehearsal for his symphony.

My nerves are in poor shape. Monday morning I'll spend a few hours at Erfurt to have a talk with the Protestant pastor, who sent me an excellent draft of an oratorio, *Les Sept Sacrements*,[22] and that evening I'll be at Wilhelmsthal, leaving again before the end of the week.

Yours ever

(Write to Wilhelmsthal, Via Eisenach.) FL

21. Probably Opus 35, in B flat minor.
22. G 52; R 530, *Septem Sacramenta*.

Sunday morning, August 12, 77
Wilhelmsthal

This evening I'll be in Bayreuth. If you are willing to write promptly, send the letter there. Perhaps I'll already be at Schillingsfürst Wednesday; but as it is an important feast day (the Assumption) I would not want to spend it in the train.

I expect to arrive in Rome Sunday morning, and will write to you without delay.

The enclosed letter from Franz Servais will interest you. The six songs of which he sent me the Milan edition are graceful and distinguished. I knew them under the title *L'Âme en fleur*, which he wisely changed to *Contemplations*, all the more so as this is also the title of V[ictor] Hugo's poems which are their text.

Mlle de Watz[dorf] has given you news of Wilhelmsthal. Evening before last I went with M. S[ach] to call on Mme de Schwartz at Eisenach. After that there was a reunion (but without M. Sach) at the home of Mlle Ramann.

Thanks to Sarring bringing and sending me punctually the newspapers the *Débats* and *L'Univers*, I had the pleasure of reading the report by Alexandre Dumas to the French Academy on the *Prix de vertu*[23] for 1877. In addition to the interest aroused by good deeds, the literary form of this report, both original and lively, pleases me greatly. I read several passages from it one evening here to Their Royal Highnesses, who seemed to enjoy them very much.

The facetious piece in the *Figaro* on Alex[andre] Dumas' confession to ex-Father Hyacinthe must be enjoying a success, though I find it repugnant. *L'Univers* published a good half of Dumas' report, probably because of the eulogy of the admirable Curé Leroy. I'll send you this issue from Bayreuth; it is already wrapped up.

Yours ever

FL

---

23. Annual award for meritorious activities and initiatives.

Friday, August 17, 77
Munich
(Marienbad)

Were it ever possible for poor FL to get angry with Lo, it could only be because of the refrain: "You are going to be angry, you are angry, you write to me as though you were angry" – – – and the brilliant variations with Riedel and Winterberger.

Fortunately, FL has become quiescent to the point of impassivity, and though not exactly enjoying either the refrain or its variations, he puts up with them in a penitent spirit.

I was at Schillingsfürst from Wednesday evening till four o'clock Thursday. Cardinal H[ohenlohe] is doing excellent charitable work there. It is an institution where more than twenty girls are being taught, fed, lodged, supervised, under the guidance of some very respectable nuns called *les petites soeurs des écoles*. I believe that they have ties with the Benedictine Order.

Moreover, Schillingsfürst is indebted to the Cardinal for embellishments both agreeable and useful in the garden of the castle, which will become a very lovely park extending as far as the nuns' house, so that the children will have plenty of space without having to go through the little town. Though H[ohenlohe] is not considered to be a theologian of the very highest order, he certainly deserves the good reputation of a prelate who is truly pious, charitable, with fine princely ways, endowed with intelligent and sensitive taste—and most sensible in his actions. With these assets, he is an honor to the Church and need have no fear of ill-intentioned gossip to which envy is no stranger.

On arriving here yesterday evening I ran into Lenbach right away and this morning went to see him in his studio. He has almost completed a magnificent (three-quarter-length) portrait of Andrássy in Hungarian costume, very colorful, with the Grand Cordon of the Order of St. Stephen.

Semper is my neighbor at the hotel; his latest severe illness has taken a great deal out of him. He and Lenbach are leaving this evening for Belgium and will attend the Rubens festivities at Antwerp.

Did you read General Klapka's speech at the Pressburg meeting? It does not lack paprika.

Please send me the three or four remaining issues of *L'Univers* in one envelope to my old Roman address: Vicolo dei Greci, 43, for I shall probably be taking the same apartment again. Don't add the *Débats* unless there is some exceptional article.

Sunday morning I'll be in Rome.

Yours ever

FL

————

August 25, 77
Rome
(Via de' Greci, 43)

The name of the street where I live since I moved from Santa Francesca Romana (in '70) has gone up in the world. It used to be Vicolo de' Greci. Now a beautiful marble inscription reads Via de' Greci. Twenty feet away stands the old Chimay house, and quite nearby the palace of the double eagle. Almost opposite my number 43, the Royal Academy of St. Cecilia has moved into an old convent of the Ursulines. Both the professors and the students are on vacation until October. Sgambati is swimming and composing at Livorno. This week I saw only one of my friends from the ranks of society: Count Charles Zaluski, Counselor of the Austrian Embassy (to the Holy See). As a respite from his diplomatic despatches he writes charming piano compositions as well as distinguished articles (*Variétés*) which appear in the *Dioscuren* at Berlin. I'll send you the one which is to appear shortly in which he describes his personal impressions of a few artists in Rome. People claim that he knows ancient and modern Greek equally well; since I know neither, we talk in French or German, which perfectly suits Zaluski whose very cultivated mind and fine Slavic sensitiveness foster the pleasure of our friendly relations. He had become a friend of

Tausig in Berlin, and when Zarembski looked me up here, Zaluski gave him a letter of introduction to me. His sister is married to Count Hugo Seilern whom you know.

These last days have been excessively hot. The papers say that the Holy Father has been a good deal incommoded by this and suffers from insomnia. His bed has been moved to the coolest room in his apartments. Nonetheless he continues to hold numerous receptions, and new pilgrimages have been announced.

I have been told that I should call on Cardinal Simeoni, born in 1816, created Cardinal in 1875 and, after Cardinal Antonelli's death, named Secretary of State of the Apostolic Holy See. A book of 393 small pages (in 12mo), which is being widely read here, entitled *Préface au conclave*,[24] contains entries on the fifty-six members of the Sacred College. The author, M. Louis Teste, has obtained a lot of information and reveals a Gallic turn of mind not devoid of malice. In particular, he is ill-disposed toward Antonelli, and even toward Hohenlohe, while writing of the latter: "One cannot reproach him in the slightest as far as his morals are concerned; he is pious and has sacerdotal virtues." Further on, my intimate relations with H[ohenlohe] are explained in a strange way, with which I cannot agree; and at the end of the volume (page 390) is a paragraph concerning Princess S – – – (add W.) [Sayn-Wittgenstein], Via del Babuino, and her salon, "where it is said that there is being hatched under the guidance of this very witty, widely read, but very mixed up woman—Polish exaltation grafted onto German obscureness—a reform of the Church!" I recall that Uncle Alexander Meyendorff (Bethsi's husband) used to say to Mme d'Agoult: "she has a German look in her eyes and a French smile." The mixture of nationalities gives spice to individuals – – – and to remarks. Without exactly recommending Teste's book to you (published this winter by Vaton, bookseller, 8 rue du Vieux Colombier, Paris), I assume that you'll enjoy reading it because of your Roman reminiscences and connections.

24. Paris, 1877.

Cardinal Simeoni, much revered for his sacerdotal virtues, received me kindly Tuesday evening at the Vatican. Yesterday morning Cardinal Hohenlohe, summoned here for a session of the Congregation and an audience with the Holy Father, very graciously called on me. Tomorrow evening I shall again be his guest at the Villa d'Este. Bronsart writes that Bülow has fairly well recovered at Kreuznach, and that after having conducted a series of philharmonic concerts in Glasgow he will accept the post of first *Kapellmeister* at Hanover, which is naturally a source of great satisfaction to Bronsart.

I have already told you that I had not failed to recommend Emmerich for the position of second *Kapellmeister* as replacement for M. Bott. Now, owing to Fischer's sudden death the situation has changed. Emmerich should manage to get along well with Bronsart and Bülow, for I cannot press more than I have, though in my reply to Bronsart yesterday I again mentioned Emmerich.

Before going there I'll try to see our old friend Baron Visconti.

I would like to be able to tell you things which will dispel your sadness – – – and I remain sincerely, and sadly too,

Yours ever

FL

Please have the enclosed card delivered to Gottschalg.

———

August 27, 77
Rome

Let me ask you to intervene promptly with Grosse (my friend and double-bass-trombone at Bayreuth) concerning the bust of Mme Moukhanoff. The sculptor Godebski is kindly presenting it to me. Herewith is his note which tells me that he has already shipped it to Weimar, where please have it uncrated and placed in your house until my return—perhaps in the round drawing room with the Bechstein. Ask Grosse to supervise the uncrating, and please advance me the small sum for the Customs and delivery to the Alexanderplatz.

I want this bust to remain at Weimar, not at Budapest or the Villa d'Este.

You know that Godebski once offered M. S[ach] a superb bust of Rossini which I believe is now in the Weimar theatre. S[ach] had some scruples about accepting it gratis; however I encouraged him to make this little effort, since this was what Godebski wished. Show S[ach] my bust of Mme Mouk[hanoff]; if he likes it, it will perhaps occur to him to acquire the other bust of Mme M[oukhanoff] (also in marble but larger) which Godebski mentions toward the end of his note, and which he is keeping in his studio. When you have received the one which belongs to me, do me the favor of writing a few kind lines to G[odebski], explaining that I have asked you to embellish your drawing room with his piece. Write to:

> M. Godebski, sculptor,
> rue de la Procession 48,
> Vaugirard, Paris

Supposing M. Sach should decide not to buy the marble, we'll write to Mme de Schleinitz. She will, I am sure, help us render the homage due to the talent of the artist, and to our admirable late friend. Her personal manner, which was infinitely graceful and subtle, in no way impaired the essence of her rare and lofty feelings. Only a boor could err on this point.

More errands! Yesterday, I heard a charming, very talented, young lady harpist—Mlle Tadolini—and promised her the two *Ave Maria*s by Arcadelt and F. Liszt,[25] transcribed for the harp by Dubez (after my piano version). They are published by Kahnt. Be so good as to ask Gottschalg to have them sent to me *subito* by Kahnt (i.e., the version for the harp).

25. Probably G 659; R 401, and G 504; R 193.

I need yet another copy of Meyer's *Hand Lexikon des allgemeinen Wissens*[26] in one volume, latest edition, plus the volume of the catalogue of my wretched works published by Härtel.[27] Kahnt could send them, together with the *Ave Maria*s, with the bill which I'll settle immediately, Via de' Greci, 43, Rome, to your very humble *Senatore*

FL

This evening I'll be at the Villa d'Este.

————————

September 3, 77
Villa d'Este

My dearest Lo is a little absentminded and didn't read my last letter carefully, nor the one from Godebski which was enclosed. Otherwise she would know: A) that it is indeed Godebski (not M. de Mouk[hanoff]) who is sending me the bust of Mme de Moukhanoff, which I asked you to keep at your home until my return; B) that I also asked you to write a few <u>kind</u> lines about this to Godebski, sculptor, rue de la Procession 48, Vaugirard, Paris. In my letter mailed here day before yesterday, I inform God[ebski] of this mark of attention on your part; C) that Godebski is presenting me with this bust, which is a smaller life-size version of another, also in marble, of which I asked him the price. I would like to find him a purchaser, and I solicit Lo's help and patronage in the form of well-turned phrases to M. S[ach] (to whom Godebski presented the magnificent bust of Rossini), and of letters to Mme de Schleinitz, and to anyone else you think appropriate, perhaps even <u>Queen Olga</u>! Were Countess Creptovitch still of this world she would have bought this bust, which is hailed as a fine work of art. Go-

26. Hildburghausen, 1873.
27. See p. 229 note 6.

d[ebski] has the title of professor at the St. Petersburg Academy, and produced many pieces in that town (especially for M. Bibikoff). I don't know whether his statue of Chopin has already been erected in Warsaw. You could ask him to send you a photograph of it. On my part, I'll speak about the matter to Mme Dönhoff, Albert Apponyi, and other admirers of Mme Mouk[hanoff]. Before undertaking this begging, though proper, tour, one must know the exact price of the bust. I'm expecting the sculptor's reply and will tell you right away.

Forgive me for this *duplicata* of my last letter, to which you did not deign to pay attention. In this M. S[ach] meets you halfway, for I had told him at Wilhelmsthal in plain language that his 500 marks for the *Wagner Verein* were no longer in your possession, and that you had passed them on to Loën with the rest of the subscriptions—the total to be invested by Loën and grow in some bank or other until Wagner publicly tells people the use to be made of the sums gathered together in several towns by the *Wagner Verein* founded after the Bayreuth performances. When Loën is back in Weimar you'll easily take care of this little business so that S[ach] is not deprived of due appreciation for his generosity, or the other subscribers for theirs either. The financial situation of Bayreuth is greatly affected by the arrangements made with the Royal Administration of Munich, and with the Vienna Opera. You know that the administration is taking over the entire cost of the complete performance, next summer, of *Der Ring des Nibelungen* at Bayreuth, and that *Rheingold* is to be performed in Vienna this winter. Later, *Siegfried* and *Götterdämmerung* will follow, for *Walküre* is much admired in high places, and the Director of the Opera has been informed that he is to stage the whole tetralogy. In Berlin, people display more reserve, almost aversion – – – M. de Hülsen is reported to have said that the success of the *Nibelungen* still seemed to him problematical, and that it was enough for him to have included *Tristan und Isolde* in his repertoire. This last is a credit to him, and the rest is beyond dispute.

I was in Bayreuth when Dannreuther brought W[agner] between 7 and 800 pounds sterling given by English enthusiasts as a contribution to making up the deficit of the 1876 performances. W[agner] had qualms about accepting this, feeling that it wasn't up to the English, but rather to the Germans to meet the costs in a case like this. He accordingly expressed his thanks and gratitude but did not accept the proffered sum. On this subject Cosima writes, "We finally returned the English money and I think we have found a formula which won't hurt the feelings of the well-intentioned givers without at the same time encouraging cynical observers."

Did I tell you a curious detail? In London, Wagner was Dannreuther's guest. The latter is only a well-regarded pianist, an excellent musician and piano teacher who charges a <u>fee</u>, and who is thus simply not in the same class as Rubinstein or Bülow. Nevertheless he lives in the charming house which was inhabited by Prince Louis Napoleon during his years of waiting. In London this seems perfectly normal and would be quite extraordinary anywhere else. Can one imagine Gottschalg occupying by himself the house of Mme Helldorf, or Sgambati (who is far more famous in Rome than is Dannreuther in London) the Villa Malta?

You're entirely and completely right to feel that notwithstanding the fact that the holder of *Patronatschein* No. 388 is emphatically honorable, there is no need to utilize the Krefeld bank, as specified in the <u>appeal</u> to the German nation signed by No. 388. Do urge Loën to transfer the modest sum which was entrusted to him through Feustel, the official channel. Let the Rhenish Provinces for their part do the best they can. Weimar, not being one of them, must continue dealing directly with the Metropolis of Great Art, Bayreuth, and with its chief Minister of Finance, Feustel. This is more in keeping with the customs of our Court.

I have not yet succeeded in settling down again to any particular work here. While the heat is less suffocating at the Villa d'Este than in Rome (where the thermometer rose to 40 degrees),[28] it is nevertheless very bad, and I spend my days catching up with my large backlog of

28. About 104° Fahrenheit.

correspondence. In the evening I play the piano a little, and engage in *conversazione* with my most eminent and amiable *padrone*.

Yours ever

FL

Godebski writes: "I will part with the life-size bust of the late Mme de Moukhanoff, for which I have just been awarded a medal of honor, for the sum of 3,000 francs."

September 13, 77
Rome

The heavy burden of my usual correspondence is made yet heavier by the letters of introduction for which people ask me from every quarter. Refusing doesn't do much good: people return to the attack, both head-on and flanking. Thus, last week I finally had to write a letter, which I had thrice refused, to Mme de Schleinitz. Alas! I don't have many illusions about my introductions; the one for Emme[rich] was of no use. Brons[art] writes that E[mmerich] showed him his new opera, which, it seems, is extremely *dilettantique* [amateurish]. Confidentially, here is the exact text of what Bronsart adds: *Indessen könnte ich Emmerich, der noch nirgends als Opern Dirigent fungierte, wenn es zur Concurrenz mit Probedirection kommt, dazu mit einladen, sobald der Kreis nicht zu gross wird, worüber ich mich mit Bülow verständigen will. Möglichenfalls wird diese Eventualität aber ganz ausgeschlossen, denn,"*[29] etc., etc.

This winter I sent Zarembski two letters, one of which was for Mme Viardot, at whose house he met Gounod. It would seem odd to me to

---

29. Meanwhile I could invite Emmerich, who still has served nowhere as an opera conductor, to take part in rehearsal competition as long as the line doesn't become too long; on this matter I want to come to an agreement with Bülow. Possibly, however, this eventuality is quite out of the question.

write once again to the latter – – – and my relations with M. Thomas only date from Loo Castle.

The most worthwhile introductions for Zarembski would be to the Russian embassy for Princess Troubetskoy and other persons in those circles, with which I am not familiar. I don't know whether Émile de Girardin still has a salon, and whether music is still sometimes played there, as formerly. Tell Zar[embski] to find out in Paris and to write to me about it to Pest (in November). Should Girardin's salon still be somewhat musical, I'll give Z[arembski] a line for the illustrious and still incandescent publicist.

I returned here yesterday evening. On the way I read a few charming pages on Chopin (published in German in the *Dioscuren* at Berlin) by Count Zaluski. Several of the études and preludes are poetically interpreted there, and the characteristic features of Chopin's enchanting genius are well defined.

Though I have not yet gone back to work, I have just written a hundred or so measures for the piano. It is a fairly gloomy and disconsolate elegy; illumined toward the end by a beam of patient resignation. If I publish it, the title will be: *Aux Cyprès de la Villa d'Este.*[30]

Yours ever

FL

With regard to Bayreuth, simply follow Cosima's advice even though it might apparently conflict with mine, as in the current business of sending the Weimar funds to Feustel, or to the "serious" banker at Krefeld. I was in favor of Feustel, but if Cosima recommends the Krefelder to you, remit them to him.

Meyer's dictionary has arrived and I have again written to Kahnt for the two *Ave Maria*s which I am awaiting.

---

30. G 163, 2; R 10e, 2.

September 27, 77
Villa d'Este

To start questioning the good which has been achieved, whether with difficulty or with ease, is a great sin. You have always been an excellent and highly intelligent mother without priding yourself on this merit, which is less common than it seems it should be. Thank our Heavenly Father for this and pray that in accordance with His divine providence He grant a happy outcome to your concern for your children. My reservations with regard to too prolonged maternal tenderness are silenced before your better wishes. May your sons be courageous and virtuous!

For the last two weeks I've been absorbed in cypresses. Those of the Villa d'Este have taken me back to Michelangelo's cypresses at the Carthusian monastery in Rome—*Santa Maria degli Angeli* (in ancient times the Baths of Diocletian, near the main station of the present railroad). Michelangelo built the cloister with its hundred travertine columns and the sublime church. He also planted the cypresses which bear his name and near which his dead body lay for some time (until it was moved to Florence, I'm told). Do me the favor of looking up in Grimm's book[31] the passage on these first and austere obsequies of Michelangelo in Rome, and let me know the page where they are mentioned.

Thus, I have composed two groups of cypresses,[32] each of more than two hundred bars, plus a *Postludium* (*Nachspiel*) to the cypresses of the Villa d'Este. These sad pieces won't have much success and can do without it. I shall call them *Thrénodies*, as the word *élégie* strikes me as too tender, and almost worldly.

Speaking of music, let me add that Härtel has sent me the proofs of the *Triomphe funèbre du Tasse* [33] (written at Monte Mario, where I arrived by the same road as that traveled in pomp by Tasso's coffin – – –).

31. *Leben Michelangelos. 2. durchgearbeitete Auflage* (Hanover, 1864).
32. G 163, 2 and 3; R 10e, 2 and 3.
33. G 112, 3; R 429, 3, first performed in New York on March 24, 1877, conducted by Leopold Damrosch, to whom the work was dedicated.

I have corrected these proofs, as well as those of <u>your</u> *Impromptu*, which will soon reach you.

Have you read the friendly letter addressed to me by Hiller in the September issue of the Berlin review *Nord und Süd*? He tells several anecdotes of our youth most wittily, and I appreciate his remembering them. They asked him for his letter in the form of a commentary on a portrait of me published in the same issue, which I'll send you if you don't already have it.

I'll be spending next week in Rome. On October 4, feast day of St. Francis of Assisi, I shall attend a solemn mass in the church of the Anima, to be celebrated in honor of my sovereign Emperor and King, Franz Joseph, to whom I am all the more indebted in that he has no time to concern himself with my music. His fairly substantial subsidy to the new Academy of Music in Pest is a noble gesture of his royal munificence. Though I did not solicit it, I note it with gratitude, and will try fully to discharge my duty even should it become difficult for me to fulfill it.

Your

FL

October 14, 77
Villa d'Este

My <u>cypresses</u> have grown taller; I've been working on them without interruption for about ten days. Then, in early October, there was the feast day of the Holy Angels. I wrote a hundred or so measures for them (for piano or harmonium) and wish I could better express my intimate devotion to the divine messengers.

Having once started blackening music paper, I wrote four more pages which will have as their epigraph: *Sursum Corda*.[34] These pieces are hardly suitable for drawing rooms and are not entertaining, nor

34. G 163, 7; R 10e, 7.

even dreamily pleasing. When I publish them I'll warn the publisher that he risks selling only a few copies.

Thanks for the information about Michelangelo's cypresses. I'm surprised that neither Grimm nor Vasari mentions them, for people indeed assured me in Rome that they had sheltered the mortal remains of the austere and sublime hero of art. In his case we feel something more than admiration—veneration—and Vasari piously called him *Il divinissimo Michel Angelo*. No one, perhaps, knew and experienced the loneliness of human genius as much as he in the course of a long life. Before this great figure I feel a sad modesty combined with shame. This too is a form of vanity! – – –

My poor brain is very tired; I almost spent these last two days in bed but I am not sick, and you know I hate people worrying about my state of health, which is always good enough. This morning I was almost uncivil to an excellent and sympathetic young deacon who sometimes practices on my piano and who asked me "if I was better?" This innocent question irritated me, for I consider that my health is always what it should be.

From my heart, your

FL

Saturday I return to Rome. Write me there until October 23. I reread with pleasure Thiers' felicitous phrase in the clever article by Cuvillier-Fleury, *la sensibilité aux grandes choses.*

———

Saturday, October 27, 77
Rome

Sgambati has composed two quintets which I consider the most remarkable works of this kind to have appeared in many a year. Only the second of these quintets has been published by Schott (Mainz). The first[35] is to appear only at the end of winter, for Sgambati has had

35. Opus 4.

to copy twice the score of more than seventy pages – – – He let us hear it recently in a very small group at his home; in the adagio there is a breath of Beethoven, and the whole writing and style of the piece reflects a master's hand. Encourage Lassen to have Sgam[bati]'s second Quintet performed at one of the Weimar *Kammer Musik* evenings. It will give you a patrician pleasure – – – in the sense of the definition by de Maistre: *Le beau, c'est ce qui plaît au patricien éclairé* [Beauty is that which pleases the enlightened patrician].

Also urge Lassen for me that he embellish his programs with the very lovely Trio by Bronsart (composed some time ago at Weimar) which has just been published by Aibl in Munich. In addition, if one felt disposed to perform new and distinguished *Kammer Musik*, I would recommend the Trio by Nápravník[36] (published by Leuckart, Leipzig), dedicated to the Grand Duke Constantine and rightly honored with a prize by the Imperial Academy of Music at Petersburg. You may recall that I played this trio last summer at the Hofgärtnerei.

I have spent this week here very much absorbed in the silly things I am writing on music paper—continually scraping, changing, and rechanging, without managing to express what I feel, and yet would like more or less to express musically.

This evening I go back to the Villa d'Este and return here November 2 in order to pack my things for Pest where I arrive in mid-November.

Forgive the lack of interest of my letters, as well as of my whole melancholy self.

With all my heart, your

FL

Wednesday we made a little music at Teano's. Sgambati and I played the *Walkürenritt* and *Les Idéales* [*Die Ideale*].[37]

---

36. Opus 24.
37. G 646; R 368.

Friday, November 9, 77
Rome

I am desperately sad and completely incapable of finding a single ray of happiness. I'm in a kind of mental depression accompanied by physical indisposition. I've been sleeping badly for weeks, which doesn't help to calm my nerves. Nevertheless I pursue my labors while trying not to become too much discouraged in my musical work, which I have resolved not to give up short of either total infirmity or death.

A few more leaves have been added to the cypresses—no less boring and redundant than the previous ones! To tell the truth I sense in myself a terrible lack of talent compared with what I would like to express; the notes I write are pitiful. A strange sense of the infinite makes me impersonal and uncommunicative. In 1840, M. Mignet in speaking of me said solemnly to Princess Belgiojoso: "There is great confusion in that young man's head." The latter is now old, but not at all confused.

People compliment me on the weight I am putting on, it seems. So long as I am alive no one will have (reasonably speaking) to complain about me or to pity me—this last would make me dreadfully unhappy – – –

Next Thursday, or at the latest Saturday, I return to Budapest. As usual I'll stop over for a few hours in Florence at Mme Laussot's.

With all my heart, your

FL

Send me news of Peterle and of his brothers. Is Clément preparing himself successfully for his role of Rubens?

If you write to me at once write to the Hôtel de Rome (for my apartment in the Via Greci has been let to others for the winter). The Bobrinskis are back but I have not yet seen them.

Teano continues to display a sincere and not at all commonplace interest in music. He and his wife continue to show me the greatest kindness. We saw each other again Saturday for lunch at M. de Keudell's, with Madame Helbig. After the dessert we played *Mazeppa* and

Hamlet[38] with Sgambati. Yesterday at a dinner at Haymerle's (Austrian Embassy) the Baroness, who had been to Bayreuth, asked me if I had the pleasure of knowing your sister (Staal) and praised her wit and amiability.

November 13, 77

Rome

Here is a copy of <u>your</u> *Impromptu*. I'll have it bound in Weimar and ask you to excuse my haste in sending it to you paperbound, just as it arrived from Leipzig yesterday evening.

In my last letter I forgot to ask you to pass on a little request from me to our friend Lassen. Mlle Timanoff keeps house, <u>artistically speaking</u>, with M. Sauret, with whom she gives many concerts. The latter having been engaged for the Court concert at Weimar on January 1, it would make Mlle T[imanoff] unhappy to be left out, all the more so because she has stayed at Weimar on several occasions. She has a most brilliant talent, and her reputation proceeds *crescendo*. So were the Grand Duchess to approve her performing on January 1, this would be a gracious and even fair thing to do.

Saturday evening I leave Rome and will be in Budapest on Tuesday.

Your ancient, faithful, and too aged

FL

Wednesday morning, November 28, 77

Budapest

Yesterday morning Bösendorfer arrived here from Vienna, and shortly thereafter another of my best friends, also from Vienna, who wanted to take up urgent matters with me. They were leaving again

38. G 644; R 366.

that evening, so I was unable to write as I had a piano class, and I have to go to bed early because of a bad cold which I brought with me from Rome.

It seems that several newspapers say I am sick. This is not at all the case, but as I wrote you from Rome I feel I am reaching the end and even succumbing—and no longer want an extension.

Keep this fairly naive confidence to yourself. Toward others I'll try to keep up a good front.

Letter writing has never been my forte. I could not adapt myself to it at sixty-six. Some die, others are born; marriage ceremonies and funeral ceremonies succeed one another. How can I handle so many letters of condolence or congratulations?

Let me tell you once again that I am extremely tired of living; but as I believe that God's Fifth Commandment, "Thou shalt not kill," also applies to suicide, I go on existing with deepest repentance and contrition for having formerly ostentatiously violated the Ninth Commandment, not without effort or humility.

Forgive me these intimate and too gloomy maunderings.

Sunday (November 18) I spent a few pleasant hours in Florence with Mme Laussot and Hillebrand. The famous sculptor Hildebrand (son of the Jena professor) has drawn two magnificent portraits of Mme Laussot and her friend in the manner of Holbein.

Princess Rospigliosi had sent me in Rome a most charming note, to which I brought a reply Monday, Nov. 19, to Lamporecchio (which is near Pistoia, on my way). She says that neither her latest treatment at Schwalbach nor the previous ones had cured her, and that she will have to start painfully all over again next summer—where, I do not know. However, her complexion is excellent and she is in delightful spirits. Moreover she does a great deal of good in her principality of Lamporecchio, an old Rospigliosi estate where Clement IX had Bernini build a superb castle, next to which the present owner has founded an educational institution run by three nuns of the third Order of Saint Dominique. More than a hundred girls are being brought up and educated there.

Being anxious to get here I spent only half a day at Lamporecchio and, like Dom Pedro, I started off again on my way before dawn so that Princess Rosp[igliosi] commented amiably that my visit resembled that of doctors, who are "more in a hurry to leave than to come" – – –

Our friend Gille informs me that you went to Jena for the Saint-Saëns concert. How do matters stand with regard to the first performance of *Dalila* at Weimar? Will it finally come to a refusal with some excuse or other, plausible or not? Is there in the company a woman singer who can measure up to the role of *Dalila*? Why not avail oneself of the good will and the outstanding talent of Mlle Brandt? This means additional expense, people say, but since when can one get something worthwhile for nothing?

Please have the enclosed letter delivered to Gottschalg, and pay him right away the 8 or 10 thalers (at the most), that being the price of his *Orgel Repertorium*[39] and of the *Choräle von Bach*, which he'll be so kind as to send without delay to Sgambati in Rome (for the organist Fischer).

Are you aware of Gottschalg's current troubles? He would have preferred a slight dose of arsenic to the silver medal with which he has been honored. In my view he deserves better in spite of his clumsiness, and I intend as the opportunity offers to repeat to M. Sach that Gottschalg is entirely worthy of wearing the cordon of the gold medal, even that of the Cross of the Falcon.

Yours ever

FL

December 9, 77
Budapest

I'm extremely happy at the success of *Dalila* at Weimar. Saint-Saëns was so very friendly as to send me a wire telling me of his pleasure, to which I would like to add still more, for I know no one among con-

---

39. A series of organ pieces edited by Gottschalg.

temporary artists who, all things considered, is his equal in talent, knowledge, and variety of skills—except for Rubinstein. However, the latter does not have the advantage of being an organist, in which capacity Saint-Saëns is not merely in the first rank but incomparable, as is Sebastian Bach as a master in counterpoint.

You don't care much for the organ—the "pope among instruments"; however, were you to hear Saint-Saëns play an organ worthy of his extraordinary virtuosity, I am convinced that you would be moved and amazed. No orchestra is capable of creating a similar impression; it is the individual in communion with music rising from earth to heaven.

I hope to hear *Dalila* at Weimar. Meanwhile I regaled myself with the six Études[40] for piano by Saint-Saëns, and with his *Jeunesse d'Hercule*,[41] in my opinion the richest of his Symphonic Poems. We'll play it together on two pianos at the Alexanderplatz and you shall explain its beauty to me.

I enclose my lines of introduction for Peterle to Glasenapp. I urge you to add a few words in French in your own hand, telling Glasenapp that you had the pleasure of meeting him at Bayreuth at Wagner's, and inviting him to spend a little time at Weimar on his return to Germany (should you find this maternal politeness excessive, it will do no irreparable harm to omit it). In the first volume of his work on Wagner whose title[42] is somewhat ponderous because of the words *in sechs Büchern* [*in six books*], which doesn't prevent the work from being really distinguished and estimable, I have just reread (chapter 13, pages 110–111), the account of our first meeting with Wagner in Paris in 1841. It's completely accurate and well described; only I hope that in the next world I'll be spared from playing the *Fantaisie du Diable aux Anges*;[43] and contrary to Vauvenargues' thought, *La servitude avilit les*

40. Opus 52.
41. Opus 50.
42. Carl Friedrich Glasenapp, *Richard Wagners Leben und Wirken. In sechs Büchern* (Leipzig, 1876–77).
43. *Fantasy of the Devil to the Angels*; cf. Wagner's review, in the Dresden *Abendzeitung* (May 5, 1841), of a Liszt concert in Paris.

hommes jusqu'au point de s'en faire aimer [Servitude debases man to the point of making him love it], I have always protested from the depths of my heart against the servitude of success.

To calm you, let me tell you that I'm in fairly good health and that people say I look better than I did last year. My chief occupation here is teaching the piano to about fifteen people (of both sexes), of whom seven or eight already show remarkable talent; let me name M. de Rössel who comes from Kharkov, as did Joseph Rubinstein five years ago (a colleague of Zarembski at the Vienna Conservatory, where he also won first prize); M. Roth, a pupil of Reinecke and several times a prizewinner at Leipzig; two Hungarians, Juháry and Aggházy. This whole young generation will be far more deserving than the two preceding ones to which I belong, while at the same time facing more obstacles than these on the road to fame and – – – to box office receipts. So I do not fail to repeat clearly to young pianists that most of them are superfluous, and that only male and female singers for opera are in demand and hence well paid.

Yesterday I sent Zarembski, who played with great success Litolff's fourth concerto (dedicated to the Duke of Gotha) at the last philharmonic concert in Vienna, a few lines of introduction to Countess Taïda Rezewuzska [Rzewuska] in Paris. She promised me that she would sponsor Zar[embski], whose praises I sang at a dinner at Prince Teano's. He, his wife, and Baron de Keudell were equally lavish in their praises, and I have no doubt that Zar[embski] will make his way brilliantly provided that he marches straight ahead without worrying about details or obstructions.

Our friend Gille writes that he has been kind enough to have some one hundred bottles of Bordeaux wine (unadulterated) shipped to me for consumption at the Hofgärtnerei. Please do me the favor of settling my little debt to Gille right away (*ca.* 140 marks), and let me know the exact amount.

Has Gottschalg sent off to Sgambati the parcel of music which I asked you to request of him, and has he also settled the bill?

If M. Sach were disposed to award the Knight's Cross (<u>not in silver</u>)

of the Order of Vigilance to Saint-Saëns, I would thank him for this good gesture which would be both appropriate and justified.

Yours ever with all my heart

FL

December 16, 77

Budapest

I am completely charmed by your first three words: "FL e. b." [sic]. My reply: Lo is a priceless treasure. Thanks for having spoken to S[ach] about the decoration for S[ain]t-S[aëns] who nobly deserves it. The most enviable prerogative of sovereigns is that of exercising the right of grace, not only toward the guilty but also to honor good people endowed with superior talent.

Also thanks for having taken care of my recommendation of Mlle Tim[anoff] for the New Year's day concert. She will probably not be accepted—and please <u>do not</u> pursue the matter further. Next Friday M. Sauret and Mlle Timanoff will give a concert here together. Two evenings before this, Sauret appears alone at the philharmonic concert at which a local pianist, M. Willy Deutsch, is to regale us with Chopin's First Concerto.[44]

Our dear de M[oukhanoff] excels on an instrument which is more widespread than the violin, the saw. He plays it with an insinuating and well-sustained *morbidezza*. You hit on the best way out in suggesting to him that he write to Mme de Schl[einitz] before he arrives in Berlin. This brings to mind a rash step by Princess Belgiojoso who, in order to please a friend, had done her the favor of writing a few lines of introduction for her roughly as follows: "Mme XXX is a ridiculous and even insufferable nincompoop. She'll tell you that she and I are on intimate terms – – – try to get rid of her politely." Unfortunately, her friend opened the letter before she should have.

De M's predecessor at Weimar, M. de Swert was here last week and was much applauded in two concerts. He was so good as to give me

44. Probably Opus 11.

the score of a German opera in four acts which are very solemn, cleverly pieced together, and most impressive – – – according to the assertions of the composer. He has been promised performances at Hamburg and even Vienna of his work entitled *Les Albigeois* (*Die Albigenser*),[45] whose success is indubitable. However, since this promise was somewhat hanging fire, de Sw[ert] thought that Weimar would show more eagerness. I cured him of this too naive illusion. In such cases, I like to quote a striking remark by Duke Sermoneta to the editor of a large work on geography, to which the Duke had been requested to subscribe some hundred crowns. In the end, backed into a corner by his tormentor, he said to him flatly, "Excuse me, Sir; I don't believe in geography."

How can one believe in the operas of the old theatrical style? But where are the snows of yesteryear?

Long live Parsifal!

Yours ever

FL

Please ask Gottschalg if he did in actual fact send off the *Orgel Repertorium*, etc., to Sgambati. I'm going to write to our friend Gille. He is recommending to me a <u>saw</u>[46] of fairly poor quality, whereas de Moukhanoff sticks to respectable <u>saws</u>. Mihalovich has promised me to look up at the Casino the article in *L'Indépendance* on *Dalila*.

———

December 31, 77
Budapest

Peterle has written me a cordial letter; please give him the enclosed brief reply. I hope it will find him completely recovered from his indisposition and in good working form. The carnival at Riga will also provide him with some pleasant entertainment. He will do well to acquire skill in the pleasures of dancing and of courtesy toward ladies and girls, without pushing attentiveness beyond that of a *galant homme*, i.e.,

---

45. Produced in Wiesbaden, Oct. 1, 1878.
46. A play on words: *scie* can mean "bore" as well as "saw".

not going too far. To observe a delicate and affable measure in relations between the two sexes befits true aristocracy to which all well-born hearts belong. Such and such marquises or princes behave like common persons and whippersnappers; on the other hand, there are bourgeois of noble character and fine manners.

Clément will be a Prince of Art. His wailing arrival on this earth was saluted by the chords of the Ninth Symphony, a good omen for his artistic vocation.

I rejoice at the thought of seeing the large cartoon of the *Cloches de la cathédrale de Strasbourg*. With your permission, I'll ask Clément to cede to me the title of ownership of his masterpiece, which I would like to place in the room I use as a refectory in the Hofgärtnerei.

At this moment we have here a magnificent exhibition of the *Sistine*, of the *Stanze*, etc., etc. I shall urge M. Eugène Aubert (the principal representative of the firm of Braun at Dornach, which reproduced so admirably the Fra Bartolommeo drawings belonging to the Grand Duchess), to favor Weimar with a complete exhibition of the works in Budapest which we admire. I may write to M. S[ach] about this.

What a miracle is contained within *Parsifal*! I read the poem last night in an ecstasy of joy.

Your comment on the feelings of obscurity which the uninitiated will experience at certain mystical passages is very true. However, with the aid of the music, the "luminous darkness" will fire the public.

In all years
Your

FL

Sunday, January 6

On your Christmas day, I'll go to the Greek Orthodox church, where there will be much music. I got to know M. le Curé at the christening of my godson Anatole de Rössel (for the Orthodox have no Saint Francis in their calendar). The father, who is still very young, is a "first-class" pianist. He spent some years at Kharkov and married a pleasant young Russian lady there who bore him little Anatole, nurses him, and lives in complete retirement with her husband in Budapest.

1878

I've sent you Father Curci's brochure. It may be of some use in Italy, but squaring the circle of conciliation between Church and State remains particularly insoluble in Rome. Elsewhere concordats are fairly possible according to the need of the times, which are still unfavorable; Cardinal Antonelli (of whom you approve) has signed several of them; they last as long as they are worth anything.

The great maxim: "In matters necessary, Unity; in matters doubtful, Freedom; in all matters, Charity," remains for all time the rule of the Holy Apostolic See, founded on the rock of Peter. Let us not ask of it that it shift with opinions which change like the wind; these can only shatter themselves against its rock of immovable and infallible dogma.

As for "freedom in matters doubtful," the Syllabus has reduced it almost to zero. Thus the noble dreams of liberal Catholics are evaporating. Our simple duty is obedience, without any reservation or commentary whatsoever.

Victor Emmanuel died like a king; like Vespasian, he believed, *decet Imperatorem stantem mori* [it befits an emperor to die on his feet]. In his last hour he first of all confessed that he had never intended, nor done anything political contrary to the faith of his ancestors.

I share in superlative degree your admiration for Pius IX, which is commonplace only for those incapable of rising above the commonplace.

Once again I owe you a thousand thanks. First, for your letter to Countess Tiesenhausen; not to succeed in no way lessens the charm and

306

merit of the attempt. I will find it difficult to accept the idea of a lottery for the bust of Mme Moukhanoff. We'll discuss it at Weimar; till then, just quietly keep the bust. Thank you also for having settled my little account with Gille. He writes that *Dalila* has been given four times. I hope to attend a fifth performance. M. Sach pleased me personally by decorating Saint-Saëns. As for the "great impertinence" which you mysteriously mention, I am convinced that it was most pertinent. Some truths just can't be expressed in dulcet tones. "Be angry, but sin not," says St. Paul.

Herewith the program of Bodenstedt's lectures on Hafiz, the Persian poets, Russian poets, Pushkin, Lermontov, etc.

Tomorrow morning, Sunday, we'll have a musical morning of the *Liszt Verein* in the drawing room of the Academy of Music (Fischplatz) (the chorus now numbers more than fifty female and forty male voices) in honor of the most illustrious and reverend president of the *Liszt Verein*, Monseigneur Archbishop Haynald.

I am sending you the program—very Hungarian except for Rossini's *Inflammatus* which Mme Kauser sings admirably.

With regard to Sarasate, I recall having said to Princess Elsi that his successes were not inferior to his talent. I gladly applaud them and am happy at the enthusiasm displayed for Sarasate by courts and towns. However his Nocturne in E flat minor by Chopin,[1] which is so generally admired, is a travesty in the worst of taste. How can one thus climb on the very first page to the higher octave like squirrels or acrobats, and then go down rapidly to the low strings, then climb and fall again, and finally swoon on a most trivial cadenza? Had you been paying attention, you would have found these acrobatics horrible – – – entirely worthy of the places to which you assign, honorifically, Mme P – – –.[2]

Yours ever

FL

---

1. Liszt wrote "mi♭ mol" and one must question his identification, as there is no nocturne by Chopin in this key.
2. Mme Pelet-Narbonne (?), landlady of the Baroness von Meyendorff.

January 25, 78
Budapest

Bodenstedt has taken into account my comments on the propriety of granting our friend Alexis Tolstoy the place in Russian literature to which he is entitled. Yesterday he informed his large audience, briefly but in most flattering terms, of the performances of *Ivan the Terrible*[3] at St. Petersburg and Weimar. To my regret, the Pest newspapers (of which I enclose the principal one in the German language, the *Lloyd*), do not print the passages of Bodenstedt's lecture which mention Tolstoy, Joukovsky [Zhukovsky] (I spell his name in the French way), and Criloff [Krylov].

Moreover, Bodenstedt has promised me to translate several poems of Tolstoy, whom he did not know personally. I told him this was a further reason to do justice to a great poet and perfect *gentilhomme* (I prefer the French word to the English "gentleman," by now used somewhat trivially, and thus quasi-discredited). *Après vous, messieurs les anglais*—as at Fontenoy—remains superbly French, and Magyar, too.

Speaking of which, here is a good maxim, more Christian than it appears, "As you shall do, I shall not do."

Let us return to Weimar and even to Apolda. Please be so kind as to complete (with 20 marks) the enclosed footnote to a letter which was addressed to the Concert Meister Liszt, and grant the latter the favor of your continuing indulgence.

He, for his part, continues to be,

Very humbly

your

FL

When is Mme Sach leaving?

––––––––

3. *The Death of Ivan the Terrible*, a play by Tolstoy, 1866.

January 30, 78
Budapest

You are certainly the wisest woman in the world; I have often said so and am happy to say it again today with regard to your comment that "to have recourse to the generosity of others is repulsive when one cannot, oneself, provide large sums" – – – So keep the bust of Mme Mouk[hanoff] at home, with no more negotiations. I hope by next May to be able to afford to buy this bust, and I shall bequeath it to the Pest museum in memory of my last meeting here with Mme M[oukhanoff] at the time of my jubilee in November 1873. It goes without saying that Clément will please me by making a drawing of the bust "in his master's studio," and I only ask that you make sure that the marble is not damaged through some unfortunate accident during its transfer from and back to the Alexanderplatz. It would be well if Clément in person were to accompany it and supervise the porters.

Saint-Saëns' idea is very noble and friendly, but I shall beg him not to pursue it further. My true friends (and Saint-Saëns is one of these few) must understand that I prefer leaving my works as they are, far from the public eye, hence unperformed. Without donning the cloak either of modesty or of pride, I feel in all humility the fatigue of old age.

Yours ever

FL

You will be pleased by Mérimée's piece on Cervantes in the December 16, '77 issue of the *Revue des deux mondes*.

When Mme Novikoff publishes her *Souvenirs* please let me know whether the "porcelain lobster," stranded at Weimar, figures among them.

February 14, 78
Budapest

I'll continue sending you *L'Univers* until the end of the Conclave, and I thank you for the *Débats*. Neither Veuillot nor J. Lemoinne shows up to great advantage in the last articles on Pius IX, the most lauded and adored of all the popes. His death in 1878, when nearly eighty-six, after thirty-two years as pope can hardly be termed a devastating blow, nor does it "represent" one of the most important revolutions of modern history, with which it merely coincides.

For many years phraseology has greatly used and abused Pius IX. In this queens who were not shepherdesses competed with shepherdesses who did not become queens; in the same way statesmen, diplomats, writers, and Catholic orators found rivals among heretics and schismatics, the indifferent, the non-believers, and the whole crowd of gossips and cretins.

The eternal glory of the pontificate of Pius IX is the doctrine of the infallibility of the throne of St. Peter.[4] This doctrine was prepared in a holy manner and, as it were, introduced by that of the Immaculate Conception of the Virgin Mother. Moreover, the Syllabus served to unclutter the paths of the Holy Ghost, who inspires and governs the Catholic Church in perpetuity. Its sublime mission goes far beyond affairs of state and stock market transactions. What does it care whether one takes over this or that patch of territory, or whether one buys "from the Turk, the Russian, or the Spaniard," etc., etc.? Unite earth with heaven and poor mankind with God; that is what our Lord and Savior Jesus Christ teaches us. So let us render unto Caesar his due, and let us belong forever to God, our Heavenly Father.

Glory and beatitude to Pius IX!

The 257th [256th] pope having died, long live the 258th [257th][5]— and until the Last Judgment may all the popes be Vicars of Christ on earth in order that they may proclaim the God of truth and mercy!

Your

FL

---

4. Pius IX convened the Vatican Council of 1869–70 which promulgated the doctrine of papal infallibility.
5. Leo XIII.

March 14, 78
Budapest

They say in Rome that a cardinal (of French origin) brought a photographer to see Leo XIII. His Holiness replied: *Questo non è tempo di fotografie. Ci penseremo un giorno* [This is no time for photographs. We'll think about it some other time] – – – Meanwhile the pictures of the Pope are not very satisfactory and hardly resemble him. When there are better ones I'll send you some. The Holy Father will probably soon charitably deign to sit for some lucky photographer.

In the supplement to *L'Univers* of March 6, which I'm sending off today, you will find the "Pastoral Letter" for Lent 1877 addressed to the clergy and people of Perugia by the Most Eminent Cardinal Joachim Pecci, now Leo XIII, happily reigning.

I had read this pastoral letter in Italian, in Rome. Queen Olga would approve of it; and next to Aristotle, Plato, Terence, Juvenal, Montesquieu, it quotes the "famous" *Revue des deux mondes* as a witness of the profound agreement (too often hidden) between "the Church and Civilization."

My childhood was spent with sheep belonging to Prince Nicolas Esterházy, my father having been the inspector of more than forty thousand of them. Consequently, I willingly submit to the crook of the shepherds of the Church – – – and for entertainment I play Wagner's *Siegfried Idyll*,[6] a marvel of enchantment!—

The arrangement for piano by Joseph Rubinstein is as successful as is possible on the piano, which lacks the sustained notes of stringed and wind instruments.

Your old tired sheep

FL

No. 2 of the *Bayreuther Blätter* (February) gives us admirable instruc-

6. Orchestral composition written in 1870 as a Christmas/birthday present for Cosima, and first performed on Christmas Day of that year in Triebschen.

tions by Wagner on the question, *Was ist deutsch?* – – –[7] I particularly recommend to Lo pages thirty-two to thirty-five.

[undated][8]

In spite of quinine, Brehmer must be right, and I hope you will merely have to nurse a neglected grippe without intermittent fever as well. No one on this earth can always be in good health nor be continually happy; Lo must therefore resign herself to the common lot of the human race, however exceptional she may be, and put up with her ill humor at not hearing the music which pleases her. Besides, Rossini's *Guillaume Tell*[9] is often given everywhere, since the famous C chest-tone of Duprez, publicized in a hundred articles, has endeared this fine work to tenors in possession, or in search, of large fees.

Speaking of *Guillaume Tell*, I recall a subtle remark of the once famous M. de Jouy, member of the French Academy and author of numerous writings, which he considered masterpieces, which were widely read and admired in France before the invasion of Romanticism. One evening I took the liberty of complimenting him on the felicitous combination of his operatic poem (?) on William Tell with the genius of Rossini. "Yes," he replied, "but only halfway, for in my poem there were two admirably contrasting and also well-harmonized elements; Rossini was successful with only one of them—the Swiss; the other one, the Austrian, he proved unable to bring to the fore although the great Prince Clément Metternich (to whom Rossini had been constantly grateful since the Congress of Verona,[10] and the homage he then rendered him in the form of his overture to *Semiramide*[11] with

7. Published also in his *Gesammelte Schriften*, x (Leipzig, 1871–1911).
8. Possibly March 1878.
9. Opera, first performed August 3, 1829, in Paris.
10. Convened October 20, 1822.
11. Opera by Rossini, first performed February 3, 1823, in Venice.

Freuet euch des Lebens [Let life be joyful], paraphrased in that overture) ought to have inspired him better on the Austrian side."

The late Grand Duchess Maria Paulowna, who so graciously tied me to Weimar, and whose name I shall never mention without blessings and gratitude, sometimes used to say, "Opinions are free," consequently each is free to say stupid or silly things according to the occasion.

Saint-Saëns has shown the most perfect and friendly understanding. He has not written me a word about the Liszt concert in Paris, of which I know nothing other than your kind message. My sole claim on this earth while I am on it, is to impersonality. At Budapest itself I avoid concerts where they perform (with almost importunate good will) my works, both good and bad. Again yesterday I was subjected to a violent *strike* [sic][12] on the matter, but I am adamant.

On April 2 I'll be at my cousin's in Vienna, on the ninth at Bayreuth, and before Easter at the Hofgärtnerei.

Your old sheep

FL

Tomorrow I'll send you the second part of Cardinal Pecci's Pastoral Letter.

N.B. The little song of the "Angels"[13] was written for Cosima's oldest daughter.

Tuesday, April 9, 78

Bayreuth

Having left Vienna Sunday evening, I arrived here yesterday before noon and will stay the week. Wagner is basking in the full sunshine of his *Parsifal*. It revives me.

12. FL may have had the German word *Schlag* in mind, and used the English word "strike" instead of "blow."

13. *Angelus! Prière aux anges gardiens* (in the *Années de Pèlerinage. Troisième année*), G 163, 1; R 10e, 1.

According to what I was told in Vienna, Mme S[ach] cannot yet be back in Weimar. Although my life has for several years been regulated like a—somewhat broken-down—clock, I hesitate to return to the Hofgärtnerei.

Write a couple of lines to your very humble

old

FL

Tuesday, June 11, 78

Paris

Arrived here Sunday morning at eleven o'clock. Am royally housed at 13 rue du Mail; Spiridion considers that the Erard house could compete with that of the king of the Netherlands.

That evening I looked up Ollivier (who had missed me at the station, for he was expecting me at the North station, whereas I arrived at the East). He, his wife, and my grandson Daniel dined at La Muette at Mme Erard's. A little before this C[araman]-C[himay] had come to call, but didn't find me in. Herewith is his note.

The first session of the international jury will take place in the palace of the legislative body day after tomorrow, Thursday morning.

Yesterday I saw Saint-Saëns again. He has suffered a terrible shock: his child[14] was killed outright in a fall from the fifth floor. Saint-Saëns is to play in London this week and only returns here after my departure, set for June 19.

Franz Servais spent an hour with me this morning. For his *Jon*[15] he will follow Boileau's wise precept: "Make haste slowly."

Zarembski is giving us a full concert today at five o'clock in honor

---

14. André, born November 6, 1875. His death occurred on May 28, 1878.
15. Opera, produced in Karlsruhe, 1899.

of the piano with two keyboards (reversed). At ten there is a reception given by the Minister of Public Instruction and Fine Arts, M. Bardoux.

Very humbly your

FL

August 29, 78
Bayreuth

When I left you I was very sad – – – with that deep sadness which reaches toward heaven and remembers only loving words. All others are forever forgotten and erased.

I promise you that my old wounds will henceforth not be heard from.

Cosima will write to you after my departure. Saturday evening I'll be in Munich, and Monday in Rome.

Eternally your

FL

The books and papers have arrived. I'll write about Sainte-Beuve's correspondence.

Sunday morning, September 1
Munich

A telegram yesterday evening told me that my old hunchbacked landlady is willing to house me once again, Via dei Greci, 43.

The day after your departure we turned back again to *Parsifal* for a while; but Wagner didn't much enjoy it, and I understand this perfectly. The creation of such a work must give one a distaste for performances in general, and a particular revulsion for those with piano accompaniment. We therefore limited ourselves to rereading thirty pages or so; and to amuse ourselves we played a few hands of whist for three. To my surprise Wagner knows very well indeed the rules and fine points of this game, which he never plays.

He and Cosima asked me to play my *Dante Symphony*[16] for them; I did so with pleasure, recalling a long and admirable letter which Wagner wrote to me twenty years ago about this composition.

Malwida von Meysenbug arrived on Wednesday and will be staying several weeks in Loulou's room. If you don't already know her third small volume of *Mémoires d'une idéaliste*, read the pages on Mazzini and Wagner.

The quotations from Sainte-Beuve's letters to Cousin and to Mme Louise Colet are in exquisite taste, both very firm and very delicate.

I have written to M. Sach and to Count Wedel. If S[ach] is annoyed with me, I can do nothing about it, but – – – it is my duty not to let him indulge in compromising illusions.

Following a word from Cosima, Lenbach fetched me at the station, yesterday evening. This morning I'll go to his studio and see his portrait of Bismarck which he recently sketched at Gastein and which people say is wonderfully successful.

At five your melancholy FL will leave for Rome and arrive there Tuesday morning.

September 12, 78
Via de' Greci 43
Rome

This evening I return to the Villa d'Este. The cypresses and the wonderful clouds at sunset will be lovely company.

Of our friends here I have only seen Baron Visconti, to whom I hastened to give detailed news of Peterle, Mimi, Sachi, and especially

16. G 109; R 426.

of the Roman Rubens, Clément. Visconti naturally asked me to convey to you his steadfast respect and homage.

Yesterday I finished transcribing the *Oster Hymne*,[17] the *Marche et Polonaise*[18] of Lassen's *Faust*. This could become a concert piece – – – I'll send you a copy when you are back from Baden, and you will be so kind as to offer it to Lassen so that he may send it on to his publisher, Hainauer.

This week I attended three or four rehearsals of the Roman Quartet which is going to the Paris Exhibition under the auspices of the Italian government, and will give several performances there in the near future. Ettore Pinelli is the leader; for the occasion he has composed a distinguished quartet. He and his three colleagues will play it in Paris as well as several others by Verdi, Bazzini, Mendelssohn, Schumann, Beethoven. Reyer will probably review these in the *Débats*.

Thanks to the kindness of M. Carlo Ducci, who between Florence and Rome has more than two hundred pianos for hire, I shall have a superb Erard at the Villa d'Este plus a fine Knaps (from Dresden) which Ducci wants to lend me in case any "first-class pianists" would like to play two pianos with me at home. Three of my Weimar acolytes, MM. Roth, Pohlig, and Blumer, who arrived in Rome a few days before I did, are capable of thus spoiling me.

Alas! I am following Berlioz' bad example and don't much listen to music for pleasure.

I saw in some paper or other a charming remark by Théophile Gautier: *La musique n'existe pas; c'est un bruit qui court.*[19]

Your

FL

I'll be back here October 4 or 5. At Baden-Baden don't forget to give Pohl and Nohl my sincere and friendly greetings.

---

17. G 496 II 1; R 176 II 1.
18. G 496 II 2; R 176 II 2.
19. Music doesn't exist; it's just a rumor (literally: "a sound going around").

Sunday, September 22, 78
(Villa d'Este)

Were you to reach down into my heart a little, you would immediately find there the feeling which is appropriate and suitable for you.
Does this comfort you? I don't know; but *expectans expectavi*. Your
habit of sounding an artificial note of superiority frequently induces in
you sourness, bitterness, and unhappiness. Self-centeredness is a wrong
attitude; while it keeps very fine company, it does not suit fine natures.
Let me believe that you are at heart a far better human being than you
like to appear. My certainty of this is confirmed by your recent tears
– – – when you left Bayreuth. Sadden yourself no more.

I've been here since Thursday (September 12). The second day after
my arrival, Cardinal H[ohenlohe] returned to Rome and came back
Monday only to leave for Rome again Friday in order to attend the
sessions of the Congregations. When he is at the Villa d'Este we have
dinner together at one o'clock, usually tête-à-tête, and we meet again
for an hour in the evening without other company. The rest of the time
I stay in my room except for the morning hour at mass. I am served
supper alone and I go to bed a little before ten.

For want of something better I continue to write my *Via Crucis*.[20]
The Fourteen Stations will amount to twenty or thirty pages of music,
which will be completed by the end of October. I will publish them
first for piano (or organ) for four hands.

You don't say whether Lassen is back at Weimar. Will the short
Faust pieces I sent you find you still at Weimar in the second week of
October?

My reading is limited to the papers you know, plus a few devotional
books, and some cantos of the *Divina Commedia* which bring me
comfort.

I have hardly opened a magnificent Erard piano installed in my sit-

20. G 53; R 534, and G 583; R 339.

ting room. I am absorbed in the *Via Crucis* and in order not to spoil its composition I refrain from playing it until the manuscript is completed.

With all my heart

your

FL

My dear old friend Augusz has died. I feel his loss very keenly.

September 30, 78

Villa d'Este

You deign to include me in your "expiations." Pius IX, of venerated and sacred memory, would have approved this word; Queen Olga would hardly contradict it. Permit me nonetheless to accept this only with considerable reserve, rather like the prison of the Vatican.

If I was wrong to flatter your egoism, will you not excuse me for having been too much flattered by it?

Very humbly

your steadfast

FL

Morning of October 1

P.S. Your lines of September 28 have just arrived. Dingeldei is not one of <u>my</u> first-class pianists; but he has a good presence, maintains good relations with the press, and thus does not have to bother about a recommendation from me. <u>Pontius</u> Lassen can send him back to <u>Pilate</u> Loën.

I'll wait until you are back at Weimar to send you my reminiscences on Lassen's *Faust*, which have already been superbly copied. Next Sunday I'll be in Rome (Via de' Greci 43) and will go back there on October 20.

Wednesday, October 23, 78
Rome

These last two weeks I have been completely absorbed in my *Via Crucis*. It is at last complete (except for the indications of the *fortes*, *pianos*, etc.) and I still feel quite shaken by it. Day after tomorrow I will go back to writing letters, a task impossible for me to undertake so long as music torments my brain. I am barely able to keep up a few indispensable though brief conversations during pauses in my work; and in the evening I feel very tired. I go to bed at 9:30 and read for another half an hour; then the wretched notes of the morning and of the day to come enter my mind and disturb my slumber. In music as in moral matters one rarely does the good one would wish, but often the evil which one would not wish.

Tomorrow morning I will send you the piece from Lassen's *Faust* (magnificently copied). Be so good as to pass it on to him; and he will also receive from me a little letter with explanations. I will also answer Lisie Wittgenstein who has told me of the death of her brother-in-law, Émile.

I shall probably have the honor of being received by the Holy Father before returning to the Villa d'Este where I shall be on Sunday. On November 4 (feast day of St. Charles) I'll be back here for three days; then I expect to spend several quiet weeks at the Villa d'Este.

Did I tell you that Sgambati has written a most serious and remarkable piano concerto[21] plus a graceful *Ouverture Festive* (for orchestra)? Yesterday he received the proofs of his first quintet, which Schott will shortly publish.

My three pianists whom you saw at Weimar, MM. Roth, Pohlig, Brunner, are hard at work here. I give them my brief instructions in the Sala Dante, which now also houses a large variety of pianos belonging to M. Ducci. In my rooms in the Via de' Greci I wish neither to see nor hear any piano.

With all my heart

FL

21. Opus 10.

I hope that Sarring has not made a mix-up with regard to your subscription to *L'Univers*. Two or three issues in duplicate for the month of October have continued to reach me here from Weimar, for I renewed my subscription as from October 1.

Tuesday, October 29, 78
Rome

Lassen's piece went off Saturday evening to your address. In order to enlarge the package I also enclosed the score, and my arrangement for piano,[22] of the *Symphonie de Harold*[23] of Berlioz. Please look after these until I write to Lassen and let you know to which publisher the *Harold* should be sent.

Religious considerations will probably keep me in Rome until November 5.

I'm working feverishly six or seven hours a day on a task which is not suited to drawing rooms.

With all my heart, your

FL

I haven't written a word to anyone in several weeks.
Write to Via de' Greci 43.

November 17, 78
(Villa d'Este)

Today, great praise of your tolerance and forbearance. You have put up with my silence; this brings my wrong-doing home to me better than a sharp sermon. As I told you, my *Via Crucis* has become longer than I expected; and scarcely had I reached the Thirteenth

22. G 472; R 138.
23. Opus 16.

Station when I was seized by an old idea. There was no other way of ridding myself of it than to write a hundred or so bars for each of the Seven Sacraments. Overbeck's admirable cartoons treat these great mysteries of the perpetually active life of Christianity with genius steeped in piety; the Nazarene artist conferred on them a development rich in edification. His drawings in the margins and on the base of the cartoons render witness to the holy concordance between the Old and the New Testaments. Had St. Thomas Aquinas been able to paint, he would not have done better than Overbeck.

My compositions are extremely simple. They limit themselves to expressing musically a few texts of the Holy Scriptures. Perhaps they can be adapted for use in church during the communion – – –

Let's go back to Lassen's *Easter Hymn*. When I sent it to you from Rome I did not have a copy of *Faust* at hand; hence I omitted the indications *Chor der Engel, Chor der Weiber, Chor der Jungen,* etc. Please ask Lassen to insert them (before sending the piece to the publisher), and hand him the enclosed letter.

Though he has not yet achieved the rank of my "pianists of the first class," the Weimarian, Pohlig, plays the whole *Faust* piece most brilliantly, and Mlle Rielke, now Mme Treuenfels, also—and others (of the third class) will follow.

Why shouldn't the most extraordinary M. Clément put his hand to it?

Did you attend Gille's philharmonic Jubilee at Jena? Tell him that I have only moderate confidence in Hamburg for the forthcoming *Tonkünstlerversammlung* and would rather be in favor of making arrangements with Schwerin.

On November 1, All Saints' Day, Leo XIII deigned to grant me a private audience. In the press there is much emphasis on the difference of mind and attitude between him and Pius IX. The new Pope stresses gravity and holy prudence. The other was less constrained, while infallibly attaining infallibility which his successors will uphold *in saecula saeculorum.*

The firm of Braun (of Dornach), which photographed Mme Sach's splendid drawings and the Sistine Chapel frescoes, has just published an impressive portrait of Leo XIII which I'll send you.

To my regret I have not received Veuillot's famous article on Mgr Dupanloup, as my subscription to *L'Univers* only runs from October 15. Since then Veuillot has brought out a summary of his thesis (not wrong, in my opinion). It can be summarized thus: if people had listened to Mgr Dupanloup, "the immense grace of the Syllabus" would have been lost, the proclamation of the fundamental Doctrine of Infallibility would have been at least postponed, and the unity of the Catholic liturgy in the entire world would have been deferred until the Greek calends.

The fine ladies of the Faubourg Saint-Germain and Saint-Honoré, Count de Falloux, and the liberal Catholics with the clique of the *Figaro* Christians claim that Veuillot has definitively "sunk himself" by his article on Dupanloup: *Vedremo; ma non mi pare* [We shall see, but I doubt it].

The great forthcoming event in the Catholic press will be the publication of the Vatican newspaper in five languages: Italian, French, English, German, Spanish. People assert that Father Curci is to be one of its chief editors. Naturally I am subscribing, and will send you outstanding issues.

My "Germanophile" and "Russophile" sentiments can only be very flattered by the support of the *Journal des débats*, and by Klaczko's articles in the *Revue des deux mondes*. Mme Malatesta will be so kind as to lend me the latter. In any case, I receive the *Débats*. Cosima will send you an issue of *La France* distinguished by an article on Busch's new book, *Bismarck und seine Leute*.[24]

Last Thursday a friendly and happy group invaded the Villa d'Este, consisting of Mme and M. Helbig, Count Gobineau, Countess Latour, Count Metternich (who was severely wounded at Castelfidardo),[25] and Baroness d'Uexküll. She mentioned having met with you and

24. *Graf Bismarck und seine Leute während des Kriegs mit Frankreich* (Leipzig, 1878).
25. Near Ancona. Battle fought on September 18, 1860, and won by the Italian troops against the Pontifical forces.

Mme Sachote at Baden-Baden. Next Saturday I'll be dining with her at the Russian Embassy where you once lived. The same day, I'll go to see the Bobrinskis who recently arrived, and Sunday evening I bury myself again here for the whole of Advent.

I will also write this week to Lisie Wittgenstein. Please apologize elegantly to her for my delay.

Did the *Seigneur ami Joseph* [prince of Caraman-Chimay] inform you of the marriage of his daughter to Count Gréfül [Greffülhe]? Mme Carolus said to me once that nothing more was lacking.

Once again I bow very lovingly before your "tolerance"

and remain truly
your

FL

Send me news of your eyes. Out of sympathy, my own are giving me a little trouble.

What are Clément Rubens' latest artistic inspirations?

A slight correction: it is not my gracious patron H[ohenlohe], but indeed Pius IX who had a taste for jokes of the kind which the "Thief" served up to you. Baron Visconti tells an anecdote on this subject fit to make one burst out laughing, over "Piff, Paff, Pouff"!

This letter may not leave until tomorrow. The *campagna* is under water and several parts of Rome are threatened by the Tiber.

November 24, 78
Rome

Let me first of all correct two omissions:

A Yes, read Ozanam's *Dante*[26] as well as Lamennais' magnificent introduction (preceding his translation of the *Inferno* which, if I am not mistaken, you have in your library at Weimar).

26. *Dante et la philosophie catholique au treizième siècle* (Paris, 1839).

B Please tell Gille that if M. Dimmler (*Musik Direktor* at Freiburg im Breisgau) asks him for the copy of my *Cantico di San Francesco*,[27] he should send it to him.

Yesterday I finally sent Pohl a few words in reply entirely along the lines of your wise letter. My old friends should know that the leisure required to write letters is seldom granted to me – – –

Feel no exaggerated scruples in keeping Amberger's *Océanide*. It will be a pleasure to find it again in your home; and although you used to claim that people did not love you for yourself, allow me to claim the contrary and to persist in this with all my heart.

FL

At your former dwelling in the *Palazzo Russo* yesterday we talked about you pleasantly with Mme d'Uexküll whom I shall see again this evening at Baron de Keudell's.

————

December 7, 78
Villa d'Este

I still can't free myself from my thickets of music paper, and will only just achieve this by Christmas eve in time to attend mass with the Tivoli Franciscans.

Meanwhile I have transcribed in memory of our four hands the *Kriemhield* [*Krimhild*] and the *Bechlarn*[28] of Lassen's *Nibelungen*, and will send you these two new pieces as soon as they are copied. M. Rubens-Clément will play them for you. Speaking of him, Count Bobrinski told me how happy he is to have such a godson whom he is shortly to ask for a cartoon or a painting; why not the *Cloches de Strasbourg*? They would produce a wonderful effect in the Roman Villa Malta, wonderfully restored, renewed, and royally decorated and arranged by Bobrinski. They say that this restoration is costing him more than two

27. G 4; R 479.
28. G 496 I, 1 and 2; R 176 I, 1 and 2.

million francs, concerning which he commented to me that he had
nothing better to spend them on. Pity that Mme Pelet shouldn't have
had the good sense to buy the Villa Malta instead of the Palazzo Dingelstedt, and to invite you to be her favorite tenant even at the risk of
having the furniture that goes with it.

Many thanks for the passage about the "Thief" from the article
Veuillot-Dupanloup. In spite of the fuss about this article I retain the
same calm opinion I already wrote you about, and which I am happy
to know you share. Would it really be a great crime to consider Mgr
Dupanloup, with all due respect, as having been a bishop of "great
zeal," great activity, great moral integrity, of universal renown – – –
but who, all things considered, was in life but one of those passersby who
never reach their goal? Can one compare such an opinion with "spitting"
on an illustrious tomb? No, and again No.

Without knowing anything about politics I believe that the decline
of the Austro-Hungarian monarchy would not be much of a contribution to the equilibrium of Europe. Hence my desire that Count
Andrássy stay Minister for Foreign Affairs as long as possible, for it
would be most difficult to find someone of equivalent nobility and
intelligence to replace him.

I have read Klaczko's remarkable articles in the *Revue*. M. d'Uexküll
had praised them moderately to me. They tell and foretell the forthcoming advent of Holy Russia, so long in preparation since Ivan III and
Ivan the Terrible – – – including the "sneers" of the shade of *l'Homo
Duplex!* General Ignatieff and Prince Dondoukoff-Korsakoff take it on
themselves in effect to traditionalize the matter pending. Basically,
neither the d'Israeli Beaconsfields, nor the Gortschakoffs or Bismarcks
will have objections other than those of the Lesson in the Breviary for
the Tuesday of the first week in Advent (*de Isaia Propheta*):

Principes tui infideles, socii furum! (Your unfaithful princes, companions of thieves).

Several dispossessed princes and others who fear to become so, find
it peculiar that the Count de Chambord should not be reigning in
France. His last letter to M. de Mun will not accelerate his enthrone-

ment. People hardly understand the meaning of "God, who returns as a master," so that a king named Henry V should rule. However, the behavior of the Count de Chambord is amply regal, as his every letter emphasizes.

Nothing could be more judicious than your thoughts on Busch's book, etc., and I flatter myself for being entirely of your opinion.

I'll send you by tomorrow's mail various copies of newspapers. Read Veuillot's article on Taine. It so happens that the French Academy has just elected Taine. Our friend Saint-Saëns should also have been elected in the Fine Arts category; on the first ballot he received thirteen votes, but on the second Massenet received eighteen which had been scattered on almost unknown names and had then rallied around the least debatable candidate. So Saint-Saëns will fill the next vacancy; for however immortal *ex officio* Academicians may be, there are frequently deaths among them which cause no displeasure to their heirs.

Did I tell you that Teano paid me a friendly call here with Sgambati last week? Next Thursday I'll be dining at the Palazzo Gaetani; there will be a *chasse-café*[29] musical event and, on the following Monday, a concert by Bertrand Roth at the Palazzo Caffarelli. Thereafter I'll be spending Christmas week here until New Year's Day and shall return to Budapest in mid-January.

Your

FL

Your letter of December 3 has this minute arrived. I hope that your four sons will behave properly and that you will derive from this the satisfaction due to the wise and very praiseworthy way you brought them up.

What a charming remark by Napoleon III concerning M. Sach "who asks questions no one could answer"!—and what an even more charming comment you add by insisting that Sach himself concocts them to this end, which is very flattering for His Highness.

---

29. Genteel slang for a liqueur after a meal which, in this case, takes the form of music.

As occasion offers I'll write to Gille (who is feeling sorry for himself) with regard to matters concerning the *Musik Verein*.

Saturday, December 14, 78

I recently spent over two weeks at the Villa d'Este, where registered letters do not reach me. As a result I was only able to answer the publisher Hainauer day before yesterday; and just as I received your letter (which was sent back to me here yesterday from Tivoli) I was writing the enclosed lines to Lassen. Please pass them on to him. Saturday or Sunday you will be receiving *Krimhild* and *Bechlarn*.

Cardinal Hohenlohe is grandly installed in the *Canonica* apartments of Santa Maria Maggiore, to which his position of archpriest of this basilica entitles him. People say that he has spent some twenty thousand francs in arranging and furnishing them. The Villa Malta is costing Count Bobrinski more than one million (over and above the purchase price). It is now a dwelling place in the finest princely taste. I dine there this evening, and on Tuesday at the Ourousoffs. Wednesday I return to the Villa d'Este.

Klaczko continues, in the *Revue*, the *Evolutions d'Orient* which Countess Malatesta is so kindly lending me.

Have you heard about the death of your friend Princess Czernicheff?

Yours ever

FL

From December 29 to January 8, write to Rome.

Herewith the program of Roth's concert next Monday at the Palazzo Caffarelli.

Tuesday, December 17, 78
Rome

Another couple of lines for Lassen (concerning the title of our pieces from the *Nibelungen* and of *Faust*),[30] which kindly pass on to him.

The manuscript went off in today's mail. Day after tomorrow I go back to the Villa d'Este for ten days or so.

Yours ever

FL

December 27, 78
Villa d'Este

I have at last written to Princess Lislie Wittgenstein and am returning to the task of dispatching letters. It is for me a sciatica far more painful than the fever of musical notes which has afflicted me uninterruptedly these last months.

And speaking of letters, I'll ask you to write one as a prelude to and recommendation of the one I am sending our friend Prince Caraman-Chimay. I would like to recommend to him one of my compatriots, a pianist of distinction, M. Agghǎzy. He has worked several years with me at the Budapest Academy and has adequately mastered Beethoven and Schumann. In Paris he teamed up with a Hungarian violinist of good standing, M. Hubay, a pupil of his father and of Joachim. These two young artists play together, and I shall recommend both of them to Chimay. Please just ask him if he is coming to Paris this winter, and when. I'll expect your reply at Pest in mid-January.

The only copy of my piano score with *sola viola* (originally written for Paganini) of Berlioz' *Symphonie de Harold* is in your house, isn't it? Please have it sent off by Sarring or Grosse together with the printed score of Berlioz to:

30. G 496; R 176.

Herrn Constantin Sander
Musik Verlag von Leipzig
Leuckart, Querstrasse

Keep the receipt until Sander has notified me of the manuscript's arrival.

So as not to cease blackening music sheets I am fulfilling an old promise I made to Lebert [Levy] (for the Cotta editions) and am arranging in proper manner (*anständigerweise*) the orchestration of the three last concertos of Beethoven,[31] with a second piano; and am having the first join in the *Tutti*, a most simple and correct procedure which occurred to none of those who previously arranged them. This little all too simple task seemed to me indispensable in order to make available to pianists the knowledge and possible effects on their instruments of these masterpieces, which are usually not unintelligently performed.

I was pleasantly entertained in reading the literary supplement of the *Figaro* (December 22) by the study on the French novel first published in St. Petersburg in the *Messager de l'Europe*. M. Zola, leader of the "naturalist" novelists, upbraids most effectively, it seems to me, the out-of-date followers of Alexandre Dumas and Eugène Sue. What he has to say on About and M. Jules Clarétie is very much to the point. No less so is his halfway sympathetic criticism of M. Léon Cladel. It makes me want to read one of the novels by this author, who was so terribly tormented by *le mot juste*, the use of periods and commas, the abolition of paragraphs, even to the point of banning identical consonants at the beginning of sentences!

In music I suffer from analogous torments—

Young Richter did indeed come to Weimar several times, but only for a few weeks.

I value his talent and thought he had a good position at the Dresden Conservatory—a town for which I hold only the musical regard it

---

31. Beethoven's opera 37, 58, and 73. Liszt's original manuscripts of the fourth and fifth concertos are in the Library of Congress.

deserves, in view of the fact that its attitude toward me has always been hostile and boorish, like certain other towns of similar size.

If I still have a few florins at my disposal by the end of January, I will ask you to send them to Richter for the complete healing of his thumb.

In the meantime the recommendation and support of the Tolls will be of greater assistance to him.

Yours ever

FL

On January 2, 79, I return to Rome and leave again on the tenth for Budapest.

Your letter of December 23 has just arrived. I am indeed grateful to M. Sach for having remembered Godebski and awarded him the Order of the Falcon.

Godebski lives at:

rue de la Procession, Vaugirard, 48
Paris

My two *Nibelungen* pieces were sent off from Rome to your address on Wednesday, December 18. Please let me know when they have arrived, and ask Lassen to follow up at Hainauer's. Should the latter have any objection to publishing them, I shan't argue with him, although my intention was to publish them simultaneously with those from *Faust*.

1879

January 1, 79
(Villa d'Este)

Your letter of December 29 finds me still here. Did you receive mine of last week? In it I anticipated your wish by giving you Godebski's permanent address:

48, rue de la Procession
Vaugirard – Paris

You say you are losing your memory – – – however, if the two pieces from Lassen's *Nibelungen* have reached you please let me know at once. They were sent off from Rome on December 18. Should the mails be at fault I'll lodge a complaint through Spiridion, who has the receipt for this <u>registered</u> letter.

Tomorrow I'll be in Rome and shall stay there (Via de' Greci, 43) until I leave for Budapest on January 11 or 12.

Herewith the explanation of the *pâté de foie gras*. Mme Street de Klindworth is extremely witty and worldly wise. At the Düsseldorf *Musikfest*, in '54 or '55, people saw in her a strange resemblance to Madame Kalergis, to the point that our peerless friend used to speak of it to me, subtly betraying her displeasure.

Sometime I'll tell you a charming remark of the late King of Württemberg about his daughter-in-law, Queen Olga. Mme de Klindworth who passed it on to me heard it with her own ears.

When you have leafed through the book by Autran please send it to me at Budapest.

Happy New Year in the best sense from

Your very humble

FL

————

January 4
Rome

First of all, thanks for your acknowledgement of my next to last letter and of Lassen's *Nibelungen* pieces, which the Rome post office had handled negligently. All is now well; so let's speak of it no more.

As for "the persecuted in music's good cause," I know some people more courageous, more senior, more sorely tried, and worthier than M. Richter of Dresden. Nohl, for example, has been quasi-victimized since his conversion to Wagner, which was too conspicuous for a biographer of Mozart. Let us see things as they are without indulging in rhetorical excesses. Bülow—above all others—Bronsart, Tausig, Cornelius, and a few others unknown to you have really suffered in the "good cause" which your very humble servant flatters himself he has been defending over the last thirty years. M. Richter is still only an acolyte with no claim to martyrdom. However, since you nobly interest yourself in him please send him right away 100 marks (from the little fund entrusted to you), but as coming from you, not from me, with a gracious note telling him that you remember having heard him at the Hofgärtnerei and that Mme Toll had recommended him to you.

For my part I cannot give more than this in such cases, of which there are too many. Turning to another matter, you continue to wrong me in imputing to me any hostility whatsoever toward the "Russian double eagle." My affectionate relations with several of your compatriots and my very marked sympathy for the group of new Russian composers: Rimsky-Korsakov, Cui, Borodin, etc., prove, it seems to me, that I am hardly afflicted by Russophobia. Moreover I owe a debt of gratitude to the public of Saint Petersburg and of Moscow, which received favorably several of my works either ignored or flayed elsewhere; and I also owe a debt of gratitude to Grand Duke Constantine for his triple telegram (on the occasion of my jubilee at Pest), in which he informed me in the most kindly terms of my nomination to honorary membership in the Saint Petersburg Academy of Music. Here I have been seeing much of the Bobrinskis for a number of years and am on sincerely friendly terms with Mme Helbig. In order to thank M. and Mme d'Uexküll for the favorable interest they took in Zarembski, I went back again to the Russian Embassy and continue doing so. Now you know that all dissembling, even the appearance thereof, is foreign to me. I worship with all my soul the God of truth and mercy. Let us pray for His blessing while trying to become ever more true, just, gentle, and humble of heart.

Your

FL

———

January 21, 79
Budapest

His Holiness having deigned to summon me Sunday at 1 P.M., my departure from Rome was delayed by one day. One of Leo XIII's characteristics is his sustained affection for his old diocese of Perugia. He talked to me about a monument which is being erected there to Maestro Morlacchi (a native of Perugia). He was for many years *Hofkapellmeister* at Dresden, where I saw him still in the year 1840. Do you know the lovely cavatina of his vanished opera *Tebaldo ed Isolina*,[1] which is preceded by a magnificent recitative, *Notte tremenda, notte di*

1. First performed February 4, 1822, in Venice.

morte? Mme Malibran, Countess Merlin, Pauline Garcia (Viardot) used to sing it admirably after the manner of one of the last great *soprani-castrati*, Velluti, whom I heard in London at the Duke of Wellington's in 1824. Until the July Revolution this *Cavatina* was at least as famous as has been since then the *Romanza* of Mme Willi Rothschild: *Si vous n'avez rien à me dire*—or *Ich grolle nicht*.

Monday morning (January 17) I was in Florence at Mme Laussot's. Her wretched husband finally died; she will be marrying Hillebrand (probably in London) next May. An excellent example for those who are slow in marrying! This will not prevent Hill[ebrand] from pushing ahead with his valuable work on the history of France under Louis Philippe and after. You know that I have for several years been spending one or two days in his room on the Lungarno when I go to Florence. This time I read there fifty or so pages of the *Cahiers* by Sainte-Beuve[2]—an exquisite little book which I recommend to you. In it I am charged with "affectation" (a reproach launched against me when I started frequenting the high society of the Paris salons and of which I hardly thought it possible to be accused), but Sainte-Beuve adds a corrective which M. Blaze de Bury and his consorts would have taken great care not to admit. I venture to confess that people err in imputing to me any egoistic urge. My faults and mistakes spring elsewhere – – –

Thanks for your kindly attitude toward the two Hungarian musicians I recommended. In my next letter I'll tell you what you will be good enough to write to Chimay (if this is appropriate—for as regards recommendations I maintain an almost excessive reserve).

As for my Budapest friends, let me tell you that Mihalovich is publishing his four ballads (score and arrangement for piano four hands) at Schott's. He'll shortly be sending them to you. Count Albert Apponyi is, in fact and because of his ability, leader of the conservative opposition – – – a thankless role, but one he fills with great dignity. Count Géza Zichy, having charmed the salons of Vienna and Paris with his left hand (Sardou used to say of him: "He has but one arm and plays

2. *Les Cahiers de Sainte-Beuve, suivis de quelques pages de littérature antique* (Paris, 1876).

four hands"!), maintains a cordial friendship toward me. I'll try to persuade him to come to Weimar next summer and it will be a pleasure for you to make his acquaintance.

M. Massenet (now a member of the Institut de France) spent the evening before last here with me. I played for him my transcription of the pieces from Lassen's *Faust*. He was impressed by the pedal-point on D flat, A flat, in the Easter Hymn. His *Le Roi de Lahore*[3] is to be given here next Saturday, in Milan on February 1, and possibly in Vienna in April. His next work, *Hérodiade*,[4] is to be first performed in Milan.

Yours ever

FL

January 31, 79

Budapest

There is more music to be heard here than usual in the Carnival season. Last week, at the theater, there was the first performance[5] of *Le Roi de Lahore*. The composer was to conduct it but it was postponed for a week, due to the prima donna's illness, and Massenet contented himself with coaching everyone at the dress rehearsal before taking off for Milan where his *Le Roi de Lahore* is to be performed in the near future. I was engaged in correcting proofs of the pieces from Lassen's *Faust* when Massenet called on me; and as he seemed interested I played them for him. He is writing a five-act opera, *Hérodiade*, with the opening performance in Milan (with the Italian text). Having been told that Massenet and Saint-Saëns were not on very good personal terms I avoided mentioning Saint-Saëns until he assured me that he considers him the most important French musician since Gounod.

3. First performed April 27, 1877, in Paris.
4. First performed December 19, 1881, in Brussels.
5. I.e., in Budapest. *See also* note 3.

Saint-Saëns is to give two concerts here in early March. It goes without saying that I'll welcome him as a highly distinguished friend.

Géza Zichy created a sensation at a recent concert (the first time that he has favored Budapest with his extraordinary virtuosity). The hall was packed and his success complete. Subsequently, the Florentine Quartet played at one of the *Künstler Abende* sponsored by Countess Alex[ander] Teleki, and is to return in March.

My compatriot-friends are showing me more and more affection. The roof of the *palazzo* of the Academy of Music is already completed. People will be moving in by the end of August and the official inauguration will take place before Christmas.

Thank you for the article by Caro on "pessimism." I always feel drawn to this kind of literature though I am rarely quite of the same mind as the learned philosophers when it is a matter of certain ideas which touch my intimate beliefs. Thus King Solomon himself doesn't impress me much with his pompous *Vanitas Vanitatum*! Confidentially speaking (for my ignorance forbids me to argue philosophy or politics with others), to consider everything as being in vain seems to me the worst of vanities. From a Christian point of view every action, every word and thought has its own value, according to whether these draw us nearer to, or farther away from Heaven – – – – The great eloquence of the Eagle of Meaux [Bossuet], or the finely honed style of M. Renan in no way persuade me of the eternal truth of these platitudes: "All desire is an illusion – – – there is no object of our desire whose supreme vanity we do not recognize once it has been grasped – – – etc., etc." May I be frank? There is a basic coarseness in this thesis which I find repugnant. M. Renan and others dress it up in seductive verbiage but don't really believe in it. To plow one's own field, *cultiver son jardin* (as M. de Voltaire used to recommend), and to discharge one's duties toward one's neighbor, starting with servants and ending with princes, these are not vain matters—nor is Dante's *Divina Commedia*, or Beethoven's Ninth Symphony. Mankind's common sense will ever protest against crushing nihilistic arguments. Renan will go on writing good French (which is no illusion). The Sisters of St. Vincent de Paul will nurse the sick, Catholic missionaries will preach the Gospel to all the nations, save when they suffer martyrdom. Scientists will make new discoveries, soldiers will shed their blood for the sake of honor, artists will produce works of beauty, etc., etc. All this is not vanity, with all due deference to King Solomon and to his glib imitators. There is, and there will ever constantly be something <u>new</u> under the sun; and in the end the Father of heavenly mercy will reward the long and persevering <u>labor</u> of mankind. This is our hope!

Forgive me this kind of homily (in secret), and do me the pleasure of taking 30 francs from the very small sum I entrusted to you, for a subscription to the *Revue politique et littéraire* of which I enclose the prospectus. Formerly I subscribed to it in Rome, but given my too frequent changes of address, please take out the subscription <u>in your name</u> (for the year '79, starting with January 1), and forward the issues to me from Weimar when you are through with them. When you see any articles in the Sunday *Figaro* or the *Débats* which would interest me do me the favor of sending them to me here through March. People here lend me *L'Univers* and the *Revue des deux mondes*.

Did you read the *Correspondance d'Eugène Delacroix* (in the December 15 issue)? I'll bring it up again with you and Clément Rubens whom Delacroix would have appreciated and taken on as a pupil.

The *Messe de Gran* will probably be performed in Vienna on Tuesday of Holy Week, April 8. I have promised to conduct it at the concert of the *Musikfreunde* in celebration of Their Majesties' silver wedding.

At Easter your very humble FL will be happy to see you again.

Herewith a couple of lines for our friend C[araman]-Ch[imay] in behalf of my two compatriots who are already excellent artists (piano and violin) MM. Aggházy and Huber. I'll simply send them a calling card with a note from F. Liszt as an introduction to Chimay as soon as you have informed me of his return to Paris. Meanwhile please deliver the note–<u>prelude</u> to him.

Yesterday evening Joseffy charmed me with his third Arabesque. I very much liked the second. He tells me that it was a fiasco at Leipzig recently. This in no way incites me to contradict myself – – – the young scamp being fully capable of weathering fiascos.

Sophie Menter-Popper (the second name is becoming a nuisance) is shortly going to Russia. I often see her here and am a very devoted friend of hers. She is a pianist of exceptional virtuosity.

———

March 7, 79
Budapest

Monsieur Prudhomme used to say: "Wherever one is one must take a leading interest in local matters." Now, the locality of Budapest absorbs me to the point that Spiridion reproaches me with losing sleep over it.

My only excuse for not writing more is that people write too much to me, and from all quarters. Deign not to take this personally and know that your letter-writing seems parsimonious to me.

Day before yesterday I received a most cordial and excellent letter from your Wolfram Caraman–Chimay. It brought back to me some lovely hours in Rome – – –

When you get these lines I'll be at Klausenburg (capital of Transylvania). From here the train journey takes eighteen hours, but I promised my old friend Alexander Teleki that we would see each other again at his house before we reach the end of the road. In '42–'43 he accompanied me to Posen, Breslau, Warsaw, St. Petersburg, Moscow. Prior to this he had received a sword blow in Berlin in a duel defending my honor. Then in '49, he was to be hanged at Arad in the most honorable and honored company in the world—that of martyrs of Hungarian patriotism – – –

Teleki was freed from his prison and escaped the gallows, I don't know how. He married a most gracious and elegant young lady— Lady Lansdale, if my spelling is correct, who had so much fallen in love with Hungary that she translated Byron's *Childe Harold* into Hungarian. Shortly after their wedding the couple came to spend a week with me in Weimar.

So on Sunday I accompany my young and very remarkable friend, Géza Zichy, poet, musician, and true aristocrat, in the real sense of the word, to which I remain attached in spite of the silliness of the numerous titled entries in the two volumes of the *Almanach de Gotha*.

From March 10 to 15 I'll be at Klausenburg, and here from the sixteenth to the thirty-first. From April 1 until the ninth I'll be in Vienna. Short of an unforseeen change, the *Messe de Gran* will be performed, with me conducting, *zur Vorfeier der silbernen Hochzeit Ihrer Majestäten* [in celebration of the eve of the silver wedding of Their Majesties], in Vienna, on April 8. On the following day your most humble FL returns to Weimar.

Saint-Saëns is here and was a complete success, which makes me happy as a sign of greater successes to come. I'll write to Gille about Wiesbaden and the jubilee (in May) of the *Riedel Verein*.

———

March 15, 79
Klausenburg
(Transylvania)

Transylvanian hospitality has a special quality of nobility and cordiality. It retains something of a bygone age. People made me aware of its charm in the course of this week, and he who has experienced it does not forget it.

Let me tell you more about my old friend Teleki (Alexander) and my young friend Zichy (Géza) with whom I came here. He spent the last three nights in the room next to mine composing over a hundred lines of verse which strike me as most remarkable. We shall shortly be setting off again and spending the evening together at the home of his brother Ernest, owner of a fine estate near Debrecen. I'll be back in Budapest Sunday evening.

Friday, March 21

Budapest

On my return here Sunday evening I found such a pile of letters that it makes my head spin. What is more I sat for two hours each day for a full-length portrait of my wretched person, painted by Countess Nemes, a distinguished artist and pupil of Angeli. This portrait is destined to grace the hall of the new Academy of Music, Radialstrasse.

Everyone in Hungary feels duty-bound to come to the aid of the many thousands of victims of the terrible floods at Szeged. Since the Lisbon earthquake there has been no other example of a large town being so much destroyed. The King went to Szeged on Monday. Funds are being raised everywhere, and I too must contribute with my ten old fingers to a benefit concert for the inhabitants of Szeged next Wednesday, March 26. Countess Andrássy has asked me to do the same thing on April 4 in Vienna at a theatrical performance at which Princess Metternich, Countess Pallavicini, etc., are to shine; but I excused myself in all humility – – – –

On April 2 I'll be in Vienna. The performance of the *Messe de Gran* is set for the eighth. If I am not mistaken, a corrected copy with pasted inserts of the score of this Mass is still in Weimar, either at the Hofgärtnerei or at your place or at Müller-Hartung's. Please be so kind as to look for it and send it to my Vienna address, Schottenhof, 3te Stiege, bei Frau Hofräthin Liszt, so that the score reaches me on April 2.

With all my heart, yours ever

FL

I'm staying here until March 31. People expect the receipts of the Wednesday concert to exceed 7,000 florins. I'll send you the program tomorrow.

Ed. note: The letters of 15 and 21 March were written as one.

March 24
Budapest

Thanks for *La Revue bleue* which I always like seeing again for old times' sake; and thanks also for the two issues of the *Débats*. The article on the Prince Imperial's campaign has a touch of Attic salt; no less the piece on Uncle Gortschakoff. If the illustrious Russian Chancellor really said, "I don't want to disappear like a lamp going out, but like a setting star," his rhetoric faltered. The public is sometimes interested in rising, but not in setting stars. And then Bismarck retorts pertinently that, whether lamp or star, *elle file*[6] – – – –

Further on in the same issue of the *Débats* pedantry is justly characterized as a form of frivolity. M. Bourdeau consciously errs in attributing this form to Germany only. It is to be found in Switzerland, in France and England and elsewhere.

I have just received your note of March 22. You must already have my last letter.

Lo's well-known infallibility dispenses with accuracy of detail. E.g., Saint-Saëns did not wait for the permission of the Aristarchs[7] to play *La Prédication de St. François aux oiseaux*[8] (not "in the wilderness") on Cavaillé-Coll's wonderful organ at the Trocadero last summer during the Paris Exhibition at a great concert attended by several thousand persons.

How he managed this I could not explain to you, but the fact remains that Saint-Saëns' success was <u>complete</u>. More than a dozen people who heard this concert assured me of this in Rome; and since then people have spoken to me about it again in the affably surprised tone of those who assume that all my feeble compositions must be hissed, or at least ignored.

Your very humble FL will be in Vienna on April 2.

6. *Filer* applies both to a shooting star (*étoile filante*) and to a smoking lamp (*lampe qui file*).
7. Critics (derived from Aristarchus, the great critic of antiquity).
8. G 175, 1; R 17, 1.

Has the score of the *Messe de Gran* (with the pasted inserts) been found in Weimar at the Hofgärtnerei or at Müller-Hartung's? If so, send it to me in Vienna, Schottenhof, 3te Stiege, to arrive by April 2.

April 6, 79
Vienna

My whole time is taken up in arranging the concert for tomorrow evening at Andrássy's; in rehearsals of the *Messe de Gran* for day after tomorrow, Tuesday, and in various matters to be settled at the Schottenhof.

I'm writing to Mme S[ach] that I'll be in Weimar a few days after Easter. Before that I shall hear the choruses from *Prometheus*, the Ninth Symphony, *Benvenuto Cellini*[9] by Berlioz, and Glinka's *A Life for the Tsar*, conducted by Bülow at Hanover from Easter Sunday through Saturday of that week.

My *Christus* oratorio will probably be performed on the Sunday after Easter at Frankfurt am Main (a not very propitious town for musical undertakings, and pretty well smothered under the false note of the critical pundits of Leipzig and its many rivals). I promised Kniese I would attend.

So I'll be only back in Weimar on Tuesday April 23.

With all my heart, your

FL

Write to Hanover—unless I wire you—beginning next Friday. As usual I shall be staying with Bronsart.

Thanks for the score of the *Messe de Gran*, which arrived on time on Wednesday.

---

9. Opera, first performed September 10, 1838, in Paris, revived by Liszt March 20, 1852, in Weimar.

Friday evening, April 18
Hanover

Tomorrow evening I'll be at Frankfurt (am Main). The *Christus* is scheduled there for Monday evening, and we'll be seeing each other again on Tuesday. Please be so good as to tell Pauline. Unless you receive a telegram from Frankfurt I'll arrive by the 3:45 P.M. train.

Bülow is doing wonders in Hanover. Yesterday's performance of *Cellini* was admirable in precision, color, and verve. Likewise the playing of the Ninth Symphony and of the choruses from *Prometheus* at Sunday's concert. I have never heard the <u>Ninth</u> interpreted with such perfection as a whole and in detail. With the exception of Wagner, Bülow is certainly the most eminent of the *Kapellmeister*.

La Revue bleue seems to me to be holding up well. The portrait of Renan by Charles Bigot is successful, and I like the nuance "*de la nuance même.*" I'll thank you to put aside for me Renan's inaugural address at the Academy together with the reply. I'll be bringing you Ollivier's two volumes,[10] of which I have read two hundred pages. Several people who are hard to please have praised this work highly to me, among them His Excellency Windhorst whom I saw day before yesterday.

Your

FL

At Frankfurt, I'll be staying at the Hôtel de Russie.
Till Tuesday.

———

[undated]

FL sends you a thousand tender messages and asks you to send him (for Bülow) *Caliban* and *Le Pape* by V. Hugo.

Bülow will call on you this afternoon. I have invited him to spend

10. *L'Eglise et l'Etat au Concile du Vatican* (Paris, 1879), 2 vols.

the evening at your house after *Hans Heiling*[11] which he wants to hear on account of Milde junior.

At the stroke of noon

your FL will be on your doorstep.

––––––––

July 23, 79

I compete with Clément. Here are some *Sospiri*[12] which prolong those of the manchon of Rome. Deign also to continue finding them not fastidious.

Your

FL

––––––––

August 22, 79
Bayreuth

FL would have to be completely heartless not to feel your absence deeply.

I am sad and cannot dispel my sadness, but as it does not serve to lighten yours I conceal it and keep it unexpressed.

Yesterday morning early I walked along the little river where we had dreamed together the evening before. For me there was left only prayer – – – –

M. Sach and his son were at the first station after Eisenach on their way to a hunt. I accompanied them in the train for a quarter of an hour. Then the illustrious and desperate Leopardi granted me his distinguished company until Bayreuth.

Of Wagner I'll only say to you that my deep and lovingly pas-

11. Opera by Heinrich Marschner, first performed May 24, 1833, in Berlin.
12. G 728; R 60, 5, for piano solo. The original manuscript is in the Library of Congress.

sionate admiration for his genius continues to increase. I leave it to others to criticize and haggle. To me he is the equal of Dante. King Louis of Bavaria and my daughter have the right perspective—adoration. To pass judgment often amounts to misinterpreting.

As I had assumed, the instrumentation of *Parsifal* remains to be written. Wagner is not going to hurry for he knows what needs doing and intends to delay the performance of the work. He is now giving a lot of time to the *Bayreuther Blätter*, which has not yet been praised by the *Revue des deux mondes*. In the next issue there will appear another incendiary piece: *Über das Operncomponieren*. Other articles[13] of the same stamp are to follow. Just recently he said to me, "Let's put an end to this beating about the bush and shamming." I am conveying accurately to you his thoughts, but not the power of his language.

Your FL is staying here until Sunday, August 31.

———

August 28, 79
Bayreuth

The third act of *Parsifal* is absolutely sublime. It makes the soul quiver and weep.

Here, we play a good deal of music. Lo would have enjoyed hearing her favorite idyll[14] properly played four hands by Wagner and FL. Also Wagner excels at whist. Nearly every evening we play three or four rubbers after dinner with Cosima and Joseph Rubinstein, an out-and-out Wagnerian of the best kind. He has just tossed into the *Bayreuther Blätter* an incendiary piece, *Über Schumanns Musik*. It casts him superbly in the role of professor or director of the principal German conservatories under the protection of the learned Hanslicks, Joachims, and their ilk, the smart lot in the major newspapers.

In the next issue of the *Bayreuther Blätter* Wagner's alarm bell against

13. Probably in Wagner's *Gesammelte Schriften*, x.
14. Surely the *Siegfried Idyll*.

the all-pervading musical and literary *médiocratie* [sic] will ring out. He wants, once and for all, to settle matters with mishmash tripe, high and low. My role of privy-counselor at Wahnfried forbids me to vex Wagner, all the more so since I share his opinion in almost every respect—theology excepted. In this field, Garibaldi seems to be a major factor. His last laconic encyclical (dated from Civita Vecchia on August 12) surpasses M. Renan, who only wanted "to organize God"! Whereas Italy's martial hero boldly declares, "Man created God, and not God man." Now we know everything, don't we? It only remains to know who will claim the copyright for having invented woman. There are those who claim that the devil had something to do with it.

Thanks for having sent me the *Débats* and *La Revue bleue*. The *Allgemeine Zeitung* (supplement of Tuesday, August 26) praises highly the Essays, *zur allgemeinen Religionswissenschaft,* by Victor von Strauss und Tornay. Gustchen will lend you the *Allgemeine* article which will perhaps make you want to read the book published by Winter, Heidelberg. I'll send you Heyse's translation of Leopardi and the *Wartburgerinnerungen*[15] by Philipp Freytag, with drawings by Schwind. Show them to Clément Rubens. They served as the program for my *Legend of St. Elisabeth*. Keep Freytag's little book in memory of our excursion to the Wartburg on Wednesday, August 20 – – – –

Lenbach recently painted a second or third portrait of Cosima. He expresses admirably without any mannerism the ideal of my daughter's personality. Sunday I'll be accompanying my granddaughter Daniela von Bülow, a grown-up lady of eighteen, who is very bright and fully worthy of her papa and mama. She is to spend several weeks with Countess Bassenheim whom she has known for about ten years, the Bassenheims who were living near Triebschen at the time of Wagner's internment.

Your sad and very humble FL spends Monday in Munich and leaves Tuesday evening for Rome.

15. *Wartburg Memories* (Leipzig, 1876).

Write to the Hotel Marienbad, Munich. I refrain from settling the question of the propriety of the copy of *Le Pape*, signed by Victor Hugo, but I do not retract.

Tuesday morning, September 2, 79
Munich

Sunday I accompanied my granddaughter Daniela who is very bright and grown-up, from Bayreuth to Munich. Lenbach, Porges, and Lévy were at the station, and we spent our time at the *Gartensalon* of the Hotel Marienbad where I used to have the honor of staying, on a friendly and quasi-regular basis with Mme Moukhanoff. Mme Wöhrmann had invited us there for that evening. Mme d'Uexküll, the wife of the ambassador, Joukowsky [Zhukovsky], and others came. Yesterday Mme de Loë and Mme Minghetti with her daughter Dönhoff arrived in Munich. This evening at six o'clock, your FL leaves for Rome.

Write to 65, Via Babuino, Rome.

Thursday evening, September 4
Rome (Via del Babuino 65)

Reassure yourself—I did not make the silly mistake of encouraging Mme W[öhrmann] to spend some time in Weimar. If such is her intention I know nothing of it. Your letter reached me Tuesday while I was writing to you. Then I went back to the exhibition with Daniela. Several people mistook her for Countess Dönhoff, and Mme d'Uexküll finds her very pretty and very charming. This opinion carries weight. After taking Daniela to the station (at two o'clock), I saw and chatted with Mme Minghetti and her daughter who looks radiant in spite of her illness. She tells me that she still has to be carried, or remain prone on a chaise lounge. She is soon to be <u>transported</u> to Ostend.

Wagner's portrait, which Peterle mentioned to you, was already known to me from Bayreuth. To my shame I'm not sure whether the painter's name is spelled Herkomm [Herkomer], but you are right in taking him to be an Englishman of the same kind as Händel. His watercolor technique is strange and produces a great effect. Don't ask me to explain it to you. Clément Rubens will take care of this, and I only hope that Schennis will soon succeed in selling his pictures at the high price which a London club paid for the portrait which was generously presented to Wagner.

Another portrait, that of Victor Hugo painted by Bonnat, is striking both for the likeness and the expression. Lo would perhaps find fault with the legs, but this stance is probably habitual to the great poet, and thus worthy of being recorded for posterity, just like Goethe's hands behind his back.

Because they hang in the great hall of the exhibition, the portrait masterpieces by Lenbach of Bismarck and Moltke are not as impressive as they should be. They would have to be at least twice life-size to stand out against the very high walls on which they hang. Lenbach is now painting Mme d'Uexküll as a Princess of Trebizond. He will shortly have the honor of painting the features of the Princess Imperial of Germany. She was in Lenbach's studio Tuesday, and graciously granted me a minute of her attention. If you go to Tegernsee do visit Lenbach's studio in Munich.

From Bayreuth I wrote to Princess Elsi[16] that my dear old friend Weitzmann could only send off to me his ingenious and learned calling cards, with musical notations in cryptic counterpoint, after his return to Berlin. I'll ask him to send you at Weimar three copies of each; please give one right away to Princess Elsi who is expecting it. Keep the second for yourself, and send the third to me at Rome. They are charming compositions, and are indeed members of the noble family of the variations on and paraphrases of the favorite and common theme:[17]

16. *Franz Liszt's Briefe*, ed. La Mara, VIII, No. 357 (Leipzig, 1893–1904), 8 vols.
17. The famous "Chopsticks" theme.

which we recently played at Lévy's in Munich with several borrowed musicians of distinction. I admit that this <u>masterful work</u> continues to charm me, and so I disseminate it more and more to the point that there will soon have to be a second edition.

Your

FL

When you see Count Wedel please thank him from me for Weitzmann's decoration, which is very appropriate.

Do you still have the article by Saint-Saëns? Lend it to me, as I would like to write a word of thanks to its author. Here I am given *Le Figaro*, so don't send it to me, but *La Revue bleue* and selected issues of the *Débats* will be welcome.

Monday, September 15, 79
Villa d'Este

Late yesterday evening I received together Lo's two little letters of September 8 and 11. I find it hard to account for this strange postal delay, and still less for Lo's massive, quasi-<u>criminal</u> confusion of No. 65 and No. 89 of the Via Babuino. Now, my Roman *pied-à-terre* is No. 65, and thus all letters may be sent to me there without any risk of "embarrassment."

I've been here since Sunday evening (September 7) in my turret which M. and Mme Sachots[18] have seen. I take my daily fare (with roast meat, good vegetables, and dessert, plus wine and coffee) every day at about six o'clock with Cardinal Hohenlohe, who asks me to remember him affectionately to you. The dining room is small, and this week I was the only guest. His Eminence has to go to Rome on Thursday for the Consistory and I'll spend three days at No. 65, Babuino, from Sunday till next Tuesday. Deign to write to me there making amends for your above-mentioned criminal confusion.

The drive in Vienna with Lenbach in your carriage certainly entitles you in perpetuity to a fine armchair in his studio in Munich. To it add a footstool for Clément Rubens and give me your frank impression of Lenbach's portraits.

Do you know the paintings by your compatriot, Valery Jacoby? Herewith the article *Un Peintre réformateur* from *La France* which will give you a high opinion of Jacoby, and of the humanitarian mission of painting in England and Russia. Tell Clément about it too, while always impressing on him "the basis" of great art. Although *Le Figaro* will have already informed you adequately on Cham,[19] I send you for good measure a few anecdotes about this good gentleman–draftsman. You'll perhaps have the chance of seeing several of his albums at Baden-Baden—among them *La Grammaire illustrée, les Cosaques*, etc., etc. I would urge M. Sach to buy them for his Academy of Painting were it not for his pronounced habits of economy.

I hope that Schulze, Wettig, and the like, as well as organ concerts, etc., will not disturb your siesta at the Villa Müller.

Irrevocably
Your

FL

None of my good friends are in Rome before the end of October.

18. Presumably the Grand Duke and Grand Duchess of Saxe-Weimar, a rare example of this curious variant of their nickname (Sach).
19. Pseudonym of Amédée, Comte de Noé, French caricaturist.

Sgambati has sent me his <u>very lovely</u> first quintet published by Schott (Mainz). The title is adorned with my coat of arms, surmounted by the <u>unicorn</u>.

Allow me to keep a few days longer the article by Saint-Saëns on the symphonic poems, to which I shall reply.

Thursday morning, September 25, 79
Rome

I returned here Sunday and am going back this afternoon to the Villa d'Este.

Cardinal Haynald is the titular head of the church of Santa Maria degli Angeli. Yesterday I attended the formal taking over by His Eminence of this admirable church, built by Michelangelo (but unfortunately left without a façade), and ministered to by the Carthusians, whose monastery is adjacent. According to the good advice of Marcel Czartoryski, I should have settled there and given proof of my religious sentiments by becoming a Carthusian in 1865, whereas I came to stay with Mgr Hohenlohe at the Vatican. Usually there's nothing so very clever in being wise in the interest of others, and Marcel didn't have to expend great efforts of imagination with regard to my novitiate as a Carthusian.

There arrived with your letter a few pleasant lines from S[ach] and his daughter Elsi in reply to a little present I sent her from Bayreuth. She tells me she has received Weitzmann's learned and delightful calling cards. Is this your doing? Do you have in your possession the two other copies which belong to <u>us</u>? I asked Weitzmann to send them to you.

I'm being interrupted by visits. So long till more letters from your very humble

FL

October 1, 79
Villa d'Este

Before returning here Thursday I again wrote you a line from Rome. Did you receive it? Your Munich letter reached me yesterday. I'm glad you spent a lovely evening <u>under</u> the *Götterdämmerung*, as well as agreeable hours at the exhibition and in Lenbach's studio. The forebears of Schennis, Papa Daubigny, and Mama Diaz are well named; perhaps you'll add to them <u>Uncle</u> Rousseau. Our young friend thus comes from a very good family, on which his works will confer added luster. You tell me nothing about Siemiradzki's new pictures. The colors seem very loud, and Makart's laurels dim the palette of the Polish painter.

Princess Marie Hoh[enlohe], whose judgment I value highly, writes that Angeli's portrait of the Archduchess Marie is very successful. He had originally let her hand rest on a fine Newfoundland dog in the midst of a landscape. Later on he erased the dog and replaced it with a book, being irritated by the praises of members of the public who admired chiefly the animal's magnificent coat to the detriment of the charming features of the Archduchess. The book will better convey respect for art and etiquette.

I'm trying to get back to work. To start with I am writing a piece for the piano, and arrangements for four hands, long promised to a Leipzig publisher, not Kahnt, who fell into disgrace at Bayreuth because his paper had done something silly – – – – People are right not to stand for anything improper, and vis-à-vis Wagner only an attitude of reverent admiration befits those who truly admire his genius.

In ten days or so I'm going to Albano. My modest ordination as <u>Honorary</u> Canon will probably take place on Sunday October 12[20] under the auspices of Cardinal Hoh[enlohe]. Calderón and Copernicus were <u>full</u> Canons. Why haggle with me over the title Honorary? Could it be because I have written more than a thousand sheets of religious music which do not please the great majority of the Canons who are addicted to what they call in Italian *gratt'orecchio* [ear-scratch-

20. Biographers generally give the end of September 1879 as the date of Liszt's appointment as Honorary Canon of Albano. Evidently it occurred later.

ing]? In spite of this it would be possible for these sheets to be and to remain <u>canonical</u>; and I shall add to their number, if God grants me life, without changing my style; for the latter comes from my very intimate and permanent Catholic sentiment.

Yours ever

FL

Continue writing to Rome, 65 Via del Babuino.

You know of the sudden death of Count Lovatelli, husband of Donna Ersilia.

————

Thursday, October 16, 79

V[illa] d'Este

Last Thursday I accompanied Cardinal Hoh[enlohe] from Rome to Albano. The trip takes two and a half hours by carriage, and by train one gains at the most half an hour, for the station is very far from Albano. Accordingly the Cardinal preferred his carriage (which is free of all rattling sounds) drawn by his two excellent horses.

The episcopal palace of Albano was built in the time of Benedict XIII. Benedict XIV stayed there several times, and Cardinal de Bernis spent some time there. The rooms are spacious and well designed. In the one I occupied there are still some fine French engravings which Cardinal Bernis left behind.

Friday and Saturday were spent in visits with H[ohenlohe] to the Seminary, the Catacombs, the Chigis (Ariccia), the Fianos, etc. The entering into possession (this is the term used) of my stall of Honorary Canon of the Chapter of Al[bano] took place very solemnly at ten o'clock in the cathedral on Sunday, October 12, feast of the Motherhood of the Blessed Virgin Mary. Some ten canons loudly intoned Gregorian plain chant in unison during celebration of the mass. An organist, of whom our friend Gottschalg would not much approve, alternated with them and indulged in agreeable *concetti* [conceits, i.e., improvisations] on his solemn instrument. Following high mass a procession took place within the cathedral (as on the second Sunday of October each year); Cardinal H[ohenlohe] carried the Holy Sacrament.

That same Sunday at one o'clock a meal for twenty-five to thirty persons was served at the episcopal palace. Neither laymen nor members of the fair sex had been invited. On the town square the municipal orchestra in brilliant uniforms with plumed headdresses provided musical entertainment which I afterward completed with a few *sonatinas* as a *chasse-café*.

I return to Rome Tuesday evening. Princess Marie Hoh[enlohe] will be there in the course of next week. Her mother is still bedridden, but is going ahead uninterruptedly with her huge work, of which six or eight large volumes have already been published.

Yours ever

FL

Please do me the favor of having 20 marks delivered to M. Goerwitz (*Schriftsteller*) at Sulza, near Weimar. He is the author of the epic and dramatic poem on the salt mines of Sulza which you liked so much. The only attribute of a great man the poor devil has is extreme want. Instruct my friend Grosse or Gottschalg to take care of the remittance of these 20 marks.

Have you received Weitzmann's wonderful calling cards? I'm expecting to receive my set from you and would like to show it to Sgambati and others of my friends in Rome.

Have you seen Mottl in Weimar?

October 25, 79
Villa d'Este

Your two last letters are admirable in heart and mind. You very shrewdly identify the good fruit in Fourier's ideas in spite of the bizarre and even grotesque rind. In 1832 I read Fourier's *La Théorie des quatre mouvements* and remember having attended two lessons in the course he was then giving in a (medical) amphitheatre in Paris. Among other things he demonstrated that true economic science would easily succeed in liquidating England's debt by using – – – matches. His oratorical talent, like his style, left much to be desired. He spoke easily and glibly but in such a way as to shed more confusion than light in the minds of the listeners. He needed disciples and popularizers of his doctrine in order to clarify it. Of these the most zealous was M. Considérant. I suppose that the *Revue* highlights the vigorous role he played. Moreover it will also doubtless show how the positivism of M. Comte and M. Littré relates to M. Fourier's ideas.

Thanks for the charming article by Renan on Hadrian, the supreme dilettante, and for Weitzmann's wonderful calling cards of accomplished canonical science and ingenuity. Since he has offered you several sets of them, please send me three of each card—twelve in all. I would like to offer one as a present to M. de Keudell and to Sgambati. On November 3 I'm dining at M. de Keudell's Palazzo Caffarelli with Sgambati, who has completed his concerto for piano and orchestra, and two or three concert études.[21] He is soon going to play them for me.

I spent the day of October 22[22] in Rome where I received some thirty telegrams and letters. The one from Bronsart refutes the report of Bülow's resignation, for Bronsart invites me to return to Hanover in the month of April in order to hear my *Faust Symphony*[23], etc., under the baton of Bülow. There are certainly various people who very much hope for his resignation, and I fear that he himself may be

21. Opus 7.
22. Liszt's birthday.
23. G 108; R 425.

one of them—among the foremost. However I hope he will continue to play his exemplary and masterly role at Hanover to the benefit of art and of worthy artists.

More than a month after it was written, the enclosed letter from Rimsky-Korsakov addressed to Santa Francesca Romana was handed to me by the lay brother porter who was awaiting the Superior's return to ask him in which country I was. My loyal devotion to Santa Francesca Romana prompted me to go to her church on Thursday before returning here. The good porter, very surprised at seeing me again, fetched Rimsky's letter which I shall answer with thanks, telling him that the *Triomphe funèbre du Tasse* was published last year in full score, as well as for piano only,[24] by Breitkopf and Härtel.

Did I tell you about my <u>brilliant</u> version, for piano with two hands, of the ravishing *Tarantelle*[25] by Dargomisky [Dargomizhsky], with *basso continuo*?

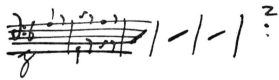

I have also transcribed (very freely) the *Polonaise*[26] from Tchaikovsky's opera. It is pompous, and will serve as a companion piece to that from Lassen's *Faust*. You will please me by influencing Lassen and Loën favorably toward the idea of a performance this winter at Weimar of Mottl's *Agnes Bernauer*.[27] He writes that his opera also has a chance of being performed shortly at Leipzig.

With all my heart, your grateful

FL

24. G 517; R 184.
25. G 483; R 148.
26. G 429; R 262, from *Eugene Onegin*.
27. First performed March 28, 1880, in Weimar.

Nov. 8, 79
Rome

Being no longer abreast of events in Paris, I don't know whether M. Renan is still an active contributor to *Le Temps*. In any case reassure your mother the Princess on the complete doctrinal consistency of this most important and serious newspaper, to which I remain particularly grateful. It was the only one in '66 of the <u>major</u> Paris newspapers to have praised my *Messe de Gran*, which was at that time rejected by my closest friends—Berlioz, d'Ortigue – – – who were urging me to continue charming salons in the role of a celebrated pianist. Many thanks —and for <u>not</u> seeing such worthless friends again.

Weitzmann is not one of these, and has in certain respects done himself harm by backing my compositions. This morning I received the enclosed letter from him. If you have no objection, please get Countess Kalckreuth to write Weitzmann (Enkeplatz 5, Berlin) a kind note telling him that you punctiliously passed on his calling cards with their ingeniously flowery counterpoint to Princess Elisabeth, and how much Her Highness enjoyed Weitzmann's enigmatic canons (for 4 hands) and other works. This mark of attention will give great pleasure to my dear old friend, who is not much of a courtier but by no means a simpleton.

I have been here all week. Princess Marie Hohenlohe arrived eight days earlier. I accompanied her on a few visits to studios. At Siemiradzki's people admire the sketch of a large painting destined to decorate the ceiling of a Polish Maecenas. You know that Siemiradzki made a splendid gift to the Cracow museum of his painting of Christian martyrs turned into human torches before the eyes of Nero to satisfy his bloodthirsty stupidity. Sie[miradzki]'s great new work is entirely symbolic. It represents *La Marche du progrés*.

The painter Richter, crowned with laurels for his recent portrait of Queen Louise praised as an outstanding masterpiece by the Court, the town, and the press, has been in Rome some days with his wife who is Meyerbeer's daughter. They will probably be coming to see me at the Villa d'Este where I return tomorrow. Although Richter looks fairly well, he is a sick man and his recovery is slow.

From the newspaper *L'Italie,* I learned that Countess Bobrinska has fractured her hip. They say it will be three months before she can walk again. You might perhaps write her a line, for she has always spoken to me kindly of you. I stopped by her house but saw neither her nor Bobrinski, to whom I am grateful for the affectionate relations I have had with them for over fifteen years. On Monday at Keudell's dinner there were present Princess Hoh[enlohe], Princess Teano and her husband Onorato, Count Gobineau, Mme Helbig, Sgambati, and Senfft von Pilsach (whom you know from Weimar). After coffee Senfft sang several *Lieder* admirably, and Sgambati regaled us with several of his compositions—among others a nocturne and an étude worthy of Chopin. What greater praise can one bestow?

Your sad and faithful

FL

Nov. 22, 79
Rome

My last letter had already been mailed when yours reached me with the very surprising news that Lassen is thinking of leaving Weimar. I hope that Mme S[ach] will persuade him to stay by paying the deficit.

Tomorrow I'll write you at length from the Villa d'Este. It goes without saying that Kömpel has not the slightest chance of being appointed *Kapellmeister* at Hanover; but the simplest things are difficult and even impossible to explain to people who don't have the common sense to have understood them beforehand.

Yours ever

FL

Nov. 30, 79

A delayed extension of my recent truncated letter.

I don't think that Lassen will leave Weimar. Are they once again offering him an honorable and lucrative post in Belgium as director of a conservatory? I doubt that he'd be happy at Hanover. The salary is meager, there is no Court, and to succeed Bülow calls for sustained hard work. Now the latter is not our good friend's weakness. He's not going to undertake something for which he has never shown any inclination. What he really likes is to be bored in a manner which suits him.

As for recommending K[ömpel] to Bronsart, I shall refrain from doing so, being aware that Bronsart already has other conductors in mind. This does not reflect on the merits of K[ömpel] whom we sincerely appreciate. Mottl is another matter. When Loën writes me about him I'll reply in the laudatory manner with which you are familiar. But once again, the loss of Lassen seems to me well-nigh impossible.

During their stay in Berlin Bülow and Cosima were on good terms with Lassalle. At that time he did not really rank in the *R.O.*, *Le Barbier de Séville*, *Revue des deux mondes* category—although the great Alexander von Humboldt commented very favorably on Lassalle's knowledge and extraordinary intellectual capacity. Ask either Bülow or Cosima which would be the best biographical book to read on Lassalle. I personally am ignorant and only know rumors of polemics involving him —in particular his biting pamphlet, quite in the *R.O.* manner, attacking a history of literature by Julian Schmidt.

You are so kind as to run errands for me and so successful that I don't hesitate to ask you to send Cosima the two enclosed notes together with the required sum of 100 marks.

An extra load of musical paperwork is taking up my time. This is a chronic disease I have to endure with no pleasure or illusion other than resignation. The world here below is much like a hospital in which the doctors themselves are sick.

It was not due to a fall from a horse, but in her own room that Countess Bobrinska (whom I have not seen since) fractured her hip. If you write to her, send the letter to Villa Malta, Pincio, Rome.

Your sad

FL

Have you any news of Bülow? Let me know, for I have heard nothing concerning his resignation from Hanover, which is very possible but contrary to my wishes. Thanks for the *Débats*, and *La Revue bleue*. I am reading them with attention.

December 16, 79
Rome

I came back here last Friday for a concert by the "Romana" musical society, popularly called the *Neri*.[28] Prince Sulmona Borghese is president, and Mustafà the chief musical director, etc. This society has at its disposal the best choruses in Rome, which Mustafà conducts in a superior manner with energy and authority. In the course of this year, Händel's *Messiah*[29] and *Israel*[30] were performed here (for the first time), as well as Spontini's *La Vestale*[31] and, I think, *Fernand Cortez*;[32] for this famous composer, in particular, belongs to the *Neri* through his pious foundations in his native town, Jesi (formerly in the Pontifical States), and Pope Gregory XVI conferred on him the title of Count of San Andrea. This is the only example I know of a musician having been made a count by a sovereign. There is an equivalent in Verdi's nomination as Senator of Italy. In France, the same dignity was conferred on Auber, but in the field of painting they went no further than Ingres. Other countries and even *R.O.* have not yet been similarly inspired.

There is in Rome another musical society known as the *Bianchi*[33] over which presides Prince Teano. It has announced the forthcoming performance of Mendelssohn's *Elijah*,[34] which I'll hear before my departure which is set for about January 9.

28. The Blacks, the extremely conservative aristocracy, close to the Vatican.
29. First performed April 13, 1742, in Dublin.
30. First performed April 4, 1739, in London.
31. First performed December 16, 1807, in Paris.
32. First performed November 28, 1809, in Paris.
33. The Whites, the more liberal aristocracy.
34. First performed August 11, 1846, in Birmingham.

My article against "Intermission Music"[35] dates from the early fifties when I was actively discharging the functions of *Kapellmeister* at Weimar, and was publishing in Brendel's *Neue Zeitschrift* various articles of Wagnerian propaganda on Berlioz, Meyerbeer, Schumann, Robert Franz. It has been suggested to me that I pull these scattered fragments together in one or two volumes, and I will perhaps attend to this later on. In the meantime I am still of the opinion that "Intermission Music" as now played is a humiliating business for the members of the orchestra and a silly pastime for the audience. It has very sensibly already been abolished in several large theatres. The torrent of custom is one thing, but when it becomes a swamp it's better to do without it.

A little barrel of Marsala has been sent off to your address. This wine can, it seems to me, compete to advantage with that served at Court. Please get Sarring to look after the cellar and the bottling.

They tell me that Countess Bobrinska is better and receives visits on her chaise longue from her friends, both male and female. I'll shortly pay her an affectionate visit.

I have written, not letters as I should have, but a few sheets of useless music which have made me entirely unsociable.

To whom it may concern, greetings!

Your very humble

FL

———

December 26, 79
(Vil[la] d'[Este])

The parallel drawn by Lo between her letters and those of Mlle Vogt is most amusing. The poor girl would tremble with pleasure at it, and would see in this the decisive confirmation of her fixed idea that only she is destined to make me completely happy.

35. Written in 1855 and in Liszt's *Gesammelte Schriften*, III, 1, pp. 136–50, where its title is *Keine Zwischenakts-Musik*—!

I'm so weary and even so harassed by the music I am writing, while composing it, revising the copy and the proofs, that afterwards I don't like to talk about it. Between mid-September and mid-December I completed three transcriptions (which I had promised) for the piano: Tchaikovsky's *Polonaise*, Dargomyzhsky's *Tic-tac Tarantelle* with repeated bass in a,a, and the *Sarabande* and *Chaconne*[36] from Händel's *Almira*, plus a distinguished arrangement for four hands of four marches by Schubert (the same marches I had arranged for orchestra)[37]—and, in particular, several compositions of religious music, among them a *Mass for Organ*[38] only (without voices). It is to appear in a week's time and I'll immediately send it to you by book post. The publication of the other pieces has been delayed until spring.

As for reading, I've almost finished the *Vie de Saint Dominique* by Father Lacordaire. It contains some fine eloquent passages and a number of felicitous expressions as, for example, with regard to the rosary, "Rationalists smile at the sight of files of people passing by, repeating the same word. He who is more enlightened understands that there is but one word for love, and that in continuing to utter it he never repeats it."

Other passages would please you less and would perhaps shock you. For my part I no longer discuss Catholic works, being by no means a preaching friar.

Rubinstein has been in Rome three days visiting his wife and children, who are in need of a mild climate and will spend the winter there. He leaves again Sunday on some tour or other. He wired yesterday that he wished to come and see me here. I replied that I shall have to go to Rome tomorrow morning and that we'll see each other there.

The Rohlfs and the learned and famous uncle, Schweinfurth, dined with me Wednesday on the terrace at the Villa d'Este. They brought me the news that Mlle Cruikshank and her sister are in Rome. The weather is magnificent. I benefit little from it (feeling a little indis-

36. G 181; R 25.
37. G 363; R 449.
38. G 264; R 384.

posed) and am writing in bed. Monday I'll be back here and will pack my bags in the first week of the new year. On January 10 I expect to be in Florence, and on the fifteenth in Budapest.

Yours ever

FL

Write until January 9 to 65, Babuino. Give me news of Bülow, about whom I have heard nothing. Thanks for Reyer's article on Berlioz.

The last time I wrote was from my bed which I took to in the afternoon of Christmas day, Thursday, at three o'clock. In order not to fail
in my promise to Mme Treuenfels (formerly Mlle Rielke) to attend
her concert, I left for Rome Saturday at eleven. At the concert (which
was at three) I found Rubinstein who is here visiting his wife for Christmas. We dined together (at the Grand Hôtel de Russie, Babuino). As a
chasse-café I banged out for him my arrangement of the *Tic-tac Tarantelle* by Dargomizhsky. Then he played four pieces admirably, among
them his famous *Galop* from *Le Démon*, as well as a very remarkable
prelude and fugue he composed in '54 at the Altenburg, together with
five other little known and technically very difficult preludes and fugues
which, in my view, are among his best pieces.

Next day Rubinstein left for Paris to confer with a poet about a
comic opera. On January 6 he conducts his oratorio *La Tour de Babel*
in Berlin, and soon thereafter will be in St. Petersburg to supervise the
final rehearsals of his new Russian opera,[1] based on a story by Lermontov (whose name I forget). His wife is spending the winter in Rome
with two of her children who look very well indeed but are of rather
delicate health. For over thirty years I have felt great esteem, even
admiration and sincere friendship for Rub[instein]. I shall continue to

1. *The Merchant Kalashnikov*, first performed March 5, 1880, in St. Petersburg.

365

do so, and wish him soon, with all my heart, one of those brilliant European successes such as *Robert le Diable*.[2]

While in Rome I made no calls, and returned here Monday. On Tuesday we had a brilliant concert, whose program I enclose, at the Palazzo d'Este. On it my name is spelt in the Parisian manner [Litz], and Mme Helbig is given the title of Princess. She played the *Héroïde Funèbre*[3] with intelligence and feeling. I particularly appreciate Mme Helbig among my very friendly acquaintances in Rome. (The German ambassador, de Keudell, came to this concert which was very well attended.)

Gounod had also sent me from London his *Marche funèbre d'une marionnette*, together with a good many of his new vocal compositions. I suppose Lassen chose it for the New Year's Day concert because of the strangeness of the title. I don't remember the other pieces, but they probably include naïve and piquant things. Let me know if you found any of either kind.

All you tell me about Martha R[emmert]'s concert and our friend Gille's new patronage of Friedmann is most charmingly and entertainingly correct.

Although I am not yet back in the saddle, and have been staying in my room these last four days (save for mass between nine and ten o'clock in the adjoining church), I go back to Rome Tuesday evening and leave again Sunday for Florence, where I shall as usual spend a day with the Hillebrands. If you write to me promptly, your letter will still reach me in Rome. On January 15 I expect to arrive in Budapest.

Yours ever

FL

I have been lent the memoirs of Prince Metternich. It seems that in his youth His Highness had little taste for a political career but a great deal for mathematics and the natural sciences, even medicine and phre-

2. Opera by Meyerbeer, first performed November 21, 1831, in Paris.
3. G 102; R 419, symphonic poem. G 642; R 364, for two pianos.

nology. When your uncle publishes his memoirs we will perhaps learn that he was particularly drawn toward painting and music, and that it was only after fierce resistance that he gave up fine arts and consented to become Grand Chancellor.

———

Friday, January 16, 80
(Hotel Hungaria)

Lo is not unaware of the fact that anything to do with my health is very displeasing to me in conversation and even more so in letters. In spite of this she continues to lecture me and "wax indignant" on this subject. So be it, so long as she finds any pleasure in doing so. Jean-Jacques [Rousseau] (I think it was) said that any man past forty who is not his own doctor must be considered an imbecile—an advantage to which I don't attach much importance.

In Florence I spent Monday pleasantly with the Hillebrands. Count von Arnim, whom I saw, is spending the winter on the Lungarno. His health, or rather his ill health, is so-so both physically and mentally.

I stopped over in Venice from Tuesday evening to Wednesday at the invitation of one of my young fans, Professor Bassani, a poet and distinguished composer. My only visit was to Princess Hatzfeldt who will prolong her stay in Venice until the summer. She seems immune to the law of aging, and remains completely fresh and graceful. Rudi Lichtenstein and his wife are living with her.

Please tell me the exact names of the composer and the (Parisian) publisher of the remarkable sonata for violin and piano which Saint-Saëns played at your house. I promised this information to Bassani (who has also just composed a sonata for violin and piano).

On my arrival here in Budapest yesterday evening, I was lodged at government expense at the Hotel Hungaria in view of the fact that my splendid apartment in the new building of the Academy of Music which was completed last summer is not yet entirely dry. Several of my friends have energetically protested against my intention to move into it this winter.

Sarasate is giving a concert this evening and Joachim is expected. Sophie Menter, my favorite pianist, is staying at the Hotel Hungaria.

Your

FL

Hillebrand will be publishing a major article in the *Rundschau* on Metternich's memoirs, and R. Lichtenstein will shortly make his first literary appearance with a novella in the Berlin review *Nord und Süd*.

———

January 22, 80

B.P.

I deplore the fact that the stoves in the Hotel Hungaria functioned so poorly during your stay here. Usually they heat properly. One of the owners of this place wishes me well; as a result the temperature of my rooms is always pleasant and carefully tended. This first week I hardly went out, and I plan to stay indoors the whole winter. My pianists (of both sexes) come here three times a week for their treatment. There are ten or twelve, of whom a third are making good progress.

Martha Remmert delights me as "a star of the first magnitude." She has more talent than others of her colleagues who are better provided with newspaper articles and concert engagements.

This morning my expensive cases of books and music arrived from Rome. I'll search for the Widor Trio[4] to send to you, but my copy may still be at Kömpel's. Send me the name of the composer of the charming sonata for violin and piano which Saint-Saëns played at your house. I thought you had the score; if not, don't bother with the name of the publisher. For me to fulfill my promise to Bassani, the name of the author will suffice.

4. Opus 19.

Autre Guitare[5] and an organ (not barrel) to boot. It seems to me that you can content yourself with the article in the *Revue des deux mondes* on Prince Metternich's memoirs. I go on reading them and will give you my impressions *viva voce*.

In Rome, when you were living in the palace of the Russian Embassy I was studying the four volumes of St. Thomas' little *Summa* [*Theologica*]. Let's turn to this reading matter again in Weimar at the chapter on the angels, having in mind Pascal's words, "Man is neither angel nor beast and unfortunately, in trying to act like an angel, he inevitably acts like a beast" (I'm quoting from memory but the gist of the thought is accurate).

Your

FL

The cask of Marsala should already have arrived at Weimar. Tell Sarring to look after it carefully.

January 24, 80

B.P.

Thanks for the information about Gabriel Fauré's *Sonata*.[6] I'll write at once to my new friend Bassani.

The principal German publisher of Tschaikowsky's works is C. Sander (Firma Leuckart) in Leipzig. He'll quickly find the idyll or elegy you are looking for.

The threatened uprising in Pest occurred on the eve of my arrival. It had been announced that it would continue on the evenings following but the military intervened with sufficient force and public order has been restored. There remain only the windows of the casino and the lamps in nearby streets smashed by rocks to cries of "Down with the dress-coat set! Long live Verhovay!" plus a few dead, some

5. "New subject," reinforced by adding an organ to the guitar. It is also the title of a short poem by Victor Hugo, following a longer one, *Guitare*.
6. Opus 13.

wounded, and others overcome by fear. Mihalovich is not one of them. Albert Apponyi who yesterday returned from the Vienna Delegation is to dine this evening with Mihal[ovich] and me at Géza Zichy's.

Joachim, whom I had not seen in more than twenty years, came and looked me up yesterday before the philharmonic concert where he played masterfully as always. Friday he gives another concert in Budapest after having delighted audiences during the week in Kaschau, Grosswardein, etc. Sophie Menter, who knows these towns, told me that the chief musical Maecenas of Kaschau is an amateur violinist who usually wears his pork-butcher's apron. She even claims that he frequently wears this apron while pigs are being slaughtered – – – –

I answer the last two lines of your letter with a maxim which I made up for my own personal use: "One must know how to wither on the vine without thereby losing one's faculties."

Yours ever

FL

———

Sunday, February 1
Budapest

What you term my "sarcasms" regarding too facile admiration can be quite easily explained.

At the Via de' due Macelli in Rome in '62, you quoted pertinently what Meyerbeer had said to you in your box at Stuttgart during a performance of Mozart's *Don Giovanni*: "That is music for all time" – – – – Consequently there is no need for the wild music of the future (so called) which is, alas, very much in our midst. Furthermore you condescended, following the example of Queen Olga, to applaud Rossini's *Le Barbier de Séville*.

Let's speak no more of the "sarcasms" nor of the accompanying unhappiness in Rome and elsewhere. I am glad that you have come to like *Roméo et Juliette*,[7] several parts of which Berlioz composed marvelously.

7. Opus 17, first performed November 24, 1839, in Paris.

Saint-Saëns' success with *La Lyre et la harpe*[8] gives me very great pleasure. I will urge M. S[ach] to invite Saint-Saëns to perform this symphonic ode at Weimar in the same way that Berlioz was formerly invited.

Without reproaching you, I complain a little of Lo's neglecting to send me certain articles she knows interest me, for example: Taine's acceptance speech and the reply of Dumas (not Alexandre).

Actually, of the French papers here I am lent only *L'Univers*, to which you will be good enough to subscribe again for three months from April 1 through June, in the semi-weekly edition as usual.

Paris [illegible] has been in my possession since I was in Rome, but I hope to find among your books Dumas' work *Le Divorce*.[9] The question is still wide open – – – –

I regret not being able to send you Widor's Trio, nor even to tell you the name of the publisher. Kahnt should know it; have Gottschalg write him a line (the latter has been roused to a Schillerian pitch of lyricism by Laura-Martha "am Clavier"). You were right to consider it superfluous to read *La Revue des deux mondes* when *Urania* and *Deutschland* were available. Besides, Widor's Trio, while distinguished, does not seem to me to be on the same level as those by Saint-Saëns and Bronsart.

Nothing new to report from Budapest. I have already told you that I saw Joachim again. Day before yesterday morning I accompanied him to the rehearsal for his concert and heard the same program that evening. He played one of Viotti's numerous concertos, the Brahms Concerto,[10] the Chaconne and Variations on one of his [Joachim's] original themes, ending with a Rondo *à la Hongroise*. This work pleases me, being both of noble inspiration and of excellent style, well proportioned and of happy effect.

As for Joachim's talent as a virtuoso, I have been of the same opinion for thirty years; no other violinist produces such an impression of ac-

8. Opus 57, for solo voices, chorus, and orchestra.
9. *La Question du divorce* (Paris, 1880).
10. In D, for violin, Opus 77. The original manuscript is in the Library of Congress.

complished perfection as he does. Certainly, charm and attractiveness
are hardly absent, but they are not scattered here and there indiscrim-
inately. In some respects Bülow who, in his execution and in other respects, has a far more individual and bold genius nonetheless resembles
Joachim in masterly concentration and a superior sense of style.

Your

FL

I want the Marsala to have your wholehearted approval. Let it rest
about a couple of weeks longer in its cask, and let the bottling operation be performed with care under the guidance of the expert whom
Beust recommended.

I'll reimburse the freight and customs costs to you as soon as I'm
back in Weimar. I need not add that I have already paid the bill for
the wine.

February 9, 80

B.P.

L'ancienne is backing down with regard to the Meiningen [orches-
tra], and more so toward Lo as concerns Naples. What an abstruse
idea to make me conduct [*de m'y faire bâtonner*][11] *Lohengrin* there! Sarring now would suffice for such an important task.

My humility has its limits.

FL

Thanks for the *Débats*. I read Klaczko's article on Dante and Michelangelo in the *Revue* and people here lend me *L'Univers* and *Le
Figaro* and even the sensational book by Dumas which *R.O.* would
approve only in secret, should she even deign to take notice of the
lucubrations of *folliculaires*.[12]

11. Liszt plays on words: *bâtonner* means to beat with a stick, and in this musical con-
text means to wield a conductor's baton.
12. A pejorative word invented by Voltaire applying to scribblers of the press.

Tuesday, February 10, 80
B.P.

Your letter, overflowing with kindness and understanding, aroused in me the same emotion as in the year '65 at the Vatican, at the hands of Ch[imay]. He was surprised at that time to hear me say that one would have to be both stupid and evil not to remain lovingly enthralled forever. Thus have your character and fate disposed of me.

Saturday, February 14

I was prevented from continuing to write to you on Tuesday. Since then you have sent me some kind of nonsense in your *Postkarte* about canceling a subscription to the *Neue Zeitschrift*, relegated by me to the waste basket together with *Urania* of inglorious memory. Besides, difficult people who only wish to know things that are true should not subscribe to any newspaper. The only role of the press—in effective control—is to entertain or amuse the public with truths and falsehoods, plus things in between. The very well intentioned Bakunin articles in the *Débats* seem to me to fall somewhere in between.

Very simply
Your

FL

The manager of the Hungaria delivers the *Débats* and *Le Figaro* to me every evening. Please merely tell me which additional pieces in them I should read.

Nothing new here except a latent ministerial crisis. Our friend Albert Apponyi is visibly growing in importance because of his merits and talents.

February 19, 80
Budapest

Yet another very good and dear letter in the true Lo key. Rest assured that my modesty is sincere enough to understand yours which in my humble opinion is greatly exaggerated but, I should add, all the more exquisite and adorable.

I sent Gille a friendly reply yesterday to the effect that my influence did not reach the point of shattering Weimar's economic tradition. Our friend Gille could have done without his last letter concerning Naumann. However, it does honor to his excellent sentiments which are unquestionable, and follows his recommendations for de Munk, Friedmann, etc.

His views on an active musical role for Jena seem to me – – – outdated. So long as Weimar had the initiative (in relation to music in Germany) Jena helped us greatly by its competition.

Now the wisdom of others has arranged matters differently.

I have asked that the Liszt concert in Vienna be postponed. It will probably take place on Tuesday in Holy Week, February 24.[13]

Herewith the triple portrait, in childhood, youth, and old age (published day before yesterday in a Budapest newspaper) of your very humble

FL

We'll discuss at your house in April, too far ahead for my taste, Alex[andre] Dumas' book *Question du divorce* and the replies of the Abbé Vidieu, Paul Féval—which I have read.

————

February 26, 80
B.P.

Please have your bookseller send me right away the magnificent illustrated edition of Montalembert's history of St. Elisabeth,[14] pub-

13. Liszt made a mistake. Easter in 1880 fell on March 28.
14. *Histoire de Sainte Elisabeth de Hongrie* (Paris, 1836). By 1880 the book was in its seventeenth edition.

lished by Mame (Paris). It is in <u>one</u> volume, large 8vo, with an appropriate binding (in red). Your most grateful FL begs you to arrange for it to reach him here before he leaves for Vienna on March 20.

The best thing is for you and Clément first to look at this fine book, and then to send it on to me from Weimar. It will arrive here in time, on March 18.

———

March 10, 80
B.P.

I come to the end of my winter in Budapest with more or less the same feelings as those Lo simultaneously conceals in Weimar. People here honor me with an almost universal goodwill. This calls for my gratitude, which is never a burden (Rousseau's remark notwithstanding) for "noble hearts."

Herewith the program of next Sunday's musical morning in the concert hall adjoining my quarters for next year, at the Royal Academy of Music in Hungary. The latter will soon, I hope, no longer lag behind in the results achieved by the older and highly reputed conservatories of music in Europe.

From March 20 until April 2, write to Vienna, Schottenhof, to your

Very humbly devoted

FL

With or without a red binding, Montalembert's *St. Elisabeth* will be of use to me in Vienna, and I thank you for seeing to it that it reaches me at the Schottenhof on March 20.

The Hungarian bonnets will be brought to you on Saturday, April 3, by

Your very obedient

FL

I'm writing to M. S[ach]. Please tell Mottl that I shall have the pleasure of attending the second performance of his *Agnes Bernauer.*

From March 20 to 30 write to Vienna, Schottenhof. I have not the slightest intention of going to Hanover next month.

March 18, 80
Budapest

You perfectly explain the inner significance of Sach's letter, and what you said to him anticipated my reply. Plato certainly remains a great philosopher, but when it's a matter of business, platonic expressions of interest don't count for much even when accompanied by the holy water of the Court. To convey the appearance rather than the reality is an old and too threadbare technique.

The three Hungarian bonnets are on their way to you by today's mail. I hope you will approve of them. If not, I'll order others at M. Porfi's shop, Wagnergasse, until the result is completely successful.

The fine book (with the appropriate red binding) on St. Elisabeth reached me yesterday. Lo is a flawless diamond—in punctuality too.

Very gratefully and humbly
Your

FL

Sunday morning, Vienna, and April 4, Weimar for the second performance of Mottl. Cordial thanks for your Dresden letter.

Monday, March 29
Vienna

Thursday evening I leave Vienna. Friday I stop over in Dresden, and Saturday evening your very humble FL will see you again.

Be so kind as to tell Pauline to have my rooms ready for Saturday evening.

———

Thursday morning [1880?]
Baden

Unquestionably Borodin is a great figure. The instrumentation of his symphony is completely successful. The work will make a good impression this evening.

Madame your sister will write to you about it. It goes without saying that I'll do my utmost here to make up to her for my moodiness at the Ziegelei (the Tuileries of Weimar).

A few hours after my arrival (day before yesterday) the Empress deigned to receive me. Her Majesty is also suffering from hoarseness so that she can only speak in a husky voice. Today at five o'clock I have the honor of dining with her in a small group, as her Chamberlain, Count Fürstenstein, informs me.

Baroness de Stockhausen of whom you approve spent the winter at Baden. I was her neighbor yesterday at a good and brilliant performance of an opera – – – which was a failure among so many others.

Your FL will be writing to you tomorrow.

At the Hôtel de l'Europe the owner did me the favor of giving me the suite (with a balcony) where your uncle lived.

Please send me *L'Univers* here. Monday evening I'll be in Frankfurt.

———

Hall (near Innsbruck)
August 27, 80

I continue to feel sad, but in a different way and more sadly. Lo is not to be distressed or become irritated at this.

At my sitting at Lenbach's day before yesterday, a visitor came in; so I did not remind him of his promise to inform you of the Wagner showings in Munich, but am writing to him this morning and giving him your Rottach address until the end of September. For safety's sake I've asked Bülow's acolyte friend, M. Spitzweg, to write or wire you two days ahead of time on the subject of these same showings. You will please me by showing him some politeness. It would be a gracious gesture if Peterle or Mimi were to call on him. Spitzweg lives at Otto Strasse 12, third floor, very near the Marienbad Hotel. If you forget this address, ask for it at the music shop Aibl where Spi[tzweg] is the manager.

Tuesday, dinner at Sach's with Tut., Pal. and L. Cranach. S[ach] talked about the recently published correspondence between Catherine and Grimm. You either know or will be reading it. Fritz will tell you about Lady Marlborough's telegram received during the dessert—and the reply.

Wednesday morning Bülow accompanied me to the station. We paused before the Bellevue Hotel which now has an external decoration of fine frescoes depicting Otto Wittelsbach, Emperor Louis of Bavaria, et al., painted by Schraudolph, son of the famous painter (Nazarene) whose major work in terms of number of frescoes is in Speier cathedral.

Your very humble FL will be in Rome Sunday.

———

Friday, September 3, 80
Rome

Tomorrow I return to the Villa d'Este. Here I have seen only the one person for whom I came in '61 and for whom I continue to return.

Wagner's sudden departure from the Villa d'Angri, rented until November, is unhappily due to ill health. He is now suffering from his third or fourth bout of erysipelas, and the doctors have ordered him to follow a cure at Gräfenberg (Silesia). In the meantime Cosima writes that they will spend a month in Siena, where I'll go and see them in mid-September.

Do you have news of Bülow? Please have Mimi or Clément ask M. Spitzweg for some, Otto Strasse 12, third floor, Munich.

Did you receive my note from Hall? I received your melancholy note only on Wednesday, and I await another, longer letter. Day after tomorrow your very humble and corrigible FL will write to you from the Villa d'Este.

Write to Albergo e Via d'Alibert, Rome. Pohlig and Friedheim (with his mother) have arrived. Reisenauer will follow.

Sunday, September 12, 80
Villa d'Este

This is only to tell you that I'll write to you next Saturday from Siena.

Day after tomorrow I return to Rome and, short of unexpected news from Cosima, I'll be with her Thursday evening. Write to Torre Fiorentina (R. Wagner), Siena (Toscana, Italia), until September 22.

I still hope that the news about Bülow in the press is false, that he has not had an apoplectic stroke, and that he will retain the use of his right hand. Should you know something accurate about him, write to me.

I have started working again a little at my music and will continue more vigorously from October until Christmas.

My sadness is haunted by many thoughts and memories which would not displease Lo, but I don't know how to express them. Guess the initials

B – FL.

Saturday morning, September 24, 80
Siena (Torre Fiorentina)

A lovely spot in the sweeping Tuscan countryside, varied and fertile, with the harmony of many hills and mountains, magnificent sunrises and sunsets, rich vegetation with pine trees, cypresses, olive trees, and vines. The Torre Fiorentina is a princely abode, with a well-kept chapel dedicated to the holy guardian angels. These last four days a Capuchin Father celebrated mass there, which the children and I attended. Afterward I took them for a stroll through the flower garden, next to which is a terraced theatre with no architecture, almost natural, a smaller version of that of the Hermitage at Bayreuth. In former times they must have given pastoral plays there. The tower does not pretend to compete with those of the cathedral and of the town hall of Siena—fifteen minutes from here; but it dominates the surroundings agreeably and contributes to the general landscape's character of amenity and contentment.

Wagner is restored to health. He is giving up the projected cure at Gräfenberg. In a week he leaves for Venice where he will spend a month or six weeks before returning to Bayreuth in November. Mme de Schleinitz, Princess Hatzfeldt, and Mme de Wöhrmann are in Venice, also Joseph Rubinstein who is dedicating his new *Fantasia on Tristan and Isolde* to Mme de Schleinitz.

Wagner hasn't worked much at the orchestral score of *Parsifal*, but he has the whole thing complete in his head, and the piano score (with numerous orchestral indications) is finished and copied. I reread this most highly sublime work, first in my room without a piano, and yesterday we went through the last part of the third act with W[agner]; he singing and I accompanying – – – – There is in the third act an idealized flower garden watered with the blood and tears of the Mystery of Good Friday, which is absolutely incredible. I know nothing comparable in music.

Rome, 5 o'clock

I'll finish my letter which was interrupted this morning. Paul Zhukovsky and I and Wagner's son Siegfried, aged eleven, went by the same train to Orvieto to admire the cathedral. The latter reveals an astonishing aptitude for architecture, and draws façades and arches, etc., very well. He is a charming and very happily gifted child. Zhukovsky spent some time at the splendid Villa d'Angri with the W[agner]s and will follow them to Venice and Bayreuth where he intends to set up his studio this winter. Cosima sang me praises of his large painting, a *Pietà*, which was shown in Paris and has just been sent off to Bayreuth (consequently I was not able to see it, nor a fine portrait, people say, of Cosima which has also been sent from Naples to Bayreuth). Over ten years ago Zhukovsky spent a few days at Wilhelmsthal and there sketched for M. S[ach] a large plan for improvements to the castle, of which only the gallery–drawing room has been carried out. Zhukovsky is now working on the cartoons for the stage sets of *Parsifal* and has promised the Capuchin Father a painting for the high altar of a new church which is being built on a hilltop near Siena. It will represent St. Francis receiving the stigmata.

Visitors are not admitted to the Torre Fiorentina. Wagner insists strongly on remaining alone with his wife and children whom he loves with passionate tenderness. Except for Zhukovsky, whose room is next to mine, I have seen no one else during these nine days. However, with the two governesses there were some ten of us at table. I showed Cosima and Zhukovsky the photograph of Clément's *Phaëton*. They found the concept and the composition most remarkable.

Happily, the bad news about Bülow in the press is false. He has lost the use of neither hand and is already actively discharging his new duties as head of the Meiningen orchestra. Gichel's father has written me a very reassuring letter on this subject from Munich.

I'll be staying here until Tuesday morning, then a couple of weeks at the Villa d'Este. Write a few lines soon

to your poor

FL

October 12, 80
Villa d'Este

My mood is not such as to soothe yours. I suffer from extreme mental fatigue against which I struggle by praying and working. These last ten days I have written a few sheets of music including a transcription of Rubinstein's famous *Lied: O wenn es doch immer so bliebe!* [O if it could only be so forever!][15] It finally worked out fairly well, not in a banal manner in spite of several inevitable trills. You will perhaps find some enjoyment in playing it for your fingers excel in trills just like the nightingale's throat.

I always greatly enjoy running errands for you. Herewith the information about the best translation of Krasiński's works from a letter of Count Kulcziki, who has promised me something more specific. You'll enjoy the French translation more. The German one you'll find at the Polish bookshop in Leipzig. Kahnt will send it to you.

On my return from Siena I found that Cardinal Hohenlohe was no longer here. He is still on a Visita Sagra (processions, confirmations, communions) in his diocese of Albano. He returned to the Villa d'Este for just one day but I'll probably see him again at Albano before winter.

And Sondershausen! Its last successful musical day of "Aranjuez"[16] was the concert whose program we had drawn up. Erdmannsdörfer will now be worried, for neither Berlin nor Vienna will appeal to him. You were so good as to introduce him to Mme de Schleinitz. He did not fail to ask me to do the same, since Mme de S[chleinitz] is considered all-powerful in the field of music in Berlin. Erd[mannsdörfer] naturally also asked me to recommend him to Princess Hohenlohe in Vienna. On the average I receive at least some twenty such letters a year, seeking the protection of the two omnipotent "principalities" in the German and Austrian empires – – – – Among Erdmannsdörfer's competitors for important posts let me mention Metzdorff. Keller-

15. G 554, 1; R 239, 1.
16. "*Die schoenen Tage von Aranjuez sind nun vorueber, meine Herren*" ("The beautiful days of Aranjuez are now over, gentlemen"), Friedrich von Schiller, *Don Carlos* (1783–87).

mann for the moment would be satisfied with Erdmannsdörfer's meager post at Sondershausen.

Pohlig is staying at the Villa d'Este and composes lugubrious and
heroic pieces. Friedheim and Reisenauer are hard at work in Rome. I
sometimes envy them certain illusions with which I have never been
afflicted. What people term my artistic career developed entirely on its
own without any pretension on my part. If I pursue it this is solely
from a sense of duty.

My aspirations and dreams lie elsewhere.

With all my heart, your old

FL

I've answered Count Beust's very kind letter concerning the gradual
move of the Hartwigs into the Hofgärtnerei. If they keep up the *matinées musicales* there on Sundays in the same rooms on the first floor,
I shall not object at all.

Mottl's appointment to Carlsruhe as *Hofkapellmeister* pleases me. M.
Sach will congratulate himself on having held back from awarding
Mottl the Falcon – – – for to go slow is the essence of the wisdom of
rulers.

October 30, 80
Villa d'Este

Here's the exact information on the publication of the complete
works of the anonymous Polish poet Krasiński, in a French translation
by Ladislaw Mickievicz, in two volumes by the Librairie du Luxem-
bourg, Paris, 1869.

In order to convey to you the very low-key enthusiasm in Rome for
the Vatican, I'm sending you the article from *L'Italie* on the Pope's
latest speech. John Lemoinne himself could not have done better than

to call Pius IX "a good country priest, apoplectic and irascible." The fact is that the current trend in religious affairs in Belgium and France and the great festival of German unity in Cologne cathedral don't seem to me to augur well for the restoration of papal temporal power in the near future. Fortunately, I am not involved in these great issues in which the cleverest people have so often failed. Simple faith, like that of the "poor in spirit," suffices for my prayers and musical work in which I persevere despite the fatigue of age. Last Friday I entered my seventieth year. It might be time to end things well – – – all the more since I have never wished to live long. In my early youth I often went to sleep hoping not to awake again here below.

You ask me whether the passage from the Ramann biography[17] concerning my mother is accurate. Yes, it is. She loved me, and in order to please her I did not enter a seminary (in 1830), for her sincere and naïve piety did not consider my vocation for the priesthood to be necessary. Thus because of her I remained a layman and have lived only too secularly. My comfort is that her benediction was vouchsafed to me until her last hour.

She liked to say: "Whatever people may say against my son doesn't offend me in the slightest, for I know what he is."

Loën, Lassen, Milde, and Ferenczy sent me a telegram on October 22. Please give each of them my friendly thanks for this evidence of their kind thoughts.

Your very humble

FL

I have written to M. S[ach]. He will pursue his ideal, which is not to be fulfilled.

———

17. Lina Ramann, *Franz Liszt als Künstler und Mensch. 1. Die Jahre 1811–1840* (Leipzig, 1880).

Tuesday, November 2, 80
(All Souls' Day)

Chateaubriand in his fine style had already exposed the injustice of denigrating the donkey, a patient, sober animal, pleasant to look at, useful, hardy, of adequate intelligence and morality, though not very skillful at cantilenas. At the time, his rehabilitation was very flattering for the burro. Now comes its glorification, for Victor Hugo sees it as the symbol of genius, an honor hitherto rendered only to the eagle and sometimes to the lion. I admit that I prefer this glorification to those, all too fashionable, of rascals such as Tiberius, Nero, and such like. Barlaam's ass deserves the respect of believers, and Buridan's[18] ass remains a model for sceptics.

Thank you for having sent me Hugo's wonderful poem to which your commentary adds the best of spices. The same applies to your comments on the feverish and relentless boredom of the salons, starting with her own, of Mme Dudeffant [Du Deffand]. Caro quotes most pertinently Pascal's thought which says in brief that you don't escape from yourself by vainly seeking the company of others. Indeed, what is to become of one on this earth if one ceases praying and loving with the least possible egoism? Otherwise, to brief illusions are added disillusions; and these last, and are not dispelled by social talents.

Very humbly from my heart,

Your

FL[19]

In order to pursue my soliloquies I'm going to stroll to the cemetery, very pleasantly located in the countryside twenty minutes from Tivoli.

---

18. Jean Buridan, scholastic philosopher of the fourteenth century. In a fable attributed to him, a donkey dies of hunger and thirst for want of being able to choose between a measure of oats and a pail of water.

19. This letter was published in *Franz Liszts Briefe*, viii, No. 388. The addressee was not identified.

November 13, 80
(Villa d'Este)

What a sweet and loving letter you have written me! It cheers me up and I thank you for it from the depths of my aching heart.

The prospect of Antwerp smiles on me. I have not yet received Verlat's letter. My reply will be positive. Short of an insuperable obstacle we will <u>together</u> look at the magnificent Rubenses in the Antwerp museum and at his Descent from the Cross. Clément-Rubens will look at them with us.

Yours ever

FL

I have nothing new for you from here. Cardinal H[ohenlohe] is still in Germany and keeps the newspaper <u>reporters</u> busy. The very important question of the union or separation of Church and State cannot be solved by palliatives—diplomatic activities on a day-to-day basis. Of necessity one will later on have to find something more definitive.

I'm writing a little poor music, but in a state of extreme depression because of my permanent conflict, for some fifteen years, with the only person who is the cause of my annual trip to Rome where I scarcely spend any time any longer.

I'll probably return to Budapest in the first few days of December.

Nov. 18, 80
(Villa d'Este)

Your letter has momentarily restored my good spirits a little and I hasten to tell you that you always have a very good and sensitive nose —slightly up in the air now and then, which well becomes you, without ever leading one into the temptation of breaking it.

Never was there a more absurd invention than that of efforts on my part to marry Mme d'Agoult, of her haughty rejection, and of the idea of converting her to Protestantism! – – – It's food for fools, hardly to be swallowed by a majority of the public which swallows so much of it.

Verlat's friendly letter and that from the Music Committee of Antwerp have reached me. I am answering them affirmatively (except for directing the festival, obviously, for fifteen years or so I have declined this honorable role in all countries). Verlat and I will serve as your Cicerones at the Antwerp museum where, as Ary Scheffer used to say, the genius of Rubens is revealed in all its brilliance and masterly exuberance.

Victor Hugo's *L'Âne* will be followed, for the benefit of the public's curiosity, by Dumas' new drama *Les Parents* (or *Lionette?*) as well as *La Moabite*, a five-act drama in verse by Paul Déroulède, author of *Chants du soldat* and *L'Hetman*, who gave a reading of it in Mme Adam's prestigious salon. *La Moabite* makes her lover gradually abjure religion, family, honor, and fatherland. As a final outcome the father, Sammgar, saves his son Misael heroically by forcing him to enter the tabernacle. Now, according to the Hebrew creed, whoever has found his way into the Holy of Holies and has seen God, dies. Sammgar returns alone saying, "Pray, he has seen God!"

The scene takes place at the time of the Judges of Israel. The Gods recognized by *La Moabite* are those

"to whom one does not have to pray, who do not have to punish, and for whom there is no evil save to make others suffer."

Your very humble

FL

Your thoughts on the correspondence of Clement XIV are entirely sound. One need not be a disbeliever to feel that temporal power is more of a hindrance than an advantage to the Holy Apostolic See. Its relations with European diplomacy will always retain something equivocal, insoluble.

December 1, 80
(Villa d'Este)

Lynen's kind invitation reached me three days ago. I have not yet replied but will accept, and since you ask my opinion, please just simply accept too. At the Antwerp Festival let us, you and I, follow Verlat's obliging lead. The idea of this festival was his; so let us not make him unhappy and let us show him our appreciation of his cordiality by reciprocating cordially without any equivocal or evasive overtones.

I have been absorbed in music sheets – – – stupidly, these last three weeks. Impossible to write letters – – – Yours gave me extreme pleasure; I am so sad and displeased with myself that a little approbation from you is needed to sustain me.

Your

FL

Do you remember M. d'Epinay? He comes to see me here with his wife and relatives. I showed him the photograph of Clément's *Phaëton*, and he too told me that your son Clément has in him all the stuff of a great painter *à la Rubens*.

Send me J. Lemoinne's reply to the charming acceptance speech by Labiche.

The press is talking about the new novel by Beaconsfield, *Endymion*. A cheap edition has been published by Tauchnitz (Leipzig).

In Hugo's *L'Âne* an astonishing scene, among others, strikes me forcefully, that of Science peering through the keyhole and unable to unbolt or break down the doors of infinite truth.

Besides Lo has rightly observed that to fight science is to beat one's nurse. To know and to achieve belong to the human condition—starting with *savoir vivre*, something we, even the most learned among us, spend our lives in learning to do badly.

December 6, 80
(Villa d'Este)

Chimay's advice is perfectly right; the best thing for you is to follow it. This seems to contradict my last letter in which I urged you to accept Mme Lynen's invitation, but this contradiction is only apparent. Politeness seemed to me to require that your first reply not be a curt refusal. When the month of May comes around (for the festival can hardly take place earlier) you'll have plenty of time to write again graciously to Mme Lynen and to ask Chimay which hotel at Antwerp he recommends.

I have replied to Verlat that I was leaving the whole business of invitations entirely up to the Committee's pleasure, and gave him no names other than those of Pohl, Nohl, Lessmann, and Schelle, as he expressly asked me to name some writers in the field of musical criticism in the German press. Even in the case of these four critics who are known for having always shown good will toward me, I am not soliciting any invitation for them from the Committee and have only mentioned them to Verlat because of his friendly zeal.

The *Sonnets de Pétrarque* of which Mme de Schleinitz spoke to you are those you know in their piano version.[20] The vocal version[21] is markedly different. It will appear in the spring in the German translation for which Cosima asked M. de Stein.

A publisher has come across some album-leaf (from at least twenty-five years ago) and wants to bring it out. I protest against outmoded things and am rewriting the *Romance Oubliée*[22] which I send you herewith. If you don't dislike it, I'll arrange it for violin and piano[23]—and you will play it with Chimay at Antwerp.

Your sad

FL

---

20. G 158 & 161, 4–6; R 10b, 4–6.
21. G 270 (later version); R 578b.
22. G 527; R 66b. The original manuscript is in the Library of Congress.
23. G 132; R 467.

December 16, 80

I don't know whether my arrangement of the *Harold* symphony by Berlioz has appeared. In this arrangement I left the principal alto (viola) part exactly as Berlioz wrote it and have restricted myself to reducing the orchestra to a score for piano. The *Marche des Pèlerins* and the *Sérénade des Montagnards* (Nos. 2 and 3 of the symphony) are successful even on the piano with viola. I played them again in Rome with Pinelli from the proofs corrected by Bülow. The edition has now probably been published by Brandus in Paris and by Leuckart in Leipzig. Ask Kömpel or Gottschalg to write a few lines to Leuckart (Musik Verlag – Constantin Sander – Leipzig), who will immediately send you a copy.

For your *glissando* exercises I once again advise you to use only the nail, either of your thumb or of your index or third finger, without even the tiniest area of flesh. Moreover, if you enjoy playing the little *Bacchanale* of the *Chants Polonais*,[24] I'll willingly arrange the *glissandos* for Lo brilliantly and comfortably.

Sophie Menter came to see me yesterday. My already long-held opinion of her is justifying itself; she is an incomparable pianist.

Several people from very different walks of life and in particular Cardinal Hohenlohe praise the Meiningen concerts to the skies, and especially Bülow's conducting. You will perhaps tell me something about them, not from hearsay but after having heard them yourself. It will be easy for you to arrange this little trip very conveniently and in good company.

Your very humble

FL

My address until January 8 is Rome or the Villa d'Este. When you see M. S[ach] tell him that we sang his praises with Fanny Lewald here this week.

---

24. By Chopin. G 480, 4; R 145, 4.

December 25, 80
(V[illa] d'E[ste])

I feel for you deeply in your sorrow.

Is your mother the Princess in Geneva? The winter there is very harsh, and I urge you to bundle yourself up well in furs.

It was a good idea of M. S[ach] to invite you to the Bülow concert at Eisenach. How I would like to be with you! Write me about it.

Last Tuesday I attended Pinelli's orchestra concert, at which the Pastoral Symphony[25] was played for the first time in Rome. On Wednesday, Sophie Menter, a pianist of the highest rank, is giving a concert at the Palazzo Caffarelli. I'll be going there, and will seize the occasion to pay a few calls, for until now I have seen no one from your world. You know that Princess Teano has been seriously ill; they say she is now convalescent. Countess Bobrinska goes out but continues to suffer a great deal as a result of the wretched accident caused by an ill-starred encounter with a dog. Mme d'Uexküll is discharging the role of nurse for her husband who is suffering sorely from merciless neuralgia.

Please send Mme Apel (Pauline) word to come to see you. She lives "an der Kunstschule, 4." Her husband is taking too long to die. On my behalf please give Pauline, who has always served me for more than twenty years zealously and with heartfelt devotion, 60 marks— and a similar little sum on her husband's death.

I have received the *Débats* with the Academy speeches of Labiche and J. Lemoinne and the article on *La Fontaine de jouvence* by Renan. Haven't I already thanked you for them? Zola's study on Flaubert is most remarkable. What interested me most is Flaubert's lengthy method of work in eager search of the *mot juste*, suitable, expressive, simple, and unique. I know similar torments in music. This or that

25. By Beethoven, Opus 68.

chord, or even pause, have cost me hours and numerous erasures. Those who know the meaning of *style* are a prey to these strange torments.

Your very humble

FL

Until January 8 write to Rome. I'll be back in Budapest on the fifteenth.

———

1881

January 7, 81
(Villa d'Este)

I spent only one day in Rome for Sophie Menter's concert. She played the whole program enclosed herewith superbly, so as to compare favorably with the three or four most famous male pianists. Her *bravura* is absolutely faultless; the rhythm and color are masterfully accented and blended. In the *Réminiscences des Huguenots*,[1] a fantasia which in my years as a virtuoso I used to play only rarely because of the trouble it cost me, Sophie M. astonished me.

Sgambati is preparing an orchestral concert which I have promised to attend. His symphony[2] will be performed and, for the first time in Rome, my *Tasso, Lamento e Trionfo*.[3] This concert was to be held on January 10; it has been postponed a few days, thereby also postponing my departure from Rome. I'll probably not reach Budapest before January 20. I'll stop off as usual in Florence for a day with the Hillebrands and will see Countess Dönhoff who is still sick.

Cardinal H[ohenlohe] has just spent three days at the Villa d'Este with his nephew—younger son of the Duke of Ratibor and Secretary at the German Embassy in Rome. He has taste and talent for painting. His sketches and water colors are charming. A young American sculptor named after a great prophet, Ezekiel, is spending this week at the Villa d'Este. He has carved a fine group which stands in a public square

1. G 412; R 221.
2. Opus 11.
3. G 96; R 413.

in Philadelphia: Religion and Liberty.[4] Since then, a Blind Homer with a rhapsodist at his feet singing the *Iliad* while accompanying himself on the lyre. Also to be seen in Ezekiel's studio in Rome is a series of statues of immortal artists (destined for America)—Michelangelo, Raphael, Dürer, Rembrandt, etc. Here he is working solely on a bust of poor me, larger than life and I hope more successful than the original.

I greatly appreciate the attention which M. S[ach] paid me at the Eisenach concert. His meticulous prudence caused him to commit a sin of omission toward Bülow last summer. I shall avoid asking His Royal Highness to make amends for it. People should know what to expect, after my thirty-five years of service at Weimar, with regard to the very rare recommendations I permit myself to make in high places.

Your sad

FL

Until January 13 write to Rome.

———

Saturday morning
January 22, 81

Shortly after my arrival here (day before yesterday), I was handed your letter of January 18. I accompany you to Geneva in heart and in thought – – – –

Be so good as to express to Monseigneur and to Count Beust my very sincere gratitude for the award of the Cross of Commander in the Order of the Falcon to Bülow, the most daring and noble artist's character I know. If he sometimes goes a little far, it's only a matter of an acute ⁄ or circumflex ∧ accent. Musically speaking, I wish for an *entente cordiale* between Meiningen and Bülow, and Weimar. It will frequently bear fruit—first of all for the unveiling of the statue of Johann Sebastian Bach at Eisenach.

4. "Religious Liberty," Fairmount Park, Philadelphia.

With regard to decorations, let the jokers who run after them chatter about them. The fact is that they are the distinctive sign of the intelligent goodwill of sovereigns. When I was decorated on the public square of Liège in '41 on the occasion of the unveiling of the statue of Grétry, the Minister said, "It is an honor for our government to decorate M. Liszt." Similarly it is an honor for Weimar with respect to Bülow.

On Sunday in Florence I saw the Hillebrands, Mme Minghetti and her daughter Countess Dönhoff who is convalescent, and Sophie Menter, the admirable virtuosa. On Tuesday in Venice I saw Rudolph Lichtenstein and his new and flawlessly tactful wife, and Mme Wöhrmann who is increasingly ailing. She wanted to spend the rest of the winter on Corfu, but will remain in Venice.

Here in my new and permanent abode I am the object of wonderful kindness and attention, which I won't describe since the press does so, but I hope you will one fine day come and see for yourself.

Very humbly

Your old

FL

February 1, 81

Budapest

Suffering, pain, and sorrow are the lot of mankind. You have experienced this while constantly displaying the most noble kind of courage, that which consists in maintaining a firm character in the face of the afflictions of our Vale of Tears in which only the merciful eye of God gleams in the depths of our hearts, while consoling and strengthening them. Since we must all live and die, let us know how to do so in noble simplicity.

FL

Bülow will be here in a fortnight, and Saint-Saëns next month. If you can find a moment write to Saint-Saëns that you will be glad to see him again in Paris. You can get his address at Durand, music publishers, 4 place de la Madeleine.

———

February 26, 81
Budapest

FL is much at fault. Stupidly he's been doing nothing these last two weeks but blackening music sheets. I've been tempted by Petőfi's The God of the Magyars. I boldly composed it,[5] then arranged it for the left hand only for my friend Géza Zichy, and also for both hands for normal pianists. For good measure I have also written a *Csárdás Macabre*[6] which I shall dedicate to Saint-Saëns. His *Danse Macabre* is worth more and is better, but I want to offer him my *Csárdás* because of its Hungarian character.

In mid-April I'll bring both pieces in print to Weimar for you. In your honor I'll arrange the *Csárdás*[7] for 4 hands. Your little bonnet from Budapest will not be in the least out of place.

Last week's musical event here was Bülow's two concerts. The first consisted of fifteen or so pieces by me (*Liszt Abend*), excluding any transcription and even any Rhapsody. This exclusion was significant. Such feats bear the stamp of Bülow – – –

The second concert consisted of Beethoven's five last sonatas.[8] The same program for the Vienna concerts. There, as here, the hall was crowded (the demand for tickets could not be met), and there was enthusiastic admiration for the astonishing genius—for multiple talents developed to this point constitute genius—of the transcendent virtuoso.

5. *Ungarns Gott*, song with piano accompaniment; G 339; R 635. *Also* G 543; R 214.
6. G 224; R 46.
7. G 617; R 301.
8. Opera 101, 106, 109, 110, 111.

One can strictly apply to him the phrase of former years, "He is music personified," from alpha to omega.

Speaking of *bon mots*, Bülow is never at a loss for them. For example he referred to a very pretty woman I know, endowed with very evident charms, as "a milk dispensary" (*ein Milch Bureau*), and to a sickly looking woman pianist as "a patient from the piano hospital," etc., etc.

Yours ever
FL

Being constantly interrupted by something or someone, I failed to enclose with yesterday's note the programs, herewith, of the two Bülow concerts in Vienna and Budapest. He will play them again shortly in Prague, Berlin, etc.

The election of Saint-Saëns to the Institute gives me great pleasure. It is a year overdue because of some intrigue or other, but all things come in time to him who knows how to wait. Berlioz had to wait longer for the same honor, and Victor Hugo was only elected to the Academy after having thrice been a candidate.

As the opportunity offers, convey once again my old and devoted affection to Monseigneur the Grand Duke, and remind him of an aphorism which he used to enjoy. Michelangelo used to say: *Chi va dietro a altri non li passa innanzi* [He who follows others will never move ahead of them].

One must stick closely to the true path.

FL

Are you reading Mérimée's letters to Panizzi?[9] These two volumes describe intimate life under the Second Empire in good French.

---

9. *Lettres à M. Panizzi* (Paris, 1881).

[undated]
[From Budapest]

Thanks for the *Figaro* on Victor Hugo, royalist, Catholic, Napo-
leonic, spiritualist. In it I found again my youthful admirations to
which I remain faithful. You know that just recently I composed music
for *Le Crucifix*[10] by Victor Hugo:

> *Vous qui pleurez, venez à ce Dieu, car il pleure.*
> *Vous qui souffrez, venez à lui, car il guérit.*
> *Vous qui tremblez, venez à lui, car il sourit,*
> *Vous qui passez, venez à lui, car il demeure.*[11]

What an adorable portrait of Sister Simplice in contrast to the virtuous Sister Perpétue! And how deeply the heart is moved by *Les
Chants du Crépuscule*:

> *Dieu est toujours là,*
> *Et l'espoir en Dieu –*
> *Espère enfant, demain,*
> *Et puis demain encore!*[12]

The French Club of Budapest, of which Count Albert Apponyi is
President and of which I am a member, has written an eloquent message with some hundred signatures to Victor Hugo on his eightieth
birthday. Regretfully I abstained from signing it for reasons of clerical
propriety.

Day before yesterday the same French Club brilliantly honored a
wealthy and witty French composer, Léo Delibes. He will conduct his

10. G 342; R 642.
11. You who weep, come to this God, for He weeps.
   You who suffer, come to Him, for He heals.
   You who tremble, come to Him, for He smiles.
   You who pass by, come to Him, for He abides.
12. God is always there,
   And hope is in God—
   Hope, child, tomorrow,
   And then again tomorrow.

opera *Jean de Nivelle*[13] here on Saturday, and I have no doubt of its complete success as was the case in Paris. Please tell our friend Loën that Jean de Nivelle who *s'en va toujours quand on l'appelle* would be a good choice for the opera repertoire next season at Weimar. Vienna and other theaters will already have given it; so there will be no risk.

Yours ever

FL

Zola has the final word on the question of divorce. His approach to the subject is perhaps slightly coarse, this being always acclaimed by the public who, as Champfort [Chamfort] used to say, rise only to low thoughts. Literature is not a universal dictatorship, day in day out, and if it fails to achieve a positive solution to the divorce question, it will not fail to find other resources.

———

[undated]

I'm writing Lassen a note. His mother's death reminds me of this simple question, what sort of world is it which we enter with the hope of seeing our father and mother die? This was better expressed in Alfred de Vigny's *Stello*. And yet we try to live as best we can, and for my part I feel it's better not to make too much of it. Let succeeding generations measure up to the task before them.

My happiest pastime in Budapest is whist in very good and friendly company. We don't usually play for stakes and, exceptionally, so as to lose at the most 10 florins or so. The faces on cards, kings, queens, knaves, and aces, have something attractive and stable about them,

13. First performed March 8, 1880, in Paris.

which is not always the case with the corresponding faces in the real world.

Yours ever

FL

Tomorrow I'll send you some printed programs with which I've been busy this week.

Day before yesterday I saw Count Andrássy whom I've admired sincerely these last fifteen years or so. He remains the most worthy and intelligent minister of the Austro-Hungarian monarchy—which is a hardy institution.

Saturday, April 2, 81
Budap[est]

Here is my itinerary for next week; tomorrow Sunday, concert for the Hummel monument at Pressburg with my excellent friend Géza Zichy. Tuesday another concert, at Oedenburg with Zichy, and the day after a trip to Raiding, my native village [fig. 4]. Thursday I'll be in Vienna where I will spend a week. Then Weimar.

Do me the favor of writing to Franz Servais that I will soon be replying affirmatively to his letter. It's only a matter of the receipts from his proposed concert covering expenses. For I cannot indulge in financial extravagance.

Your very humble, devoted

FL

From April 5 to 12 write to Vienna, Schottenhof.

Monday, April 11, 81
Vienna

Thursday morning I'll be at Nuremberg and will come to Weimar Sunday to wish you a happy Easter.

FL

(Write to Nuremberg [Bavaria], Hotel Zum Rothen Hirsch, until April 15.)

———

Wednesday, April 27
Berlin

On his own, without telling me, Bülow yesterday sent you a few Berlin newspapers. I commented to him afterward that you didn't pay much attention to my little successes and would even prefer <u>fiascoes</u> to them, should these make me stay more at home.

Her Majesty the Empress and Queen deigned to attend the most successful performance day before yesterday of my oratorio *Christus*. She also deigned to receive me most graciously yesterday, and the Emperor granted me a brief and most friendly exchange of words and of memories of the past.

Yesterday Countess Schleinitz gave a musical evening. Marianne Brandt, M. Sauret, and your very humble servant between them shared the program, in which I had proposed to Martha Remmert that she participate. However, she was prevented from doing so by a swollen hand and a certain untimely fit of nerves. I regret this for her sake, as it was a very favorable opportunity, which may not soon occur again, for her to appear before influential circles in Berlin.

I talked with Lord and Lady Russell (their name has now changed) about Rome and you. I'll be seeing them again today at dinner at the Széchenyis.

I'll tell you orally in about ten days time why I can't stop off at Weimar tomorrow.

Tomorrow evening (eight o'clock) I leave Berlin, probably with Bülow, and pass through Weimar by night so as to arrive in Freiburg just in time for the final rehearsals for the May 1 and 2 concerts.

On May 8 or 9 I return to the Hofgärtnerei where I will stay until our departure for Antwerp. The Festival Committee has fixed the date of Thursday, May 26, Ascension Day, for me. We'll have to leave on the twenty-second or twenty-third.

With all my heart
Your

FL

Herewith the news report on the Tchaikovsky quartets.

———

Wednesday, May 4, 81
Carlsruhe

You are cross with me, Madam. Not one word from you at Freiburg. I am not expecting any at Baden-Baden where I shall stay until Saturday morning.

I'm sending my thanks to the gentlemen of Antwerp, and will be there May 24—afterward for the concert of Franz Servais at Brussels the twenty-eighth—and next Monday at Weimar.

Very humbly
your old

FL

———

[undated]
Saturday morning

My thoughts are with *Tristan* – – – for the rest, I continue to improve. This morning, my first bath. Before dinner (two o'clock) I'll take a fifteen-minute walk. Zhukovsky has settled down here in a house very near Wahnfried; also, but for one week only, young Baron von Stern, Professor (*Privat Docent*) at the University of Halle where he is giving a course on Schopenhauer's philosophy.

After the performance of *Die Meistersinger* in Munich we expect the arrival of Mme Judith Gautier, a very lovely person with a charming mind. If you see her give her a thousand affectionate and admiring messages from me. She is not at all of the *demi-monde* and remains a woman of merit.

I have urged Cosima to read Paul de Saint-Victor's book.[14] Please send me the title which I have stupidly forgotten.

Next Saturday your old and sad FL will be on his way to Rome.

I've just finished correcting proofs and copies for Fürstner and Bock. Yesterday we resumed our whist.

[undated]

Your last note but one (of the four seasons) did not reach me. I suppose that in it you gave me the title for which I had asked, of the book by Paul de Saint-Victor on Aeschylus. Be so kind as to send me this title again.

I'll be staying here another four days nursing certain new ailments which are not very serious, but annoying.

Mme Judith Gautier spent three days with the <u>Sun</u> of Bayreuth [Wagner]. She is finishing her translation of *Parsifal*[15] (excellent, they say).

14. Probably *Les Deux Masques: tragédie-comédie. Les Antiques, Eschyle,"* published 1880.
15. From Wagner's German.

Friedheim's concert in Weimar was a greater success than expected. It even seems that it was well attended, according to what I was told by someone who heard it, M. Bénédictus, who came here day before yesterday to join Mme Gautier.

Send news soon to your perpetual

FL

As extra fare I'm reading a strange "contemporary" novel which is somewhat lascivious from the beginning. Princess Metternich and our friend Fredrow [Fredro?] appear in it strongly caricatured. The hero is *Le Roi vierge*, which is also the title of this book[16] (now banned in Bavaria) by Catulle Mendès.

Zhukovsky continues to work on his fine paintings of *Parsifal*. We see each other all the time and play whist in the evening.

I'm very pleased with Grosse. In spite of his girth he looks after me nimbly and affectionately.

October 7, 81
Bayreuth

Zhukovsky's paintings inspired by *Parsifal* seem to me most successful. The forest and temple will figure on stage sets painted by the well-known Brückners, at the Bayreuth performances and probably elsewhere, for M. Neumann is going to carry out his very timely and fruitful project of the international Wagner theatre. Following the artistic and material success of the *Nibelungen* in Berlin, there is no doubt that Neumann will do excellent business in London and Paris, Wagnerism being the order of the day and fortunately highly fashionable. Performances will everywhere be in German with the same German orchestra and cast of singers.

For the French translation of *Parsifal* and the adaptation of the text to the music, Mme Gautier had as private counselor M. Bénédictus, a Parisian German, with some Swedish blood they say, a Wagner en-

16. (Paris, 1881).

thusiast and recognized worshipper of Mme Gautier. She did not fail to make Wagner play for her on the piano a few fragments of *Parsifal*. Her <u>soul</u> understood all in spite of the irregular fingering of the performer. We have also had a performance at M. Jäger's of several scenes from the second and third acts of *Tristan*. He sings admirably this role which M. Porges, who accompanies him perfectly on the piano, made him study thoroughly. The audience consisted of only three persons, Cosima, Wolzogen, and your very humble FL. Mme Jäger sang the duet in the second act with her husband. Wagner goes out only to get some air in his brougham with a jump seat, which he bought recently, and to which are harnessed two white horses of Hungarian origin. In general he retains the good humor of a great, a very great man, outwardly caustic and with the myriad coils of genius within. He is ill at ease with others and his relations with them are to him superfluous. He loves his wife and children; it is up to his true friends to understand the life-style he requires and to take care not to bore him.

Read his article in the last (September) issue of the *Bayreuther Blätter*. You will find in it, first of all, flattering praise of the little known works of Count Gobineau on "races," *Les Religions et les philosophies dans l'Asie Centrale*, followed by a most astonishing mystical passage on the blood of Our Lord Jesus Christ. Queen Olga and the *Revue des deux mondes* do not go that far. They observe the first of the cardinal virtues, Prudence. Much good may it do them!

I go back to Zhukovsky to tell you that it would be wrong for intelligent people to treat him henceforth as a dilettante. His pleasant ways and good company do not prevent him from working hard as a serious and worthy artist. I like to believe that he will be an honor to his name and to his country.

By the time you receive these lines I'll be on my way to Rome. Write to <u>Via e Hôtel Alibert.</u>

> With all my heart,
> Your old
>
> FL

Your "four seasons" letter has definitely gone astray—a rare misdeed by the post office.

Friday, October 14, 81
Venice

Daniela and I have been here since yesterday staying with Princess Hatzfeldt and Mme de Schleinitz, who returns to Berlin in November. Venice remains incomparably attractive to me. I saw again with rapture the church and lion of St. Mark.

Day after tomorrow I'll be in Rome.

Before leaving Bayreuth I wrote to M. S[ach] and, this morning, to Loën. I hope neither of them will object to the performance of *Quentin Durward*[17] at Weimar (at the end of '82). It seems to me completely appropriate from every point of view. I told Gevaert that the grand-ducal management will gladly take care of the minor expenses of the German translation which his Paris publisher, who is a neighbor of the *marchand de galettes* opposite the *Gymnasium* and not very forceful, re-fuses to assume. Richard Pohl will do the translation perfectly and reasonably.

When you see Loën please tell him I forgot to ask him for an ex-tension of leave (two or three weeks) for Grosse, whose good and af-fectionate services I appreciate. I await a word from you on Loën's attitude, which I like to assume is favorable.

Having spent Wednesday night at Verona, I found old memories again there yesterday morning, the admirable tombs of the Scaligers, several churches, and magnificent views of the Adige.

With all my heart, as always,
Your

FL

---

17. Opera by François Auguste Gevaert, first performed March 25, 1858, in Paris.

November 3, 81
Rome (Via e Hôtel Alibert)

Cardinal H[ohenlohe] having contracted a fever at Tivoli in July, people fear that I'll also have one in November. The reasoning hardly seems probable, but as I go to Rome only in order to see one person I refrain from arguing the point, and shall spend a few weeks at the Hôtel Alibert, where I have found very adequate rooms for Daniela and myself. We have the sun in the morning and a view on the Villa Medici in the Pincio (the French Academy) with trees in the foreground. My idea would be to return in December to the Villa d'Este – – – and its cypresses, my close companions these dozen years.

From the end of September until October 27 Princess H[ohenlohe] stayed here at her mother's. She had brought with her Conrad, her eldest son, a charming young man of seventeen, and her daughter Mlle Dorothea, aged nine, most wide-awake and sensible. She prefers the basilica of St. Paul to that of St. Peter, etc. The grandmother was delighted by her grandchildren. Otherwise, she follows her old custom of spending most of the year in bed.

To my regret the Cardinal had just left Rome when I arrived there. He was in need of a change of air to get rid of the fever from which he suffered for a couple of months. His recovery is taking place at Domodossola (on Lago Maggiore),[18] the principal seat of the Rosminian Fathers, of whom Cardinal H[ohenlohe] is the protector. They say that this new order, founded by the illustrious and very venerable Rosmini, has a future. Up to now it does not have many members. However, they own one or two houses in London, another in Rome, and they stand out through their learning, a result of the doctrine of their founder who was no stranger even to the field of aesthetics. His great publication[19] encompasses all the sciences and the arts. From the Catholic point of view it resembles the great work of Lamennais (the sequel to his *Essai sur l'indifférence en matière de religion*, several volumes of philosophy placed on the Index except for the first one). Rosmini, while

18. In fact Domodossola is some twenty miles west of Lago Maggiore.
19. *Opere* (Naples, 1842–49), 16 vols.

not winning the favor of the Holy See, did not, as did Lamennais, leave the Church, and simply missed becoming a Cardinal even though he had already been nominated to this eminent dignity, because of the untimely publication of his pamphlet on *Les cinq plaies de l'Eglise*.

High society is not yet back in Rome save for Princess Teano, Mme Boutenieff, and her daughter Cocona whom I'll soon be seeing again. You know that there is much talk of informally appointing Boutenieff to the Russian Legation at the Vatican.

This last fortnight my music sheets have completely absorbed me. I have again corrected, and added some sixty bars to my *Cantico di San Francesco*. In its present state I consider it one of my least bad works. In addition I am working on a *St. Christophe*[20] for baritone voice (like the *Cantique de St. François*)[21] and a small final chorus of angels. I had long been haunted by this idea, and at last I have written it. The actual performance will last barely fifteen minutes; but I was afraid of its dragging and wanted to move ahead in broad lines without any padding.

Wagner, his wife, and the children arrive in Palermo tomorrow. Daniela will be staying on here with me for some time.

I won't speak of the more than a dozen tributes and over a hundred letters and telegrams I received on October 22. I'll be spending a couple of weeks writing letters. The tribute of the "Musical Associations" from Vienna covered with at least four hundred signatures is magnificent. The one from Weimar is also outstanding. I'll thank Loën for it as soon as possible, pending which please transmit my cordial friendship to him and to Lassen.

I have received the letters you sent me at Tivoli.

With all my heart,
Your unchanging old

FL

M. Renan paid me the honor of coming to see me. He must already be back in Paris, and he is bringing out another book on the Church

20. G 47; R 483.
21. G 28; R 494.

(as a sequel to his preceding books on St. Paul). I also see other un-
believers, specifically Moleschott (Senator and professor at Rome University), with whom we played whist yesterday, for since Daniela
excels at this game, we play nearly every evening after supper which is
served at eight o'clock. At half-past ten (at the latest) we go to bed.

> November 29, 81
> Rome

Stupidly, I took literally what you told me about an "Epistle to the
Romans" by Renan, and asked several acquaintances to find this epistolary piece for me. No one had ever heard of it. I finally became
aware of my error when I received the portion of the new volume on
Marcus Aurelius, for which many thanks. Not that I incline toward
the wisdom of stoical non-involvement. I admire its heroic aspect but
do not feel up to practicing it sincerely. Pain is not to me the same
thing as pleasure, or even peaceful absence of suffering. Everything
passes, as we well know, but until this happens one is either at ease or
ill at ease. As for a certain contempt of things and men, I only understand this within very narrow limits, beginning with one's self; but the
gentle and wise Marcus Aurelius seems to me to have uttered a truly imperial stupidity in counseling us to *divide* up each thing in our thoughts
so as to become imbued with the emptiness of everything. To reduce
music to single sounds, to isolate the features of a beloved person, is
this to philosophize? Away with this method; let us look for the whole,
the harmony. It is there we will find beauty and truth. I far prefer Job's
heart-rending lamentations and resignation to the vanity of Solomon's
Vanitas Vanitatum, and especially the sublime gentleness of the Sermon
on the Mount, which sheds a divine light on our sufferings here below.

When something to my taste appears in the *Débats*, please send it to
me. I am being lent *Le Figaro*. The last issue, of Saturday, November
26, contains things which greatly interested me: the admirable letter
from Lacordaire to Sainte-Beuve on the seminary of Issy, as well as

Zola's short article on the rocky tomb of Chateaubriand on the Bé of
Saint Malo. Nearby, Mme Judith Gautier owns and lives on a romantic
rock.

Do you know the photographs of the paintings by Vereshchagin on
the last Russian war? These caused much stir, and even brought in a
lot of money recently in Vienna. Siemiradski is working here on a prodigious picture representing the progress of humanity. Someone in
Cracow commissioned it from him for a large sum. Speaking of com-
missions, there's an American in Rome named John Field (like the celebrated composer of nocturnes) who had the good sense to commission
two pieces from Sgambati on the basis of a fee of 5,000 francs for each.
Sgambati is free to choose their medium and title and retains the right
to publish them for his own profit. He started off with a string quartet[22]
(without piano) which I heard at a preliminary rehearsal. It is a most
distinguished work, very serious and, to my mind, very superior to
other modern quartets praised by critics in the press.

The Bobrinskis are not yet back, I am told, but Cocona B[ariatinska]
invited me to dinner. She is magnificently installed, Via e Palazzo
Buffalo. We spoke of the charms of Weimar which I appreciate all the
more for being deprived of them. The other evening, while strolling
with Daniela at the Villa Pamphili, I unintentionally exclaimed, "Oh!
the Wäwicht! Oh! Ober Weimar! Oh! the Akerwand!" At Cocona's
I saw again Mme Venevitinoff (eldest daughter of one of my best
friends in former times, Count Michael Wielhorsky), Mme Boutenieff,
Cocona's mother, and Baron d'Uexküll whose very charming wife
promises to return at the end of December.

I don't go out much, and since October 23 I've done nothing but
write music. Nothing of importance or of interest to others. My idio-
syncrasy with regard to letters increases and is becoming an intolerable
sickness. Of more than a hundred letters and as many telegrams that I
received this month, I have answered barely five. I'll have to write at
least thirty; this will be my penance in Advent.

22. In D flat, Opus 17.

3. Liszt and his daughter (by Marie d'Agoult) Cosima, who, after her divorce from Hans von Bülow, married Richard Wagner

4. In 1881 Liszt visits his birthplace, Raiding, Hungary (*see p. 400*)

My young pianists (six in all) come regularly twice a week. Friedheim clearly stands out. He doesn't look like someone who's happy, quite the contrary, and I would like to help him with his career, but it is not often easy for talents to succeed and this depends on capricious good luck. However, I hope that if Friedheim is patient and perseveres he'll succeed in carving out a place for himself. He is assured of my sincere recommendation.

I am tormented by a great worry, and even worse than that. Let me ask you for a service. Ask my Grosse to come to see you, and tell him that I cannot find the little black leather wallet containing Princess W[ittgenstein]'s letters and a few others. I had carefully put it aside the eve of my departure from Weimar, recommending that it be safely packed together with two other (larger) cartons filled with various letters which I am also missing. After you have conferred with Grosse, ask Pauline to have the drawers of my desk (which belongs to you) opened for you, and try to find the wallet which is roughly the size used for banknotes. If it stayed behind in Weimar it can only be in one of those drawers, where you will spot it at once – – – –

Please send it off to me in a good envelope and with the seals required for registered mail. Be so kind as to make another parcel of the two brown cartons which must have stayed behind with the wallet, and send them to me also by the most secure means.

With all my heart,
Your old

FL

Deign to write to me soon, and forgive me if the insistent hammering of my superfluous compositions is paralyzing my correspondence.

December 6, evening, 81
Rome

Day before yesterday I met Countess Stroganoff (born Potocka) and her husband. They will spend the winter here, and told me that the Bobrinskis have been at their Villa Malta for several days. The famous doctor masseur Metzger (Amsterdam) seems to have done wonders for Countess Bobrinska. She now walks, rides horseback, etc. I haven't yet seen the Bobrinskis again, having returned to Rome before them. I shall wait for the Count to call and will only be as forthcoming to him as he is to me.

Friday I lunch at Baron Keudell's with the heir to Mecklenburg and his wife, a beautiful woman and daughter of the Grand Duke Michael. One of my little piano solos served as a *chasse-café*.

Herewith an extract from Prince Caraman–Chimay's speech at the prize-giving ceremony of the Brussels Conservatory, in his role as President of the Commission. I am very flattered by what he was kind enough to say about my *Faust*, and ask you to thank him when you write him, which I will do at the first free moment.

I have received several flattering invitations from Belgium for next year. I've replied by making reasonably justified excuses.

This afternoon's concert in my honor, of which I enclose the program, was a complete success both as a performance and in terms of the favorable attitude of the large audience. When you used to hear my Dantesque Symphony at the same Sala Dante some fifteen years ago, it seemed to the great majority of the audience a tissue of extravagance. People assure me that this is no longer the case.

Sgambati played my Concerto in A[23] wonderfully.

As ever your old

FL

Because of the *Goethe Marsch*[24] please pass on the program to M. S[ach].

23. G 125; R 456.
24. G 115; R 433.

December 15, 81

Rome

Following your orders, I open the series of my weekly letters of "fifteen lines" each. If there are sixteen or thirty you will not be cross.

First of all, thank you most sincerely for your fruitless search for the black wallet. Perhaps I'll find it in the crate which was sent to Budapest.

The best way not to expose letters to the indiscretion of others is to burn them immediately after reading them, as I shall do with yours henceforth. If they have already been opened by the secret police at the post office or by the janitor, there is no remedy.

You would not have been bringing water to the Tiber by sending me Renan's letter to the Romans, for none of my acquaintances here has read it, nor could lend it to me. In order to avenge myself against your water which was not brought to the Tiber, I am tomorrow having a little cask of Marsala sent to your name and address at Weimar.

Le Figaro of December 6 contains a charming article on Hébert's fine portrait of Princess W[ittgenstein]. Mme Ollivier is mentioned in it, and is to spend two months here with her husband who is very busy with important matters of Church and State, with which he dealt in masterly fashion in his two remarkable books on the last Council, already known to you.

The "fifteen" and thirty lines have been exceeded – – – –

Your very humble and bowing

FL

Have you heard Lassen's *Circe*?[25]

---

25. Incidental music to Calderón's *Circe*, 1881.

[undated]

There may be something original in reproaching me for being "solemn." Being innocent of this, I ignore the reproach while admitting that various kinds of *sans-façon* behavior, even if fashionable, displease me just as dirty linen does and even more, for with it goes a contempt for others which is highly unseemly and cheap in the bad sense.

Bravissimo! for your charming comparison of a parrot cage with the frequent thematic repetitions in Haydn's symphonies. I share this impression in spite of the great respect due to the creator of the modern symphony and quartet.

Without being solemn I repeat to you that the Symphony in G-minor,[1] the one known as *Jupiter*,[2] together with the superb *Zauberflöte*[3] overture by Mozart are the peaks of instrumental music before Beethoven. Let us admire them in an appropriately respectful manner, or let us not discuss any music any more.

Your old

FL

Errands don't count in the "weekly fifteen lines."

So please give my friend Grosse (the trombone player) 12 thalers from me and 20 marks to Pauline Apel for New Year's Day.

After New Year's I'll send you my little news from Rome. I return to Budapest on January 15.

Hitherto my information about a teacher of painting in Rome for Clément bears out what I already told you concerning the dearth of teaching in the field of painting here. There remain the incomparable models, the Sistine Chapel, the *Stanze*, etc., which Clément will do well to study thoroughly. On the practical side he will do better in Brussels, Antwerp (with Verlat), or Munich than in Rome.

---

1. KV 550.
2. KV 551.
3. KV 620.

1882

Once again I'm very late – – – –

Last Tuesday I accompanied Cardinal Hohenlohe to Albano where I spent three days with him at the episcopal palace, formerly inhabited and improved by Cardinal de Bernis. H[ohenlohe] seems fairly pleased with his trip to Germany, and would not object to the idea of administering a large diocese there. People are talking a lot about it but this does not mean that it will happen. Our old friend Schlözer is awaited here as balm for the *modus vivendi*, all very complicated. This will call for lots of ink and brain-racking. The Holy Apostolic See is patient and endures through the ages like God Eternal. Pius IX used to say wittily, "Yes, St. Peter's boat is completely sound, but not the crew."

These last six weeks I have seen much of Émile Ollivier and his very witty second wife. He is working on the sequel of his excellent book *Le Concile du Vatican* (two volumes) which I urge you to read. You will find many true and very well written things there.

My departure from Rome has been postponed until January 20. I'll spend a day in Florence and one in Venice before returning to Budapest.

Thank you from my heart for your letters, which your faithful and very humble FL begs you to multiply.

I'll write again this week about certain trifling matters.

Wednesday, January 18
Rome

There are several pitiful aspects to the correspondence between Benjamin Constant and Mme Récamier. What is the point of playing the bashful lover when one can only sing an old tune in a hoarse voice? Mme Récamier could not transform herself into Laura, mother of many children, any more than Constant into Petrarch, for he lacked the great gift of writing admirable sonnets. Even less could she aspire to the role of Beatrice, not having died in her tenderest youth. Now, as I used to say to Daniel Stern, much to her annoyance, it is Dante who created and immortalized Beatrice, and not Beatrice Dante. Ladies with false ideals falsely imagine the opposite.

The correspondence of B.C. and Récamier thus turns into the artificial atmosphere of the salon, with Prince August of Prussia, Prince Montmorency, and the Viscount de Chateaubriand, the illustrious genius of *Le Génie du christianisme* – – – This charms the salon loungers; and the *coquetterie angélique* merits all the enchantment of the idle for whom stupidity takes the place of pride.

Nothing is truer than what you say about Russia. One must belong to one's country, loyally and courageously. Peterle and your three other sons will give you the satisfaction of following your guidance and advice. We were speaking of this the other day with Princess Cocona Bariatinska. Her reputation as a woman of charming and lively wit is well established here. M. S[ach] would gladly frequent her salon in Rome which is much frequented.

Since Bobrinski has not called on me, I will refrain from making a call at the Villa Malta—the most magnificent in Rome and in the best taste. Not being in a position to return every invitation, I only accept those of others with appropriate modesty.

Your very humble FL will stay here until January 27.

Please convey my cordial greetings to Peterle.

I shall shortly write to Mme Stte [Sachette] to thank her for her very kind note.

What is being given at Weimar? Is Lassen's Circe-Devrient still casting her spells there?

January 20, 82

Rome

As a postscript to my note of yesterday let me add with regard to Benjamin Constant's letters to Mme Récamier that it seems to me inadmissible for any man to exploit a woman in love for purposes of business and of his own reputation.

Ventre-saint-gris, as Henry IV used to say, let us not degrade the male sex to such a degree of ridiculous shortcoming. Lauras who pose as Beatrice only have to look for their Petrarch and Dante. There is always something base in ambiguous situations, however charming the wit injected into them.

Thanks for Pressensé's article on Minghetti's book.[4] Ollivier knew the book and I've passed the article on to him. It is well written and, without saying too much, concludes essentially in favor of the separation of Church and State—a thorny question which seems in France to be on the road to a practical solution in the not too distant future.

Ollivier is also working on a book on the same question, which Bonghi has just discussed masterfully from the Italian point of view of a possible but much delayed agreement.

Your very humble FL

will be leaving Rome on Saturday (January 28).

I'm postponing until we see each other again the answer to your question about which painter would be best qualified to guide Clément's studies and aspirations in Rome. Hitherto I have found no one better suited than Müller-Hartung or Gottschalg for giving music lessons to *messieurs vos fils*, to whom please convey my cordial greetings.

---

4. *L'Etat et l'Eglise* (Paris, 1882). (Italian: *Stato e chiesa* [Naples, 1878].)

January 29, 82
Florence

I arrived here yesterday evening, and a few well-wishing compatriots are keeping me here another day. Tomorrow Venice, Thursday Vienna, Sunday Budapest. If you are writing straightaway to me, send the letter to Vienna, Schottenhof (as of old).

I carried out your errand for Co[cona] Bari[atinska]. Her reputation as a witty, charming, and intelligent woman is *crescendo*. She doesn't mind Rome contributing to this, and everyone is happy.

I've been seeing Mme Minghetti fairly often. She is a woman of unusual attainments and of marked superiority, whatever the circumstances.

Since Bobrinski has forgotten to call on me, I have refrained from leaving cards at the Villa Malta, that very princely abode, highly elegant and entirely worthy of all possible Imperial Highnesses. It is to Bobrinski's credit that he has not only improved and restored, but has renovated at heavy cost the old Villa Malta of King Ludwig I of Bavaria. It was falling into ruin and now it is flourishing with I know not what oak of Goethe, and flawless luxury and comfort.

Whom do you think I met in Rome day before yesterday? Mme Pelet de Narbonne, your Weimar landlady. She was almost lamenting not to be able to count on your lease in the years ahead.

I share your impressions on reading Schopenhauer, and remember having mentioned to you for the first time in Rome, long ago at the Sciarra ball, the quidam Schopenhauer, who has since risen to such heights. Please tell me in your next letter what penalty Schopenhauer intends to substitute for the abominable social crime of the death penalty.

It is obvious that we are all more or less guilty, deranged, or crazy, but it does not follow that we ought to be guillotined, hanged, or, as an act of mercy, shot.

Your very humble

FL

Friday, February 3, 82
Vienna

I have your letter. The day after I left Rome Daniela went back to her mother's at Palermo where Wagner will stay until the end of April. Adelheid v. Schorn accompanied Daniela to Naples, where Mlle Corsani (of the Wagner household) is waiting in order to accompany her to Palermo.

Your knowledge, great and reliable though it be, may be found wanting with regard to new railroad lines. Owing to the shortcut of Pontebba between Venice and Vienna completed two or three years ago, it is now simpler to go to Budapest via Vienna.

Thus there is not a trace of "flitting about," which would be more than laughable, flatly absurd at my age. Between Verona and Rome, Venice is a detour of only one and a quarter hours at the most. Other interpretations of my very short stays in Venice and Vienna are of the saucy variety which I don't much care for.

The replacement for the conceited scoundrel Spiridion has a fine name: Achille. He looks after me much better than his predecessor, and the recommendations people had given me about him are justified. His shortcoming is that he speaks only Italian and French, but he is going to concentrate on studying German, and pending his success I put up with the shortcoming.

You reply evasively to my question about the penalty which Schopenhauer had in mind to substitute as an improvement in lieu of the social crime of the death penalty. Let's drop the subject if it's only *verba volant* [empty words].

Tomorrow evening your very humble FL
will be in Budapest.

Bülow gave a Brahms concert here yesterday of which I enclose the program. The audience was large and very responsive. The performance was admirable.

Bülow's Budapest concert is scheduled for February 10.

Tuesday, February 14, 82
Budapest

If Buddhism is but a form of Christianity "minus the hope of a better life" in the hereafter, I confess that all its subtle, benign, compassionate, and soporific philosophy is to me something like an embalmed corpse. Now, neither the science of the Egyptians nor the ingenious and elegant method of embalming by M. Ganal has succeeded in restoring mummies to life. I am astonished at your finding "conclusive arguments" in Schopenhauer against immortality of the soul. To say that it is not possible to demonstrate *ex professo* the nature of life in the hereafter amounts to not saying anything at all, for our end as well as our beginning does not fall within the competence of man. But who would be qualified to determine on the basis of the blindness of the comprehension of the mortal race the supreme rights of God's mercy? It remains eternal! What do our lapses, our malignity, our faults and sorrows matter, which sometimes lead us to wish for the annihilation of our being, by God's grace created immortal? Ah! Let us not abjure our heavenly heritage; this would be infamous. "Conclusive arguments" against the infinity of the divine breath which animates us are hateful delusions. Believe me on this point, very dear Lo, without further vain inquiry, and do not let yourself be led astray by, or fall into false doctrines which are, alas!, all too fashionable. Night shall never prevail over day, nor evil against good. Let us hope and love in Jesus Christ, God crucified. This is the real truth.

Sunday I accompanied Bülow to Pressburg. He is in his best mood, not as we saw him at Meiningen. His present concert tour does not include Romania. He plays again in Vienna this evening, then in Prague and Cracow. On March 1 his orchestra will play in Dresden, then once again in Leipzig, etc.

Send me news of Bronsart's *Frühlings Fantasie* and of Raff's great new work performed in Weimar. Is it already in print? Do you know the exact title?

Friday, February 17

Budapest

I don't want to importune you any more with questions concerning semi-capital punishment which Schopenhauer suggests substituting for the guillotine and the gallows. You will clarify *viva voce* at Weimar that which I still do not understand in your explanation.

Géza Zichy is soon going to play in several charity concerts in Munich, Nuremberg, Wiesbaden, and even Erfurt, and it would please me if you were to go there to applaud him. I'll let you know the date of the Erfurt concert, which you will in any case learn ahead of time at Weimar. Loën and one of the prominent lady patrons of some "charitable project" at Weimar could invite Zichy to play the day after his Erfurt concert, at the theatre or at the Erholung at Weimar.

I believe he would accept with good grace.

Yours ever

FL

Postscript to my lines of yesterday.

Géza Zichy's reputation is not just parochial Hungarian. He is an astonishing artist of the left hand, which is remarkably dexterous to the point that the greatest pianists would be hard put to it to match him with their five [sic] fingers. Moreover, Zichy ranks among the best aristocrats (and I use this word here in its truly fine sense), takes an effective interest in fine arts and letters, delivers speeches at the Academy, and has already published some highly distinguished poems – – –

It thus seems fitting to me that he be invited to Weimar, since the fact is that in the course of his little tour (a fortnight) in Germany, from February 24 to March 7, he is also playing in behalf of some charity at Erfurt—this coming March 6 or 7. Mme "Regierungs Präsidentin Krampetz" (or Crampetz?) is listed as the principal lady patron of the concert and is in correspondence with Zichy. I naturally did not say a word to him about Weimar, but if you approve of my suggestion please bring Count Beust around to the idea of inviting

Zichy either for a charity concert or for a soirée at Court at which the musical program would be given solely by the very celebrated one-armed man. If they decide on a soirée, the simplest would be for the Grand Duke to send me shortly a brief and forthcoming note which I'll pass on to my friend Zichy. I am convinced that Their Highnesses will take pleasure in making his acquaintance in person and will appreciate his talent. You know that the Prince of Wales has invited him to London where he can be very sure of success.

Your very devoted

FL

Munkácsy is arriving here this evening. He will be given a magnificent reception at a session of the Academy of the Plastic Arts, entertained at banquets, one or two concerts, and a fancy dress ball as well.

February 27, 82
B.P.

I am writing to M. S[ach]. No need to worry about any ambitions on G[éza] Z[ichy]'s part for a decoration. He belongs to the not very numerous category of the best aristocrats, and you know that I always use this term etymologically, as a title for all that is preferable here below. The abominable song *Les aristocrates à la lanterne* remains a bloodstained disgrace of the great French revolution. One might perhaps find its excuse in an examination in strict conscience of the causes of the eruption of the volcano. By now the aristocracy has sufficiently paid for its insolence. The night of August 4 remains a glorious date for it: work and merit are its lot for the future.

G[éza] Z[ichy] has just read before an academy here an epic poem in Hungarian of more than a thousand verses. It had a brilliant success, and I presume that in another three or four years he will completely give up the piano in order to devote himself at his leisure to literature.

Thanks for your adroit approach to M. S[ach]. To tell the truth I had no other object in this little incident than to render service to the Court of Weimar. I didn't say a word about it to Z[ichy], but am today sending him the second page, which concerns him, of the letter from M. S[ach], "the most princely and charming Maecenas," as Berlioz puts it in his *Lettres intimes*. I am quoting this remark to S[ach] as well as another one, not flattering for me. At the time when Berlioz was attacking the *Messe de Gran* and condemning it as "the negation of art," my two old friends, he and d'Ortigue, were disowning me at their leisure in Paris (in the winter of '66), concluding with 99 percent of the public that I was very wrong to concern myself with composition, since I had no talent and should limit myself to my success as a pianist. Not to follow this peremptory advice amounts, in the religion of art, to final impertinence. My sincere catholicism does not prescribe that I should seek the absolution of people who dislike my music, such as it is. Opinions and sensations are free and I make no claim whatever to imposing mine on anyone. To go on working is enough for me.

Here Munkácsy has been gloriously feted this whole week. Hungary is proud of him, and his perfect modesty does not forbid him to feel the legitimate pride of a great artist. Tomorrow he goes to Munkács, his native town, accompanied by outstanding literary and other figures of the country—Jókai, Pulszky, my old and close friend Teleki (Sandor), etc. You know that in his early years Munkácsy was a carpenter. Thereafter his painting vocation was responsible for his enduring for some time the trial of suffering from hunger. Now here he is, at the pinnacle of success, from which he will in all probability never step down. The next painting he has in mind is a Crucifixion. Sketches of two figures for this painting are already on exhibition here. Before mid-March he will be back in his splendid house in Paris.

I have not seen the arrangement for four hands of Bülow's *Nirvana Symphony*,[5] and do not even know whether this work, which I ad-

5. Opus 20.

mire, has been published other than as a score. Ask Bock (Berlin) or Kahnt (Leipzig) for the arrangement for four hands.

Vostrissimo

FL

March 3

I have spent several days writing a *Hungarian Rhapsody*,[6] to be published for Munkácsy. This explains the delay in sending off these lines.

———

March 11, 82
Budapest

I've already told you that the delay in sending off my last letter is entirely my fault. Being absorbed in the Munkácsy rhapsody, I imagined that the letter had already reached you, when to my stupefaction I found it in my desk drawer. The Munkácsys left yesterday and are to dine in Vienna at the Reusses' today or tomorrow. Before the end of the week they will be back in their *palazzo* in Paris. Thousands of people from all classes, including workers and peasants, continue to throng to the showing of *Christ before Pilate*. Never has such a success been seen before. The price of admission is a florin. Receipts must already exceed 30,000 florins and be growing daily.

Zichy is also bringing in excellent receipts and arousing brilliant *furore* at his charity concerts. I have received very enthusiastic telegrams and letters (not from him) from all the towns where he has played—Munich, Nuremberg, Wiesbaden, Carlsruhe. You will certainly enjoy hearing him, and I have no doubt of his complete success at the Court soirée at Weimar. Please let me know how it went.

I often see Cardinal Haynald. He attends concerts at which we are usually neighbors and we also see each other at the homes of mutual

6. G 244, 16; R 106, 16, *Zu den Munkácsy Festlichkeiten in Budapest* (Hungarian Rhapsody No. 16). The original manuscript, lacking the end, is in the Library of Congress.

acquaintances. His Eminence tells me he saw Princess Elsi at her sister's (in Vienna), and Hay[nald] intends to pay a visit to our illustrious Court in July. A cardinal at Weimar—that will be something new. Within living memory no Prince of the Church wearing the purple has appeared there. It's a pity that Mlle Cruik[shank] no longer holds her boudoir, open air reading group, and writing class, near the Alexander Platz lawn. She would have so much charmed and edified His Eminence!

I have read de Broglie's articles on diplomacy, and *L'Ecclésiaste* (Cohelet) by Renan in the *Revue des d[eux] m[ondes]*. The latter constitutes a most attractive skeptical mirage. My dullness of mind prevents me from agreeing with the axiom "vanity of vanities," which seems to me of extreme vanity. Shorn of moral law and its practice, life is but a sad delusion. Thus Renan's quotations of the fine passages from Spinoza and Kant on stable happiness and on duty suit me much better than the ingenious system of pseudo-philosophy of those who are disgusted – – – – A harsh but not unjust word by Carnot on Talleyrand: "If he despised men so much, this is because he studied himself deeply." To hold those in error in scorn remains sound Christian advice on condition that we are not lacking in gentleness and humility of heart.

In Easter week your old FL will be near you.

———

April 4, 82
Budapest

I had a slightly bad – – – epistolary conscience. Your telegram of yesterday has intensified it. What can be done when one is stupidly writing music as I have been doing these last two weeks in spite of many displacements and without any free time for letter writing?

Paris will have relieved your tedium a little, but I am grateful to Peterle for not running down Weimar in vulgar fashion.

Tomorrow I go to Kalocsa, a Hungarian town of ten or twelve thousand inhabitants. It is slightly known in Europe, thanks to its Archbishop, Cardinal Haynald, who has very graciously invited me to spend Holy Week and Easter in his very princely residence. You recall that Cardinal Haynald was good enough to preside in Budapest over the fifty-year jubilee of my career as an artist.

Your very humble FL
will be back in Weimar before April 20.

Send your next letter to Budapest where I return for two days after Kalocsa.

———————

Sunday, April 16, 82
Vienna

I ought finally to follow one of your old pieces of advice and compose *The Lamentations of Jeremiah*. The lamentable state of mind for this would hardly be lacking. Unfortunately Palestrina has written songs on these texts which have been consecrated by the Sistine Chapel and by universal admiration, and it would be improper to follow these with a new version condemned and vilified by all good judges, especially by those who hardly know the texts. Gounod cleverly avoided the problem of competing with Palestrina, and succeeded in rejuvenating musically several verses from Jeremiah by making them apply to the Paris disasters of 1871, when Paris was grieving no less than ancient Jerusalem. The great Ode–Lamentation *Gallia*[7] remains, in my opinion, one of Gounod's best works. For my part I'll fall back on Job who has the additional advantage of conversing personally with God, not in the name of a devastated city.

What's all that about? the most wise Lo will ask. So I'll say no more

7. For soprano, chorus, orchestra, and organ, 1871.

and only warn you that your very humble FL will be back in Weimar next Wednesday.

Please have Pauline get my rooms ready for Wednesday.
I'll wire you again the day before.

———————

May 5, 82
Brussels

Lo is always completely gracious, admirable, bewitching, not as an exception but both in principle and effect.

In spite of the dire prognostications of Mme S[ach] and Z[ichy], the *Elisabeth* went off adequately. Mlle Kufferath, who sang the role of Elisabeth, had a great success and was warmly applauded.

You will tomorrow receive the program with the French text of *The Legend* as well as the article from *L'Indépendance*.

Thank you for the Academy speech of Renan, "the unctuous skeptic." He proves with elegance that Truth is a great flirt, and that it rather enjoys respectable absurdities. In the last resort, "*l'acide droit* 'restera l'aride droit, l'acide gauche restera l'aride gauche.' "[8]

No reproach, but another time please send me the speech of the newly elected member of the Academy. That of Pasteur would interest me. You know that I have the good taste of liking fine academic French.

I'll bring back to you the books you are expecting, and Massenet's *Hérodiade*, an opera whose fifty-fifth performance was given here Tuesday under the composer's baton with brilliant success. I was there and will tell you about it. The following day Massenet and my valiant friend Saint-Saëns (who came expressly for this from Paris) attended the *Elisabeth*.

Yesterday there was a brilliant evening at the Zarembskis, who are

8. A play on the words *le droit* (legal right) and *la gauche* (political left).

more pleasantly installed in a charming small and suitably furnished house than you are at Mme Pelet's in Weimar.

This evening I'll be at Antwerp and will give your kind regards to Verlat, and your compliments to my kind hosts the Lynens. On Saturday there is a concert at Antwerp with a chorus of <u>eight hundred</u> children. I'll send you the program.

Weimar on Tuesday.

Your very humble

FL

July 3, 82
Freiburg

Being a traveling salesman—not a minister plenipotentiary of the four postern-gates, as the personage in Rome used to say—being, as I say, a traveling salesman in music, I'll tell you at once about yesterday's concert. I regret that Clément was not there to hear *Les Cloches de Strasbourg*. He would have thought more highly of the musical composition which inspired his magnificent drawing. At Jena, our most excellent friend Gille was unable to measure up to all the aspects of the performance of that – – – lopsided work which Wagner calls *Ein geistiger Spuk* [a witty ghost] – – – please do not translate this word by <u>spitting</u>, as M. Blaze de Bury would be capable of doing in the *Revue des deux mondes*. All honor to whom honor is due on condition that he be entitled to it and be neither a boor nor a rogue, however much readers from high and distinguished society may care for articles in the fashionable press.

The performance at Freiburg of the *Messe de Gran* was the best I have heard, after that in Antwerp (and before it, in Vienna). Both the singers and the orchestra performed not only with scrupulous accuracy but appropriate piety as well.

Your very humble FL
will be in Zurich Saturday evening.

Tuesday, July 11, 82
Zurich

One of the privileges of intimacy is sharing cares together. Yours touch me closely, and I shall try to lighten them as much as I can.

Last Wednesday I was at Baden-Baden for a Liszt concert. As Uncle Gort[schakoff] was occupying his quarters at the Hôtel d'Europe, I could not have them this time. I saw no one of your circle at Baden. I was agreeably surprised to find Mme Héritte there. She is back from a trip to Italy, has published (in Leipzig) her work *Feu du ciel*, composed on Victor Hugo's *L'Orientale* [*Les Orientales*], yearns for the glory of the great composers, writes scores waiting to be performed, and is shortly returning to Stockholm where she settled last year as a professor of voice. She teaches the well-known Garcia method which has prevailed everywhere for more than fifty years in theatres and salons.

The Grand Duke of Baden sent me at Freiburg a very gracious telegram from Meinau.

The gentlemen of the Zurich committee are behaving in exemplary manner with regard to the *Musikfest*. The audiences are large; in spite of the heavy costs there will be a profit of 2,000 marks for our *Musik Verein*. This honors the compatriots of M. de Palézieux whom I will ask to settle matters between M. S[ach] and Gille with regard to the tickets for several seasons of the Jena Concerts. One can, without acting like a nabob, limit Court expenditures to what is properly necessary.

Your very humble FL
will be in Bayreuth Saturday evening.

Saint-Saëns is here as well as Sophie Menter and Mme Jaëll.

———

Thursday morning, July 20
Bayreuth

M. Gross, Bayreuth Minister of Foreign Affairs, was so kind as to negotiate with your man who has coaches for hire.

For 25 marks a day you will have an adequate carriage for the four first performances of *Parsifal*. I asked if one also had to pay for the days between the performances. M. Gross assured me that one did <u>not</u>. Consequently the whole price will be 100 marks, plus the driver's tip.

Saturday I attended the first dress rehearsal of Acts I and II of *Parsifal*. "Masterpiece" is an inadequate word. From the opening to the final bars it progresses from the sublime to the more sublime.

FL is very humbly waiting for your telegram with the hour of your arrival at Bayreuth on July 25.

Please convey to Mme de Schleinitz and her husband my faithful and respectful friendly greetings.

———————

Friday [July 21]
[Bayreuth]

Changing Peterle's tickets is not the slightest trouble.

The Siegfriedstrasse runs past the Villa Wahnfried.

I wrote to you yesterday on the matter of the coach which has been settled by M. Gross.

Till Tuesday evening.

FL

———————

[August 24]
Thursday evening
Bayreuth

This time Lo's consummate skill in the field of itineraries has been found wanting. At Eisenach the stop was only a quarter of an hour, thirty minutes at Meiningen, and a little longer at Lichtenfels. At <u>one</u>

o'clock I arrived at the Bayreuth station where I immediately made the acquaintance of Count B. Gravina, a gentleman of the most pleasing —even very handsome—appearance, like a <u>Sicilian</u> Oscar Wedel.

Tomorrow (feast day of St. Louis and double birthday and name day of King Ludwig of Bavaria) the civil marriage contract between Gravina and Blandine von Bülow will be signed at Wahnfried. After tomorrow their marriage will be blessed at a mass in the Catholic church. Afterward the young couple leaves for the husband's home, Palermo—via Frankfurt, the Rhine, and Switzerland.

Peterle is favorably remembered at Wahnfried. Tell him this.

Your old

FL

Saturday, August 26, 82
Bayreuth

Between ourselves, M. S[ach] can hardly "behave properly," for he seeks everywhere his – – – illusory advantage. This is the way with princes, and it is not too stupid given the stupidity of people, with which I sincerely associate myself. As for M. S[ach], my ties to him of more than thirty years count for naught. He'll ignore them whenever he feels like it—and I'm entirely prepared for this. In any country a princely mess of things may suit people, but I don't have to become involved either in Weimar or elsewhere. My line of conduct will remain straightforward without any pretentions.

My telegram of this evening tells you that your old servant FL is returning to Weimar Wednesday.

Wagner himself will conduct the final performance of *Parsifal* on Tuesday, so it would be most unseemly for me to leave the day before.

If Schenniss [Schennis] comes this will please me, and I will very willingly take him to the banquet which Wagner is giving for the artists after the performance on Tuesday evening at ten o'clock—but I do not undertake to obtain a free ticket for *Parsifal* for anyone, having barred myself from ever becoming involved in such matters.

If Schennis intends to arrive in time Tuesday, he must leave Weimar by the 1.00 A.M. train so as to reach Bayreuth at 1.00 P.M. The performance begins at four.

September 27, 82
Weimar

Forgive me for all the unhappiness I have very unintentionally caused you over the last ten years. My wrongs and my faults grieve me deeply. Grant them full forgiveness and let us remember the good and great thoughts we have shared, the lovely and adorable music we have heard together – – – – Let us remember our lofty moments together and let us remain unshakable in the sublime communion of Love—the life and light of souls in time and eternity.

May the blessing of Jesus Christ rest on you and your children.

FL

Friday morning, September 29

As we were returning sadly from the station yesterday with Zhukovsky, we met M. Sach at the door of the Hofgärtnerei. I suggested that he go right in and see my portrait, without going up my stairs. "Already done," he replied, "I've just been to Zhukovsky's studio and consider your portrait a very good likeness; only I'll tell the painter" (who was present at this little exchange by the front door) "that he has treated you as fate generally treats mortals: harshly." Without further elaborating on this thought S[ach] repeated, "Yes, harshly." Zhukovsky offered no excuses and went back into his studio after talking for a few minutes more with S[ach] outdoors. In my room he told me about his trip to Biarritz, and he will first stop off at Baden-Baden for the birthday of his sister the Empress. Your name was not mentioned but I have no doubt that he will call on you at Baden. In his brief speech at the meeting of the naturalists (*Naturforscher*) at Eisenach he quoted the maxim which he claims is from the Koran (?): "Silence is golden, speech is silver" – – – and added pleasantly for me, "I have wrought enamel."

At the dinner for four (the fourth being M. von Cranach) at the *Maison Romaine*, S[ach] distinguished himself greatly by speaking volubly and very pleasantly. The topic of the conversation was chiefly painting, Lucas Cranach, the galleries of Rome, Madrid, Seville. He insisted so much and so repeatedly on his desire to see Zhukovsky settle down at Weimar that the latter did not know how to get out of it, however flattered he must have been by the invitation. Neither the picture of Saint Francis of Assisi he has promised to the Capuchins of Siena, nor Countess Gravina's portrait awaiting completion induced S[ach] to drop the subject. Equally in vain I also timidly attempted an intermezzo by saying that I had seen in your home an excellent portrait of Turgenev drawn by Fredrov. On this subject S[ach] quoted a painful remark by Fredrov, "I suffer from three handicaps; I am poor, a nobleman, and Polish."

Finally S[ach] cordially embraced Zhuk[ovsky], all "garlanded," who almost committed himself to return and take over the studio at the *Kunstschule* next February. Somewhat incautiously, he had previously said that it was the finest studio he had occupied in all his life. This provided S[ach] with a splendid opening: "Well, I offer it to you and ask you to settle down there."

"And of Caron (Arthur Schen.) not a word"!

If you will be so good as to receive my old friend R. Pohl (chief editor of the *Badener Zeitung*) you will please your sad but not hateful

FL

I shall see Mme S[ach] at the concert of the astonishing d'Albert this evening and will return the pair of gloves left behind at your home to the *bastille* of G[ustchen].

Monday, October 2, 82
[Weimar]

Gustchen was in bed and could not see me when I brought her the pair of (pearl gray) gloves which she claims are not hers. She came to see me yesterday evening and we waxed melancholy together over your absence – – – Tomorrow we'll be seeing each other again at Ettersburg as she is accompanying Mme S[ach] there this afternoon. Mme S[ach] returned to Weimar expressly to see Zhukovsky's portrait and I met her in the studio. The comment: "The portrait is a very good likeness and the style historic," is beginning to go the rounds. If I am not mistaken this picture will add to Zhukovsky's reputation, already rated as very good and brilliant thanks to the stage sets for *Parsifal*.

Saturday evening after eight o'clock at my house a preliminary game of whist, improvised for three—Gille, Zhukovsky, and FL. As Adelheid does not know how to play she did needlework. At the next game (Wednesday) Lassen and Mme Merian will play together. Yesterday, Sunday, she assembled all the whist partners together for dinner and regaled us with excellent dishes and wines, including a kind of Tokay, unknown to me, and which is not a dessert wine. Zhukovsky was again due to dine at five o'clock at Ettersburg with Loën who will take him there and bring him back in a Court coach.

I will convey to him your Roman errand. Before he can perform it, we will probably see each other again in Venice.

The tasks I face of correcting (manuscripts and proofs) increase to the point that your very sad FL will only be able to leave Weimar in another two weeks or so.

If, in the course of a stroll, Clément happens to come across "R. Wagner" by Mme Judith Gautier at the well-known bookshop, Marx, in the Kurhaus, please send it to me.

Sunday, October 8, 82
W[eimar]

Barely a couple of lines today, tr. ch. [très chère] Lo. The Tolls came to see me yesterday. I told them about your note of introduction which Martha Remmert will be presenting. At Loën's on Thursday I dined with Toll's successor, M. de Höltzke, who is already in very good odor at Court. His appearance and manner are most agreeable and entirely free of pompousness. Did I tell you that the coach in which he went to Ettersburg was drawn by four horses?

I just cannot get through my papers and corrections of music. This week too will be given up to it. I also expect two visits from publishers with a few thalers.

Be so good as to have someone inquire at Lungarno Nuovo, 50, whether Mme Hillebrand and her husband are back. If so, convey to them my faithful and friendly greetings. Hillebrand could also give Clément-Rubens good information on various artists and works of art in Florence.

T.v.

FL

Zhukovsky's portrait is a real and complete success. He has been asked for a *recapita* [sic] for the Weimar museum and he seems disposed to paint one. This evening we're having another whist game. Tomorrow he'll be at his sister's at Wiesbaden. We'll probably be seeing each other again at Frankfurt and will pursue our way together in ten days or so via the St. Gotthard as far as Venice.

October 20, 82
Weimar

Some friend of mine wrote to me over thirty years ago, *Je vous félicite de posséder un château (Nonnenwerth) au bord des Reins.*[9] Speaking of

9. I.e., the kidneys, instead of the Rhine, *du Rhin.*

spelling mistakes, a steadfast correspondent informs me that she is suffering from *maux de Rheins*. So be it. Count Beust, who has entirely recovered, told me yesterday that he had received a charming letter from you. His daughterW. and Gust[chen], with whom we mourned your absence are with Mme S[ach] at Heinrichsau. Baroness Pelet de Narbonne favored me with her visit yesterday. Her objective was the private doors of your apartment in her house. She was a little embarrassed by the information I gave her on this subject and deeply regrets your departure.

After your sons' high school years you had to leave Weimar. Rome was indicated for Clément-Rubens. May he look at Michelangelo and Raphael. May he draw and paint there, and may you enjoy your stay in the Eternal City.

Your

FL

I shall probably stay here another ten days or so and spend November and December in Venice.

November 4, [1882]

Rubinstein will be conducting his *Les Macchabées* at Leipzig tomorrow and has wired that he is coming to see me Tuesday.

Were you able to hire the person Achille recommended?

[unsigned]

November 15, 82
Nuremberg

Herewith the notes for Madame Helbig and for Siemiradski. You know that he has very generously presented his large picture, "Nero's

Torches," to the Cracow museum. If I am not mistaken he is hard at work on paintings commissioned from St. Petersburg.

Sunday your very humble Sarring II[10] will be in Venice.

Siem[iradski]'s studio is in that ugly street of studios behind the Babuino.

Please <u>seal</u> my two letters before presenting them.

———

Wednesday, Nov. 29, 82
Venice

That's good! Lo has reverted to her <u>minor</u> key, neither grumbling nor overloaded with <u>double-sharps</u>—translate it into the German *Doppel-Kreuz* so as to get the double meaning.

Not to have sent off the letter I had started in Weimar six days earlier was doubtless a mistake. All the same one could find several excuses; first of all I was expecting a letter from you which never arrived, then I felt really very low for almost a week. Wagner suffers from the same nervous ailment as I, and more often. For the thirtieth time I repeat that there is never any reason to worry about me, and beg you earnestly to refrain from so doing.

I am housed in princely style at the Vendramin palace where family life is peaceful, complete, and not boring. Wagner goes out only for a stroll and dispenses with making or receiving calls. Cosima stays quietly at home, knowing that her husband prefers this. Thus, with a few exceptions, we are always by ourselves. For dinner (two o'clock) and supper (eight o'clock) we are nine at table, including Siegfried's young tutor and Mlle Corsani, whom you saw at Wahnfried. For three years

10. FL himself.

she has been part of the household as lady-companion and teacher of Isolde and Eva. Some music, but not too much, before or after supper. Somewhat for my sake, the evening usually ends with two or three games of whist.

Princess Hatzfeldt has very kindly invited me to dine (at half-past six) every Thursday. Her dining room, most elegantly appointed, is less spacious than yours at Weimar. The late Baron Visconti would have approved of the menu of the dinners at which six or seven people are present. After coffee, whist. The Princess likes to play. One of our leading partners is the very celebrated Pasini. He is all the rage now and has just sold his large watercolor of the interior of the church of the Frari (in Venice) for 50,000 francs. A good example for our friend Schennis to follow, as well as a precedent set by Pasini, who is the widower of a rich woman (born Warschauer, very closely related to the Mendelssohns), who left her daughter a dowry of over a million. The young lady plays the violin and piano agreeably, they say, and will be spending the winter here.

Your compatriot, M. de Wolkoff, is prolonging his stay in Venice and his Venetian watercolors are greatly prized. He recently disposed of some in London for 20,000 francs. Last year I made his acquaintance here at Princess Hatzfeldt's, but this time we have not yet seen each other again. He is said to be a very witty man, fond of paradoxes to the point of maintaining that Dante's reputation is much outmoded and exaggerated.

From one day to the next we are expecting Zhukovsky, for whom I have sincere affection. He intends to paint a second portrait of me; but, on reflection, I shall not send the first to Toronto, as the gift seems to me disproportionate. It will suffice to have a large photograph of it made for the Canadian recipient, and to add a frame costing 200 francs. Zhukovsky will dispose of the painted portrait as he likes. He will perhaps offer it to M. S[ach] for his Weimar museum.

Lenbach, having made the necessary arrangements for his stay of several months in Rome, has gone to Munich whence he writes to my daughter that he will make a brief stop here at Christmastime on his way back to Rome. I will urge him strongly not to treat Clément too much as a <u>baron</u>, but to look on him as a vigorous candidate for the high aristocracy of art, which excludes <u>upstart</u> dilettantes and only recognizes the <u>successful</u>.

When I have talked with Lenbach I'll send Clément a line.

If you will kindly lend me Maxime Du Camp's article (October 15) for a few days, you will be doing me a favor. I know no subscribers here to the *Revue des d[eux] m[ondes]*, and it is contrary to my strongly stay-at-home habits to frequent reading rooms or clubs.

Heckel has published as a pamphlet his resounding Eisenach speech, part of which you know through the press. The pamphlet is some twenty pages longer. Shall I send it to you? You will easily find in Rome the third volume of George Sand's correspondence, in which I recommended to you the letters to Napoleon and his cousin, and especially the long philippic to Mazzini.

In late September at Weimar I corrected the final proofs of the Tivoli pieces which you request. They are to appear, or perhaps already have, in the third volume of my *Années de Pèlerinage*[11] at Schott's (Mainz). A tiff between the publisher and myself might dissuade him from sending me my three or four author's copies – – – When I know that the work is on sale I'll send it to you.

A second edition of the Munkácsy rhapsody is being published with the additions and changes I made for Mlle Ranouschevitch. You'll receive the second improved version from Budapest.

Thank you for the program of the benefit concert for the *danne[g]giati dalle inondazioni* [flood victims] under the baton *del Maestro* Cavaliere Pinelli. There is nothing surprising in the fact that Maestro Ponchielli, renowned in Italy because of the success of his opera *I promessi sposi*,[12] should, in his hymn to the St. Gotthard, have inserted "God Save the Queen" in honor of the English and German stockholders of the colossal tunnel. This is entirely appropriate, for the official English anthem has become equally official in Germany and is accepted as such in

11. G 163; R 10e.
12. First performed August 30, 1856, in Cremona.

Prussia, Bavaria, Württemberg, etc. (including Sondershausen), with the text *Heil dir im Siegerkranz*. Austria alone has its own anthem, composed by Haydn: *Gott erhalte Franz den Kaiser!*[13]

At Sgambati's *da camera* concerts you'll hear a good many of the works performed by Lassen, Kömpel, etc., at the Erholung. I urge you to subscribe to this concert series. They represent a definite improvement in instrumental music in Rome and are attended by the right people.

Your melancholy but reassured

FL

Please convey my affectionate thanks to Siemiradzki, and again express to Mme Helbig my homage and my cordial friendship.

Wednesday evening, December 6
Venice

I am replying at once to the last lines of your letter. Passive expectation is the proper attitude and posture on both sides. More would be excessive, and less superfluous. That self-respect should be involved is natural, but the maxims of La Rochefoucauld which reduce all feelings to that of self-respect do not provide the real key. Something indefinite rises above it which must be nobly upheld—to the point of heroism.

Your very humble and truly devoted

FL

Thanks for the article by Du Camp which I'll discuss in my next letter. I am prevented from continuing this one by several interruptions.

13. Haydn used it also in his String Quartet, Opus 76, No. 3.

1883

January 7, 83
Venice

Forgive and forgive, very dear one, and guess, which won't be very hard, that in the last couple of weeks I've been doing nothing but write music. The oars of a *Gondole Lugubre*[1] beat on my brain. I have tried to write them and had to rewrite them twice, whereupon other lugubrious things came back to mind and, willy-nilly, my scrawls on music sheets continued to the exclusion of all else.

Let's not talk any more about "selfish heroism"; it is out of place in embassies where "watertight compartments," as Renan ingeniously phrased it, prevail. All the same, heroism exists here below and in a great many ways even in the lower strata of society. Not to recognize this amounts to impertinent stupidity.

Renan is perhaps cloaking himself a little in convention and jargon when he writes that, all in all, four women have loved him – – – his mother, his sister, his wife, his daughter – – – – There must be some other, less legitimate lady, and I think I told you Balzac's theory that no man with fewer than seven women in his life has achieved the perfect state of a complete being. It remains to be known how many men ladies require in order to become complete too?

The passages concerning the St. Sulpice seminary, and Renan's insistence on remaining a Sulpician in an entirely different world have great charm. They vibrate with a note of strict honesty as regards him-

1. G 200; R 81.

441

self, and of indulgence toward others. I recaptured several times in
them the personal impressions of my youth. However, I think that if
my confessor had not advised against my entering a seminary—and I
ardently wanted to do so when I was eighteen—I would never have
left ecclesiastical life, and would have devoted myself entirely to the
holy duties of priesthood. Later on, music gripped me unrelentingly
to the point where even failure could not change matters. This is the
lasting spell of my vocation – – – –

I am returning to you by this same mail the three issues of *La Revue*,
and urge you to read the remarkable piece on Count Gobineau in the
December issue of the *Bayreuther Blätter*, which you receive. The author of these fine pages has signed them "Wahnfried." Beginning January 1, the *Bayreuther Blätter* will appear only on a quarterly basis—
hence four deliveries a year instead of twelve.

With regard to the performance of his symphony, composed in '52[2]
and which turned up again unexpectedly in Dresden, Wagner has
written a very witty letter to his publisher, Fritzsch. This performance
was the event of the closing days of last year in Venice, where Wagner
himself conducted it as well as the five or six preliminary rehearsals in
honor of his wife's birthday—*Vigile de Noël*. The charming hall of the
foyer of the *Fenice* was brilliantly lit, but the public was excluded by
higher authority of the *grandissime Wort- und Tondichter*, as the King
of Bavaria calls him. Thus the audience was reduced to only nine or
ten people—Cosima, her children, the tutor Hausburg, the assistant
conductor of the orchestra, Humperdinck (who had come expressly
from Paris to place himself again at Wagner's orders), Mlle Corsani,
who has for two years (Naples, Palermo, Bayreuth) been filling the
role of reading companion to Cosima's daughters, plus Zhukovsky,
excellent and perfect friend of the Wagner household of which he has,
as it were, very nobly become a vassal. His portrait of me is having no
less success in Venice than in Weimar. Pasini—whom you will see
again in Rome in April—and Wolkoff have <u>sincerely</u> congratulated

2. Correct date of composition: 1832.

him on it, with some slight criticisms which Zhukovsky took into account by reducing the laurel grove and the armchair decoration.

I reminded Pasini that M—— had given you the watercolor of a pretty Roman girl – – – today it would cost at least 5,000 francs; for you know that Pasini's latest large watercolor fetched 50,000 francs, and the price of the next one will not be lower.

As for the price of paintings, I would mention the 15,000 florins for the portrait of Countess Duchatel, wife of the French ambassador in Vienna, painted by Makart. He has painted a large portrait of Countess Maria Dönhoff at the piano, or rather at Bach's *Well-tempered Clavier*, with garlands in profusion. She told me yesterday that it was a kind present from Makart. It has been admired here at the Palazzo Vendramin, for I begged Mme D[önhoff] to have it unpacked, and you will see it in Rome, where the graceful live original will herself be next week. There was a rumor in Vienna that Mme D[önhoff] was marrying Lenbach: mere drawing room chitchat. She has other things to bother about.

On another subject, your *commérages* [gossip] have distracted me from my somber thoughts.

Thanks for your last letter to which I reply that Lo has this time done nothing wrong and that the entire fault lies with her very humble

FL

I'll send you Wagner's letter as soon as it appears.
Saturday I return directly to Pest without passing through Vienna.

January 10, 83
Venice

Countess Dönhoff will give you the latest news of the old and young inhabitants of the Palazzo Vendramin. She will do it so wittily that you will be greatly amused.

In spite of my guilt, due almost entirely to my being absorbed in music—no longer being able to write both letters and music notes—I remain unvaryingly and with all my heart, reproaching none other than myself, your saddened and aged servant

FL

Monday evening I'll be in Pest.

January 15, 83
Budapest

Countess Dönhoff has already handed you my latest message from Venice, which repeats things you already know. A young lady of high society of former times, having erred, wrote to her mother: "I am guilty but not criminal." Except for the difference in sex, the same applies to me.

I left Venice at a quarter past two on Saturday and arrived here peacefully yesterday before noon—less than twenty-two hours on the way. My reading matter during the trip was the second volume of Taine's *Voyage en Italie* (*Venise*), written in strong and lively French with rarest subtlety. I recommend that you read the first volume (*Rome*) in which you will find remarkable comments and descriptions. To this add, if only by way of contrast, *Rome chrétienne*[3] by the late Mgr Gerbet.

If you still have with you the three issues of the *Revue des deux mondes* which you kindly sent to me in Venice (with the articles by Du Camp and Renan), you would please Cosima by lending them to her and sending them to the Palazzo Vendramin. Here people lend me *La Revue*, but when there are any articles in the *Débats* which suit my reading habits please forward them to me.

---

3. Olympe-Philippe Gerbet, *Esquisse de Rome chrétienne* (Paris, 1844–50). After Gerbet's death in 1864 the work was completed (3rd vol.) by Augustin Bonnetty.

Wagner's letter about his youthful Olympian Symphony will reach you directly from Venice.

How harshly you deal, my very dear Lo, with Sg[ambati]'s *clairs de lune*. There is in them something of penumbra and even of the dawn. When you rise earlier, you will become aware of these while not yet fully awake. On the other hand I don't take much issue with your impressions and opinions, specifically your forecast that Sgambati will soon become doctrinaire in music. It is his natural inclination, which is noble, not precipitate. In Italy especially, it is now preferable to the opposite trend. *R.O.* would approve.

I am again suffering from the fever of writing music. Is this senility? Let others decide.

The conversation between Princess J. and M. Sach is one of your happy inspirations. Now and then it is hard to decide which of the two should receive the palm.

Do you know Vereshchagin's paintings? Over thirty of them are being shown here at the Kunsthaus (next to my lodgings). I'll go and see them tomorrow and will tell you about them.

Your old

FL

Tell me about the pleasure Sgam[bati] takes in our beloved Russian music.

January 25, 83

Budapest

Do you know Vereshchagin's paintings? He depicts India and the Russo-Turkish war with strikingly original color and poetic realism, quite in keeping with the mood and trends of our *fin de siècle*.

Vereshchagin's wife is a heroine. She kept a diary of her very dangerous trip to India. I'll send it to you on the chance that it may interest you. It runs only to a hundred or so beautifully printed pages with illustrations. In the meantime, have your son Clément read you the enclosed piece on Vereshchagin's pictures.

The *Pester Lloyd* is not Russophile just now. Notwithstanding this, it is doing me the honor of attacking me because of my alleged anti-Semitism, recently and erroneously discovered in the second edition of my book on the Gypsies.[4]

In any case, Vereshchagin will remain one of your glorious compatriots; and you know my strong sympathy for the great musical talents there are in your great country, which it does not yet appreciate at their true value.

Vereshchagin's paintings, which I admire, are on exhibition here in the Kunsthaus next to my lodgings at the Royal Academy of Music. They had previously been shown in London, St. Petersburg, Paris, Brussels, Vienna, Berlin, etc. The opinions of critics are divided with regard to them, as, in medicine, between allopaths and homeopaths. The golden mean belongs to the philosopher's stone and to Lo.

The Tivoli pieces,[5] which were proofread at Weimar, have not yet appeared. A silly squabble between the publisher and myself has delayed their publication. As soon as they come out I'll send them to you.

La Nouvelle revue (not yet *R.O.*) prints, in its issues of December 15 and January 1, hitherto unpublished letters from Lamennais to M. de Vitrolles. If you are in a mood to read them, you will receive them.

Please convey my affectionate respects to Mme Minghetti and her daughter.

Your perpetually incorrigible

FL

---

4. First published in French in 1859 (*Des Bohémiens et de leur musique en Hongrie*), then, years later and greatly expanded, in German, translated by L. Ramann (*Die Zigeuner und ihre Musik in Ungarn*). The latter is now vol. VI of Liszt's *Gesammelte Schriften*. It exists also in an English translation by Edwin Evans, *The Gipsy in Music*.

5. The *Années de Pèlerinage. Troisième Année*, G 163; R 10e, published in 1883 by Schott.

[undated]

The atmosphere of Rome is very favorable to Lo's letter-writing talents. Nothing could be more subtle or striking than her comments on Hoh[enlohe] and Hüb[ner], two persons about as different from each other as Cardinals Billault and Bonaparte.

The "Travel Sketches in India," by M. and Mme Vereshchagin, will reach you very soon, together with three issues of *La Nouvelle Revue* containing the letters from Lamennais to his intimate friend Baron de Vitrolles, whose intimacy sometimes went awry. I'm adding to the parcel the third volume of my *Années de Pèlerinage* with *Les Cyprès de la Villa d'Este* and the three *Sonnets de Pétrarque* (for voice) just recently published by Schott, Mainz.

When you have read the issues of *La Nouvelle Revue* (that of January 15 publishes the last, somewhat spiritualist, novella by Turgenev, *Après la mort*), please send them to Cosima (Venice), and the Vereshchagin "Travel Sketches" to your very humble servant,

FL

Of the painters of battle scenes the French now place MM. Detaille and de Neuville in the front rank. Together they have painted a series of pictures of striking episodes—like *The Last Cartridge*—from the war of 1870.

If it suits you I'll be glad to write a note to Lenbach for Clément, so that he should not be treated as a baron, which means being more or less politely shown the door. Besides, the admirable Madame Minghetti is the best spokesman where Lenbach is concerned.

February 14, 83
Buda

As usual, your flair was sound in picking Bonghi as a guide and commentator for the wonders of Rome. I have only just met Bonghi but I hold him in high esteem for a few of his articles (in particular that in the *Revue Hillebrand*) and of his speeches, which I have read with care.

You and Lenbach have little in common. He is too Germanic for your cosmopolitanism. However, on the chance that it should suit you I'll send you the lines of introduction for Clément to hand him.

Did you attend Father Curci's lectures? Schlözer and Hübner, and others from the world of high society won't have missed them. These lectures are an integral part of intellectual high life [sic] and of what we call "*Reine Olga.*" Curci is the Heckel of militant catholicism; ask him, when you have the chance, whether he has come across his *Alali* [*alalie*][6] which Heckel had unfortunately failed to discover.

If Sgambati can only travel with his family, the wisest thing for him will be to stay at home.

With all my heart

FL

Did you receive the parcel with the three issues of *La Nouvelle Revue* (to be returned to Cosima) and the superfluous sheets of music?

February 20, 83

Budapest

Your Wagner telegram touched me. The press is full of obituary notices on the great poet-musician (*Wort- und Tondichter*, as the King of Bavaria rightly called him), the supreme dramatist of an Ideal never realized before him in complete art: poetry, music, and the stage. Compared with this triple achievement the colossi, Beethoven and Goethe, are sublime fragments. From *Tannhäuser* and *Lohengrin* to the *Nibelungen* and *Parsifal*, complete art has been revealed. To see Wagner

6. Acquired or accidental muteness.

only as a celebrity or showpiece strikes me as a somewhat silly misconception. The branches of his genius rise from deeper roots. In him the superhuman dominates.

I suggested to my daughter that I join her in Venice and escort her back to Bayreuth. She replied in the negative.

Between her and me there are bonds and dates far removed from ordinary relations.

Until Easter
your very humble FL will be staying here.

[undated]

I entirely agree with your arrangements. So Weimar is firm for May. I'll probably go to Cologne and even Brussels before then. Bayreuth is a special matter which I can't yet settle.

Your disappointment in Curci's lectures is no great surprise to me. You know St. Gregory of Nazianzus, Bossuet, Demaistre [de Maistre], Lacordaire, and the admirable lectures, not widely enough read, of Father Felix; hence other preachers and apologists only provide you with repetitions more or less dressed up in rhetoric.

When I see you again I'll venture to tell you of a striking point of resemblance between Lo and Napoleon I.

Very humbly
Your
FL

Yesterday evening I read Gounod's *La Rédemption*,[7] and *La Lyre et la harpe* by Saint-Saëns. The second work has more substance than the first, which seems to me somewhat anemic.

Our Rendano from Weimar is to give a concert here in which I take an interest because of the really <u>audacious</u> works on the program.

7. A sacred trilogy, 1881, for solo voices, chorus, and orchestra.

More than fifty thousand people went to the Vereshchagin exhibition. The thirty or forty paintings are now going to Moscow. Next week we'll have an exhibition of the drawings and paintings of Michael Zichy who spent several years in St. Petersburg.

March 18, 83
Pressburg

You have sent me a good and sweet word about your return to Weimar in June. It is not my custom to be ungrateful, and I never am, even in exceptional cases. If I have not thanked you before this for your latest letter, the fault lies once more with that tyranny of music which I endure without illusion but with obstinacy. In the last two weeks I have done nothing but blacken large and small score-paper. To what end? I'll tell you when we see each other again.

Cardinal Hoh[enlohe] writes that you are one of those women, too rarely found, with whom one can enjoy a pleasant conversation. I appreciate the truth of this very justified opinion and remain forever,

Your very humble

FL

Tomorrow evening I'll be back in Budapest. Please write to me there until the end of the month.

Even more than Liberty, Wagner's works, including *Parsifal*, must circle the globe. Fashion and simple-mindedness triumph over outworn critics—not to mention the wonderful character of the works themselves.

I'll send you Mme Sand's letters to Flaubert published in *La Nouvelle Revue*. They are short, but have a splendid touch of genius and spontaneity.

Read in the latest issue (March) of the *Bayreuther Blätter* the letter which Wagner wrote shortly before his death to H. v. Stein, and the latter's dialogue between Solon and Croesus.

Saturday, March 31, 83
Budapest

You rightly guessed that it was not once again a case of an eel or a Grill (a fish pseudonym for the wondrous invention of Lo) lurking under a rock, but simply of writing music, which is very inimical to the prompt scribbling of letters.

This time it's a matter of a work of importance to Hungary: the Royal Anthem.[8] Lo will consider this superfluous, but I endorse Voltaire's comment: *Le superflu, chose très nécessaire.* Consequently I have spent over a week writing down on paper the popular air of this Royal Anthem, adapting to it an old Hungarian version (not the Rákóczy). I will need another week to write the various versions for piano, voice, and orchestral score. Music is a tremendous burden.

Day after tomorrow, Monday evening, your very humble FL will be in Vienna, and in Weimar on April 8.

April 9, 83
Weimar

Mme Voigt let me know yesterday that the apartment (Marienstrasse), about which you have already inquired, is available beginning May 15. I enclose herewith the letter which I suggested that Mme Voigt write to you. Please answer it without delay. The price seems to me exorbitant. Perhaps one should have recourse to bargaining,

---

8. His *Ungarisches Königslied* (Magyar király-dal), G 93; R 563.

which is something almost improper, but sometimes of practical value.

Yesterday, on her birthday Mme S[ach] deigned to receive at noon some thirty members of the Court. There was no official dinner. That evening Mme S[ach] attended the performance of *La Jolie Fille de Perth*[9] (by Bizet), a *Carmen* that has only just blossomed, innocent of all guilt. Once and for all, I lack the taste needed to enjoy this kind of opera, even *Carmen*. I feel obtuse and often out of place.

With regard to Count Beust (who is again very sick) asking when you are coming back, I replied that I was expecting you here only in June. I'll arrange my stay in Weimar and elsewhere so as to conform as much as I can to Lo's dictates.

From May 2 to 9 I'll be in Leipzig for *Die Tonkünstler Versammlung*, of which you'll receive the program, which is this time very rich. M. S[ach] will put in an appearance in his role of sponsor of this institution, which is surviving successfully after twenty-four years despite many obstacles. It is not difficult to commemorate the illustrious dead with Mozart's *Requiem*[10] and the oratorios of Händel, Bach, and Mendelssohn, etc., but except for the theatre, living composers can only wait, and – – – die. Now, the particular function of the *Tonkünstler Versammlungen* is precisely to stress for the living their right to live.

Please return the issues of *La Nouvelle Revue* with Mme Sand's letters, to M. Saissy, Directeur de *La Gazette de Hongrie*, Ferencz-József Rakpart, 10, Budapest (Hongrie).

With all my heart, your very humble

FL

I tell people about Clément's fine appearance, with his Russian fur cap, and bearing the standard of the Artists' International Club in Rome at the celebration in honor of Raphael.

---

9. Opera, first performed December 26, 1867, in Paris.
10. KV 626.

April 17, 83
W[eimar]

Gustchen pulled off a small *coup d'état*. She simply decided to inform M. de Hadeln that you are reserving quarters at the Castel Helldorf, either on the ground floor or the second floor (?) from July 1. You are subject to the short-term inconvenience of taking rooms at the Hotel Erbprinz, or Russie.

Rosenoff, not being here, was not able to transmit your message to Mme Voigt; but Gustchen boldly took it on herself to go off and find her in order to cancel the apartment which you had thought of renting. All things considered, in spite of the nuisance of several weeks at the hotel, it seems to me that you will be better off at the Castel Helldorf than elsewhere. Gustchen asked me to influence you in agreeing to this and is sending you details of her imperious negotiation.

With all my heart, your very humble and expectant

FL

Herewith two programs of the very successful concerts which lacked only your approbation and presence.

———

April 28, 83
Weimar

In spite of the unfortunate inconvenience of spending a month in the old-fashioned Hotel Erbprinz, Gustchen's arrangements for the Castel Helldorf still seem to me the best possible.

FL will show himself to be more punctual than Sarring and will await you here from mid-May on. Day after tomorrow I shall be in Marburg, where they are celebrating on May 1 the 600th anniversary of the consecration of the church of St. Elisabeth. On this occasion, my *Légende* (which has already become hackneyed) is to be performed.

From May 2 to 7, I shall be in Leipzig in honor of *Die Tonkünstler Versammlung*. There will be four or five concerts of which I'll send you the program.

Perpetually
Your very humble
FL

Please write to Hôtel de Prusse, Leipzig.

Sunday [1883?]
Wilhelmsthal

Nothing new to report from here. Wilhelmsthal has been from time immemorial favored by frequent rains which have not ceased these three days. I don't pay much attention to them, and stay put in my room.

However, an innovation has been introduced into Their Royal Highnesses' evenings. I am so flattered by it that I dare not tell you – – – –
Wednesday morning your very humble FL will be back.

October 1, 83
Weimar

Mme Jaëll wrote you yesterday about your Ingres painting. Goupil, a man of major importance, asserts that this portrait of a cardinal was never painted by Ingres; hence its market value will be greatly reduced.

To my cordial greetings to R. Pohl please add my recommendation that he complete as soon as possible the translation of the libretto of *Quentin Durward*. Loën and Lassen are waiting for Pohl's German text in order to start rehearsing Gevaert's opera. I want the performance to take place at Weimar without unnecessary delay.

The superb Steinway piano (very *forte*) awaits you. Mme Jaëll, Lassen, Reisenauer, and your very humble servant have all tried it at Loën's, who is keeping the instrument destined for Your Highness until her return. Solos and pieces for 4 hands will follow in the house (opposite the Hofgärtnerei) nicknamed *commode renversée* [upside-down bureau] by the sharp-tongued Weimarians.

Your very aged, constant

FL

You have read in the *Débats* of September 28 Deschanel's second article on Renan's memories of his childhood and youth.

Alas! Thanks to King Solomon we know that everything here on earth is Vanity of Vanities. To this Renan introduces nuances in good French.

———

[1883?]

Today, one word only: Lo is adorable. Take this word in its true sense, and know that your latest lines revived for me one of my rare and loveliest hours in Rome, that in which Chimay brought me at the Vatican an explicit letter from Lo, about which I commented to the generous messenger: not to understand would be too unworthy!

Tomorrow I'll write to you about Maxime Du Camp, Renan, and conventional—or true—"heroism." The latter survives in varying degree according to the inspiration – – – –

Your
FL

———

1884

Rendano will be most welcome at the *Tonkünstler Versammlung* (first week in June) at Weimar. Give him my cordial greetings. I am asking Riedel to include Rendano's concerto in the program. It is a vigorous, original, and remarkable work which I greatly appreciate, while being of the opinion that the ears and pens of the leading critics will not receive it favorably.

Hans Richter recently praised Sgambati's symphony[1] sincerely to me. The Vienna performance was fairly well received but in the *Presse* [*Wiener Neue Presse*], Hanslick was critical. Hence it is a failure. The public is easily discouraged by a newspaper article. With few exceptions, people believe what they read. The Horoxes [Horrockses][2] of the press call the tune and mold opinion.

In Budapest Anton Rubinstein regaled us with two concerts, each consisting of fifteen to seventeen numbers. At the first concert, two Beethoven sonatas, and Schumann's great Sonata in F minor;[3] several études, preludes, and nocturnes by Chopin, a few pieces by Tchaikovsky and a charming little composition by Liadoff. In Vienna, Rubinstein has just given half a dozen concerts with large box-office receipts and enthusiastic audiences. He will soon play in Paris, Lyon, Bordeaux,

1. Opus posthumous.
2. Arthur Horrocks, an Englishman living in Weimar, widely known for his narrow-mindedness.
3. Opus 14. Its original title was *Concert sans orchestre*.

and then in Sweden. It is astonishing how he continues to be an extra-ordinary virtuoso, but his personality definitely betrays fatigue. His eyes are growing weak and he is to undergo a cataract operation.

Have you already read the poems of Leo XIII?[4] They were pub-lished at Udine in one volume, with an excellent Italian translation by Brunelli.

When you return to Gran you will find something new, very worth seeing. The architect Lippert has built a propylaeum (eight huge col-umns) in front of the basilica, has admirably restored the old chapel of the king, Saint Stephen, and has built the new and pompous palace of Cardinal Simor, Prince Primate of Hungary.

With all my heart
Your
FL

You know that Daniela is engaged to M. Brandt (from Darmstadt). Bülow and Cosima approve this marriage.

Please send me the name, with the exact spelling, of the author of the three volumes on the Reformation which you read in Weimar.

February 5, 84
BP

Il fait le plus beau temps du monde
Pour aller à cheval et sur l'onde,[5]

wrote Malebranche in a verse which has remained famous because of its defects.

I wish you this most lovely weather in Rome, together with Roman radiance.

On arriving here yesterday I found your *Débats*, and thank you for

4. This Pope was noted for his Latin poetry.
5. "It's the most lovely weather in the world / To go horseback riding and sailing."

this kind surprise. *Le Figaro* announces the engagement of Chimay's son (brother of the beautiful Viscountess Greffülhe) to Mlle de Béhague, whose mother recently married the Count de Kerjègu.

Marriages, births, troubles, pleasures, vanities, a thousand things, and halves and quarters of things, errors and miseries are the lot of human life so long as it does not steep itself in abnegation and in the infinity of divine love.

At Nuremberg, a telegram from Gille informed me of Achille's death. I feel affection for him. In response to my request, a stone cross will be placed on his tomb which will be blessed by the Catholic priest at Weimar.

Your sad

FL

February 25, 84
Pressburg

I came here yesterday for the fifty-year jubilee of the priesthood of Monseigneur Heiller, long senior priest at Pressburg and recently ordained bishop. I arrived here yesterday. This morning at the very pompous service in the cathedral I conducted my *Coronation Mass.* Heiller is one of the most worthy men I know, whose nature and constant practice it is to do good. The fine restoration of the cathedral is one of his achievements.

Tomorrow I return to Budapest, and next Sunday I shall probably pay my very humble visit to the Cardinal Primate of Hungary, Simor, at Gran. His Eminence is rightly granting his patronage to a talented architect, Lippert. I'll write to you about the propylaea of the basilica and the other works, which Lippert (with whom I am on good terms) has carried out at Gran under the Cardinal's orders.

Another cardinal, Haynald, has no thought whatever of my being at odds with him as somebody or other has claimed – – – – Since I do not consider myself to be a troublemaker, I am never at odds with anyone, even when circumstances might warrant it – – – – It seems to me better to be patient, save in absolute extremity.

As in former years, I see Cardinal Haynald frequently and can only be grateful to him for his continuing kindness toward me.

Did you receive your inscribed copy of the *Trois Valses Oubliées*?[6] Know that I am adding to it a *postscriptum* in print, which I will give you at Weimar. "After all! no one is perfect, Your Honor," as someone accused of having killed his father and mother said in court!

Your most imperfect

FL

Tell me on which day Charles, with whom I am very pleased, is to return to Weimar.

A Hungarian gentleman is entering my service on March 1, which would hardly prevent Charles from staying with me up to the day you decide. Having to pay two servants is no trouble at all.

———

March 12, 84
Budapest

Your Charles went back yesterday to Weimar and is at your service. I was very pleased with him and think that you will appreciate him more than his predecessor Sarring, who dabbled in painting. Artists never know how to please. On the one hand they are carried away by their talent; on the other hand the yoke of reality inflicts endless troubles on them. Charles is not an artist, but he has a cultivated mind, and used to read aloud newspapers and pamphlets in German intelligently to me in the evening; for my eyes are growing so weak that it is becoming almost impossible for me to use them for more than a few hours in the day. Too much time spent on music sheets affects my sight.

6. G 215; R 37. The original manuscript of No. 1 is in the Library of Congress.

March 25

The same excess prevented me from continuing this letter. For Christmas I intend to give myself a big negative present, that of writing no more music.

Thank you for your Roman musical chronicle. Rendano will be welcome at Weimar. I shall find room for his concerto even though the program is heavily loaded, and will include in good position your favorite quartet[6a] by Sgambati.

With regard to the Bülow incident[7] in Berlin, I'm sending you Lessmann's article with the two authentic texts by Hülsen and Bülow. The latter's "palinode" letter, in which he apologizes to Messrs. Renz, Salomonsky, Herzog, Schumann, circus directors, and states that he had no intention of insulting them by calling the Royal Berlin Opera the "Hülsen circus," is a minor masterpiece of wit. I also enclose the *Pester Lloyd* piece on this incident.

Wagnerism spreads and triumphs everywhere. In the *Débats*, Reyer describes his first audition of *Tristan und Isolde* at Weimar with our friend Lassen – – – – and now, twenty years later, the performance of one act of *Tristan* at the Concerts Lamoureux. A definitely different impression!

In the charming pages on Mme de Schleinitz in the short book *Berlin Society*, which first appeared in *La Nouvelle Revue* under the pseudonym of Count de Vasili,[8] Wagner is awarded the title of the Bismarck of German art.

You have read this book, whose sale is forbidden in Budapest. People say that the greater part was written by Mme Adam, who has been here for several days and is much lionized and stared at. One of my friends told me that she owes her considerable importance at this time

---

6a. *See* p. 410 note 22.

7. Cf. Liszt's *Briefe* VII, No. 392. In this letter to Princess Carolyne (dated March 12, 1884), Liszt writes: "Bülow, the declared anti-Semite, has just made a savage attack against the Royal Theatre of Berlin which he calls 'the Hülsen circus.' The incident has stirred up a row and I fear that this row will harm Bülow's career."

8. Pseudonym of Juliette Adam, founder of *La Nouvelle Revue*.

to her secret role as a Russian agent. She is engaged in research for a book on Hungary. Her work will no doubt create a sensation.

At the beginning of the book of letters from Flaubert to George Sand, you will find an excellent piece by Maupassant on Flaubert. The file of the stupidities of the most famous writers is a source of painful instruction.

Alas! Alas! I imitate Cardinal Barberini who, according to his cousin the late Count Lovatelli, spent fifteen years of his life translating *Kyrie eleison*!

What a harrowing account of the political exiles in Siberia by Prince Kropotkin! I am sending it to you; and in the same issue *Le Figaro* publishes a comical fragment of Heine's *Memoiren* featuring an account of his grandparents' wigs. For many years now my mood has not at all been inclined toward the humorous style, and I willingly leave to others the pleasure of finding it amusing.

FL

The parcel of newspapers is so large that I am sending it off to you under separate cover.

On Tuesday of Holy Week I shall probably be going to Kalocsa to stay with His Eminence Haynald.

—————

April 11, 84
Budapest

Our letters crossed. I want to greet you while you are still in Rome.

No news from here other than the disagreeable weakening of my sight. To write is becoming as difficult for me physically as mentally. Hence I am very far behind, not only in answering letters but in my promises to the publisher Kahnt, who is to bring out the *Stanislaus* fragment, announced in the program of the next *Tonkünstler Versammlung*.

Tomorrow we will have a Brahms concert. The most fortunate of all composers, thanks to the omnipotent protection of the critics, will himself conduct his new symphony[9] and others of his works. Next Monday we will hear his *Deutsches Requiem*.[10]

I'll probably go to Kalocsa Wednesday of Holy Week and stay there until Easter Monday.

In the next issue of her *Nouvelle Revue*, the most illustrious Mme Adam will publish the account of her <u>very brilliant</u> stay in Hungary.

I have struck up a slight acquaintance with the author of *La Païenne*.[11] In matters of free thinking she could, as they say in billiards, spot points to princes and princesses of like opinion.

Yours ever

FL

If Dorothea were willing to bring me forty or fifty cigars <u>Forti Napolitani</u>, not Cavours, she would do me a favor. However, she will have to declare this shipment at the Austrian customs and pay a small duty, so as to avoid an exorbitant fine.

I'll be staying in Budapest until April 8.

Tuesday, April 22, 84
Vienna

From Kalocsa, where I spent six days—from Wednesday of Holy Week until Easter Monday—at Cardinal Haynald's, with whom, despite certain rumors, I have never quarreled, I had nothing else to write about other than the church services. These I attended regularly for at least four hours daily. This is not of much interest to you, but so long as there are human beings here below, their best course will be to say *Kyrie eleison, Christe eleison!* and *Pater noster!*

9. Opus 98.
10. Opus 45.
11. Juliette Adam, *Païenne* (Paris, 1883).

There is a splendid remark by Napoleon I to Larevellière-Lépeaux, leader of the theophilanthropists: *Vous voulez du sublime, Monsieur; eh bien, dites votre Pater.*

The illustrious Mme Adam is not of this opinion, and claims that Apollo suffices for everything. So be it for those, among whom I do not number myself, who are content with this.

Here I saw again Princess Reuss who has invited me to dinner tomorrow. I'll be leaving Thursday evening and will wire you from Leipzig.

Your old

FL

I hope that at Weimar *les neiges d'antan* have already melted.

———

Sunday morning, July 13
Bayreuth

Henschel's authority and Gille's very accurate itinerary notwithstanding, I only arrived here yesterday at half past three. The train from Lichtenfels to Neumarkt had been much delayed. Fortunately Daniela had heard about the accident *subito*, and surprised me by coming to fetch me at Neumarkt with her two sisters, Isolde and Eva, and her husband to be, M. Brandt. The other sister, Blandine, and her husband, Gravina, will be at Meiningen for a few more days, where Bülow is housing them and looking after them with paternal kindness. My room in the house of Mme la Conseillère des Forêts (*Forsträthin*) Fröhlich is perfectly convenient and pleasant. In eight days' time Zhukovsky will be my next-door neighbor.

Mme de Schleinitz, her husband, and her mother are expected here on the nineteenth. The Villa Fantaisie is no longer at their disposal, as a Prince Hercolani is negotiating for its purchase.

Thursday morning
July 16

Your letter reached me yesterday.

Half the days are taken up by rehearsals. I have attended all those for orchestra. A stand with a lamp, and the score, has been set up for me in the first row of seats. I'll make use of it again tomorrow and the day after.

The performance is progressing very well indeed.

J. Rubinstein arrived (from London) day before yesterday, all dashing and dandified – – – – Greatly to my regret Zhukovsky cannot come. He is writing a detailed letter to Daniela about his poor state of health which is keeping him in Baden-Baden where you will probably see him again. If so, please give him my devoted greetings.

[unsigned]

Wednesday morning, July 23, 84
Bayreuth

Day before yesterday, Monday, they gave *Parsifal*, the first performance in this year's series. The voices and the orchestra were worthy of the highest praise. The house was filled and the audience enthusiastic. Two august personages were present, the Queen [Olga] of Greece and the brother of the reigning Duke of Hesse (Darmstadt), Alexander (?). I am told that in former years lovely ladies courted him. Not having the honor of being known either to His Royal Highness or to Her Majesty the Queen of Greece, I cannot tell you more.

Yesterday there was a *ricevimento* at Wahnfried at which my daughter did not appear. Ambassador Sabouroff and I had a little talk together about our unforgettable friend Mme Moukhanoff.

Mme de Schleinitz is a very gracious and effective patron of the Bayreuth performances. Yesterday I sent off to you the *Festblätter* which came out in the last few days. They are in any case worthy of attention and study because of the illustrations and even more so because of the text.

La Revue des deux mondes will take note of this in a few years' time. Meanwhile:

Expectans expectavi [I have waited in expectation]

FL

August 1, 84
Bayreuth

Nothing new here other than the continued success of *Parsifal*. The tenth performance, one week from today, Friday, August 8, will be the last. If you are returning to Weimar, I'll go back there. Otherwise I shall have to follow another and more distant road.

Your very humble old

FL

Sunday evening, August 3, 84
Bayreuth

You will receive my telegram tomorrow morning.

There will be a *ricevimento* here Thursday evening. It would make me happy if you came.

In any case I will be waiting at the station. Please wire the time of your arrival

to the very humble

FL

August 27, 84
Munich

This time I arrived an hour and a half earlier than stated on my timetable. This is a fairly rare occurrence, they tell me, to the point that Gravina, Levi, and Gross (from Bayreuth) came to fetch me at the station while I was having dinner at the Hotel Bellevue. Daniela and Eva stayed in Bayreuth, Mme de Schleinitz and her mother at Fantaisie. The Gravinas, Isolde, and Siegfried are here. I was in their box yesterday evening for *Rheingold*. I don't wish to criticize, but really both the staging of this masterpiece and the sets are most inadequate and tawdry. We had an entirely different impression of *Rheingold* at Bayreuth. Extraordinary works are hardly suited to ordinary stage productions. When the grandiose and the sublime are lacking, only the carcass is left.

Wagner was a thousand times right not to build his Bayreuth theatre along the lines of the Grand Operas of Berlin, Vienna, Milan, Paris, where the singers have to exert themselves, not to the advantage of art, in halls which are far too large. Audiences of fifteen hundred are large enough. Nowadays, it is only a matter of box-office receipts. Triviality and brutishness!

On the way I read two hundred well-written pages by Hippeau on *Berlioz intime*.[12]

Sad, oh sad!

Berlioz has ensconced himself in his fulminations against "cretins and scoundrels" and in his illusions. His letters to General Lwoff [Lvov] seem to me lamentable.

Your

FL

---

12. Paris, 1883.
Ed. note: For reproduction of original of this letter, *see* endpapers of this volume.

Sunday, August 31, 84
Munich

Lenbach is painting a fourth portrait of your very humble servant. Tomorrow I have a sitting. Day after tomorrow I'll wire M. S[ach] asking whether I will find him at Wilhelmsthal or at the Wartburg on Wednesday. Otherwise, your FL will be returning straight to Weimar.

———

Thursday morning, October 30, 84
Vienna

At Nuremberg I spent a day and a half with L. Ramann discussing music: theory methodical, practical, aesthetic. I left Nuremberg at 11:00 P.M., on Sunday, arrived here Monday at 10:00 A.M., and have seen only my cousin, her two children, and Bösendorfer—a rare friend.

On leaving Weimar I wrote Princess Marie Hohenlohe a note about my visit here. She sent a reply as early as Monday to the Schottenhof to say that if my cousin was not afraid of scarlet fever, from which her daughter was recovering, she would be glad to see me again.

Accordingly I called on her Tuesday. Otherwise I called on no more than three people.

To my very pleasant surprise I ran into Countess Dönhoff at *Die Meistersinger* on Tuesday. She is in Vienna (her favorite spot) in order to look after her old tutor Martino, who has just had a very serious operation.

Yesterday evening there was a small gathering of eight people at Standhartner's. Mlle Standhartner being a very good pianist, Madame Dönhoff parsifalized four hands with her, and as for me I accompanied her fairly badly in Zarembski's Polish dances.[13] In addition, Hellmesberger played my *Romance Oubliée* admirably. His Exc. Baron Hoffmann, who came in after dinner, told me that he is giving *Cellini* again this winter. In March Rubinstein will conduct his *Néron*.

Your FL will be at Pressburg in three hours, and in Budapest by nine.

13. Opus 21.

I'm very much annoyed by the disappearance of the two newspapers you were so kind as to send me. I read at once half the speech by Saint-Saëns at the formal session of the Institut, but because of the small type I postponed the Duc d'Aumale's speech until the following day, and next morning I was unable to lay my hands on the two newspapers which I will try to find.

Please have your Karl send me at Budapest two copies of the photograph on sale at Held's of my room at the Hofgärtnerei.

Thursday, November 5, 84
Tetétlen

I left Vienna Thursday and stopped off for a few hours in Pressburg, on which I have no more to report than on Budapest. Saturday I arrived here. The little house next to Zichy's, which he built with me in mind, provides me with a slightly more roomy lodging than the Hofgärtnerei. I am told there is a room for Gille.

We are waiting for Teleki in order to settle our excursion into regions unknown to you—Szatmár, Nagyban [Nagybánya]. Ábrányi and Bösendorfer will be with us.

I'll probably be back in Pest a few days ahead of time, for Bülow's concert (with his Meiningen orchestra) on November 22.

Thanks for the fine summary of the Russian article which Lo made for me. The author is right in dating my sympathy for Russian music —not that which used to be sung in the imperial chapel and made Mme Catalani cry and Berlioz, almost, too—from the year '42. The vitality and charm of Glinka's operas attracted me. I often used to see Glinka at my home, for he rarely went out in society. I transcribed the *Marche Tcherkesse*, and used to play at the St. Petersburg theatre another transcription of *Russlan*, very brilliantly arranged by Vollweiler—an artist who died too young. For this performance, which was not much applauded, I used a recently invented piano with two keyboards, of which the second imitated stringed instruments. Countess Dönhoff, whom one of my friends used to call Sakuntala, does not suffer at all from Roman fever. She suffers rather from W̲e̲g̲ than from Heimweh, as Mme Moukhanoff used to say. She intends to return to her lodgings, Via Gregoriana, shortly before Christmas.

Your very humble

FL

Continue to write to Budapest.

November 13, 84
Tetétlen

My two visits, to Szatmár and Kolto, have been canceled. Monseigneur Bishop Schlauch is with the delegation in Budapest, and my most excellent friend Alexander Teleki—my traveling companion in Russia, in '43—is in bed. He has just published a few admirable lines dedicating his third volume to me.

Tetétlen's only landscape is the plain and the Puszta. The garden landscaping is recent. People on horseback hunt a few unfortunate hares and spend hours playing c̲r̲o̲q̲u̲e̲t̲ (I don't know how to spell this word); these two forms of entertainment are alien to me. But in the evening I enjoy a game of whist with partners as skillful as Lassen. Even better, in the morning, a chapel serviced by an aged Franciscan to whom I yesterday explained the *Cantico del sol[e]* (with Messer *lo frate sol[e]*, *suor Luna, frate Vento e Fuoco*).

Except on Sundays and High Feast days, only I attend mass, and the only Catholics are about ten employees of Zichy. The thousand or so inhabitants of the village are Protestants.

My cottage, about a hundred paces from Z[ichy]'s residence, which also has only one floor, is most convenient. I'll be staying there until

Monday next when I return with Géza Zichy and his brother Ernest to Budapest, where I will hear Bülow's concerts.

Thanks for the photograph of the Hofgärtnerei. Your very humble FL ever lives in his thoughts across the street from you.

Thursday morning, December 4, 84
Budapest

Your sagacity and perspicacity are rarely at fault. Thus they had rightly guessed that I'm going to undertake a friendly task in behalf of Géza Zichy. This is the orchestration and rearrangement of a long ballad: "The Enchanted Lake" (*Zaubersee*),[14] in which the composer has introduced three charming melodies which, however, do not combine happily. He is as ignorant of the difficult art of transitions as he is of that of orchestration – – – – The instrumented ballad will run to about thirty printed pages. In order to complete them as I promised, I will stay here until Monday evening and only arrive in Rome Wednesday or Thursday.

The cold is intense. I have hardly left my room since Sunday.

Thanks for the extracts from Taine, Metternich, and Pailleron's very original address at the Academy.

When will *planton* [*piantone*][15] again discharge the duties he likes best, of reading and playing music in duet with you?

Unvaryingly yours

FL

December 6

Please write to the Hôtel Vittoria, Rome. I shall perhaps end by returning to the Hôtel Alibert because of its proximity to the Babuino. Crossing the Piazza di Spagna is no fun for me.

14. G 377; R 451, *Der Zaubersee*.
15. Army orderly; i.e., FL.

The little enclosed announcement is causing something of a stir here. Anyway, I'll take advantage of it to spend more time in my room.

FL

Wednesday I'll be in Rome.

———

Friday, December 12, 84
Rome

Finally I wrote from Budapest, asking that the quarters I occupied two years ago with Daniela be reserved for me—except for her room. So please write to Hôtel e Via Alibert, Rome (Italy).

Following Mme Hillebrand's invitation I spent a day with her in Florence. Her husband's death has left an aching void in her life; but being a woman of intelligence and character, she accepts the new situation courageously, without outwardly betraying undue melancholy. I paid no visits in Florence where I only saw, at Mme Hillebrand's, Buonamici Mackenzie—a remarkable composer of Scottish origin. His opera *Colomba*[16] (after Mérimée's novel) was a marked success in London, as were his dramatic cantata *Jason*,[17] a symphony, and a symphonic composition (after a ballad by Keats),[18] of which I recommend to you the arrangement for four hands. Mackenzie, whose age is between thirty and forty at the most, has already published other works, among them some Scottish rhapsodies. He is a gentleman, and comes to Florence fairly often, which his financial means permit—in order to work there more comfortably than in London.

I also saw again an ex-professor of the *Kunstschule* at Weimar, Boecklin, whose reputation is now firmly established. His personal income permits him to build a house with a fine studio in Zurich.

16. First performed April 9, 1883, in London.
17. Opus 26, 1882.
18. *La Belle Dame sans merci.* Opus 29, 1883.

When you see Monseigneur again, ask him whether he has visited the exhibition in Berlin of the works of the highly reputed sculptor Hildebrand. Hil[debrand] is from Weimar, and M. S[ach] ordered a statue from him during his stay in Florence.

Sgambati was waiting for me at the station, and we'll go on seeing each other as good friends. His symphony was given with full orchestra at a large Court concert, an unprecedented event.

Unvaryingly your

FL

———

Friday, December 19, 84
Rome
(Hôtel Alibert)

The note you sent to the Hôtel Vittoria was immediately forwarded to me at the Hôtel Alibert. One gets some sun in the morning, and I have a fairly good fire during the day and in the evening; so there is nothing to complain about. I have not been out for three days. Sunday I left cards on MM. de Keudell and Schlözer, at whose house there was a *pranzo diplomatico* on Tuesday, followed by a very fashionable [sic] musical soirée. Mme de Hegermann, formerly Mme Moulton (one of the most elegant figures of Paris in the last ten years of the empire), now the wife of the Danish Minister in Rome, sang delightfully some Grieg *Lieder*, one or two romances by Massenet, and at our lively insistence, after letting herself be asked several times, Gounod's *Medjé*,[19] which Schlözer dotes on. M. de Lilienkron, the son whom you saw in Weimar, played a Chopin nocturne on the cello and a caprice by Popper. M. and Mme de Keudell were so kind as to introduce us to the first movement of the Brahms Quartet[20] (in C minor, 9/8) playing it for four hands with perfection. Finally, fried chicken having been served on the

19. A *chanson arabe*, 1865.
20. Opus 51, No. 1.

table, I played my <u>fried chickens</u>, after recalling how, in former days, they were invented and made famous in Paris by Princess Metternich.

We were eight for dinner: Mme Hegermann, Mme Lilienkron, and six gentlemen (Arco had another invitation); and Mme de Keudell, who is nursing her baby, arrived with her husband for the soirée to which no one else had been invited. Thus we had music in private.

The next day, Wednesday, I saw the Keudells and Schlözer again for dinner (at Santa Maria Maggiore) with Cardinal Hohenlohe, almost younger looking and in fine ecclesiastical humor despite his resignation from the bishopric of Albano.

This evening I shall have the honor of dining in the same grand company at the Palazzo Caffarelli.

Count Bobrinski has sent me word. I was out when he came to see me. Yesterday I returned his call at the Villa Malta without finding him in. Thus the "thermometer of public health in Rome," as to which you wish to reassure your family, is more than satisfactory.

Umilissimo servo

FL

———

Sunday, December 28
Rome

My social life in Rome continues. I think I already told you that after the dinner and private musical evening at our friend Schlözer's, Cardinal Hohenlohe invited a few people to dinner: the German ambassador and his wife, the quasi-ambassador Schlözer, etc. Starting with oysters accompanied by Château d'Yquem and ending with *timbale glacée*, the meal was excellent and the conversation lively. Likewise at the Palazzo Caffarelli, where Mme Helbig and Sgambati played *Die Ideale* beautifully, and Sgambati regaled us with several new and short, but charming, fantasies.

At Count and Countess Bobrinski's I made the acquaintance of your cousin Ernest. His reputation as a wit is very well established here. I am told that his sallies have hurt his career – – – –

Wednesday evening there was a fine Christmas tree at M. de Keudell's, at which only the staff of the two German embassies and your very humble servant were present.

On the evening of Christmas day there was a family dinner at the house of Duke Sermoneta. Counting Donna Ersilia's children, the family numbers at least fifteen or so members. Sermoneta's third son, Roffredo, who is my godson, has an extraordinary talent for music. He played for us in very praiseworthy fashion my transcription of Mendelssohn's *Lied, Auf Flügeln des Gesanges*.[21]

I have told everyone of your forthcoming arrival here. So, more soon.

Your very humble

FM

---

21. G 547, 1; R 217, 1.

1885

The bad reputation of Italian railroad cars seems to me exaggerated. I was perfectly comfortable in second class from Florence to Nabresika. During this fourteen-hour trip I was almost always left alone (with Mihal). On Wednesday I was able to read, have a bite to eat, meditate, and sleep as I wished, and to do the same that night and the following day in a better Austrian coach until Budapest. This does not mean that I find any pleasure in traveling, quite the contrary. I do it only from a sense of duty, possibly illusory – – – – my tastes are most sedentary, and few people are as satisfied as I to stay quiet and think. Since my youth, Victor Hugo's lines have remained in my memory:

> *Reste à la pauvreté*
> *Reste à la solitude*
> *Et ne te fais étude*
> *Que de l'éternité.*[1]

I have been seeing some of my friends here who are not averse to company. Géza Zichy stays in his room nursing a bad cold he caught as he was leaving after one of his successes. Albert Apponyi too. Mihalovich is expecting the success of his opera *Hagbarth und Signe*,[2] which has already been given in Dresden, and will be given again here in

---

1. Remain poor, / Remain solitary, / And reflect only / On eternity.
2. First performed March 12, 1882, in Dresden. A performance in Hungarian was given on January 17, 1886, in Budapest.

Hungarian in the spring. Cardinal Haynald is slightly unwell but attends social functions in spite of his sharp differences with the Prime Minister, Tisza.

The event of the Budapest stage is the performance of Erkel's new grand opera: *Istvăn Király*[3] announced for the end of February. This same composer has already had the satisfaction of more than two hundred performances here of his *Hunyady László*[4] and about a hundred of his *Bánk-Băn*,[5] not counting other less favored works; but none of them has up till now had the good fortune of crossing the Hungarian frontier, so that his name and his compositions remain unknown even in Vienna.

Steadfastly your very humble old servant

FL

————

February 26, 85

Budapest

I am again guilty of being late, and for the same reason—or rather for the same fault as formerly. This fault is writing music, a task which tires me greatly and which I only carry out unhappily, finding my talent very inadequate for the lively expression of my thoughts. Everything seems to me listless and colorless – – – –

In this month of February I have written some forty pages of Hungarian music: A) a Rhapsody[6] for the album of the Exhibition which is to open on May 1. It will be entirely national, so that there will be only Hungarian works and objects in great quantity, and some of them

3. First performed March 14, 1885, in Budapest.
4. First performed January 27, 1844, in Budapest.
5. First performed March 9, 1861, in Budapest.
6. G 244, 18; R 106, 18.

of great value. Munkácsy is sending a painting. Antique and modern gold and silverware will be magnificently represented.

B) Modestly, let me mention another Rhapsody[7] written for my old friend Ábrányi—plus a *Csárdás Obstiné*[8] and a very Magyar Funeral March.[9]

The social event in Pest for the month of February was the fancy dress ball given by Countess Ladislas Festetics (formerly Princess of Monaco). She wore a costume as Catherine de Médicis which people claim cost 20,000 florins, not counting the additional value of the diamonds and pearls. The Duchess of Coburg, as Elsa, and Countess Georgina (?) Károly, as Catherine Cornaro, rivaled the mistress of the house in luxury and charm. Albert Apponyi was dressed as Marquis Posa, maliciously called Huguenot by the press. His last opposition speech in the Chamber of Deputies on the imminent reform of the Upper House is a masterpiece of eloquence and of parliamentary style. It was extremely applauded and admired; but for the time being the President of the Council, Tisza, is firmly rooted in, and supported by, the highly powerful auxiliary of the Jewish financiers, without whom all credit is destroyed. War and peace between nations rest in their hands. They control the stock exchange and public opinion through the press—two sovereignties which the most majestic sovereigns cannot match.

Speaking of which, I recall a remark by Cardinal Antonelli (someone, incidentally, whom I admired only moderately in spite of his spurious popularity among diplomats, princes, and princesses): *Les journaux, ce sont les Jouifs.*

Too bad for the Christians, for letting themselves be thus dominated!

Tomorrow I'll write to Countess Bobrinska to tell her about my present of paprika. This red spice has certain advantages over the best peppers. It can be pleasantly used with fish and meat, with almost any sauce, and does not have the bite of cayenne pepper.

---

7. G 244, 19; R 106, 19.
8. G 225, 2; R 45, 2.
9. G 206; R 84.

Taste it at the Villa Malta.

Please give Peterle my warmest greetings.

FL

It won't be long before I write to you again. My eyes are better. I read "Bonnet" before going to sleep.

———

March 3, 85
Budapest

My constant advice is never to worry about poor me.

I exist, after a fashion—and as long as this lasts my only worries concern another world.

Day before yesterday, M. Sach wrote me a few friendly lines from Vienna where, as you know, he is being feted, coddled, courted, and almost glorified. We had given each other no sign of life in nearly four months and I thought that the letter I sent to Biarritz in October had earned me his marked disfavor. S[ach] has kept his disapproval within bounds and deigns not to forget that I served him faithfully for some thirty years.

Did the way I signed my telegram yesterday amuse you? <u>Grill</u> is the name you invented and applied to an excellent Hungarian fish, known only under a quite different name.

The inability to speak which Mother Nature has imposed on fishes often makes me feel envious.

As ever your not very loquacious

FL

Do please convey my steadfast attachment to Duke Onorato Sermoneta.

Thank you for the Victor Hugo *Saint-Victor*. When my eyes and my weariness permit I read Taine's *Les Origines de la France contemporaine*. Some politicians with good minds assert that it is a masterpiece.

March 25, 85
Budapest

A very highly born young lady, having let herself be abducted by her lover, wrote to her mother: "I am guilty, but not a criminal." Well, I confess to being both guilty and almost a criminal because of my delays in writing. Need I repeat that it is once again my silly music which has, this whole month, kept me from writing letters. Those of which M. R[endano] spoke to you were invented. Tomorrow I'll reply personally to Rendano about matters concerning the founding of a conservatory in New York.

I had intended (as in the last two years) to spend Holy Week with Cardinal Haynald at Kalocsa. A church concert here prevents this. Other local tasks will keep me in Budapest during Easter week, and it will be only after mid-April that your incorrigible, too aged servant FL will have the pleasure of seeing you again in Weimar.

Please convey many messages of devoted friendship to father, son, and grandson (Roffredo, my godson, who is already a good musician) to Duke Sermoneta.

Saturday, April 11, 85
Budapest

From Holy Thursday to Easter Monday I was, as for the past two years, a guest of Cardinal Haynald at Kalocsa. He assured me that he had recently told Princess Reuss in Vienna that he would be coming to

Weimar about the middle of July in order to pay his respects to the Grand Duke.

In spite of a heavy cold I'll be day after tomorrow, Monday evening, in Pressburg where Rubinstein is being so kind as to give a benefit concert for the monument to Hummel, a native of Pressburg. Rubinstein and Leschetizky will play the Sonata in A flat for four hands,[10] one of the best works of the celebrated late *Kapellmeister*, whose piano compositions were formerly far more prized and played in salons and in public than those of Beethoven.

Your very humble FL will arrive in Vienna Tuesday evening and will spend five or six days at the Schottenhof.

The first performance in Vienna of Rubinstein's *Néron* will take place in the course of next week.

———

Wednesday, April 15
Vienna

Monday I attended the brilliant concert given by Rubinstein in Pressburg for the monument to Hummel. Saturday I will attend the dress rehearsal here of Rubinstein's *Néron*. Next Monday I'll stop over in Leipzig for a few hours in order to settle with Riedel the program for the Karlsruhe Festival, and will wire you as soon as I arrive in Leipzig.

The success of *Der Trompeter von Säckingen*[11] and of *Feldprediger*[12] is modest compared with that of the *Wiener Walzer*. I'll tell our friend Loën that this tiny ballet of only three scenes has, people assure me, already brought in 72,000 florins to the box office. Recently the *Wiener Walzer* was given as an epilogue to Gluck's *Orpheus*.[13] Both in Hades

10. Hummel's Opus 92.
11. Opera by Viktor Ernst Nessler, first performed May 4, 1884, in Leipzig.
12. Opera by Karl Millöcker, first performed October 31, 1884, in Vienna.
13. Opera, first performed October 5, 1762, in Vienna.

and in the Elysian Fields the hall was half empty. Subsequently it was sold out.

Your very humble

FL

Perhaps I'll be arriving in Leipzig Sunday morning at eleven. I'll let you know without delay. Please ask Pauline to prepare my rooms for Sunday evening.

Wednesday, June 3, 85
Strasbourg,
c/o M. von Putkammer

In telegraphic style I write to Your Highness: Monday (May 25), excellent performance of *Die Götterdämmerung* at Mannheim. Paur had held about a hundred rehearsals, counting partial rehearsals with voices, and bassoons.

Mlle Reiss's house is furnished in princely manner and in good taste. M. S[ach] and Wedel would approve.

I made the short trip from Mannheim to Karlsruhe with my two granddaughters, Isolde and Eva, and their aunt Frau Ritter.

During the Karlsruhe *Musikfest*, which was a great success from every point of view, the Grand Duke was worthy of the highest praise. He avoided both polite banalities and stiff or clumsy condescension. I am deeply grateful to him. Mottl was admirable.

In spite of my two letters of regret, here I am at Strasbourg. This evening we'll have a fine performance of the enclosed program.

Day after tomorrow morning your very humble FL will be in Antwerp.

Write to Antwerp, c/o M. Lynen.

Wednesday, June 10, 85
Antwerp

Yesterday I sent you the program of Sunday's concert, a brilliant performance by an excellent orchestra (from Brussels) conducted with great intelligence and warmth by Franz Servais. On Monday my Mass for male voices[14] was extremely well sung at the church of St. Joseph. Peter Benoit, the musical Rubens of Antwerp, conducted, and he had rehearsed conscientiously. Yesterday, Tuesday, I had the honor of greeting the King and Queen at the exhibition. In the evening there was a splendid fête with rich costumes and *tableaux vivants* at my most hospitable *padrone di casa*, Lynen. More than 150 people had been invited, including a few Ministers from other countries accredited to Brussels: Chotek, Maffei, Villeneuve, and Montebello. There was a fancy dress ball on the garden lawn with electric lighting, to the general satisfaction and enjoyment of all.

Tomorrow I'll spend the day at Halle with the Servais. The Prince of Caraman, whom I missed in Brussels (Saturday), will be coming to Halle with his daughter and son. There we will hear Zarembski's new Quintet,[15] said to be most remarkable, as well as several of his new compositions for four hands, plus an unpublished quartet by Joseph Servais. I shall ask Franz to play an Act from his *Jon*.

Saturday evening I'll be at Aix-la-Chapelle, where Kniese is organizing a Liszt concert for Sunday, and on Tuesday evening in Weimar your very humble FL will come to give you details about his peregrinations.

Your very humble

FL

————

14. G 8; R 485.
15. Opus 34.

Thursday, July 16
Weimar

These brief lines are responsive to your wishes. I immediately conveyed your message to Karl—who reads periodicals to me. He has
already sent off to you the *Débats* and the rest.

Herewith the latest piece by Dr. Pfeiffer, plus a review of the brilliant success of Mlle Schnobel's concert, which I attended at Sulza,
while recalling my previous visits to these parts – – – –

M. S. came to see me day before yesterday morning. His son had invited me to dinner on Sunday at Ettersburg. I regretted because of a
previous engagement.

A telegram from Bülow has informed me that he is held back in
Meiningen by gastric flu.

Klindworth, who is now and rightly so a musical personality in
Berlin, was here with me yesterday with the already very famous
Eugène d'Albert.

Very humbly

FL

[Saturday] July 25, 85
W[eimar]

While awaiting your categorical answers on Ionic and Lydian modes
—plus the various rhythms which Plato prohibited in his *Republic*, Karl
reads the German newspapers to me very well nearly every evening.
In the venerable *Die Allgemeine* there is an analysis of the new novel,
Cruelle Enigme, by Paul Bourget (a correspondent of the *Débats*).

The theme, with its infinite variations, remains eternal: love. The
author is pessimistic with regard to the fair sex. He draws upon a verse
of Alfred de Vigny: *Ah! plus ou moins la femme est toujours Dalila*—and
worse still, from the same poem by de Vigny, which I can no longer
quote, entitled *La Colère de Samson*.

Neither Samson nor Delilah is today at Ettersburg.

For this anniversary of the birth of the Hereditary Grand Duchess, we have been invited, at three o'clock, to a picnic (*Gartenfest*). There will probably be many children on the lovely lawn, with a view of Ettersburg, laid out by the late Prince Pückler.

Very humbly

FL

Monday

Clément has told you about my musical excursion to Halle on Saturday. The performance of Grell's Mass (with sixteen parts) was admirable, and the work deserves unqualified respect. In both cases one must have Germans.

Yesterday morning M. S[ach] wrote me a friendly little note of reproach. He went with Mme S[ach] to Frankfurt where he talked with the King of the Netherlands. M. S[ach] has invited me to dinner at the Roman House.

FL is very humbly following your <u>ukase</u> partially but with complete obedience.

August 2, 85
W[eimar]

Princess Elsi was moved to Ettersburg today. Her convalescence is slow. If you have not already read some very laudatory lines on Princess E[lsi] in the *Illustrierte Zeitung*, Leipzig, of July 25, I'll show it to you when you return. On the same day there was a small dinner at Ettersburg in honor of the birthday of the Hereditary Grand Duchess. The mother-in-law and father-in-law were present. Beust won general approbation by talking about the article on Elsi in the *Illustrierte*.

The hereditary couple went to Scheveningen yesterday. Gille leaves

Wednesday for Wiesbaden, having been told by Bodenstedt that there is no longer any danger.

The articles in the *Débats* which you so kindly sent delight me, for they conform perfectly to the opinion I have several times expressed, at the risk of being refuted or even of starting an argument – – – –

Personally, I hardly knew Veuillot, but in spite of his anti-musical nature I held him in much higher esteem than one usually professes for celebrities.

Your very humble abandoned

FL

———

Tuesday, 9 o'clock
[August?]

Today the Munich theatre starts at a quarter past five. I will wait for you here until five.

Would you like to keep the Höhle *pianino* in one of your rooms? It has already had the honor of staying under your roof.

Please let me know your orders at once, because of the porters who are going to arrive here with the Ibach *pianino*.

Your very humble

FL

———

October 18, 85
Schloss Itter
c/o Sophie Menter

Lassen is on the road to recovery; however, he will have to request an extension of his leave. Dr. Wiederhold, director of electric treatments at Wilhelmshöhe, calls Lassen's illness a congestion of the marrow of the spine. I don't know enough to be able to distinguish between the known diseases of the marrow of the spine, but it seems that they differ considerably, for one recovers from some of them and usually dies from the others.

In any case Wilhelmshöhe is the best place for Lassen in his present condition. He benefits from strolls in the admirable park, his appetite is good, he sleeps well, is even able to write a little, and plays dominoes with Adelheid who nurses him like a sister of mercy. Their apartment consists of two pleasant rooms which communicate with each other through an open door. They dine at the doctor's table. For supper L[assen] contents himself with a glass of lemonade while regretting the beer of Weimar and, contrary to his habit, goes to bed at ten o'clock and rises at seven.

To my great pleasure *The Barber of Bagdad*[16] was a complete success at the two first performances on Thursday and Friday. I was only able to attend the one on Friday. Baron Perfall and Levi assured me that this remarkable and charming work (perhaps a little too subtle for the general public) will remain in the repertory of the Munich theatre. Gura was most excellent in the part of the "Barber," and his colleagues were very satisfactory.

Alex[ander] Ritter's one-act opera was also very well received. In my time at the Weimar theatre Ritter had enlisted as a volunteer in the violin section. For several years he has been a member of the Meiningen orchestra. The title of his opera is *Der faule Hans.*[17]

I'm sending you herewith a fairly explicit article from the *Allgemeine Zeitung* (*Beilage* [supplement] of Sunday, October 18) and will ask you to pass it on to Baron Loën. The other Munich papers were also very favorable to the two operas of Ritter and Cornelius.

Saturday I dined at Levi's. The guests were Mme Raff and her very intelligent daughter; Mme Cornelius, widow; Mme and M. Ritter; etc.

Do you know a book by Count Leo Tolstoy entitled *Ma Religion*

16. See p. 277.
17. First performed October 15, 1885, in Munich.

(published by Fischbacher, Paris)? Levi greatly admires the chapter on a parallel between Christianity and Judaism, and considers that nothing as convincing on this dualism has hitherto been written.

Be so kind as to correct a culpable act of negligence on my part. The album bound in red, containing thirty *Lieder* dedicated to the Grand Duchess, was accidentally left behind on one of the pianos at the Hofgärtnerei. Please fetch it and ask Mlle de Watzdorf to return it to the sovereign.

Because of the floods at Rotzen and Ala plus Sophie Menter's departure, tomorrow, for Christiania, I'm in a complete confusion. Hence not possible to give you an address until your very humble FL shall have again written to you.

Tuesday [October?]
Florence

After arriving here yesterday morning I wrote at once to Count Arco to thank him for having so obligingly (on your insistence) made my trip easier. Tomorrow in less brilliant fashion I shall go to Budapest, whence your incorrigible old FL will write to you without delay.

November 16
Rome

I was writing you these lines during a most sad awakening at the Villa d'Este. The bells of the Franciscan church were tolling some Mass of the Dead, and I was immersing myself in my memories.

Among the best of these, musically speaking, are our four hands together. I protest against the calumnies you wrongly express about them.

Here, I have again seen the Keudells, Schlözers, Mme Helbig—ever lively and courageous—Sgambati, and Rendano.

Dräseke's *König Helge* has something of the sublime, especially in the *élan d'amour* repeated thrice *crescendo* – – – – and I don't find it very implausible that Helge should not have willingly swallowed Hebe's cup. Had this ballad appeared as a posthumous work of Schubert or Schumann, it would have had greater success. Unless they appear over a well-known name, the finest works risk passing unnoticed or unappreciated by the public.

Tomorrow I'll write to Loën to ask him to recommend Posse, an admirable harpist, to the Grand Duchess, so that she should deign to include him in the program.

[unsigned]

November 24, 85
Rome

No man can know, let alone feel a mother's grief.[18] It is not forbidden to condole with deep respect – – – –

Your son Pierre has written me some warm and noble lines. Be so good as to give him my enclosed reply, as I do not have his address.

The religion of sorrows with the supreme hope of divine mercy is that of Christians. Let us keep it faithfully with all our soul.

FL

18. Clément von Meyendorff, son of Olga von Meyendorff, had just died.

December 9, 85
Rome

[incomplete][19]

. . . to officiate there on Christmas day.

I don't go out much. To my regret I was unable to go to the Bobrinskis, who kindly asked me to dinner.

I will be in congenial company at Sermoneta's on Sunday evening.

Your sorrowing

FL

December 23, 85
Rome

Since one must live, one tries to do so as best one can short of mor-
tifying oneself greatly.

The only news I have for you is that Grand Duke Constantine has
written me very graciously inviting me to come to St. Petersburg.
You may recall that during my jubilee in Budapest, His Imperial Highness honored me with an explicit telegram which created a sensation at
the time. His letter, which I received yesterday, strikes the same note
of warm good will, and I'll probably go to Saint Petersburg in mid-April
after London.

Very humbly

FL

My weakness of sight is going from bad to worse. Soon I shall no
longer be able to write.

19. Of this letter only the closing few lines remain.

December 28, 85
Rome

I continue to see people you know here. They have been displaying the same affectionate feelings toward me for more than twenty years. It is not my nature to be ungrateful.

Cardinal Hohenlohe has retired to the Villa d'Este, and did not officiate at Christmas in the basilica of Santa Maria Maggiore of which he is Archpriest. People talk a lot about his financial troubles. I don't believe much in these, knowing that he has several strings to his bow. The death of his trusted servant Antonio has greatly affected him and is a source of inconvenience to him.

I frequently see Minister von Schlözer. He retains his brilliant intellectual liveliness and is completely romanized. The other evening at Cardinal Czacki's he assured us that if Bismarck had lived in Rome a little he would never have thought of the laws of May. Also a distinguished Roman prelate said: *Sua Eccellenza Schlözer è veramente un sant'uomo* [His Excellency Schlözer is truly a saintly man]—a title no one contests.

Did I tell you that at Duke Sermoneta's, M. and Mme de Keudell played excellently my *Salve Polonia*[20] four hands? – –

The Bobrinskis do not waver in their affability toward

your "not sick"

but sorrowing and sad FL

---

20. G 604; R 330.

1886

January 27, 86
Palazzo Malipiero
Venice

On the way here, Stavenhagen read me a good many pages from *Ma Religion* by Leo Tolstoy. This work may please people who enjoy fuzzy thinking. If, as on pages twenty-one and following, one advances the proposition *Ne résistez pas aux méchants* as the central and supreme axiom of Christianity, this means continually straddling the false and the absurd. Indeed we must resist evil men by whatever means we can if we are not to suffer the worst fate here below. Without government, without judges, without military power, without resistance to evil, what kind of society can be organized? Are we to open our doors wide to thieves and bare our throats supinely to murderers?

I have already pointed out to you the strange inconsistency of the philological chicanery of Tolstoy, on the word "resurrection." The Gospel teaches us that the Pharisees believed in resurrection; the Sadducees denied it. Jesus said to the good thief on the cross: "Tomorrow[1] thou shalt be with me in Paradise," and thus did our divine Savior finally proclaim the dogma of immortality.

This evening I shall be at my cousin's at Giorzia—and Sunday in Budapest.

Very humbly

FL

1. Not "Tomorrow," but "Today" in Luke 23:43.

My *padrona di casa*, Princess Hatzfeldt, is of a kindness which never ages, but continues to grow younger with the years.

February 18, 86
Budapest

Before hearing from you, I had written to beg you to write <u>large</u> because my eyes are growing steadily weaker.

Please tell Rendano that I invite him to drink the excellent Calabrian wine at Weimar this summer before or after the *Tonkünstler Versammlung* which will probably take place at Sondershausen.

The *Messe de Gran* is to be given in Paris on March 25 at the church of Saint-Eustache. The conductor will be M. Colonne and they assure me that everything will go well, unlike the unfortunate performance of the same mass in the same church in '66.

Your very humble FL will write again shortly.

February 24
Budapest

When I happen to be discourteous, this is much against my will.

To have regretted the very gracious invitation of Grand Duke Constantine—the head of all Russian music institutes—would have been worse than discourtesy: boorishness.

In about a week I shall receive the reply which will decide either my trip to Saint Petersburg or my return from London to Weimar.

Meanwhile I am confined to my room by a heavy cold. Because of the growing weakness of my sight I can only write seldom, even notes which are easier for me than letters.

I spend a couple of hours a day with my students, several of whom continue to distinguish themselves to the point of soon achieving the rank of "first-class" pianists—

They are so kind as to play new pieces for me, in print or in manuscript; yesterday the efflorescent *Voix du Printemps* (for four hands) by Mme Jaëll, and a Danish concerto, a massage of the ear.

Very humbly

FL

Monday, March 8
Budapest

Next Friday I'll be in Vienna (Schottenhof), and four days later in Liège. "The Siren" is president of the *Société d'Emulation* which is organizing a large concert for March 17. On the twenty-fifth, the *Messe de Gran* will be given in Paris. I'll let you know whether it was better performed and received this time than formerly, in '66.

According to the old proverb, a rolling stone gathers no moss. Nevertheless I shall be rolling from Paris to London on April 1 and then to Saint Petersburg.

Very humbly

FL

When you see Mme Helbig, please ask her if she received my letter from Venice (late January). As for the antagonism between R. and S., it will be difficult for R. to emerge the winner.

Friday, March 19, 86
Antwerp (c/o Lynen)

At the end of this month the entire Russian Court will be in the Crimea. Consequently I am postponing my trip to Saint Petersburg until October or November.

Day before yesterday the Liszt concert was given at Liège, with the *Messe de Gran*, the Concerto (in A), and a rhapsody remarkably well played by Mme Falk-Mehlig. Between these two compositions, two of my *Lieder* in which the singer was applauded.

Countess Mercy–Argenteau, courageous and active patroness of the new Russian music, now knows Russian and translates with enthusiasm the *libretti* of Cui's operas into French. The *Prisonnier du Caucase*[2] has already been given several times in the Liège theater, and people count on a success for *Angelo*[3] in Brussels.

Borodin's two symphonies appear on various programs in this country. Belgium is taking the lead. Aside from the Wagner:

Hérodiade (Massenet)
Sigurt[4] (Reyer)
Néron[5] (Rubinstein)
Les Templiers[6] (Litolff)

were first performed in Brussels or Antwerp.

Very humbly

FL

Tomorrow evening I'll be in Paris at the Hôtel de Calais, rue des Capucines.

———

Saturday morning, April 3

The success in Paris exceeds all expectations. At the home of Parisis, of *Figaro*, the admirable and great man M. de Lesseps reminisced to

2. Opera by Cui, first performed February 16, 1883, in St. Petersburg.
3. Opera by Cui, first performed February 13, 1876, in St. Petersburg.
4. First performed January 7, 1884, in Brussels.
5. Here Liszt seems to have erred. *Néron* was first performed November 1, 1879, in Hamburg.
6. First performed January 25, 1886, in Brussels.

me about his trip with you. He remains astonishingly vigorous, and a short time ago Mme de Lesseps presented him with their eleventh child.

Yesterday, after the second performance of the *Messe de Gran* at Saint-Eustache, attended by thousands of people, the emotion was lively and deep.

This evening your very humble FL will be in London.

———

April 13, 86
Westwood House
Sydenham (near London)

I intended leaving today, but the second performance of *Elisabeth*, which will take place at the Crystal Palace next Saturday, is keeping me here another week.

The two Liszt Concerts (as they are usually called), with a large orchestra, in addition to *Elisabeth* were a complete success, also a third and fourth, without orchestra.

I saw your sister again, first at *Elisabeth* last Tuesday, then at lunch at her house; and day before yesterday at dinner at the Prince of Wales's, where she said to me something strikingly true: "England is a country of small constraints and of great freedoms."

Tuesday evening, your very humble FL will be in Antwerp.

———

Sunday, April 18, 86
Westwood House
Sydenham (near London)

I was kept here by the second performance of *Elisabeth* at the Crystal Palace. Day after tomorrow I'll be in Antwerp by evening at the Lynens (Boulevard Léopold), and in Paris a week later. This time I'll be staying with my illustrious friend and compatriot, Munkácsy. His portrait of me is considered a masterpiece. Also the bust carved here by the most renowned sculptor in England, Böhm.

Forgive me for talking to you even indirectly about my sad face.

Before leaving Antwerp, your very humble FL will write to you.

The performance of *Elisabeth* at the Trocadéro (Paris) has been postponed to May 8. Before this there will be two concerts with all-Liszt programs.

In mid-May I'll be back at the Hofgärtnerei.

———

Wednesday, April 21, 86
Antwerp (c/o M. Lynen)

My very humble thanks for your letter which I received this morning. I'll be staying here until Easter Tuesday; then for a couple of weeks, with my illustrious compatriot and friend, Munkácsy—avenue de Villiers 53, Paris.

The performance of *Elisabeth* at the Trocadéro has been announced for May 8, before which there will be two concerts with all-Liszt programs.

I hardly expected such successes in Paris and London; but since they come to me spontaneously I cannot grumble. This would be boorish of me.

I'll give you details orally at Weimar in mid-May.

FL

In view of the growing weakness of my eyes, please write large.

———

Paris, May 2, 86
53 avenue de Villiers
(c/o M. de Munkácsy)

My enslavement by the public continues. It occurs more and more discreetly, so as to call for my warmest gratitude. In mid-May we'll have a heart-to-heart talk about it at Weimar.

Very humbly

FL

Paris, May 11, 86
53 avenue de Villiers
(c/o M. de Munkácsy)

I'll reach Weimar only next Sunday, May 16. Please be so good as to let Pauline and Mme Hartwig know, so that my quarters at the Hofgärtnerei should be ready toward noon Sunday.

Very humbly

FL

July 2
Bayreuth

Please ask the most illustrious Volkmann the names of the two doctors in Kissingen to whom he was so good as to recommend me. Stradal will go to Kissingen ten days or so before me to reserve my rooms, and I would like to give him the names of these two doctors.

Daniela is to be married tomorrow, Saturday, at Wahnfried before the civilian authorities—the Mayor and the notary, plus the witnesses.

The following day, Sunday, the religious wedding will take place in the Protestant church. The same evening the couple will leave for Switzerland and will pay a call on the father and father-in-law, Baron H. von Bülow.

Monday evening your *umilissimo servo*, FL, will
be at Colpach (Grand Duchy of Luxemburg).

———

Tuesday, July 6, 86
Colpach Castle
Grand Duchy of Luxemburg

What an astonishing improvement in calligraphy! I was able to read your last letter easily, without the slightest hesitation.

The *ricevimento* of more than eighty persons on Saturday evening for the signing of the marriage contract at Wahnfried was a complete success. The Mayor delivered a warmhearted address. In addition, the buffet, plentifully provided with cold dishes, contributed to the animation of the guests.

The next day, Sunday, in the very crowded Protestant church, before the exchange of the marriage vows, the pastor delivered an excellent homily on the thirteenth [sic] Epistle of St. Paul to the Corinthians —an admirable definition and glorification of love (*Caritas*!).

At noon there was a luncheon for thirty guests in the restaurant of the Wagner Theatre.

The bridal couple will arrive in Geneva today in order to call on Bülow. In a couple of weeks they will return to Bayreuth, and in August will settle in Bonn where, next autumn, Thode will begin, as *Privat Dozent*, to give his course at the university on the history of the plastic arts.

Colpach is an ancient and roomy house of two floors, rather than a castle. The rooms are well laid out and richly and elegantly furnished. The principal charm of the countryside lies in forests of oak, beech, ash, and pine. In the old vaulted chapel on the ground floor, Cardinal Haynald celebrated mass yesterday and today. He leaves again tomorrow for an audience with the King in Brussels.

Very humbly

FL

———————

Monday, July 12, 86

No incident occurred here after last Wednesday's dinner with Cardinal Haynald and the Bishop of Luxemburg. The days follow and resemble each other. Munkácsy is working here on a fairly large painting representing his studio in this house, with three young ladies and a view of the garden. He and I have one thing in common, which is that work makes us surly and sleepy. Fortunately his wife is neither the one nor the other, but always in the best of spirits.

We are usually about ten at table: the father and mother of Mme Munkácsy, Viscount de Suse and his wife, and two agreeable young ladies, pleasant friends of the lady of the house.

After luncheon and dinner, Stavenhagen, who excels at billiards, plays with M. de Suse. As for me, I play only two or three hands of whist in the evening with three ladies, and go to bed at ten thirty after the prescribed massages, infusions, and bathing of my eyes (not very effective).

Stavenhagen writes very well indeed my German letters, which I dictate, and Mme Munk[ácsy] the _____.[7]

Next Monday I shall spend a few hours in Luxemburg, and on the following day *sera de retour à B*[8]

[unsigned]

———————

7. FL wrote *alemandes* (sic) but presumably meant to write *françaises*.

8. This unsigned letter simply ends with the words, *"sera de retour à B"*. The next (and final) letter suggests that Liszt may have intended to write "Bayreuth."

Saturday, July 17, 86
Colpach

To my physical condition, already so pleasant, has now been added these five days a most violent cough which plagues me day and night. To comfort me, the doctor says that this type of cough is very tenacious. So far, neither cough medicine nor infusions, nor mustard plasters, nor foot-baths have rid me of it.

Stavenhagen will accompany me to Bayreuth, where Göllerich will take his place as secretary, for I can now only dictate letters.

He reads to me in German the continuation of Thode's book, and Mme Munkácsy keeps me abreast of the *Revue des deux mondes*, and has also read to me the articles in the *Débats*, which I thank you for having sent me.

I knew M. Zeller only by name and was not aware that he had published five volumes of history.

Thank you also for having written to Zhukovsky. I'll probably see him again at Bayreuth next Thursday, for Adelheid told me that she wanted to attend the two or three first performances at the same time as her friend from Brussels, Mme Tardieu, and Lassen.

One cannot imagine that Zhukovsky will deny himself the pleasure of accompanying Ad[elheid] to *Parsifal*.

I have promised to attend a concert in my honor at Luxemburg Monday evening, and on Wednesday your very humble FL will be at Bayreuth (Siegfried Strasse).

INDEX

INDEX

ABOUT, Edmond François Valentin (1828–85), French journalist, novelist, and playwright, 330

Ábrányi, Kornél (1822–1903), Hungarian pianist, composer, and author, 107, 108, 116, 236, 249, 468

Achille, *see* Colonello, Achille

Adam, Juliette (b. Lamber) (1836–1936), French author and editor, pseuds. Lam Massine, Juliette Lamber, Count Paul Vasili, 387, 460, 462, 463

Adelung, Mme d', wife of Russian official at Court of Württemberg, 104

Aeschylus (525–456 B.C.), 64

Agghazy, Károly (1855–1918), Hungarian pianist and composer, pupil of Liszt, 302, 329, 338

Agoult, Countess Marie Catherine Sophie d' (b. Flavigny)(1805–76), Liszt's first great love and mother of his three children; wrote under pseud. Daniel Stern, 22, 29, 32, 56, 63, 64, 101, 144, 153, 237, 285, 386, 416

Aibl, Joseph, founder of music publishing firm in Munich, 296, 378

Albert, Eugène d' (1864–1932), Scottish-German pianist and composer, pupil of Liszt, 433, 483

Albrecht, Prince and Princess, 276

Alembert, Jean Le Rond d' (1717?–83), French mathematician and philosopher, 121

Alexander I (1777–1825), emperor of Russia (1801–25), 120, 255

Alexander II (1818–81), emperor of Russia (1855–81), 110, 222, 259

Alton-Shée, Edmond d' (1810–74), peer of France, 144

Amberger, Gustav (1831–96), German landscape painter, 325

Ambros, August Wilhelm (1816–76), Austrian musicologist and critic, pianist, and composer, 122

Andrássy, Count Gyula (1823–90), Hungarian statesman and Austrian diplomat, 32, 34, 87, 106, 250, 251, 255, 283, 326, 343, 400

Andrássy, Countess, 341

Angeli, Heinrich von (1840–1925), Hungarian-Austrian painter, 341

Antokolsky, Mark Matveevich (1843–1902), Russian sculptor, 157

Antonelli, Cardinal Giacomo (1806–76), Vatican secretary of state, 53, 99, 143, 201, 216, 285, 306, 477

Apel, Pauline, 11, 47, 103, 107, 236, 275, 377, 391, 411, 415, 427, 481, 497

Apponyi, Count Albert György (1846–1933), Hungarian statesman, 103, 105, 107, 110, 113, 127, 128, 136, 227, 236, 262, 289, 335, 370, 373, 398, 475, 477

Apponyi, Georgina, sister of Albert, 136

Apponyi, Countess Thérèse (d. 1874), musician, close friend, and protectress of Liszt; wife of Count Antal, Austro-Hungarian statesman and envoy to Paris, 34, 36, 127

Aquinas, Saint Thomas (1225–74), 265, 322, 369

Arcadelt, Jacob (1514?–75?)
Ave Maria, 287

Arco, Count, 487

Arenberg, Duchess Eleonore Ursula d' (1845–1918), 44

Aristotle (384–322 B.C.), 311

Arneth, Alfred von (1819–97), Austrian historian, 155

Arnim, Count Harry Karl Kurt Eduard von (1824–81), German diplomat, ambassador at Rome, 216, 231, 233, 367

503

Auber, Daniel François Esprit (1782–1871), 254, 361
    La Muette de Portici, 29
Aubert, Eugène, representative of Braun, of Dornach, 305
Auersperg, Princess Frederika (Sister Raymondine) (b. 1820), 44
Auersperg, Princess Wilhelmina (1826–98), wife of chamberlain at Austrian Court, 127
Augusta (1811–90), empress of Germany as wife of Wilhelm I; sister of Carl Alexander, grand duke of Saxe-Weimar, 6
August Wilhelm, prince of Prussia (1722–1858), 416
Augusz, Baron Antal (1807–78), Hungarian statesman and art patron, musician, close friend of Liszt, 54, 56, 107, 319
Aumale, Duke Henri Eugène Philippe d'Orléans (1822–97), statesman and author, fourth son of Louis Philippe, king of France, 468
Autran, Joseph (1813–77), French poet, 333

BACH, Johann Sebastian (1685–1750), 190, 261, 264, 301, 394, 443, 452
    Fugue and Prelude in A minor, 276; *The Well-tempered Clavier*, 235
Baden, Grand Duke Friedrich of (1826–1923), 429
Bakunin, Mikhail Aleksandrovich (1814–76), Russian author and anarchist, 373
Balázs, Mme, Hungarian singer, 112
Balzac, Honoré de (1799–1850), 101, 441
Barberini, Cardinal, 461
Barbier, Paul Jules (1825–1901), French playwright and librettist, 187
Bardoux, Agénor (1829–97), French politician, 315
Bariatinska, Princess Cocona, lady-in-waiting to the empress of Russia, wife of Prince A. Bariatinski, field marshal, member of Russian Imperial Council of State, 162, 182, 211, 410, 416, 418
Bartolommeo, Fra (1475–1517), Florentine painter, 305

Bassani, Ugo, Italian author and composer, 367–69
Bassenheim, Countess, 347
Batta, Alexander (1816–1902), Dutch cellist, 242
Bauffremont, Prince Paul de (b. 1827), divorced Valentine de Riquet, countess of Chimay, who then married Prince George Bibesco, 221
Bazzini, Antonio (1818–97), Italian violinist and composer, 317
Beatrice Portinari (1266–90), 416, 417
Bechstein, Friedrich Wilhelm Karl (1826–1900), founded German firm of piano manufacturers, 188, 226, 227, 234
Beethoven, Ludwig van (1770–1827), 118, 138, 161, 175, 193, 204, 245, 267, 272, 296, 317, 329, 415, 448, 480
    Concertos, piano, Nos. 3, 4, 5, 330; Mass in D, 120; Sonatas, Ops. 101, 106, 109, 110, 111, 396; Symphonies: Ninth, 120, 305, 337, 343, 344, *Pastoral*, 391; *Variations on a Theme by Diabelli*, 60
Béhague, Mlle de, 458
Beidler, Isolde (1865–1919), daughter of Cosima and Richard Wagner; m. Franz Beidler in 1900, 279, 438, 463, 466, 481
Belgiojoso, Princess Cristina Trivulzio di (1808–71), Italian patriot, friend of Liszt, 297, 303
Benedict XIII (Pope, 1724–30), 354
Benedict XIV (Pope, 1740–58), 354
Benedict, Saint (480?–543?), 18
Bénédictus, Louis, French composer, 404
Benoît, Peter (1834–1901), Belgian composer and conductor, 482
Berlioz, Hector (1803–69), 111, 118, 136, 163, 193, 264, 317, 358, 362, 364, 390, 397, 423, 466, 468
    Benvenuto Cellini, 343, 344, 467; *Roméo et Juliette*, 370; *Symphonie de Harold*, 321, 329; *Symphonie Fantastique*, 277; *Les Troyens*, 249
Bermani, Venetian official, 232
Bernard Tolomei, Saint (1272–1348), 18
Bernini, Giovanni Lorenzo (1598–1680), 231, 299

Bernis, Cardinal François Joachim Pierre de (1715–94), French prelate and statesman, 354, 414

Berry, Duchess Caroline de (1798–1870), French aristocrat at whose home in Paris Liszt played as a youthful prodigy, 46

Bessel, Vasili Vasilievich (1842–1907), Russian music publisher in Saint Petersburg, 248

Betz, Franz (1835–1900), German baritone, 195

Beust, Count F. H. de, grand marshal of the Weimar Court, 8, 10, 11, 16, 51, 111, 191, 219, 372, 383, 394, 421, 436, 452, 484

Bey, singer, 186

Bibesco, Princess Georges (b. de Riquet, Countess Caraman-Chimay) (b. 1839), 222

Bibikoff, V., equerry of Grand Duke Constantine, 289

Bièvre, Marquis Georges François, maréchal de (1747–89), French author, 29

Bigot, Charles, artist, 344

Billault, Cardinal, 447

Birker, Benedictine abbot, 95

Bismarck, Prince Otto Eduard Leopold von (1815–98), 62, 80, 204, 205, 216, 251, 316, 342, 349, 460, 490

Bizet, Georges (Alexandre César Léopold) (1838–75)
 Carmen, 254, 263, 452; *La Jolie Fille de Perth*, 452

Blackford, Harriet Ely, pseud. Fanny Lear, 206

Blaze de Bury, Baron Henri (1813–88), French music critic and editor, 163, 209, 210, 335, 428

Blum, musician, 202

Blumer (Brunner?), pupil of Liszt, 317

Bobrinska, Countess, 19, 22, 23, 28, 96–99, 102, 140, 141, 146, 147, 149, 152, 159, 163, 168, 171, 172, 182, 206, 207, 210, 324, 334, 359, 360, 362, 391, 410, 412, 474, 477, 489, 490

Bobrinski, Count A., an official of the Russian Imperial Court and member of the Council of the Empire, 17, 19, 22,

23, 96–99, 140, 149, 159, 163, 168, 206, 210, 324, 325, 328, 334, 410, 412, 416, 418, 473, 474, 489, 490

Bock, *see* Bote and Bock

Bock, M. de, maréchal de noblesse de Livonie, tutor of the sons of Olga von Meyendorff, 77, 82

Bodenhausen, Mme de, 90

Bodenstedt, Friedrich Martin von (1819–92), German poet and translator, 69, 113, 307, 308, 485

Boecklin, Arnold (1827–1901), Swiss painter, 471

Böhm, Sir Joseph Edgar (1834–90), Hungarian-British sculptor, 496

Boileau-Despréaux, Nicolas (1636–1711), French critic and poet, 246, 314

Boissier, Marie Louis Gaston (1823–1908), French classical scholar, 263

Boiste, Pierre Claude Victoire (1765–1824), French scholar and lexicographer, 127

Bojanowski, Paul von (d. 1915), editor of the *Weimarer Zeitung*; head of the grand ducal library in Weimar, 54, 252

Bombelles, Count, 113

Bonaparte, Princess Julie, marchesa di Roccagiovine (1830–92), granddaughter of Lucien Bonaparte, 141, 143

Bonaparte, Cardinal Lucien (1828–95), 447

Bonghi, Ruggiero (1828–95), Italian scholar, author, statesman, 167, 417, 447

Bonnat, Léon Joseph Florentin (1833–1922), French painter, 349

Bonnechose, Cardinal Henri Marie Gaston de (1800–83), archbishop of Rouen, 52

Borghese, Prince Paolo of Sulmona (1845–1920), 361

Borodin, Alexander Porphirievich (1833–87), 281, 334, 377, 494
 Symphony No. 1 in E flat, 203, 222

Bösendorfer, Ludwig (1835–1919), Austrian piano manufacturer and music patron, 261, 270, 298, 467, 468

Bossuet, Jacques Bénigne (1627–1704), French priest and orator, 247, 337, 449

Bote and Bock, music publishing house

in Berlin founded in 1838 by Eduard Bote and Gustav Bock, later taken over by Bock family, 403, 424

Bott, Jean Joseph (1826–95), German violinist, conductor, and composer, 276, 286

Bouguereau, Adolphe William (1825–1905), French painter, 242

Bouhers, singer, 191

Bouillet, Marie Nicolas (1798–1864), French scholar and lexicographer, 62

Bourdaloue, Father Louis (1632–1704), French Jesuit theologian, 173

Bourdeau, Louis (1824–1900), French philosopher and author, 342

Bourget, Paul Charles Joseph (1852–1935), French novelist and critic, 483

Boutenieff, 408

Boutenieff, Mme, 408, 410

Boutenieff, Mlle Cocona, 408, 410

Brahms, Johannes (1833–97), 80, 419, 461 Concerto, violin, Op. 77, 371; *Ein Deutsches Requiem*, 462; Symphony No. 4, 462

Brandt, Fritz, on theatre staff in Bayreuth, transferred to Weimar, 457, 463

Brandt, Marianne (Marie Bischoff) (1842–1921), Austrian contralto, 149, 151, 186, 226, 276, 277, 300, 401

Brandus, French music publisher, 390

Braun, lithographic firm in Dornach, 305, 322

Brehmer, Dr. Hermann (1826–89), Liszt's physician, 280, 281, 312

Breitkopf & Härtel, music publishers in Leipzig, 56, 120, 161, 229, 288, 293, 357

Brendel, Karl Franz (1811–68), German critic and editor, 362

Brid'oison, character in Beaumarchais' *Le Mariage de Figaro*, 48

Broglie, Jacques Victor Albert de (1821–1901), French statesman and author, 425

Bronsart von Schellendorf, Hans (1830–1913), German pianist and composer, pupil of Liszt, 187, 190, 198, 240, 244, 276, 277, 286, 291, 333, 343, 356, 360, 371 *Frühlings Fantasie*, 420; *Trio*, 296

Bronsart, Ingeborg von (b. Starck) (1840–1913), Swedish-German pianist and composer, wife of Hans, pupil of Liszt, 277

Brückner, Max and Gotthold, of Coburg Court theatre, scene painters, 404

Brunelli, Geremia, Italian poet, 457

Bülow, Blandine Elisabeth von, *see* Gravina, Countess Blandine

Bülow, Daniela Senta von, *see* Thode, Daniela

Bülow, Baron Hans Guido von (1830–94), German pianist, conductor, composer; a favorite student of Liszt; in 1857 married Liszt's daughter, Cosima, who later divorced him to marry Wagner, 26, 34–40, 56, 60, 65, 75, 79, 83, 91, 111, 138, 139, 142, 143, 146, 150, 153, 217, 219, 220, 244, 245, 247, 286, 290, 333, 343, 344, 356, 360, 364, 372, 378, 379, 381, 390, 391, 394, 396, 397, 401, 402, 419, 420, 457, 460, 463, 468, 470, 483, 498 *Carnevale di Milano*, 26; *Nirvana Symphony*, 423; *Des Sängers Fluch*, 277

Buridan, Jean (d. after 1358), French scholastic philosopher, 385

Busch, Moritz (1821–99), German author, 323, 327

Byron, Baron George Gordon (1788–1824), 64, 109, 201, 339

CABANEL, Alexandre (1823–89), French painter, 242

Caetani, Princess Ada of Teano, wife of Onorato, 22, 218, 302, 359, 391, 408

Caetani, Duke Michelangelo of Sermoneta (1804–82), Italian patriot and Dante scholar, 22, 98, 140, 304, 474, 479, 489, 490

Caetani, Prince Onorato of Teano (1842–1917), Italian statesman, son of Michelangelo, 140, 141, 143, 163, 243, 256, 296, 297, 302, 327, 359, 361, 478

Caetani, Roffredo (b. 1871), son of Onorato, and Liszt's godson, 474, 479

Calderón de la Barca, Pedro de (1600–81), Spanish dramatist and poet, 353

Calixtus III (Pope, 1455–58), 151

Calvin, John (1509–64), 67, 80

Caraman-Chimay, Prince of, *see* Riquet, Joseph de

Card, Father Ronald de, 14

Carl Alexander (1818–1901), grand duke of Saxe-Weimar (1853–1901), 3, 4, 8, 11, 14, 16, 24, 32, 33, 39, 47, 49, 60, 70, 87, 89, 108, 111, 135, 144, 145, 150, 164, 171–173, 179, 191, 224, 239, 243, 257, 264, 266, 277, 282, 422

Carl Augustus (b. 1844), hereditary grand duke of Saxe-Weimar, son of Carl Alexander and Sophie, 33, 106, 113, 135

Carnot, Lazare Hippolyte (1801–88), French politician, journalist, and historian, 425

Caro, Elme Marie (1826–87), French philosopher and author, 16, 214, 337, 385

Caroline (1768–1821), queen of England, wife of George IV, 237

Catalani, Angelica (1780–1849), Italian singer, 468

Catherine II (1729–96), empress of Russia (1762–96), 255, 378

Catherine of Siena, Saint (1347–80), 19

Caux, Marquise de, *see* Patti, Adelina

Cavaillé-Coll, Aristide (1811–99), French organ builder, 342

Cervantes Saavedra, Miguel de (1547–1616), 309

Chambord, Count Henri Charles Ferdinand Marie Dieudonné d'Artois de, duke of Bordeaux (1820–83), Bourbon claimant to French throne as Henry V, 45, 46, 105, 190, 326, 327

Chambord, Countess de, 158

Chamfort, Nicolas-Sébastien Roch (1741–94), French writer and wit, 399

Champagny-Rospigliosi, Princess Fanny (b. Cadere)(1825–99), Liszt considered her the most intelligent woman in Rome, 28, 86, 119, 227, 231, 299

Charles, *see* Lehmann, Charles

Charles, Princess, *see* Marie Louise, Princess Charles

Chateaubriand, Viscount François René August de (1768–1848), 201, 385, 410, 416

Cherbuliez, Charles Victor (1829–99), French novelist, pseud. G. Valbert, 237

Chérémétieff, Mme, composed a minuet dedicated to Liszt, 161, 182

Chevicz, de, Russian diplomat, 160

Chigi, Prince Mario (1832–1914), 354

Chimay, *see* Riquet, Joseph de

Cholmelay, Countess Isabel, 232

Chopin, Frédéric François (1810–49), 175, 289, 292, 303, 307, 359
    Concerto No. 1 in E, Op. 11, 303; Nocturne in C minor, 54; Nocturnes, 265; Prelude No. 24, 210; Sonata No. 2 in B flat minor, Op. 35, 187, 281

Chotek, Count, Austro-Hungarian minister to Belgium, 482

Cicero, Marcus Tullius (106–43 B.C.), 144, 263

Cimosa, conductor in Trieste, 168

Cladel, Léon Alpinien (1835–92), French symbolist author, 330

Clarétie, Jules (1840–1913), French journalist and novelist, 330

Clement II (Pope, 1046–47), 93, 152

Clement IX (Pope, 1667–69), 231, 299

Clement XI (Pope, 1700–21), 9

Clement XIV (Pope, 1769–74), 121

Coburg, Duchess of, 477

Cocona, Princess, *see* Bariatinska, Cocona

Colet, Louise (b. Revoil)(1808–76), French writer, 316

Colonello, Achille (d. 1884), Liszt's valet, 419, 436, 458

Colonne, Edouard (1838–1910), French conductor and violinist, 492

Comte, (Isidore) Auguste (Marie François)(1798–1857), French mathematician and philosopher, 356

Considérant, Victor Prosper (1809–93), French social scientist and reformer, 356

Constant de Rebecque, Benjamin (1767–1830), French author and politician, 416, 417

Constantine Nikolaevich, grand duke (1827–92), son of Emperor Nicholas I, brother of Emperor Alexander I, 296, 334, 489, 492

Copernicus, Nicolaus (1473–1543), 353

Coquerel, Athanase Josué (1820–75), French clergyman and author, 245

Cornaro, Caterina (1454–1510), member of noble Venetian family, queen of Cyprus, patroness of art and literature, 57

Cornelius, Mme, wife of Peter, 486

Cornelius, Peter (1824–74), German composer and author, close friend of Liszt, 177, 217, 241, 333
    Barber of Bagdad, 277, 278

Corsani (Corsara?), Mlle, governess of Eva and Isolde Wagner, 419, 437, 442

Cossmann, Bernhard (1822–1910), German cellist, teacher, composer, played under Liszt in Weimar orchestra, 60, 65, 91

Coudenhove, Countess, wife of Count Karl and daughter of Mme Moukhanoff-Kalergis, 117, 273

Cousin, Victor (1792–1867), French philosopher and author, 209, 316

Cranach, L. von, aide-de-camp at Weimar Court, 378, 433

Cranach, Lucas (1472–1552), 433

Creptovitch [Khreptovitch], mother of Princess Bariatinska, 288

Croesus (d. 546 B.C.), king of Lydia, 451

Cruikshank, Mlle, 62, 363, 425

Cui, César Antonovich (1835–1918), 203, 334, 494
    Angelo, 494; *Le Prisonnier du Caucase*, 494

Curci, Father Carlo Maria (1810–91), Italian priest and author, 167, 172, 306, 323, 448, 449

Cuvillier-Fleury, Alfred Auguste (1802–87), French author and journalist, 124, 237, 295

Czacki, Cardinal Wlodimiro (b. 1834), 490

Czartoryska, Princess Marcelline (b. Radziwill)(1817–94), Polish noblewoman, pupil of Chopin, and follower of Liszt, 86

Czartoryski, Prince Marcel, 352

Czernicheff, Princess (b. Titoff), 57, 101, 141, 159, 172, 176, 179, 182, 211, 328

DANNREUTHER, Edward George (1844–1905), German-English pianist and critic, 289, 290

Dante Alighieri (1265–1321), 22, 29, 64, 153, 158, 324, 337, 346, 372, 416, 417, 438

Dargomizhsky, Alexander Sergeevich (1813–69), Russian composer, 357, 363, 365

Daubigny, Charles François (1817–78), 353

David, Ferdinand (1810–73), German violinist, composer, and teacher, 76, 78, 79, 198

Decazes, Louis Charles Élie Amanieu (1819–86), French statesman and diplomat, 255

Delacroix, Ferdinand Victor Eugène (1798–1863), 338

Delibes, Clément Philibert Léo (1836–91), 398
    Jean de Nivelle, 399

Déroulède, Paul (1846–1914), French author, playwright, and politician, 387

Descartes, René (1596–1650), 55

Deschanel, Émile Auguste Étienne Martin (1819–1904), French critic and author, 455

Detaille, Jean Baptiste (1848–1912), French painter, 447

Deutsch, Willy, pianist, 303

Devrient, Otto (1838–94), German theatre director, 240, 241, 278

Diabelli, Anton (1781–1858), Viennese music publisher and composer, 60

Diaz de la Peña, Narcisse Virgile (1807–76), French painter, 353

Dimmler, music director at Freiburg im Breisgau, 325

Dingeldei, Ludwig, pupil of Liszt, 319

Dingelstedt, Franz von (1814–81), dramatist and poet, director of Weimar Court theatre and of the Vienna *Burgoper* and *Burgtheater*, 39, 40, 60, 234, 238, 241, 248, 326

Dingelstedt, Mme de (b. Jennie Lutzer), singer, wife of Franz, 34

Disraeli, Benjamin, earl of Beaconsfield (1804–81), 251, 255, 388

Döllinger, Johann Joseph Ignaz von (1799–1890), German theologian, 43

Dondoukoff-Korsakoff, Prince, member of Russian Imperial Council of State, 326

Dönhoff, Countess Maria (b. Camporeale), member of Liszt-Wagner circle, 34, 57, 85, 101, 117, 124, 138, 273, 289, 348, 393, 395, 443, 444, 467, 469

Donndorff, Adolf von (1835–1916), German sculptor, 261

Door, Anton (1833–1919), Austrian pianist, 31

Doria, Prince, 24

Dorr, Anton, *see* Door, Anton

Dotter, Mlle, singer, married Julius Elkan, banker, 191, 197

Doudan, Ximénès (1800–72), French writer, 251, 253

Dräseke, Felix August Bernhard (1835–1913), German composer and author, friend and disciple of Liszt, 488
   Scherzo, 277

Dubez, Peter (1849–1890), harpist, member of Budapest opera, 287

Du Camp, Maxime (1822–94), French journalist and teacher, 439, 440, 444, 455

Ducci, Carlo, piano dealer, 317, 320

Duchatel, Countess, wife of French ambassador at Vienna, 443

Du Deffand, Marquise Marie (1697–1780), celebrated for her salon, 385

Dumas *fils*, Alexandre (1824–95), 102, 206, 211, 282, 371, 372, 374, 387

Dumas *père*, Alexandre (1802–70), 213, 330

Dumas, Jean Baptiste André (1800–84), French chemist and scholar, 371

Dunkl, Johann Nepomuk (1832–1910), music publisher in Budapest, pupil of Liszt, 107

Dupanloup, Mgr Félix Antoine Philibert (1802–78), bishop of Orléans, French prelate, and politician, 41, 42, 105, 127, 238, 323, 326

Duplessis-Mornay, *see* Mornay, Philippe de

Duprez, Louis-Gilbert (1806–96), French tenor and composer, 312

Durand, Marie-Auguste (1830–1909), French organist, composer, and music publisher, 396

Durazzo-Pallavicini, Count, 153

Dürer, Albrecht (1471–1528), 394

ECKERT, Mme, wife of Carl Anton Florian, German violinist, pianist, conductor, and composer, 196

Ehrlich, Alfred Heinrich (1822–99), Austro-German pianist, composer, and author, 253, 258

Eichel, d', official of Court of hereditary grand duke of Weimar, 264

Eitner, Robert (1832–1905), German musicologist and bibliographer, 60

Elisabeth Amalie Eugénie (1837–98), empress of Austria (from 1854) and queen of Hungary (from 1867), 235

Elkan, Julius, *Hofbankier* to the Weimar Court, 73

Elsi (Elisabeth), Princess (b. 1854), daughter of Grand Duke Carl Alexander and Grand Duchess Sophie, 307, 349, 352, 358, 425, 484

Emmerich, Robert (1836–91), German conductor and composer, 286, 291

Erard, Mme, wife of Sébastien, 314

Erard, Sébastien (1752–1831), founded French firm which manufactured pianos and musical instruments, 201, 314

Erdmannsdörfer, Max von (1848–1905), German conductor and composer, 382, 383

Erkel, Ferenc (1810–93), Hungarian composer, conductor, and pianist, 476
   Bánk-Bán, 476; *Hunyady László*, 476; *István Király*, 476

Essipoff, Annette Nikolaevna (1851–1914), Russian pianist, married Theodor Leschetizky, 247, 270

Esterházy, Prince Nicolas [Nikolaus], 122, 311

Esterházy, Prince Paul Antal (1786–1866), Austro-Hungarian diplomat, 110

Esterházy, Prince Paul Anton (1843–98),

grandson of Paul Antal, 106, 110, 122

Esterházy, Princess, wife of Paul Anton, 122

Étex, Antoine (1808–88), French sculptor, painter, and architect, 83

Ett, Kaspar (1788–1847), German organist and composer, 16

Eugénie (1826–1920), empress of France (1853–71), 124

Eulenburg-Wicken, Count Botho Heinrich zu (1804–79), Prussian government official, 241

Ezekiel, Moses Jacob (1844–1917), American sculptor, known as Sir Moses Ezekiel after being decorated by Germany and Italy; friend of Liszt, 394

FALLOUX, Count Frédéric Alfred Pierre de (1811–86), French politician, 323

Farina, Jean Marie (1686–1766), Italian chemist and merchant, 228

Fauré, Gabriel Urbain (1845–1924)
Sonata, 369

Fausti, Deacon Colomba, 221

Favre, Pierre (1506–46), French Jesuit theologian, 29

Faxelles, see Hillebrand, Karl

Félix, Father Célestin-Joseph (1810–91), noted preacher, 449

Feodora, Princess Hohenlohe-Langenburg (b. Princess of Leiningen)(d. 1872), 50

Ferenczy, Ferenc (d. 1881), Hungarian tenor of Weimar Court opera, 111, 384

Ferrari, Mgr, 26

Festetics, Countess Ladislas, 106, 477

Feustel, Friedrich, Bayreuth banker, friend, and supporter of Wagner, 256, 257, 290, 292

Féval, Paul Henri Corentin (1817–87), French novelist and playwright, 374

Field, John, 410

Fischer, Carl Ludwig (1816–77), German conductor, 286

Flaubert, Gustave (1821–80), 136, 140, 391, 450, 461

Florentine Quartet (1867–80), founded in Florence, 31

Flotow, Friedrich von (1812–83)
Martha, 97

Földvári, Emma, Hungarian aristocrat, 265

Fortunato, see Salvagni, Fortunato

Fourier, François Marie Charles (1772–1837), French social scientist and reformer, 356

Frances, Saint, of Rome (1384–1440)(b. Francesca Bussa di Leoni), founded Benedictine Oblate Congregation of Tor di Specchi, 18

Francis of Assisi, Saint (1182–1226), 172–73

Franck, César Auguste Jean Guillaume Hubert (1822–90)
La Rédemption, 188

Franz, Robert (1815–92), German composer, organist, and conductor, 72, 80, 85–86, 89, 161, 163, 167, 178, 362

Franz Josef I (1830–1916), emperor of Austria (1848–1916), 47, 106, 230, 235, 274, 294, 338, 340, 341

Frédault, Dr. Félix, 265

Frederick II, the Great (1712–86), king of Prussia (1740–86), 62, 92

Fredro, Count Alexander (1793–1876), Polish playwright, known as "the Polish Molière," 49, 57, 67, 404, 433

Freytag, Philipp (1840–1905), author, 347

Friedheim, Arthur (1859–1932), German-Russian pianist and composer, pupil of Liszt, 379, 383, 404, 411

Friedrich, Father Johannes (1836–1917), German theologian and historian, 157

Friedrich Wilhelm III (1770–1840), king of Prussia (1797–1840), 120

Friedrich Wilhelm IV (1795–1861), king of Prussia (1840–61), 241

Fritzsch, Ernst Wilhelm (1840–1902), music publisher in Leipzig, 22, 39, 77, 80, 442

Frommann, Alvine, 111

Fugel, Baron, 192

Fürstenstein, Count, 377

Fürstner, Adolf (1833–1908), founder of music publishing firm, 143, 403

GABLENZ, Baron Ludwig von (1814–74), Austrian field marshal, 123

Gaetana, Mlle, singer, 243

Gaetani, *see* Caetani

Gambetta, Léon (1838–82), French statesman and lawyer, 15

Garcia, Manuel del Popolo Vicente (1775–1832), Spanish singer, teacher, and composer, father of Maria Malibran and Pauline Viardot, 429

Garibaldi, Giuseppe (1807–82), 347

Gaul, Kitty, American student of Liszt, 104, 117, 222, 247

Gautier, Judith (1850–1917), French novelist and poet, daughter of Théophile, 253, 404, 405, 406, 410, 434

Gautier, Théophile (1811–72), 317

Gelasius II (Pope, 1118–19), 151

Gerbet, Mgr Olympe Philippe (1798–1864), French cleric and author, 444

Gérome, Jean Léon (1824–1904), French painter and sculptor, 242

Gevaert, François Auguste (1828–1908), Belgian music scholar and composer, 191, 192, 242

   Quentin Durward, 406, 454

Giedroyć, Prince Romuald (b. 1842), Russian nobleman and writer, 241

Gille, Carl (1813–99), German lawyer and court official at Jena; close friend of Liszt and first curator of Liszt Museum at Weimar, 22, 31, 39, 42, 48, 64, 73, 79, 87, 112, 190, 222, 252, 256, 259, 276, 278, 280, 300, 302, 304, 307, 322, 325, 328, 340, 366, 374, 428, 429, 434, 458, 463, 468, 484

Gioberti, Vincenzo (1801–52), Italian philosopher and politician, 169

Girardin, Delphine de (b. Gay)(1804–55), French poet and author, pseud. Vicomte Charles de Lannay, 166, 170

Girardin, Émile de (1802–81), French journalist and editor, 292

Glasenapp, Carl Friedrich (1847–1915), German author, biographer of Wagner, 301

Glinka, Mikhail Ivanovich (1804–57), 142, 213, 222, 468

   A Life for the Tsar, 139, 146, 343

Gluck, Christoph Willibald von (1714–87), 249, 256

   Orpheus, 480

Gobbi, Henrik (1842–1920), Hungarian composer and teacher; his career furthered by Liszt, 116

   Liszt-Cantata, 111

Gobineau, Count Joseph Arthur de (1816–82), French author, orientalist, and diplomat, 323, 359, 405, 442

Godebski, Cyprien (1835–1909), French-Russian sculptor, 286–88, 291, 331, 332

Goerwitz, poet, 355

Goethe, Johann Wolfgang von (1749–1832), 22, 29, 64, 102, 167, 181, 198, 200, 201, 203, 212, 238, 249, 349, 448

Goldmark, Carl (1830–1915), 254

   Die Königin von Saba, 254

Göllerich, August (1859–1923), German pianist and teacher, pupil of Liszt, 500

Gomes [Gomez], Antonio Carlos (1839–96), Brazilian composer

   Il Guarany, 28

Gortschakoff, Princess (b. Stourdza), wife of Constantine, 143, 218

Gortschakoff, Princess Agatha (b. Bakhmétieff), mother of Olga von Meyendorff, 358, 391

Gortschakoff, Prince Alexander Mikhailovich (1798–1883), diplomat, minister for foreign affairs and chancellor of the Russian Empire; uncle of Olga von Meyendorff, 249, 251, 255, 342, 367, 429

Gortschakoff, Constantine, son of Alexander, 220

Gotha, Duke Ernst II of (1818–93), also a composer, 302

Gottschalg, Alexander Wilhelm (1827–1908), composer, organist, and scholar, pupil and long-time friend of Liszt, 6–7, 24, 41, 48, 61, 74, 93, 215, 252, 258, 259, 260, 264, 286, 287, 290, 300, 302, 304, 354, 355, 371, 390, 417

   Orgel Repertorium, 300, 304

Gottschall, Rudolph von (1823–1909), German author and journalist, 272

Götz, Hermann (1840–76), German composer
    Der Widerspänstigen Zähmung, 189, 263

Gounod, Charles François (1818–93), 291, 336, 366, 426
    Faust, 97; *Gallia*, 426; *Marche Funèbre d'une Marionnette*, 366; *Medjé*, 472; *La Rédemption*, 449

Goupil, Adolphe (1806–93), art dealer in Paris, 454

Gratry, Father Auguste Joseph Alphonse (1805–72), French priest and philosopher, 14, 15, 120

Gravina, Count Biagio (1850–97), Italian nobleman; married Blandine von Bülow, 431, 463, 466

Gravina, Countess Blandine Elisabeth (1863–1941), second child of Cosima and Hans von Bülow, wife of Biagio, 431, 433, 463

Greffülhe, Viscountess Elisabeth, daughter of Prince Caraman-Chimay, 458

Greffülhe, Viscount Henri Charles (b. 1848), 324

Gregorovius, Ferdinand (1821–91), German historian, 152, 153, 154, 162, 219

Gregory VII (Pope, 1073–85), 65

Gregory XI (Pope, 1370–78), 18

Gregory XVI (Pope, 1831–46), 18, 361

Gregory of Nazianzus, Saint (325?–390?), a founder of the Eastern Church, bishop of Constantinople, 449

Greith, Karl (1828–87), German composer and organist, 16

Grell, Eduard August (1800–86), German organist and composer, 484

Grétry, André Ernest Modesti (1741–1813), Flemish-French composer of Walloon descent, 395

Grieg, Edvard Hagerup (1843–1907), 472

Grillparzer, Franz (1791–1872), Austrian poet and playwright, 6

Grimm, Baron Friedrich Melchior von (1723–1807), German-French author, 378

Grimm, Hermann (1828–1901), German art critic, teacher, and author, 167, 293, 295

Gross, Adolph, banker in Bayreuth, promoter of Wagner *Festspiele*, 429, 430, 466

Grosse, Eduard, trombonist and double bassist in Weimar Court orchestra; devoted to Liszt, who asked many services of him, 51, 55–57, 59, 95, 97, 100, 102, 104, 109, 184, 188, 195, 211, 215, 230, 232, 287, 329, 355, 404, 406, 411, 414

Grün, Count, 100

Grün, Mme, German mezzo-soprano, 195

Guérin, Mgr Paul (b. 1830), French cleric, 110

Guibert, Cardinal (1802–86), archbishop of Paris, 238

Guiraud, Ernest (1837–92), French-American composer, born in New Orleans
    Piccolino, 263

Guizot, François Pierre Guillaume (1787–1874), French statesman and historian, 45, 80, 253

Gura, Eugen (1842–1906), German bass-baritone, 486

Gustchen, *see* Watzdorf, Augusta

HAAS, M., Paris clockmaker, 155

Hadein, Baron de, official of the Weimar Court, 453

Hadrian (76–138), Roman emperor (117–38), 356

Hafiz, Shams ud-din Mohammed, 14th-cent. Persian lyric poet, 307

Haft, Mlle, violinist, 270

Hainauer, German music publisher, 317, 328, 331

Hamman, Edouard Jean Conrad (1819–88), Belgian painter, 191, 192

Händel, Georg Friedrich (1685–1759), 349, 452
    Almira, 363; *Athalie*, 48; *Israel*, 361; *Messiah*, 361

Hanslick, Eduard (1825–1904), Viennese music critic and aesthetician; opposed to Liszt-Wagner school, 61, 113, 258, 346, 456

Hardtmuth, photographer in Weimar, 113

Härtel, *see* Breitkopf & Härtel

Hartog, Edouard de (1829–1909), Dutch-French composer, 242

Hartung, German publisher, 166

Hartwig, 383, 497

Hase, Georg Oscar Immanuel von (1846–1921), grandson of Gottfried Christoph Härtel and member of music publishing firm Breitkopf & Härtel, 199

Hatzfeldt, Princess, 367, 492

Hausburg, Siegfried Wagner's tutor, 442

Haydn, Franz Joseph (1732–1809), 63, 414, 440

Symphonies, 414

Haynald, Cardinal Ludwig (1816–91), archbishop of Kalocsa, became cardinal in 1879; friend of Liszt from 1856, 4, 103, 107, 124, 127, 129, 131, 157, 248, 250, 307, 352, 424–26, 458, 459, 461, 462, 476, 479, 499

Hebbel, Friedrich (1813–63), German poet and playwright, 20, 25

Hébert, Antoine Auguste Ernest (1817–1908), French painter, director of the French Academy at Rome, 98, 413

Heckel, Emil, music dealer in Mannheim, founder of first *Wagner Verein*, 252, 439, 448

Heemskerck van Beest, Jacob Eduard (1828–94), Dutch painter, 242

Hegermann, Mme de, wife of Danish minister at Rome, 472

Heiller, Mgr, 458

Heine, Heinrich (1797–1856), 187, 461

Helbig, Mme Nadine (b. Princess Schakovska) (1847–1915), pupil and friend of Liszt; wife of the archaeologist Wolfgang, 140, 163, 182, 210, 256, 297, 323, 334, 359, 366, 436, 440, 473, 488, 493

Hélène, princess of Mecklenberg-Schwerin, married Louis Philippe's oldest son, duke of Orléans, 31, 61

Helldorf, Baroness Thérèse von; she and her husband were close friends of Liszt in Weimar, Liszt was guest at their estate in Schwerstedt, near Weimar, 5, 8, 11, 13, 33, 41, 43, 46, 48, 69, 70, 74, 290

Hellmesberger, Joseph (1828–93), Austrian violinist and conductor, 467

Hellmesberger Quartet (1849–87), chamber music quartet of Vienna, 31

Henry IV (1050–1106), king of Germany and Holy Roman Emperor, 65

Henry IV (1553–1610), king of France (1589–1610), 417

Henry V, *see* Chambord, Count de

Henschel, Sir George (1850–1934), German singer, composer, and conductor; knighted in Great Britain, 89, 463

Hercolani, Prince Alfonso (b. 1850), 463

Héritte, Louise Pauline Marie (1841–1918), French singer, teacher, and composer; daughter of Pauline Viardot, 429

Herkomer, Sir Herbert (1849–1914), German-English painter, 349

Herzog, circus director, 460

Heus, binder and stationer, 104

Heyse, Paul von (1830–1914), German novelist, playwright, and poet, 166, 347

Hildebrand, Adolf von (1847–1921), German sculptor, 166, 232, 299, 472

Hildebrand, Bruno (1812–78), German economist and author, 166

Hillebrand, Joseph (1788–1871), German literary historian and philosopher, 177

Hillebrand, Karl (1829–84), German journalist and historian, pseud. Faxelles, 29, 63, 65, 100, 166, 177, 196, 197, 299, 335, 366, 367, 393, 395, 435, 471

Hillebrand, Mme, *see* Laussot, Jessie

Hiller, Ferdinand (1811–85), German composer and conductor, 219, 221, 223, 224, 225, 228, 240, 294

Hippeau, Edmond Gabriel (1849–1921), French critic, 466

Hoffmann, Baron Leopold von (1822–85), intendant of Vienna Court theatre, 467

Hohenlohe, Princess Thérèse (b. Countess Thurn) (1817–93), wife of Prince Egon, 158

Hohenlohe-Langenburg, Prince Hermann Ernst Franz Bernhard (1832–1913), 52, 95

Hohenlohe-Schillingsfürst, Amélie (b. 1821), sister of Cardinal Hohenlohe, 95

Hohenlohe-Schillingsfürst, Prince Constantine von (1830–96), German-Austrian statesman, m. Princess Marie von Sayn-Wittgenstein, 106

Hohenlohe-Schillingsfürst, Princess Dorothea (b. 1872), daughter of Constantine and Marie, 462, 467

Hohenlohe-Schillingsfürst, Cardinal Gustav Adolf, Prince of (1823–96), German priest and prelate; close friend of Liszt, 50, 52, 53, 73, 93–95, 106, 172, 203, 229–31, 233, 283, 318, 324, 328, 351–54, 382, 386, 390, 393, 407, 415, 447, 450, 473, 490

Hohenlohe-Schillingsfürst, Princess Marie von (1837–1920), daughter of Princess Carolyne von Sayn-Wittgenstein; wife of Constantine, 25, 26, 28, 31, 202, 353, 355, 358, 382, 407, 467

Hohenlohe-Schillingsfürst, Princess Thérèse (1816–84), 95

Hohmann, Father, priest of Liszt's parish in Weimar, 109, 113

Holbein, Hans (1497?–1543), 299

Höltzke, C. de, Russian diplomat at Weimar, 435

Homer (fl. 850? B.C.), 64, 185, 394

Horace (Quintus Horatius Flaccus) (65–8 B.C.), 246

Horrocks, Arthur, Englishman living in Weimar, officer in grand duke's army, 456

Hubay, Jenő (1858–1937), Hungarian violinist, teacher, and composer, 329, 338

Huber, Johannes (1830–79), German Catholic theologian and philosopher, 208, 338

Hübner, Emil (1834–1901), German classical scholar and philologist, 10, 447, 448

Hugo, Victor Marie (1802–85), 40, 75, 133, 136, 154, 187, 188, 211, 263, 274, 282, 344, 348, 349, 385, 387, 388, 397, 398, 429, 475, 478

Hülsen, Baron von (1815–86), intendant of the Berlin Court theatre, 150, 218, 289, 460

Humboldt, Alexander von (1769–1859), German geographer and scientist, 360

Hummel, Johann Nepomuk (1778–1837), Hungarian composer, pianist, and conductor, 219, 400, 480
	Sonata in A flat, 480

Humperdinck, Engelbert (1854–1921), 442

Huss, John (1369?–1415), Czech religious reformer, 157

Huszár, Imre (1838–1916), Hungarian magnate and politician, 107

Hyacinthe, Father, see Loyson, Charles

IBACH, Johannes Adolf (1766–1848), German piano and organ manufacturer, founded Ibach & Söhne, 485

Ignatieff, General P., member of the Russian Imperial Council of State, 326

Ignatius, Saint (799?–878), patriarch of Constantinople, called Nicetas, 10

Ingres, Jean Auguste Dominique (1780–1867), 361, 450

Isoard, Mgr Louis-Romain-Ernest (1820–1901), French priest, later bishop, 208, 275

d'Israeli, see Disraeli, Benjamin

Ivan III, *the Great* (1440–1505), grand duke (1462–1505), 326

Ivan IV, *the Terrible* (1530–84), Russian ruler (1533–84), 157, 326

JACOBY, Valery (1836–1902), Russian painter, 351

Jaëll, Alfred (1832–82), Austrian pianist and composer, 56, 219

Jaëll, Marie (b. Trautmann) (1846–1925), Alsatian pianist and composer, wife of Alfred, 56, 113, 219, 270, 429, 454
	Voix du Printemps, 493

Jäger, Mme, German singer, wife of Ferdinand, 405

Jäger, Ferdinand (1838–1902), Viennese tenor, 405

Jagwitz, Mlle de, pianist, 265

Janet, Paul (1823–99), French philosopher, teacher, and author, 52, 55

Janin, Jules Gabriel (1804–74), French journalist, critic, and novelist, 82

Janina, Olga, 30, 115, 149, 151, 163, 178

Jauner, Franz (d. 1900), director of Vienna Court opera, 218, 274

Joachim, Amalie (b. Weiss)(1839–98), Austrian singer and teacher, wife of Joseph, 56

Joachim, Joseph (1831–1907), Austro-Hungarian violinist and composer, 56, 329, 346, 368, 370–72

Joinville, Prince François Ferdinand d'Orléans (1818–1900), third son of Louis Philippe, king of France, 55

Jókai, Moritz (1825–1904), Hungarian poet and novelist, 106, 423

Joseffy, Rafael (1852–1915), Hungarian pianist, teacher, and composer; pupil of Liszt, 338–39
    Arabesque No. 3, 338

Joukowsky, Paul, *see* Zhukovsky, Paul

Joukowsky, Vasily, *see* Zhukovsky, Vasily

Jouy, Victor Joseph Étienne de (1764–1846), French author and librettist, 312

Juhary, Hungarian pianist, pupil of Liszt, 302

Juvenal (60?–140?), 263, 311

KAHNT, Christian Friedrich (1823–97), music publisher in Leipzig, 110, 287, 292, 353, 371, 382, 424, 461

Kalckreuth, Countess, wife of Count Stanislaus, director of Weimar Art Academy, 15, 358

Kalergis, Mme Marie von Moukhanoff, *see* Moukhanoff-Kalergis, Marie von

Kálnoky, Count Gustav Siegmund (1832–98), Baron von Körös-Patak, Austro-Hungarian statesman and diplomat, 22, 26

Kant, Immanuel (1724–1804), 425

Karácsonyi, Count Guido, Hungarian magnate; good friend of Liszt from youth, 107, 185

Karl I (1823–91), king of Württemberg (1864–91), 76, 332

Károly, Countess Georgina (b. Erdődy), 57, 477

Kate, Herman Frederik Carl ten (1822–91), Dutch painter, 191, 242

Kaulbach, Wilhelm von (1805–74), German painter, 241

Kauser, Berta (b. Gerster), singer greatly admired by Liszt, wife of American consul at Budapest, 307

Keats, John (1795–1821), 471

Kellermann, Berthold (1853–1926), German pianist, teacher, and composer, pupil of Liszt, 382–83

Kerjègu, Count de, 458

Kertbeny, Karl (1824–82), German-Hungarian author and translator, 57

Keudell, Baron Felix Max Leopold Robert von (1824–1903), German statesman, ambassador at Rome; composer, 141, 143, 163, 182, 210, 216, 218, 297, 302, 325, 356, 359, 366, 412, 472–74, 488, 490

Klaczko, Julian (1825–1906), Polish critic and author, 323, 326, 328, 372

Klapka, General György (1820–92), Hungarian military commander, 284

Klindworth, Mme de, wife of Karl, 332

Klindworth, Karl (1830–1916), German pianist, conductor, and teacher; his adopted daughter, Winifred, married Wagner's son, Siegfried, 91, 111, 483

Knežević, Spiridion, Liszt's valet after Miska Sipka, 196, 200, 211, 249, 275, 314, 332, 419

Kniese, Julius (1848–1905), German conductor and composer, 343, 482

Kömpel, August (1831–91), German violinist, concertmaster in Weimar, 69, 70, 161, 164, 216, 242, 359, 360, 368, 390, 440

Konneritz, Mme de, 16

Kopf, sculptor, 171, 174, 177

Kovachi, Mme, harpist, 192

Krampetz, Mme, 421

Krasiński, Count Zygmunt (1812–59), Polish poet, 382, 383

Krebs, Marie (1851–1900), German pianist, 247

Kretschmer, Edmund (1830–1908), German composer, conductor, and organist, 199

Die Folkunger, 199

Kropotkin, Prince Pëtr Alekseevich (1842–1921), Russian geographer, philosopher, and revolutionist, 461

Krylov, Viktor Aleksandrovich (1838–1906), Russian dramatist, 308

Kufferath, Antonia (1857–1939), Belgian singer, 427

Kulcziki, Count, 382

LABICHE, Eugène Marin (1815–88), French playwright, 388, 391

La Bouillerie, Mme de, 46

Lacordaire, Father Jean Baptiste Henri (1802–61), French Dominican monk and author, 363, 409, 449

La Fontaine, Jean de (1621–95), French fabulist and poet, 198, 256

Lagrange, Marquis Adelaïde Edouard Le Lièvre de (1796–1876), 82

Lamartine, Alphonse Marie Louis de Prat de (1790–1869), French poet and statesman, 106, 124, 128, 228, 258, 260

Lamennais, Father Hugues Félicité Robert de (1782–1854), French priest and philosopher, friend of and advisor to Liszt, 324, 407, 408, 446, 447

Lamoureux, Charles (1834–99), French violinist and conductor, founded the "Concerts Lamoureux" in Paris, 1881, 460

Larderelles, Count, French diplomat in Rome, 24

Larevellière-Lépeaux, Louis Marie (1753–1824), French politician, 119, 463

La Rochefoucauld, Duke François de (1613–80), 440

Lassalle, Ferdinand (1825–64), German socialist and disciple of Karl Marx, 360

Lassen, Eduard (1830–1904), Danish composer and conductor; succeeded Liszt as music director and opera conductor at the Weimar Court, 7, 20, 25, 41, 90, 92, 111, 113, 127, 148, 149, 165, 174, 179, 191, 197, 211, 212, 215, 216, 221, 222, 224, 226, 228, 229, 234, 236, 239, 240, 251, 252, 254, 257, 262, 264, 267, 277, 278, 281, 296, 298, 317–19, 321, 322, 325, 328, 329, 331–33, 336, 357, 359, 366, 384, 399, 417, 434, 440, 454, 455, 460, 469, 485, 486, 500

Circe, 413

Lasteyrie du Saillant, Count Ferdinand Charles Léon (1810–79), French archaeologist and politician, 253

Latour, Countess, 323

Lauckhard, Dr., head of the school system in Weimar, 41

Laura de Noves (1308–48), Petrarch's beloved, 416

Laussot, Jessie (b. Taylor)(1827–1905), English friend of Liszt, married successively Eugène Laussot and Karl Hillebrand, 26–28, 63, 138, 139, 166, 227, 231, 232, 297, 299, 335, 471

Laveleye, Baron Émile Louis Victor de (1822–92), Belgian economist and author, 16, 30

La Villemarqué, Viscount Théodore Claude Henri Hersart de (1815–95), French scholar, 62, 76

Lazareff, 168

Lear, Fanny, *see* Blackford, Harriet Ely

Legouvé, Ernest (1807–1903), French playwright and author, 228, 263

Lehfeld, musician, 253

Lehmann, Charles, servant of Olga von Meyendorff, 459

Lemoinne, John Marguerite Émile (1815–92), French journalist, 22, 29, 214, 215, 237, 267, 309, 383, 388, 391

Lenau, Nikolaus (1802–50), pseud. of Nikolaus Niembsch von Strehlenau, Hungarian-German poet, 72

Lenbach, Franz von (1836–1904), German portrait painter, 28, 101, 103, 107, 124, 196, 283, 316, 347–49, 351, 353, 378, 438, 439, 443, 447, 448, 467

Lenormant, Amélie (*ca.* 1810–93), French authoress, 63

Leo XIII (Pope, 1878–1903), 310, 311, 313, 320, 322, 334, 383, 457

Leopardi, Count Giacomo (1798–1837),

Italian poet and classical scholar, 248, 345, 347

Leopold II (1835–1909), king of Belgium (1865–1909), 482, 499

Lermontov, Mikhail Yurievich (1814–41), Russian poet and novelist, 307, 365

Leroy, Curé, 282

Leschetizky, Theodor (1830–1915), Polish pianist, teacher, and composer, 480

Lesseps, Mme de, 495

Lesseps, Viscount Ferdinand Marie de (1805–94), French diplomat, responsible for construction of Suez Canal, 220, 494

Lessing, Karl Friedrich (1808–80), German painter, 157

Lessmann, Otto (1844–1918), German critic, editor, and pianist, 389, 460

Leuckart, music publishing firm in Leipzig, 122, 296, 369, 390

Levi, Hermann (1839–1900), German conductor, 348, 350, 466, 486, 487

Lévy, Hermann, *see* Levi, Hermann

Lévy, Michel, publisher, 52, 116

Levy, Sigmund (1822–84), German pianist, editor, and teacher, 330

Lewald, Fanny, *see* Stahr, Fanny Lewald

Liadov, Anatol Konstantinovich (1855–1914), 456

Lichnowsky, Mgr Robert, canon of the cathedral at Olmütz, 153

Lichtenstein, Prince Rudolph von (1833–88), 367, 368, 395

Lieven, Princess Dariya Khristoforovna de (b. von Benkendorff)(1785–1857), wife of Russian ambassador in Berlin, 44–45

Lindsay, Lord Alexander William Crawford (1812–80), British nobleman, bibliophile, and author, 255

Lippert, Josef Erwin Ritter von (1876–1902), Austrian architect, 457, 458

Liszt, Blandine, *see* Ollivier, Blandine

Liszt, Cosima, *see* Wagner, Francesca Gaetana Cosima

Liszt, Eduard Ritter von (1817–79), Austrian government official; youngest son of Georg-Adam Liszt, who, though born later than Franz, was the composer's

uncle; FL often referred to him as his *Onkelvetter* (uncle-cousin) and welcomed his friendship and counsel, 10, 12, 33, 54, 57, 77, 87, 100, 236, 245, 246, 274, 313

Liszt, Franz (b. Raiding, Hungary, October 22, 1811; d. Bayreuth, July 31, 1886)
Die Allmacht, 5; *"Am stillen Herd"* (from *Die Meistersinger*), 36; *Angelus,* 313; *Années de Pèlerinage,* 439, 446, 447; *Arbre de Noël,* 229; *Auf Flügeln des Gesanges,* 474; *Aux Cyprès de la Villa d'Este,* 292, 293; *Ave Maria,* 287, 288, 292; *Ave Maria* (trans. of Arcadelt's), 287, 288, 292; *Bach's Fugue and Prelude in A minor,* Transcription of, 276; *Beethoven Cantata,* 31, 42; *Der blinde Sänger,* 204, 207, 213, 248, 253, 256; *Cantico del Sol di San Francesco d'Assisi,* 325, 408; *Cantico di San Francesco,* see above; *Chants Polonais: Bacchanale* (trans. of Chopin's), 390; *Christus (Weihnachts Oratorium),* 30, 33, 34, 76, 185, 343, 344, 401; *Les Cloches de G . . . ,* 75; *Les Cloches de la Cathédrale de Strasbourg,* 148, 150–51, 428; Concerto in A, 412, 494; *Concerto Pathétique,* 129, 277; *Coronation Mass,* 124, 127, 458; *Le Crucifix,* 398; *Csárdás Macabre,* 396; *Csárdás Obstiné,* 477; *Danse Macabre,* 217, 221; *Dante Sonnet,* 153; *Dante Symphony,* 166, 316, 412; *Elégie,* 192; *Faust* (trans. of Lassen's): *Marche et Polonaise,* 317–20, 331, 336, 357; *Oster Hymne,* 317–20, 322, 331, 336; *Faust Symphony,* 356, 412; *Festpolonaise,* 226–30; Four Schubert Marches, 363; *Funeral March* (dedicated to Göllerich), 477; *Goethe Marsch,* 412; *Gondole Lugubre (Die Trauergondel),* 441; *Gretchen* (see also *Faust Symphony*), 197; *Hamlet,* 298; *Harold en Italie,* 321, 329, 390; *Héroïde Funèbre,* 366; *Hungarian March,* 58, 65; *Hungarian March (Sturmmarsch),* see *Marche Hongroise*; *Hungarian Rhapsody,* 65; *Hungarian*

Rhapsody, 476; *Hungarian* (Ábrányi) *Rhapsody*, 477; *Hungarian* (Munkácsy) *Rhapsody*, 424, 439; *Hymne de l'Enfant à son Réveil*, 124, 191, 197; *Die Ideale*, 83, 296, 473; *Impromptu* (Nocturne), 229, 294, 298; *Jeanne d'Arc*, 213; *The Legend of St. Elizabeth*, 48, 126, 190, 221, 272, 276, 277, 347, 427, 453, 495, 496; *Lenore*, 204; *Marche Hongroise* (*Sturmmarsch*), 213; *Mass for Four Male Voices*, 482; *Mass for Organ*, 363; *Mazeppa*, 26, 75, 297; *Messe de Gran*, 55, 88, 103, 105, 183, 239, 338, 340, 341, 343, 358, 423, 428, 492–95; *Nibelungen* (trans. of Lassen's): *Bechlarn*, 325, 328, 331–33, *Krimhild*, 325, 328, 331–33; *O! wenn es doch immer so bliebe*, 382; *Orpheus*, 6, 26, 71; *Polonaise*, from *Eugene Onegin*, 357, 363; *Prometheus*, 132, 239, 343, 344; *Psalm 13*, 8, 183; *Rákóczy March*, 69; *Reiter Marsch*, 210 (see also Four Schubert Marches); *Réminiscences des Huguenots*, 393; *Requiem*, 191; *Romance Oubliée*, 389, 467; *St. Cecilia*, 166, 170, 213, 276, 277; *St. Christophe*, 408; *St. François de Paule*, 197, 408; *St. Stanislaus*, 103, 214, 217, 461; *Salve Polonia*, 490; *Sarabande* and *Chaconne*, from Händel's *Almira*, 363; *Schlummer Lied im Grabe*, 147, 160, 163; *Septem Sacramenta*, 281, 322; *Soirées de Vienne*, 79; *Sonnets de Pétrarque*, 389, 447; *Sospiri*, 345; *Sursum Corda*, 294; *Symphonie de Harold*, see *Harold en Italie*; *Szózat*, 106; *Tarantelle*, 357, 363, 365; *Tasso, Lamento e Trionfo*, 393; *Der traurige Mönch*, 204; *Triomphe Funèbre du Tasse*, 293, 357; *Tristan und Isolde* (*Isolde's Death Scene*), 182; *Trois Valses Oubliées*, 459; *Tscherkessen Marsch*, from Glinka's *Russlan und Ludmilla*, 213, 468; *Ungarisches Königslied*, 451; *Ungarns Gott*, 396; *Via Crucis*, 214, 318–21; *Wartburg Lieder*, 96, 113; *Weihnachtsbaum*, 214; *Der Zaubersee*, 470

Liszt, Maria Anna (b. Laager)(1788–1866), mother of Franz, 58, 83

Litolff, Henry Charles (1818–91), French composer and pianist
Concerto No. 4, 302; *Les Templiers*, 494

Littré, Maximilien Paul Émile (1801–81), French scholar and lexicographer, 356

Lo, FL's nickname for Olga von Meyendorff, *passim*

Loë, Baroness Franziska von (1833–1908), 240, 241, 348

Loën, Baron August Freiherr von (1828–87), German theatre director, from 1867 intendant of the Weimar Court theatre, 19, 20, 26, 35, 36, 38–42, 80, 95, 111–13, 144, 147–50, 153–55, 171, 174, 185, 191, 199, 200, 222, 225, 226, 241, 243, 252, 257, 259, 262, 264, 267, 272, 275, 277, 278, 289, 319, 357, 360, 384, 399, 406, 408, 421, 434, 435, 455, 480, 486, 488

Loën, Baroness von, 111

Longfellow, Henry Wadsworth (1807–82), 148, 150, 151, 155

Lopuchin (Lopukhin), Princess, 210

Louis IX (1214–70), king of France (1226–70), 80, 431

Louis XVI (1754–93), king of France (1774–92), 205

Louis Philippe (1773–1850), king of France (1830–48), 17, 144, 260, 335

Louise (1776–1810), queen of Prussia, 358

Lovatelli, Countess Ersilia (b. Caetani)(b. 1840), wife of Jacques, 99, 140, 354

Lovatelli, Count Jacques Colombo (d. 1879), 140, 354, 461

Loyola, Saint Ignatius of (1491–1556), Spanish soldier and ecclesiastic, founder of the Society of Jesus, 170

Loyson, Charles (1827–1912), known as Father Hyacinthe; French priest excommunicated in 1869, 5, 7, 14, 19, 23, 27, 37, 43, 70, 77, 78, 83, 84, 204, 245, 282

Lübke, Wilhelm (1826–93), German art scholar and critic, 258

Ludwig I (1786–1868), king of Bavaria (1825–48), 418

Ludwig II (1845–86), king of Bavaria

(1864–86), grandson of Ludwig I, enthusiastic supporter of Wagner and his operas, 21, 49, 196, 248, 279, 346, 378, 431, 442, 448

Ludwig, Otto (1813–65), German author and librettist, 186

Luxemburg, bishop of, 499

Lvov, General Alexis Feodorovich (1798–1870), composed Russian national anthem, "God Save the Czar," 466

Lynen, Mme, wife of Victor, 389

Lynen, Victor, resident of Antwerp and friend of Liszt, 388, 428, 482, 495–96

Lysberg, Charles Samuel (1821–73), Swiss pianist and composer, 67

MACKENZIE, Sir Alexander Campbell (1847–1935), Scottish composer, violinist, and teacher, 471
    La Belle Dame sans merci, 471; *Colomba*, 471; *Jason*, 471

Maffei di Boglio, C.A., Marquis de, Italian minister to Belgium, 482

Maistre, Count Joseph de (1753–1821), French philosopher, statesman, and author, 61, 121, 296, 449

Makart, Hans (1840–84), Austrian painter, 57, 353, 443

Malatesta, Mme, 163, 323, 328

Malebranche, Nicolas de (1638–1715), French philosopher, 457

Malibran, Maria Felicia (b. Garcia) (1808–36), Franco-Spanish mezzo-contralto and composer, 243, 335

Maltitz, Baron Apolonius von (1795–1870), German poet, playwright, and novelist; Russian minister to Saxe-Weimar and Dresden, 247

Marchand, Alfred (1842–95), 208

Marcus Aurelius (121–80), Roman emperor (161–80), 409

Marguerite, Princess (b. 1851), hereditary princess of Italy, 220

Maria Anna (b. 1837), Princess Frederick Charles of Prussia, 210

Maria Paulowna (1786–1859), grand duchess of Weimar, 86, 313

Maria Theresa (1717–80), archduchess of Austria, queen of Hungary and Bohemia, mother of Marie Antoinette, 155

Marie Alexandrine, *see* Reuss, Princess Marie

Marie Antoinette (1755–93), queen of France, 29, 155

Marie Henriette (1836–1902), queen of Belgium, 482

Marie Louise, Princess Charles of Prussia (1808–77), sister of Grand Duke Carl Alexander of Saxe-Weimar, 53, 266

Marlborough, Lady, 378

Marschner, Heinrich August (1795–1861), German composer
    Hans Heiling, 345

Masetti, Countess, 153

Massé, Victor (Félix Marie) (1822–84), French composer
    Paul et Virginie, 263

Massenbach, Baroness de, lady-in-waiting to Queen Olga of Württemberg, 104

Massenet, Jules Émile Frédéric (1842–1912), 327, 336, 427, 472
    Eve, 188; *Hérodiade*, 336, 427, 494; *Le Roi de Lahore*, 336

Materna, Amalie (1844–1918), Austrian soprano, 195, 262

Mauderode, de, official of Weimar Court, 16

Maupassant, Guy de (1850–93), 461

Mazade, Charles de (1821–93), French journalist, 42

Mazzini, Giuseppe (1805–72), Italian patriot, lawyer, and politician, 63, 64, 134, 316, 439

Mecklenburg, Grand Duchess Catherine of (1827–94), 50

Mecklenburg, Grand Duke George of (1824–76), 50, 52

Mehlig, Anna (Falk-) (1846–1928), German pianist, pupil of Liszt, 247, 494

Meiningen, Duchess of, daughter of Princess Feodora Hohenlohe-Langenburg, 50, 95

Meli, Giosuè (1807–93), Italian sculptor, 18

Mendelssohn-Bartholdy, Jakob Ludwig

Felix (1809–47), 161, 225, 241, 317, 452
  Elijah, 361
Mendès, Abraham Catulle (1841–1909), French poet, novelist, and critic, 404
Menter, Sophie (1846–1918), German pianist and teacher, pupil of Liszt, 114, 129, 247, 270, 272, 339, 368, 370, 390, 391, 393, 395, 429, 485, 487
Mercy-Argenteau, Countess Louise (d. 1890), music enthusiast, promoted new Russian school in Belgium and France, 494
Merian-Genast, Émilie (1833–1905), German *Lieder* and oratorio singer, friend of Liszt, 11, 46, 90, 186, 191, 197, 434
Mérimée, Prosper (1803–70), French novelist, government official, and politician, 109, 111, 113, 115, 116, 124, 309, 397, 471
Merlin, Countess, 335
Mérode, Mgr Francis Xavier de (1820–74), archbishop of Mélitène, 99–100, 143
Metternich, Count, 323
Metternich, Prince Klemens Wenzel Nepomuk Lothar von (1773–1859), Austrian statesman and diplomat, 21, 34, 312, 366, 368, 369, 470
Metternich, Princess Pauline (1836–1921), 21, 274, 341, 404
Metzdorff, Richard (1844–1919), German composer, 146, 153, 174, 179, 188, 189, 203, 204, 214, 225, 254, 271, 382
  Rosamunde, 146, 199, 204, 212, 221, 225, 254; *Symphonie Tragique*, 277
Metzger, Dr., 412
Meyendorff, Alexander von (1798–1865), Russian chancellor, uncle of Felix, 285
Meyendorff, Alexander (Sachi) von (1869–1964), youngest son of Olga, 195, 246, 316
Meyendorff, Elisabeth (Bethsi) von (b. d'Hogguer), wife of Alexander, 285
Meyendorff, Baron Felix von (1834–71), Russian statesman and diplomat, accredited to Russian embassy in Rome, ambassador at Weimar, husband of Olga, 9, 141, 143

Meyendorff, Klemens (Clément) von (1863–85), third son of Olga, 12, 13, 17, 31, 51, 53, 81, 96, 105, 106, 173, 177, 195, 215, 278, 280, 281, 297, 305, 309, 317, 322, 324, 325, 338, 345, 347, 349, 351, 375, 379, 381, 386, 388, 414, 417, 428, 434–36, 439, 446–48, 452, 484, 488
Meyendorff, Michael (Mimi) von (1861–1940), second son of Olga, 51, 77, 81, 96, 139, 195, 215, 316, 378, 379
Meyendorff, Baroness Olga von (b. Princess Gortschakoff)(1838–1926), *passim*
Meyendorff, Peter (Peterle) von (1858–1918), eldest son of Olga, 51, 81, 96, 107, 139, 149, 185, 195, 215, 246, 252, 297, 301, 304, 316, 349, 378, 416, 425, 430, 431, 478, 488
Meyerbeer, Giacomo (Jakob Liebmann Beer)(1791–1864), 241, 358, 362, 370
  L'Africaine, 225; *Dinorah*, 175; *Le Prophète*, 199, 225; *Robert le Diable*, 366
Meysenbug, Malwida von (1816–1903), German writer, friend of Liszt and Wagner, 267, 316
Michael, Grand Duke, 140, 412
Michaud, Canon, 42
Michelangelo Buonarroti (1475–1564), 59, 163, 168, 293, 295, 352, 372, 394, 397, 436
Michelet, Jules (1798–1874), French historian, 126
Mickievicz, Ladislaw (1838–1926), 383
Mignet, François Auguste Marie (1796–1884), French historian, 297
Mihalovich, Ödön Péter József (1842–1929), Hungarian composer, head of Royal Academy of Music in Budapest, 58, 61, 105, 107, 124, 138, 186, 191, 227, 254, 262, 271, 304, 370
  Ballads, 335; *Hagbarth und Signe*, 475; *Wieland der Schmied*, 271
Milde, Hans Feodor von (1821–99), German singer, member of Weimar Court opera, 111, 186, 191, 384
Milde, Rosa von (b. Agthe)(1827–1906), German singer, wife of Hans, member of Weimar Court opera, 111, 186, 191

Millöcker, Karl (1842–99), Austrian conductor and composer
Feldprediger, 480

Minghetti, Princess Laura, wife, successively, of Prince dei Camporeale and Marco Minghetti; mother of Countess Dönhoff, 34, 140, 141, 143, 163, 182, 218, 220, 348, 395, 418, 446, 447

Minghetti, Marco (1818–86), Italian statesman, 417

Miska, *see* Sipka, Miska

Moleschott, Jacob (1822–93), Dutch physiologist, professor in Rome, and Italian senator, 409

Molière, pseud. of Jean-Baptiste Poquelin (1622–73), 276

Moltke, Helmuth von (1800–91), Prussian field marshal, 349

Monbelli, Mme, singer, 31

Monsabré, Father, 237

Montalembert, Mlle de, daughter of Charles and niece of Mgr de Mérode, 100

Montalembert, Charles Forbes (1810–70), French journalist and politician, 206, 226, 272, 374, 375

Montebello, Marquis Gustave Louis Lannes de (1838–1907), French diplomat, ambassador to Belgium, 482

Montesquieu, Charles-Louis de Secondat, baron de La Brède et de (1689–1755), French lawyer, author, and philosopher, 311

Montijo, Countess Marie-Manuela de, mother of Empress Eugénie, 124

Montmorency, Prince, 416

Morlacchi, Francesco (1784–1841), Italian conductor and composer, 334
Tebaldo ed Isolina (cavatina), 334

Mornay, Philippe de (1549–1623), called Duplessis-Mornay, French Huguenot leader, 80

Morton, Lady, 210

Mottl, Felix (1856–1911), Austrian conductor and composer, 355, 360, 376, 383, 481
Agnes Bernauer, 357, 376

Moukhanoff, Serge de, 154, 159, 160, 162

Moukhanoff-Kalergis, Mme Marie von (b. Countess Nesselrode)(1822–74), art patron and gifted pianist, close friend of Liszt, 8, 13, 21, 30, 44, 45, 67, 69, 72, 76, 81, 85, 97, 100, 101, 104, 108, 109, 117, 136, 139, 142, 147, 159, 163, 172, 176, 179, 193, 196, 200, 210, 240, 271, 286–88, 291, 307, 309, 332, 348, 464, 469

Moule, 64

Mozart, Wolfgang Amadeus (1756–91), 254, 256, 333, 414
Don Giovanni, 205, 370; *Requiem*, 452; Symphonies: in G minor, 414, *Jupiter*, 414; *Die Zauberflöte*, 414

Müller-Hartung, Karl (1834–1908), German conductor, 216, 235, 252, 260, 341, 343, 417

Mun, Count Adrien Albert Marie de (1841–1914), French politician and social reformer, 326

Munk, de, musician, 374

Munkácsy, Mme, wife of Mihály, 499, 500

Munkácsy, Mihály von (Michael Leo Lieb)(1844–1900), Hungarian painter, 41, 422–24, 439, 477, 496, 499

Mustafà, Domenico (1829–1912), Italian conductor and composer, 361

NAPOLEON I (1769–1821), emperor of France (1804–15), 46, 86, 119, 200, 255, 265, 449, 463

Napoleon III (1808–73), emperor of France (1852–70), 18, 46, 83, 86, 290, 327, 439

Nápravník, Eduard (1839–1916), Czech-Russian composer and conductor
Trio, 296

Narvaez, Duke Ramón Maria of Valencia (1800–88), Spanish general and statesman, 125

Naumann, Karl Ernst (1832–1910), German composer, organist, and theorist, 374

Nazarene, school of painting in Germany, founded in 1812, 378

Nemes, Countess Elise (b. Baroness Ransonnet)(1843–99), Hungarian painter, 341

Nero (37–68), Roman emperor (54–68), 358, 385

Nesselrode, Count Karl Robert (1780–1862), Russian statesman and diplomat, chancellor of Russia, 67

Nessler, Victor Ernst (1841–90), German composer
    Der Trompeter von Säckingen, 480

Neumann, Angelo (1838–1910), Austrian theatre director and singer, 404

Neuville, Alphonse Marie de (1836–85), French painter, 447

Nicetas, *see* Ignatius, Saint

Nicholas I (1796–1855), emperor of Russia (1825–55), 163, 255

Nicolai, Carl Otto Ehrenfried (1810–49), German composer and conductor
    Die lustigen Weiber von Windsor, 189

Nietzsche, Friedrich Wilhelm (1844–1900), 36, 38–40, 100, 101, 136, 137, 167, 212, 217

Nisard, Jean Marie Napoléon Désiré (1806–88), French journalist and literary critic, 120

Nohl, Carl Friedrich Ludwig (1831–85), German musical scholar, editor, and author, 161, 201, 203, 204, 245, 333, 389

Normann, music director in Dessau, 80

Novikoff, Mme Olga Alekseevna de (b. Kiréeff) (1840–1925), Russian journalist, pseud. "O.K.," 34, 309

OBRENOWICH (Obrenovitch), Princess, 85

Odescalchi, Prince Ladislaus (1805–85), 99

Olga (1822–92), queen of Württemberg, wife of Karl I, daughter of Emperor Nicholas I of Russia, 55, 57, 61, 66, 79, 93, 150, 153, 163, 172, 173, 212, 214, 222, 226, 258, 259, 288, 319, 332, 360, 361, 370, 372, 405, 445, 448

Olga Konstantinova (1851–1926), queen of Greece, 464

Ollivier, Mme (b. Gravier), second wife of Émile, 162, 314, 413, 414

Ollivier, Blandine Liszt (1835–62), Liszt's oldest child, married Émile, died as a result of childbirth, 83

Ollivier, Daniel (b. 1862), Liszt's grandson, son of Émile and Blandine, 314

Ollivier, Émile (1825–1913), French statesman and politician, prime minister under Napoleon III; married Liszt's daughter Blandine, 52, 59, 64, 128, 162, 314, 344, 415, 417

Orgeny, Anna Maria Aglaja d' (b. Görger St. Jorgen) (1841–1926), soprano, 270

Orléans, Bishop of, *see* Dupanloup, Mgr Félix Antoine Philibert

Orléans, Princes of, 190

Ortigue, Joseph Louis d' (1802–66), French music critic, 358, 423

Ossuna, Duke of, 185

Overbeck, Johann Friedrich (1789–1869), German painter, 322

Ozanam, Antoine Frédéric (1813–53), French historian and author, 217, 324

PAGANINI, Niccolò (1782–1840), 329

Pailleron, Edouard (1834–99), French dramatist and poet, 470

Palestrina, Giovanni Pierluigi da (*c.* 1525–94), 16, 426

Palézieux, M. de, 429

Pallavicini, Princess, 18, 341

Pana, Mgr, 100

Panizzi, Sir Anthony (1797–1879), Italian-British scholar and librarian, 397

Parisis, writer for *Figaro*, 494

Pascal, Blaise (1623–62), 10, 15, 32, 33, 42, 60, 173, 190, 204, 269, 369, 385

Pasdeloup, Jules Étienne (1819–87), French conductor, 253

Pasini, Alberto (1826–99), Italian painter, 438, 442, 443

Pasteur, Louis (1822–95), 427

Patti, Adelina (Marquise de Caux) (1843–1919), 127

Pauline, *see* Apel, Pauline

Pauline, Princess Ida Maria Olga Henrietta Katherina (b. 1852), hereditary grand duchess of Saxe-Weimar, wife of Carl Augustus, 484

Paur, Emil (1855–1932), Austrian conductor, violinist, and composer, 481

Pavlova, Karolina Karlova (1807–93?), 204, 207

Pawloff, Mme, *see* Pavlova *above*

Pedro II, Dom (Pedro de Alcántara) (1825–91), emperor of Brazil (1831–89), 300

Pelet-Narbonne, Mme, Baroness von Meyendorff's landlady in Weimar, 247, 307, 326, 418, 428, 436

Pelletier, Mgr Victor, 238

Perfall, Baron Karl von (1824–1907), German theatrical manager and composer, 486

Périgueux, Bishop Nicolaus Joseph of, 119

Pérot, Alfred, 105

Peter the Great (1672–1725), emperor of Russia (1682–1725), 255

Petőfi, Sándor (1823–49), Hungarian poet and patriot, 396

Petrarch, Francesco (1304–74), 103, 154, 389, 416, 417

Pfeiffer, Georges Jean (1835–1908), French pianist and composer, 483
Agar, 188

Pflughaupt, Robert (1833–71), German pianist, pupil of Liszt, 176

Pictet de Rochemont, Adolphe (1799–1875), Swiss philologist, 226

Pinelli, Ettore (1843–1915), Italian violinist, conductor, and composer, 172, 202, 317, 390, 391, 439

Pinner, Max (1851–87), American pianist and teacher, pupil of Liszt, 163, 174, 222, 226, 227, 234, 271

Pirch, Baroness de (b. Princess Thurn und Taxis), wife of Baron William de Pirch-Wobinsin, Prussian minister at Weimar, 230

Pius IX (Pope, 1846–78), 24, 25, 78, 84, 99, 106, 141, 143, 167, 229, 230, 238, 285, 306, 310, 319, 322, 324, 383, 384, 415

Plato (427?–347 B.C.), 311, 376, 483

Plötz, Baroness de, friend of Princess Wittgenstein in Weimar, 82

Plüddemann, Martin (1854–97), German composer, conductor, and author, 258

Pohl, Richard (1826–96), German critic and author, close friend of Liszt and champion of the Liszt-Wagner school; wrote a critical biography of Liszt; pseud. Hoplit, 65, 92, 161, 201, 204, 245, 256, 325, 389, 406, 433, 454

Pohlig, Karl (1858–1928), German conductor, pianist, and composer, pupil of Liszt, 317, 320, 322, 379, 383

Ponchielli, Amilcare (1834–86), 439
I promessi sposi, 439

Pontmartin, A. de (1811–90), French journalist and critic, 140

Popper, David (1843–1913), German-Czech cellist and composer, husband of Sophie Menter, 472

Popper, Sophie, *see* Menter, Sophie

Porges, Heinrich (1837–1900), Czech-German critic and editor, 192, 348, 405

Portaels, Jean François (1818–95), Belgian painter, 191, 192

Posse, harpist, 488

Potocka, Countess Maria (b. Rzewuska), 66

Preller, Friedrich (1804–78), German painter, 179

Pressensé, Edmond Déhault de (1824–91), French Protestant clergyman and politician, 105, 417

Proruoli, Countess, 143

Prudhomme, Joseph, fictional character, 128, 339

Pückler-Muskau, Prince Hermann von (1785–1871), adjutant to grand duke of Saxe-Weimar, 6

Pulszky, Ferenc von (1814–97), Hungarian statesman and author, 423

Pushkin, Aleksander Sergeevich (1799–1837), 307

QUEEN OLGA, *see* Olga, queen of Württemberg

Quinet, Edgar (1803–75), French author, politician, and philosopher, 126, 170, 188

R.O., *see* Olga, queen of Württemberg

Racine, Jean Baptiste (1639–99), 75

Radowitz, Joseph Maria von (1839–1912), German diplomat, 216, 266

Radowitz, Mme Nadine Ozerow (1840–1912), 216

Raff, Doris (b. Genast)(1826–1902), actress, wife of Joseph, 486

Raff, Joseph Joachim (1822–82), German composer, close friend of Liszt; for some years acted as his secretary, 142, 225, 420

   Im Walde, 68

Ramann, Lina (1833–1912), German authoress and teacher, biographer of Liszt, and editor of his *Gesammelte Schriften*, 93, 194, 246, 282, 384, 467

Ranouschevitch, Mlle, 439

Raphael (1483–1520), 59, 211, 394, 436, 452

Ratibor, Prince Franz of (b. 1849), diplomat, 393

Ratzenberger, Theodor (1840–79), German pianist and conductor, pupil of Liszt, 239, 261, 265

Ravignan, Father Xavier de (1795–1858), French Jesuit priest, 113, 115, 121, 124, 128, 136, 140, 173

Raymondine, Sister, *see* Auersperg, Princess Frederika

Rayneval, Count A. de, French minister at Weimar, 232

Récamier, Jeanne Françoise Julie Adelaïde (b. Bernard)(1777–1849), French social leader and wit, 63, 65, 416, 417

Reine Olga, see Olga, queen of Württemberg

Reinecke, Carl Heinrich Carsten (1824–1910), German composer, pianist, and conductor, 302

   La Fée des Alpes, 272

Reisenauer, Alfred (1863–1907), German pianist and composer, pupil of Liszt, 379, 383, 455

Reiss, Mlle, friend of Liszt in Mannheim, 481

Rembrandt Harmenszoon van Rijn (1606–69), 394

Reményi, Ede (1830–98), Hungarian violinist, 107

Remmert, Martha (b. 1854), German pianist, pupil of Liszt, 247, 260, 265, 270, 271, 366, 368, 401, 435

Rémusat, Count François Marie Charles de (1797–1875), French statesman and author, 253, 272

Renan, Joseph Ernest (1823–92), French philosopher and historian, 80, 93, 134, 245, 337, 344, 347, 356, 358, 391, 408, 409, 413, 425, 427, 441, 444, 455

Rendano, Alfonso (1853–1931), Italian pianist and composer, 449, 456, 460, 479, 488, 492

Renz, circus director, 460

Reuss, Edouard Guillaume Eugène (1804–91), Alsatian-French Protestant theologian, 173

Reuss, Prince Henry VII, von (b. 1825), German statesman and diplomat, 206, 424

Reuss, Princess Marie (b. 1849), daughter of Grand Duke Carl Alexander of Saxe-Weimar, wife of Henry, 206, 207, 226, 227, 229, 424, 463, 479

Réville, Albert (1826–1906), French Protestant clergyman, 214

Reyer, Ernest (Louis Étienne Rey)(1823–1909), French composer and critic, 187, 272, 317, 364, 460

   Sigurt, 494

Richter, Gustav (1823–84), German painter, 358

Richter, Hans (1843–1916), Austro-Hungarian conductor, 31, 56, 80, 88, 107, 165, 186, 195, 330, 333, 456

Riedel, Karl (1827–88), German conductor and composer, president of the *Wagner Verein*, 22, 56, 57, 173, 203, 222, 243, 283, 456, 480

Rielke, Mlle, *see* Treuenfels, Mme

Rimsky-Korsakov, Nikolai Andreevich (1844–1908), 203, 334, 357

   Sadko, 222

Riquet, Joseph de, prince of Chimay and Caraman (Caraman-Chimay)(1808–86), Belgian statesman and diplomat, ambassador to Rome; friend of Liszt, 51, 54,

87, 160, 329, 335, 338, 339, 373, 389, 412, 455, 458, 482

Ritter, Alexander (1833–96), German-Russian composer, 486
    Der faule Hans, 486

Ritter, Mme Franziska Wagner, wife of Alexander, niece of Richard Wagner, 481, 486

Robert (1027–1110), abbot of Molesmes, founder of Cistercian Order, 18

Rochussen, Charles (1814–94), Dutch painter, 191, 242

Rohlfs, Friedrich Gerhard (1831–96), German explorer, 363

Romuald, Saint (950?–1027), founder of Camaldolese Order, 18

Rosa, Salvator, senator, 19, 24, 162

Rosmini-Serbati, Antonio (1797–1855), Italian philosopher, 7, 407

Rospigliosi, Princess, *see* Champagny-Rospigliosi, Princess Fanny

Rössel, M. de, pianist, pupil of Liszt, 302, 305

Rössel, Anatole de (b. 1877), godson of Liszt, 305

Rossi, Ernesto (1829–96), Italian actor and playwright, 124

Rossi, Countess Marie, 85, 129

Rossini, Gioacchino Antonio (1792–1868), 225, 312–13
    Le Barbier de Séville (*Almaviva*), 205, 360, 370; *Le Comte Ory*, 175; *Guillaume Tell*, 312; *Inflammatus*, 307; *Semiramide*, 312

Rostopchin, Count Fëdor Vasilievich (1763–1826), Russian soldier, politician, and author, 107

Rosty, Baron, 168

Roth, Bertrand (1855–1938), Swiss pianist and composer, pupil of Liszt, 302, 317, 320, 327, 328

Rothschild, Baron Amschel Salomon (1803–74), member of the banking firm, 78

Rothschild, Baroness Willy de, 335

Rousseau, Jean-Jacques (1712–78), 55, 167, 353, 367, 375

Rubens, Peter Paul (1577–1640), 280, 386, 388, 482

Rubinstein, Mme, wife of Anton, 365

Rubinstein, Anton Grigorevich (1829–94), Russian pianist, composer, and conductor; as pianist reputed to be second only to Liszt, 31, 34, 35, 40, 90, 185–87, 225, 244, 247, 263, 290, 301, 363, 365, 382, 436, 456, 467
    Concerti: No. 5, 186, No. 3 in G, 270; *Le Démon*, 263, 365; *Les Macchabées*, 186, 436; *The Merchant Kalashnikov*, 365; *Néron*, 187, 263, 467, 480, 494; Symphony, Op. 95, 186; *La Tour de Babel*, 186, 365

Rubinstein, Joseph (1847–84), Russian pianist and composer, assistant to Wagner at Bayreuth, 184, 195, 302, 311, 346, 380, 464

Ruland, Karl (1834–1907), German official, director of the Weimar Museum, 57

Russell, Lady, 81, 401

Russell, Odo William Leopold, Baron Ampthill (1829–84), British diplomat, ambassador to Berlin, 81, 135, 401

Rzewuska, Countess Taïda, 302

SAAR, Ferdinand von (1833–1906), Austrian poet, novelist, and playwright, 65, 261

Sabouroff, P. de, Russian ambassador to Germany, 464

Saint-Pierre, Abbé Charles Irénée, Castel de (1658–1743), French cleric and author, 238

Saint-Priest, Count Alexis de Guignard (1805–51), French author and diplomat, 121

Saint-Saëns, Charles Camille (1835–1921), 212, 220, 223, 242, 248, 300–1, 303, 309, 313, 314, 327, 336, 337, 340, 342, 350, 352, 367, 368, 371, 396, 429, 468
    Danse Macabre, 217, 224, 248, 254, 396; *Études*, 301; *Improvisation sur la Beethoven-Cantata de Franz Liszt pour piano*, 71; *Jeunesse d'Hercule*, 301; *La Lyre et la harpe*, 371, 449;

Samson et Dalila, 199, 204, 212, 227, 272, 300, 301, 304, 307; *Timbre d'argent*, 272; Trio for Piano and Strings in F, 371; *Variations*, 277

Saint-Victor, Count Paul Bins de (1827–81), French literary critic and author, 55, 403

Sainte-Beuve, Charles Augustin (1804–69), French author and critic, 52, 113, 184, 315, 316, 335, 409

Saissy, Amadé (1844–1901), French journalist, editor of the *Gazette de Hongrie*, 452

Salm, Prince Leopold (1833–93), 95

Salomonsky, circus director, 460

Salvagni, Fortunato, one of Liszt's several valets, 11

Salviati, Antonio (1816–1900), Italian mosaicist, 19, 24

Sand, George (b. Dupin) (1804–76), pseud. of Amandine Aurore Lucie, Baroness Dudevant, 88, 439, 450, 452, 461

Sander, Constantin, music publisher in Leipzig, 330, 369

Sanguszko, Prince Paul (1834–76), 136

Sarasate, Pablo de (1844–1908), Spanish violinist and composer, 261, 307, 368

Sardou, Victorien (1831–1908), French playwright, 335

Sargana, Mlle, harpist, 163

Sarring, Liszt's domestic servant in Weimar, 77, 79, 149, 280, 282, 321, 329, 362, 369, 372, 437, 453, 459

Sauret, Émile (1852–1920), French violinist and composer, 298, 303, 401

Sayn-Wittgenstein, Princess Carolyne Jeanne Elisabeth von (b. Iwanowska) (1819–87), Polish-Russian noblewoman and Liszt's second love. In 1848 she followed him from Russia to Weimar where they lived together for 12 years. After their attempt to marry (1861) failed, she settled in Rome, became a religious fanatic, and wrote many volumes devoted to religion and theology, 14, 26, 31, 35, 46, 56, 78, 83, 86, 89, 94, 96, 98, 119, 130, 131, 134, 135, 156, 158,

161, 164, 201, 202, 204, 207, 228, 279, 285, 329, 355, 407, 411, 413

Scaliger, Joseph Justus (1540–1609), Italian scholar and editor, son of Julius, 406

Scaliger, Julius Caesar (1484–1558), Italian physician and scholar, 406

Scaria, Emil (1838–86), Austrian bass-baritone, 195

Scheffer, Ary (1795–1858), Dutch-French painter, 387

Schelle, Karl Eduard (1816–82), German music critic, 389

Schennis, Friedrich (Hans F. Emanuel) von (1852–1918), German painter, 349, 353, 431, 438

Schirmer, Mme, wife of Gustave, 219, 220, 223, 251

Schirmer, Gustave (1829–93), German music publisher, founder of the firm of G. Schirmer in New York, 219, 220

Schlauch, Mgr Lörine (1824–1902), Hungarian cleric, 469

Schleinitz, Baron Alexander von (1807–85), German statesman, 81, 463

Schleinitz, Baroness Maria von (b. von Buch), great friend and supporter of Liszt and Wagner, wife of Alexander, 21, 34, 57, 81, 140, 144, 146, 172, 174, 177, 179, 196, 222, 241, 287, 288, 291, 303, 380, 382, 389, 401, 406, 430, 460, 463, 464

Schlözer, pianist, 69, 271

Schlözer, Kurt von (1822–94), Prussian minister to the Vatican; friend of Liszt, 415, 448, 472, 473, 488, 490

Schmidt, Gustav (1816–82), German conductor and composer, 199

Schmidt, Heinrich Julian (1818–86), German journalist and literary historian, 360

Schnobel, Mlle, musician, 483

Schöll, Gustav Adolf (1805–82), archaeologist, author, and librarian at Weimar, 54

Scholz, Bernard (1835–1916), German conductor and composer
    Golo, 199

Schopenhauer, Arthur (1788–1860), 167, 403, 418–21

Schorn, Adelheid von (1841–1916), German writer and friend of Liszt and Princess Carolyne von Sayn-Wittgenstein, who allegedly stationed her in Weimar to keep an eye on the composer. The Meyendorffs called her "die dämliche Providenz," 48, 174, 179, 212, 214, 217, 223, 230, 419, 434, 486, 500

Schott, Mme Betty (b. Braunrasch) (1820–75), wife of Franz, 120, 146

Schott, Franz Philipp (1811–74), German music publisher, of firm B. Schott & Söhne, Mainz, 120, 252, 255, 257, 262, 295, 335, 439, 447

Schraudolph, Claudius von (1843–1902), German painter, 378

Schraudolph, Johannes von (1808–79), German painter, member of the "Nazarene" school of painting, 378

Schubert, Franz Peter (1797–1828), 5, 79
Rondo, 69

Schulz-Beuthen, Heinrich (1838–1915), German composer and teacher, 87

Schulze and Sons, J. F., German firm of organ builders, 351

Schumann, circus director, 460

Schumann, Clara (b. Wieck) (1819–96), pianist and composer, wife of Robert, 56, 239, 276

Schumann, Robert Alexander (1810–56), 84, 111, 254, 317, 362
Manfred, Op. 115, 272; Sonata in F minor, 456

Schuré, Edouard (1841–1929), French scholar and critic, 194, 248, 271

Schwartz, Mme Espérance de (b. Brandt) (1821–99), philanthropist and author, pseud. Elpis Melena, 56, 73, 282

Schwind, Moritz von (1804–71), German painter, 347

Sciarra, Princess, 24, 100

Scribe, Augustin Eugène (1791–1861), French playwright and librettist, 254

Ségur, Count Anatole de (b. 1823), author and poet, 107

Ségur, Count Philippe-Paul de (1780–1873), French general and historian, 107, 116

Ségur, Countess Sophie Rostopchine de (1799–1874), mother of Anatole, 107

Seilern, Count Hugo (1840–86), brother-in-law of Count Charles Zaluski, 285

Seitz, Robert, Weimar music publisher, 217

Semper, Gottfried (1803–79), German architect, 283

Senff, Barthol (1815–1900), music publisher in Leipzig, 186, 263

Senfft von Pilsach, Gottfried Arnold (1834–89), German singer, and doctor of jurisprudence, 359

Sermoneta, Duke of, *see* Caetani, Michelangelo

Servais, Franz Matthieu (1847–1901), Belgian pianist and composer, 55, 60, 80, 100, 102, 103, 112, 282, 314, 400, 402, 482
Contemplations, 282; *Jon*, 314, 482; *Tasso*, cantata, 100, 103

Sgambati, Giovanni (1841–1914), Italian composer and pianist, student of Liszt, 26, 141–43, 160, 163, 202, 255, 284, 290, 295–96, 298, 300, 302, 304, 320, 327, 352, 355, 356, 359, 393, 410, 412, 440, 445, 448, 472, 473, 488
Piano concerto, Op. 10, 320, 356; Études, 356; Grand Quintets: No. 1, 295, 320, 352, No. 2, 202, 203, 295; *Ouverture Festive*, 320; Quartet in D flat for Strings, 410, 460; Symphonies: Op. 11, 393, Op. posthumous, 456

Shakespeare, William (1564–1616), 64

Shelley, Percy Bysshe (1792–1822), 271

Siemienski, Lujan (1804–77), Polish poet, 217

Siemiradzki, Henryk (1843–1902), Polish painter, 353, 358, 410, 436, 437, 440

Simeoni, Cardinal (b. 1816), 285

Simor, Cardinal János, prince primate of Hungary (1867–91), 457, 458

Singer, Edmund (1830–1912), Hungarian-German violinist and composer, played under Liszt in Weimar orchestra, 60, 65

Sipka, Miska (d. 1875), Liszt's valet, 11, 62, 74, 88, 175, 180, 182, 183

Sivori, Ernesto Camillo (1815–94), Italian violinist and composer, 31

Snoukaert, Baron, 215

Solon (638?–559? B.C.), 451

Sophie (1824–97), grand duchess of Saxe-Weimar, wife of Grand Duke Carl Alexander, 3, 4, 10, 11, 14–16, 24, 33, 39, 42, 49, 99, 109, 135, 150, 171, 176, 187, 189, 191, 207, 219, 227, 266, 282, 298, 305

Spinoza, Baruch (1632–77), 425

Spiridion, *see* Knežević, Spiridion

Spitzweg, Eduard, succeeded Joseph Aibl as head of Aibl music publishers, 378, 379

Spohr, Rosalie (1829–1919), harpist, friend of Liszt, 197

Spontini, Gasparo Luigi Pacifico (1774–1851), Italian opera composer, 249, 361
    Fernand Cortez, 361; *La Vestale*, 361

Staal, Baroness von, wife of Russian diplomat, ambassador to Württemberg; sister of Olga von Meyendorff, 104, 298, 377, 495

Stahr, the Misses, probably sisters of A. W. T. Stahr, 93

Stahr, Adolf Wilhelm Theodor (1805–76), German scholar and author, 194, 195

Stahr, Fanny Lewald (1811–89), German novelist, wife of Adolf, 194, 390

Standhartner, Dr. Josef, Viennese physician, 467

Stavenhagen, Bernhard (1862–1914), German pianist, conductor, and composer, pupil of Liszt, 491, 499, 500

Stein, Prioress Amelie von (d. 1878), sister of Adelheid von Schorn's mother, 212

Stein, Baron Heinrich von (1857–87), German philosopher and poet, 389, 437, 451

Steinway, Christian Friedrich Theodore (1825–89), of piano manufacturing firm, Steinway and Sons, New York–Hamburg, 188, 234

Stephen I, Saint (975?–1038), king of Hungary, 457

Stern, Baron von, 403

Stern, Daniel, *see* Agoult, Marie d'

Stockhausen, Mme (b. Beulwitz), 260, 265, 377

Stradal, August (1860–1930), German-Bohemian pianist, pupil of Liszt, 497

Strauss, David Friedrich (1808–74), German theologian and philosopher, 60, 62, 63, 65, 67, 80, 101

Strauss und Torney, Victor Friedrich von (1809–99), German diplomat and author, 347

Street, Agnes (b. Klindworth)(d. 1896), pianist, close friend and pupil of Liszt, recipient of his *Briefe an eine Freundin*, 332

Stroganoff, Mme (b. Potocka), 98, 412

Sue, Eugène (1804–57), French novelist, 330

Suse, Viscount de, 499

Swert, Jules de (1843–91), Belgian cellist and composer, 303–4
    Die Albigenser, 304

Széchenyi, Countess Alexandra (b. Countess Sztáray-Szirmay)(1843–1914), wife of Imre, 119, 122, 227, 401

Széchenyi, Countess Béla (b. Erdődy)(d. 1872), 57

Széchenyi, Dénes, member of distinguished Hungarian family, 36, 37, 56, 57, 103, 227

Széchenyi, Count Imre (1825–98), Hungarian statesman and diplomat, ambassador to Berlin; also composer. Liszt arranged his *Einleitung und Ungarischer Marsch* for piano solo, 4, 5, 33, 58, 65, 107, 123, 227, 401

Széchenyi, Countess Marietta, wife of Dénes; singer, 105

Szymanowska, Marie (b. Wołowska) (1789–1831), Polish pianist and composer, 201

TACITUS, Cornelius (55?–after 117), 64

Tadolini, Mlle, harpist, 287

Taillandier, René Gaspard Ernest (Saint-René-Taillandier)(1817–79), French journalist and scholar, 62, 120, 140

Taine, Hippolyte Adolphe (1828–93), French critic, philosopher, and aesthetician, 109, 111, 113, 327, 371, 444, 470, 479

Talleyrand-Périgord, Charles Maurice de, prince de Bénévant (1754–1838), French statesman, 104, 207, 425

Tappert, Wilhelm (1830–1907), German critic and author, 258

Tasso, Torquato (1544–95), 79, 293

Taubert, Karl Gottfried Wilhelm (1811–91), German composer, pianist, and conductor
Noveletten, 90

Tauchnitz, Christian Bernhard (1816–95), German publisher, 388

Tausig, Carl (1841–71), Polish pianist and composer, possibly Liszt's most brilliant student, 13, 21, 111, 247, 285, 333

Tchaikovsky, Pëtr Ilich (1840–93), 142, 203, 357, 363, 369, 402
Symphony No. 2, 277

Teano, Prince and Princess of, *see* Caetani, Onorato and Ada

Teleki, Count Alexander (Sándor)(1821–92), Hungarian patriot and author, 339, 340, 423, 468, 469

Teleki, Countess (b. Hon. Jane Frances Bickersteth), wife of Alexander, 337, 339

Tennyson, Lord Alfred (1809–92), 76

Terence (190?–159 B.C.), 311

Teste, Louis (1844–1926), 285

Theiner, Father Agostino (1804–74), Italian priest, papal archivist, and church historian, 26, 143, 157

Thern, Karl (1817–86), Hungarian conductor, composer, and teacher, 235

Thiers, Louis Adolphe (1797–1877), French statesman and historian, 17, 45, 105, 141, 143, 295

Thode, Daniela Senta (1860–1940), eldest child of Cosima and Hans von Bülow; wife of Henry, 313, 347, 348, 406–9, 419, 457, 463, 471, 497

Thode, Henry (1857–1920), German art historian and professor, 498, 500

Thomas, Charles Louis Ambroise (1811–96), 191, 192, 242, 292

Tiberius (42 B.C. – A.D. 37), Roman emperor (A.D. 14–37), 385

Tiesenhausen, Countess, 123, 306

Timanoff, Vera (1855–1942), Russian pianist, pupil of Liszt, 247, 270, 298, 303

Tisza, Kálmán (1830–1902), Hungarian statesman, prime minister of Hungary, 477

Titian (1477–1576), 57

Toll, Count de, Russian ambassador at Weimar, 247, 331, 435

Toll, Countess de, 333

Tolstoy, Mme, wife of Alexis, 35, 97, 137, 207

Tolstoy, Alexis Konstantinovich (1817–75), Russian lyric poet, novelist, and playwright, 35, 37, 46, 97, 137, 194, 196, 204, 206, 207, 212, 248, 253, 256, 308

Tolstoy, Count Leo Nikolaevich (1828–1910), 486, 491

Trefort, Ágoston von (1817–88), Hungarian statesman and minister of culture, 230

Treuenfels, Mme (b. Rielke), pupil of Liszt, 202, 322, 365

Troubetskoy, Princess, 292

Turgenev, Ivan Sergeevich (1818–83), 433, 447

Turino, cellist, 163

UEXKÜLL, Baron d', Russian ambassador to Rome, 96, 218, 219, 326, 334, 410

Uexküll, Baroness d', 216, 218, 219, 323, 325, 334, 348, 349, 391, 410

Ullmann, conductor, 31

Unger, Georg (1837–87), opera singer famous for interpretation of role of Siegfried, 195

Unruh, Baron d', official of the Berlin Court, 252

Urspruch, Anton (1850–1907), pianist and composer, pupil of Liszt, 55

Usedom, Mme d', wife of Count d'Usedom, Prussian diplomat, ambassador at Rome, 153

VARZIN, physician, 260
Vasari, Giorgio (1511–74), Italian painter, architect, and art historian, 295
Vasili, Count, *see* Adam, Juliette
Vaton, French publisher and book dealer, 285
Vauvenargues, Marquis Luc de Clapiers (1715–47), French soldier, writer, and moralist, 301
Végh, János von Vereb (1845–1918), jurist and composer of songs and piano pieces, 254
Velluti, Giovanni Battista (1780–1861), Italian male soprano, 335
Venevitinoff, Mme, 410
Verdi, Giuseppe Fortunino Francesco (1813–1901), 254, 317, 361
　　Festival Requiem, 142, 254; String Quartet, 254
Vereshchagin, Vasili Vasilievich (1842–1904), Russian painter, 410, 445–47, 450
Verhovay, Gyula (1849–1906), 369
Verlat, Charles (1824–90), Belgian painter, a director of Weimar *Kunstschule*, painted a portrait of Liszt, 90, 280, 281, 386–89, 414, 428
Vespasian (9–79), Roman emperor (69–79), 306
Vespignani, Virginio (1808–82), Italian architect, 24
Vestris, Maria Caterina Violante (1732–91), Italian dancer and singer, 42
Veuillot, Louis François (1813–83), French journalist and editor, 17, 25, 29, 37, 40, 78, 87, 88, 118, 119, 123, 144, 190, 198, 201, 237, 265, 309, 323, 326, 327, 485
Viardot-Garcia, Michelle Ferdinande Pauline (b. Garcia)(1821–1910), sister of Maria Felicia Malibran; French lyric actress and singer, student of Liszt, 10, 270, 291, 335
Victor Emmanuel (1820–78), first king of Italy (1861–78), 306
Vidieu, Abbé, 374
Viel-Castel, Louis de (1800–87), French diplomat and author, 107
Vieuxtemps, Henri (1820–81), Belgian violinist and composer, 242

Vigny, Alfred Victor de (1797–1863), French poet and man of letters, 399, 483
Villemessant, Jean Hippolyte Auguste Cartier de (1812–79), French journalist, founder of *Le Figaro*, 222–23
Villeneuve, Count de, Brazilian minister to Belgium, 482
Vincent de Paul, Saint (1581?–1660), 80
Vinci, Leonardo da (1452–1519), 167
Vinet, Alexandre (1797–1847), Swiss Protestant theologian, 204
Viotti, Giovanni Battista (1755–1824), Italian composer and violinist, 371
Visconti, Baron Pietro Ercole (1802–80), Italian commissioner of antiquities, curator of Vatican art collection, 24, 97, 99, 101, 141, 286, 316, 317, 324, 438
Vitrolles, Baron Eugène d'Arnauld de (1774–1854), 446, 447
Voigt, Mme, 451, 453
Volkmann, Richard von (1830–89), German surgeon and author, 497
Vollweiler, Carl (1813–48), German pianist and composer, 468
Voltaire, pseud. of François Marie Arouet (1694–1778), 50, 79, 92, 119, 337, 451

WAGNER, Eva (1867–1942), daughter of Richard and Cosima, 438, 463, 481
Wagner, Francesca Gaetana Cosima (1837–1930), Liszt's second daughter; m. Hans von Bülow in 1857, from whom she was divorced in 1869; m. Richard Wagner in 1870, 26, 50, 54, 55, 66, 67, 78, 80, 81, 84, 91, 93, 130, 135, 136, 139, 149, 151, 153, 160, 165, 169, 170, 173, 180–84, 187, 192, 196, 198, 234, 236, 237, 247, 249, 252, 255, 256, 266, 268–70, 275, 278, 279, 290, 292, 313, 315, 316, 323, 346, 347, 360, 379, 381, 389, 403, 405, 408, 437, 442, 444, 447–49, 457, 464
Wagner, Isolde, *see* Beidler, Isolde
Wagner, Siegfried (1869–1930), German composer and conductor, son of Richard and Cosima, 380, 437, 466
Wagner, Wilhelm Richard (1813–83), 8, 20–22, 29, 30, 32, 42–44, 50, 54, 59, 61, 77, 80, 91–93, 111, 130, 141, 144, 161,

163, 165, 169, 176, 177, 181–83, 187, 192, 195, 199, 218, 234, 236, 247–49, 252, 253, 255–58, 261, 262, 266–70, 274, 275, 278, 279, 289, 290, 301, 312, 313, 315, 316, 333, 344–47, 349, 353, 379–81, 403–5, 408, 419, 428, 431, 434, 437, 442, 443, 445, 448, 450, 451, 460, 466, 494 *Lohengrin*, 32, 35, 189, 199, 231, 372, 448; *Die Meistersinger*, 66, 403, 467; *Parsifal*, 87, 279, 305, 313, 315, 346, 380, 381, 404, 405, 430–32, 434, 448, 450, 464, 465, 500; *Der Ring des Nibelungen*, 91, 141, 256, 262, 274, 289, 404, 448: *Das Rheingold*, 289, 466, *Siegfried*, 289, *Die Walküre*, 274, 289, *Walkürenritt*, 129, 272, 296, *Götterdämmerung*, 262, 289, 353, 481; *Siegfried Idyll*, 311, 346; *Tannhäuser*, 85, 91, 448: *Sängerkrieg*, 91; *Tristan und Isolde*, 144, 289, 403, 405, 460

Wales, Prince of (1841–1910), later Edward VII, king of Great Britain (1901–10), 422, 495

Watzdorf, Augusta von (Gustchen), court lady to grand duchess of Weimar and niece of Weimar minister of state, 14, 24, 33, 165, 171, 194, 282, 347, 434, 453, 487

Weber, Carl Maria Friedrich Ernst von (1786–1826), 184, 256

Wedel, Count Oscar de, son-in-law of and successor to Count Beust at Weimar Court, 191, 192, 194, 232, 234, 252, 316, 350, 431, 481

Wedel, Countess de, 241

Weitzmann, Karl Friedrich (1808–80), German musicologist, teacher, and composer, 349, 352, 355, 356, 358

Wellington, Duke of (1769–1852), 335

Wenzel, Johanna, *see* Zarembski, Johanna von

Werthern-Beichlingen, Countess de, wife of grand chamberlain of Weimar Court, 49

Wettig, 351

Widor, Charles Marie Jean Albert (1844–1937), French composer and organist Trio, 368, 371

Wiederhold, Dr., head of sanatorium in Wilhelmshöhe, 485

Wielhorsky, Count Michael Jurjew (1788–1856), Russian singer, composer, and art patron, 410

Wieniawski, Henryk (1835–80), Polish violinist and composer, 191

Wilczek, Count Johann Nepomuk Joseph Maria (1837–1922), 180

Wilhelm I (1797–1888), emperor of Germany (1871–88), 19, 87, 401

Wilhelmj, August Daniel Ferdinand Victor (1845–1908), German violinist and teacher, 78, 195

Willem III (1817–90), king of the Netherlands (1849–90), 192, 242, 243, 484

William III of Prussia, *see* Friedrich Wilhelm III

William IV, *see* Friedrich Wilhelm IV

Windhorst, Ludwig (1812–91), German statesman and lawyer, 344

Winter, German publisher, 347

Winterberger, Alexander (Sacha) (1834–1914), organ and piano virtuoso, pupil of Liszt, 283

Witt, Franz Xaver (1834–88), German priest, composer, critic, and editor; reformer of Catholic Church music, 16

Wittelsbach, Otto, 378

Wittgenstein, Princess, *see* Sayn-Wittgenstein, Princess Carolyne Jeanne Elisabeth von

Wöhrmann, Mme, 348, 380, 395

Wolff, Pierre Etienne (1809?–82), French pianist and teacher, one of Liszt's first pupils in Paris, then in Geneva, 67

Wolkoff, Alexander, Russian artist and scientist, 438, 442

Wolkonska, Princess (b. Lvoff), 218

Wolzogen, Baron Hans Paul von (1848–1938), German author, scholar, and editor, 249, 258, 405

Württemberg, *see* Karl I

XAVIER, Saint Francis (1506–52), Spanish Jesuit missionary, 170

ZALUSKI, Count Charles, Austrian
diplomat and composer, 284, 292
Zarembski, Johanna von, wife of Julius,
pupil of Liszt, 230
Zarembski, Julius von (1854–85), Polish
pianist and composer, pupil of Liszt,
202, 210, 216, 218, 220, 226, 227, 230,
244, 271, 279–81, 285, 291, 292, 302,
314, 334, 427, 482
    Fantaisie, 279, 281; Polish dances,
    467; Quintet, 482
Zedlitz, M. de, 268
Zeller, Jules Sylvain (1819–1900), French
historian, 500
Zhukovsky, Paul von (1845–1902), Russian painter and architect, 348, 380, 381,
403–5, 432–5, 438, 443, 463, 464, 500

Zhukovsky, Vasili (1783–1852), Russian
poet and translator, 308
Zichy, Countess Anna, 87
Zichy, Count Edmond (1811–94), Hun-
garian officer; art patron and museum
founder, 78, 185
Zichy, Count Ernest (1846–1919), 341,
470
Zichy, Count Géza (1849–1924), Hun-
garian pianist and composer, pupil of
Liszt, 335, 337, 340, 370, 396, 400, 421,
422, 424, 427, 468–70, 475
Zichy, Count Michael (1827–1906), Hun-
garian painter, 450
Zola, Émile (1840–1902), 330, 391, 399, 410
Zumbusch, Kaspar von (1830–1915),
German sculptor, 267

HAEC OLIM MEMINISSE JUVABIT